¡A SU SALUD!

Peterson

¡A SU SALUD!

SPANISH FOR HEALTH PROFESSIONALS

CLASSROOM EDITION

Christine E. Cotton
Elizabeth Ely Tolman
Julia Cardona Mack
University of North Carolina at Chapel Hill

Revised and Expanded by Elizabeth C. Bruno

Yale University Press
New Haven and London

This book was originally accompanied by a DVD. The video program is now available at Yalebooks.com/Salud. To access it, use the password cotton09.

Publisher: Mary Jane Peluso
Editorial Assistant: Elise Panza
Project Editor: Timothy Shea
Production Editor: Ann-Marie Imbornoni
Production Controller: Karen Stickler

Cover Designed by James J. Johnson
Editing, Interior Design, and Composition by Victory Productions

The Library of Congress has cataloged the DVD edition as follows:

Cotton, Christine E.
"A su salud": Spanish for health professionals / Christine E. Cotton, Elizabeth Ely Tolman, Julia Cardona Mack.—Classroom ed. / revised and expanded by Elizabeth C. Bruno.
p. cm.
Revised and expanded ed. of: 1st ed., 2005.
Includes bibliographical references and index.
ISBN 978-0-300-11966-4 (pbk.: alk. paper)
1. Spanish language—Conversation and phrase books (for medical personnel)
2. Medicine—Terminology. I. Tolman, Elizabeth Ely. II. Cardona Mack, Julia. III. Bruno, Elizabeth C. IV. Title.
PC4120.M3C68 2009
468.3'42102461—dc22

2008056011

ISBN 978-0-300-21445-1 (pbk. with online media.)

Printed in the United States of America.

A catalogue record for this book is available from the British Library.

This paper meets the requirements of ANSI/NISO Z39.48-1992 (Permanence of Paper).

10 9 8 7 6 5 4 3 2 1

CONTENTS

Unidad 1b

Unidad 2a

Unidad 2b

Unidad 3a

Unidad 3b

Unidad 4a

Unidad 4b

SCOPE AND SEQUENCE

There are 8 units in the course materials.

The focus of the methodology is *language in use*. Every unit is organized around specific *tasks*. The structures increase in difficulty as the units progress and the tasks become more complicated.

Design of language lesson within each unit

ACTION	DVD SEGMENT	CUADERNO
a. thinking (reading) about a topic		*Note to the Student, Notes from the Field,* readings from outside sources
b. observing a scene	*Historia, En la práctica, Analizar, Escuchar*	
c. expressing understanding	*En la práctica*	*En la práctica, Vocabulario, Principios*
d. expressing personal thoughts on specific readings or discussions		*Principios, ¡A conversar!,* readings from outside sources
e. correcting (repairing) expressions (using material developed in *d.*)		*Vocabulario, Principios ¡A conversar!* readings from outside sources
f. developing control of language through exercises		*Principios, ¡A conversar!,* readings from outside sources
g. self-testing		*Vocabulario, Principios, Comprobación*
h. exploring further	*Analizar, Escuchar, En la práctica*	*Vocabulario, Principios, Más allá, ¡A conversar!*
i. creating new material (personalizing, individualizing)		*Vocabulario, Principios, ¡A conversar!*

PROGRESSION OF UNITS

UNIT	LANGUAGE TASKS	SPANISH LANGUAGE STRUCTURES	HEALTH Issues	HEALTH Tasks
1a	■ Identifying yourself and others ■ Asking questions ■ Watching for facial expressions and body language	■ Nominal phrases ■ Nouns, articles, adjectives ■ Subject pronouns ■ Order of words in the sentence	■ Accidents ■ Poverty ■ Social isolation	■ Physical exam ■ Discussing pain ■ Speaking under stress ■ Developing rapport
1b	■ Describing present environment ■ Questioning the message to ensure communication	■ Verbal phrases ■ Regular verbs in the present tense ■ Contrast between *ser* and *estar* ■ Irregular present tense	■ Diabetes ■ Nutrition ■ Immigration	■ Home visit ■ Building bridges between cultures

UNIT	LANGUAGE TASKS	SPANISH LANGUAGE STRUCTURES	HEALTH Issues	HEALTH Tasks
2a	■ Establishing time and circumstances of an action ■ Asking for corroboration to avoid misunderstandings	■ Verbs in the present progressive ■ Past participles as adjectives ■ Present perfect ■ Adverbs ■ Distinction between *por* and *para*	■ Wellness ■ Alternative health practices ■ Diet and exercise ■ Gang violence	■ Discussing alternative health practices ■ Establishing a climate of trust ■ Using "teachable" moments
2b	■ Telling a story in the past ■ Taking statements as a whole	■ Verbs in the preterit ■ Verbs in the imperfect ■ Contrast between the preterit and imperfect ■ Conjunctions	■ High risk pregnancy ■ Domestic violence	■ Conducting the prenatal intake exam ■ Assessing patients' and clients' strengths
3a	■ Establishing agent and object (who did what to whom) ■ Communicating with children	■ Gender and number ■ Object, reflexive and reciprocal pronouns ■ Relative clauses ■ Verbs in the future	■ Child health ■ Immunization ■ Informed consent ■ Differing national standards of health care ■ Workplace accidents	■ Discussing informed consent ■ Working with children ■ Discussing immunizations
3b	■ Ordering someone to do something, convincing ■ Giving clear commands	■ Formal and informal commands ■ Conditionals	■ HIV/AIDS ■ Communicable diseases	■ Dealing with HIV treatment issues and prevention ■ Giving bad news across language and culture
4a	■ Comparing, rejecting and denying, conflict avoidance ■ Expressing agreement and/or negation	■ Passive voice and impersonal sentences ■ Negative expressions ■ Comparisons of equality and inequality	■ Mental health ■ Substance abuse in adolescents ■ Patient confidentiality ■ Dosage ■ Rheumatoid arthritis	■ Assessing mental health ■ Explaining correct dosage across language and culture ■ Working with adolescents
4b	■ Expressing your opinions, feelings ■ Distinguishing subjective elements from facts ■ Using names and titles to establish or reduce distance in a relationship	■ Present and past subjunctive	■ Social support ■ Professional networking	■ Maintaining social support at a distance ■ Developing respectful provider/patient relationships ■ Developing connections with agencies and community organizations focused on Latino health issues

COMPONENTS OF *¡A SU SALUD!*

WHAT ARE THE COMPONENTS AND WHERE DO I BEGIN?

The three components of *¡A su salud!* were designed to be viewed as parts of a whole rather than as ancillaries to each other. Recognizing that print, multi-media products, and the web all have different capabilities, and that students have different learning styles, the authors of *¡A su salud!* decided that although the content of the course would center around the *Historia*, none of the components would be more essential than any other. As you will see from the descriptions below, each of the three components contains important information and exercises designed to help you strengthen your Spanish skills.

THE DVD

All activities on the DVD are centered around the *Historia*, the *telenovela*-style drama in eight episodes. On each unit of the DVD you will find activities broken down into various categories. To complete the activities, refer to the instructions and questions for each activity in the textbook:

- ***Historia***—This segment contains the unit's episode of the drama, as well as a summary of the last episode (except for *Unidad 1a*). You should always watch the *Historia* segment for each *unidad* before beginning any other work on the *unidad*.
- ***Personajes***—The primary characters of the *Historia* introduce themselves in this segment.
- ***Escuchar***—These segments presents a variety of situations that are directly connected to events that have taken place in the *Historia*. These are intended to give the student an opportunity to discuss more profoundly these issues. Note: *Escuchar* segments are only included in the "a" units.
- ***Conversar***—These segments gives the students a chance to "listen in" on a conversation between two or more characters from the *Historia*. Each conversation ends with a question posted directly to the student. Note: *Conversar* segments are only included in the "b" units.
- ***Analizar***—These segments, much like those of *Escuchar*, are a series of short videos in which the characters discuss an issue or situation from the *Historia*.
- ***En la práctica***—These video clips present conversations between a health-care provider and a patient and/or client. In each case the conversation revolves around a condition or circumstance in which cultural differences can influence how one interprets or reacts to a particular situation.
- ***Lengua***—These exercises use a combination of new video and clips from the *Historia* to help you apply the language lessons you have learned within specific health and cultural contexts.
- ***Entrevista***—These clips contain unscripted conversations with native speakers of Spanish. The clips in the "a" units are interviews with actual healthcare provides. The "b" clips are conversations with some of the professional actors from the *Historia*. In both cases, the student has the opportunity to hear unscripted, conversational speech from native speakers from a variety of regions of Latin America.

THE TEXTBOOK

You will find grammatical explanations, exercises, and information designed to help you better understand the *Historia* (and ultimately, your patients and clients!) in the textbook. Each unit of the textbook contains the following sections:

- **Note to the Student**—This section provides you with strategies for learning and using language in a variety of contexts.
- ***Vocabulario***—This section provides you with several opportunities to practice using the terms featured in the unit.
- **Useful Terms and Expressions**—This section provides lists of health-related vocabulary words and expressions used in the grammar explanations and exercises from the *Principios* sections of the textbook.
- ***Principios***—This section provides you with detailed explanations of the grammatical structures featured in the unit and opportunities to practice using these structures.
- ***¡A conversar!***—This section provides the student with a variety of opportunities to practice his/her speaking skills. Each of the conversation starters draws directly on a particular segment of the DVD or on the *episodios*.
- ***Más allá***—This section contains further reflections on how communication goes beyond grammar and vocabulary.
- ***Entrevista***—This section, presented in English, is designed to help you better understand the unit's *Entrevista* on the DVD.

This edition also includes articles related to health issues. To read these articles online, go to www.yalebooks.com/salud.

THE WEB

On the web you will find both your class site and the *Recursos* website. Although all of you will have access to the *Recursos* website, not all of you will have a course website. This will depend on your instructor and institution.

- **Course site**—This site may contain your syllabus, ways to communicate with your classmates and your instructor, discussion forums, extra exercises to help strengthen your language skills, and links to helpful websites.
- ***Recursos***—Found at yalebooks.com/salud/recursos, this site serves as a portal for *¡A su salud!* and contains links to helpful language, culture, and health sites. Your instructor may also occasionally direct you to specific sites within *Recursos*.

This book was originally accompanied by a DVD. The video program is now available at Yalebooks.com/ Salud. To access it, use the password cotton09.

UNIDAD 1a

NOTE TO THE STUDENT

Dear student,

Welcome to the textbook of ***¡A su salud!*** *We want this textbook to be a comfortable place where you can learn about the Spanish language and its uses, and where you can practice at your own pace. We hope you'll come to it often as you work your way through* ***¡A su salud!****, adding your own thoughts in the margins and making our words your own.*

PEDAGOGY

Language in Context

When people have an ardent need to communicate, they will, even if they don't speak the same language. Gestures, symbols, and something even more basic, like intuition, have served in many instances. All this tells us that language is much more than what traditional grammar books and dictionaries contain. In this textbook you will practice Spanish in *context*, which means that as you work with vocabulary and grammar, you will want to stay connected to those other aspects of language that also carry meaning: where the conversation is taking place, who is speaking, the physical state of the speakers, the gestures that accompany the words, what happened earlier in the conversation, the purpose of this exchange, and so on.

Self-monitoring

At the beginner level, we learn what makes a language work. At the intermediate level, we learn to make it work for us. Repeating over and over what others say or what you know to be correct will certainly help you to become familiar with how language works. In order to become a proficient and effective speaker, however, you must be able to listen to what you say and correct your own mistakes, change the message to make it more expressive, and generally help your listener understand you.

To assist you in developing this self-monitoring skill, the textbook will help you become more aware of the process of language acquisition and your own habits of learning and communicating.

Culture

As speakers relate to each other, their speech reflects the worldview and the traditional behavior of the group of speakers that shares their language. This is what we call "culture" in *¡A su salud!* It is an important tool in understanding language. In a healthcare environment there is a culture for every profession, a distinct way of seeing and doing things. The immigrant experience also has its singular characteristics, which will be part of the equation in many activities as you work your way through this textbook.

Spanish in the United States

¡A su salud! brings you closer to the Spanish language spoken in the United States by immigrants who have little or no command of English. This population is varied and changing. Geographic origin, educational level, social class, age, time in the United States, and living conditions are some of the many factors that can influence the type of Spanish you'll hear. It's wonderful to know that all these variants are still mutually intelligible, and with time and a sharp ear, you'll learn to recognize the clues that tell you so many things about your patients and clients.

METHODOLOGY

In this textbook, as in the DVD, the authors encourage you to follow these principles of second language learning:

- **Memorizing** is important in the process of learning a language. It gives you the building blocks for structures and helps you "monitor" your performance.
- **Drills** help your mind get used to things and make connections between them. "Practice makes perfect," they say, and regular brief practice is better than long spurts of practice, followed by long droughts of forgetting.
- **Applying what you learn** to your personal environment keeps your knowledge current and accessible and strengthens your language performance. To speak a language well you have to continue working with it, much in the way that you keep any skill sharp. See if you can bring the new things you're learning in *¡A su salud!* into your conversations with patients, clients, and co-workers.

We will try to explain to you as often as possible the reasons for the activities that we'll offer in this textbook. Knowing why one is doing something helps to connect the immediate action to others that went before, motivating performance and improving the outcome.

THE READINGS

Throughout the textbook you will find some readings in Spanish and some in English with Spanish sections. The purpose of these readings is to allow you to make the most of your skills as an adult learner.

Children who are learning his native language do not know how to read and will make use of the tools that their brain provides: constant repetition, total memorization, absolute focus on the source of language, and so on. They can't say, "Write that phrase down, so we can see how it's put together." You, on the other hand, have been using written text as a source of information and as a jumping off point for learning for a long time.

Readings provide you with practice in "total language" —vocabulary in longer phrases, phrases in logical paragraphs, paragraphs that form a conversation, and so on. Your experience finding meaning in the longer streams of language helps your brain become familiar with Spanish in use. You may never talk about illness and wellness to a Spanish-speaking provider in Spanish, and even if you did, memorizing long articles in your field of expertise will only provide you with long strings of memorized language, not the tools you need for effective communication.

VOCABULARIO

This is a review section. The audio segments associated with the vocabulary section in the textbook are available for listening on the *Recursos* Web site. You can find *Recursos* at *yalebooks.com/salud/recursos*. If you understand the *Vocabulario* section on the *Recursos* website without difficulty, you may not need to work on this section in the textbook. On the other hand, practicing the language with elements that are very familiar helps you become fluent, like practicing your scales helps you to play Mozart!

Below are the words from this unit's *Vocabulario* segment at the *Recursos* website. After you've listened to them, write beside each one its English equivalent. If you have any doubt about the words' exact meanings, look them up in a good Spanish-English dictionary. (A "good" dictionary for an intermediate language student does not fit in your coat pocket!) There are interactive links to some good dictionaries on the *Recursos* website. Remember to compare the meanings that you have written down with those found on the *Recursos* website.

Use this space to add new, useful words that you found in the unit, but were not included in *Vocabulario!*

picar: to bite

Verbos

acabar to end, to finish, to run out

bajar to go down, to get off

chocar to crash

congelarse to freeze, block, suspend

cuidar to take care of

darse cuenta to realize

pelear to fight

poner al día to bring up to date

Adverbios y adjetivos

además in addition

acabado finished, worn out

casi almost

cuidado care

de cualquier forma in any way

peligroso dangerous

Sustantivos

el agujero hole

el azúcar sugar

el calentador heater

el dulce sweet

la feria de salud health fair

la glucosa glucose

el golpe hit

la meta goal

el obstetra obstetrician

la oreja ear

la pobreza poverty

la receta recipe/ prescription

¡A PRACTICAR!

1A-VOC-1

Match the Spanish words with their equivalents in English. If you need help, review Unidad 1a Vocabulario *at the* Recursos *website before continuing.*

1 acabar	9	**a** to bite
2 calentar	5	**b** to care for
3 chocar	3	**c** to crash
4 congelarse	8	**d** to fight
5 cuidar	1	**e** to finish
6 darse cuenta	4	**f** to freeze
7 golpear	2	**g** to heat
8 pelear	7	**h** to hit
9 picar	6	**i** to notice, realize

1A-VOC-2

Fill in the right word for each blank. Be careful with the proper agreement between the new word and the rest of the sentence.

Duna y Ashleigh a menudo trabajan juntas. Hoy ellas van a visitar a una señora que vive en una parte muy **(1)** peligroso *(dangerous)* de la ciudad. Hay problemas de salud **(2)** además *(besides)* de viviendas insalubres. Aquí viven inmigrantes y gente del pueblo en una gran **(3)** probeza *(poverty)*. Jaime, médico **(4)** obstetra *(obstetrician)*, dice que su **(5)** meta *(goal)* principal es mejorar las condiciones de vida de estas personas. Todos son buenos, trabajadores, industriosos, pero también son muy pobres. Para mejorar las condiciones del lugar los vecinos tienen ? que **(6)** darse cuenta *(notice)* de los problemas y trabajar juntos para resolverlos. Duna y Ashleigh piensan que **(7)** casi *(almost)* todos quieren y pueden trabajar juntos.

1A-VOC-3

Read through the paragraph carefully, noting the use of the vocabulary words you have been studying. Write below in English what the paragraph says. If you need help, review Unidad 1a Vocabulario *on the* Recursos *website and the section on Word Order in* Principios *in the textbook.*

Duna habla con Carmina sobre las condiciones de salud en que se encuentran la señora y sus dos niños:

"Mira, Carmina, esta señora vive en un apartamento pobre y oscuro con sus dos hijos. Los niños son pequeños, pero no pelean y además parece que no se dan cuenta de la pobreza. Son niños felices. Creo que el padre no vive con ellos, pero la señora los cuida muy bien ella sola. De cualquier forma, ella busca un apartamento nuevo en donde vivir."

talk w/Carmina about
the conditions of health

1A-VOC-4

DVD

Review Historia 1a *on the DVD and watch Jaime answering the phone. Imagine what the person on the other end is saying. Write a paragraph in Spanish explaining what you think is going on.*

Me parece que...

USEFUL TERMS AND EXPRESSIONS

This section introduces new vocabulary and expressions related to themes found throughout *Historia 1a* of the DVD and at the *Recursos* website.

SUSTANTIVOS

La gente

el/la cliente	client
el/la empleado/a	employee
el/la enfermero/a	nurse
el/la farmacéutico/a	pharmacist
el/la intérprete	interpreter
el/la médico/a	doctor
el/la paciente	patient
el/la pediatra	pediatrician
el personal	staff
el/la técnico/a	technician
el/la trabajador/a social	social worker

El cuerpo

el brazo	arm
la cabeza	head
el cuello	neck
la frente	forehead
la garganta	throat
el hueso	bone
la muñeca	wrist
la nariz	nose
la pierna	leg
el tobillo	ankle

Las condiciones físicas

la cortadura	cut
el descanso	rest
el dolor	pain
la enfermedad	illness
los escalofríos	chills
la fiebre	fever
la hinchazón	swelling
la infección	infection
la magulladora	bruise
las náuseas	nausea
el plomo	lead
el resfriado	cold
la sensibilidad	tenderness
el síntoma	symptom
los sentimientos	feelings
el veneno	poison

El equipo

la camilla	stretcher
el collar	collar
las muletas	crutches
la placa	x-ray
la radiografía	x-ray
la tablilla	splint
el yeso	cast

VERBOS	
apretar	to squeeze
dañar	to harm
enfermar(se)	to get sick
envenenar	to poison
extender(se)	to extend
hinchar(se)	to swell
lastimar(se)	to hurt oneself
marear(se)	to faint
masticar	to chew
molestar	to bother
perder el conocimiento	to lose consciousness
radiar, correr(se)	to radiate
regresar	to return
sentir(se)	to feel
suceder	to happen
violar	to violate, rape
vomitar	to vomit

ADJETIVOS Y ADVERBIOS	
agudo/a	sharp
alérgico/a	allergic
angustiado/a	distressed
débil	weak
en peligro	in danger
estable	stable
fuerte	strong
herido/a	wounded
inquieto/a	restless
intensivo/a	intensive
izquierdo/a	left
mareado/a	dizzy
profundo/a	deep
sangrando	bleeding
torcido/a	sprained

Study the vocabulary above before you begin *Principios* because it will be useful when practicing the grammar points of the unit. Remember that this section is not intended to be an exhaustive list of all relevant terms, but rather an exposure to some of the basic vocabulary used in health care. The definitions given here are limited to the way the words are used in exercises found in *Principios*. Look the words up in a good Spanish-English dictionary if you want to know other meanings, how to pronounce them, the contexts in which the words can be found, sayings and common expressions using these words, and their derivatives (adjectives from nouns, nouns from verbs, etc.).

PRINCIPIOS

For an English speaker the grammar of Spanish is "familiar," because many of the structures in English and Spanish are the same. English and Spanish also share many cognates, words that have the same origin and similar meanings. These connections will make learning some Spanish structures and vocabulary easier for you, but they will also lead you astray. This will happen especially where a structure in English is also found in Spanish but is used differently, is not used as often, or is not used in the same context.

Native speakers do not analyze language the way conventional grammar books do. Still, linguists analyze structures and write grammar books for learners, because learners find it useful to see the language they're learning "deconstructed." As we take the structures apart, describe how they function, and guide you through the exercises that put them back together in a meaningful context, you will learn to "monitor" your own speech production. Developing a watchful use of language is the big accomplishment of the intermediate learner. The trick is to use your intuitive sense of language (from English) and also the grammar of Spanish to watch over your Spanish speech.

"Intermediate" means that you already know what the language is "about" (for example, that nouns are masculine and feminine, that *-s* signals plural, that verbs have "endings" which relate to who's the subject, etc.) After a brief review, you are ready to focus on applying what you've learned about the Spanish language to actually speaking in Spanish. We opted to begin this course with the noun phrase because it is an easy point of entry.

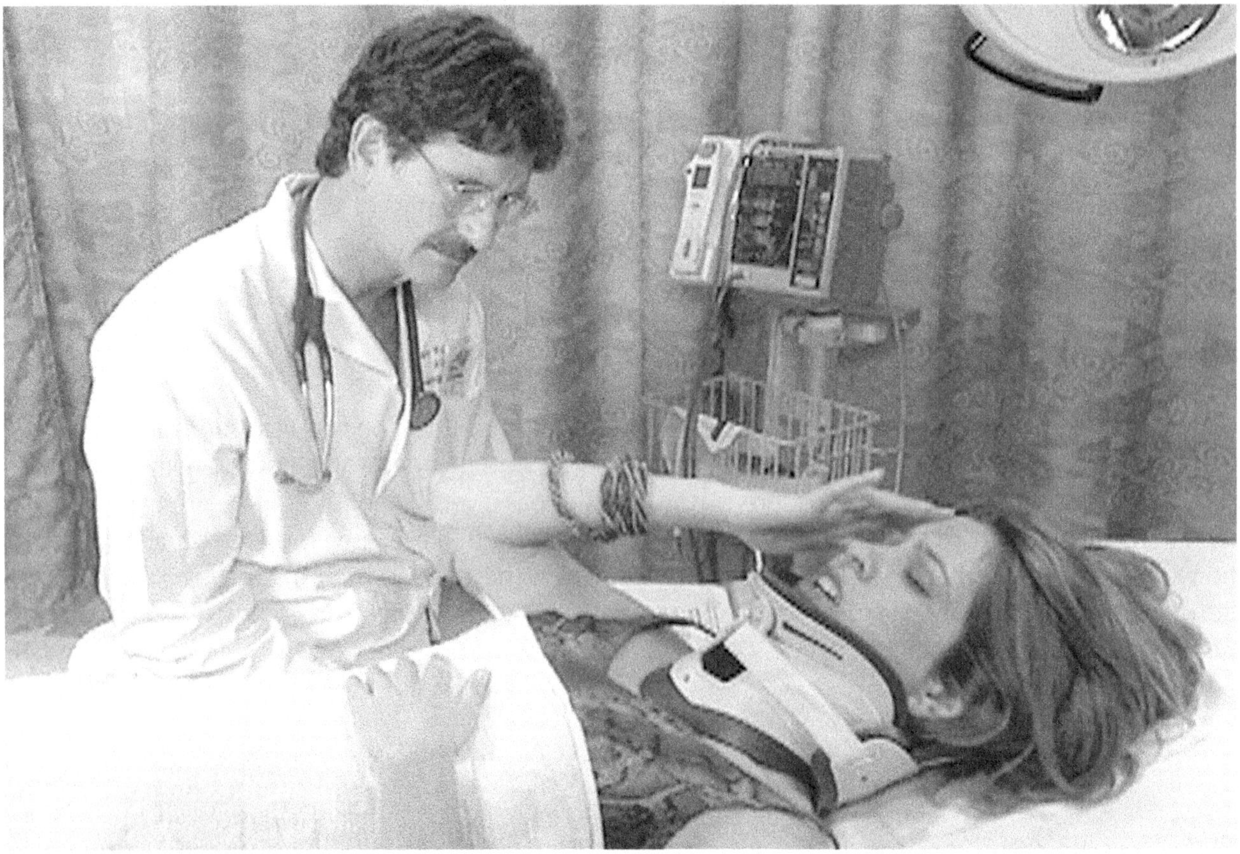

IDENTIFYING YOURSELF AND OTHERS

Unfamiliar surroundings and individuals often cause us to be uncomfortable, apprehensive, and reluctant to express true feelings. To alleviate such awkward situations, we search for something with which we can identify or for someone who might understand us as individuals. We are more likely to confide in someone when we perceive real concern for, or interest in, us as people. In the healthcare environment roles are clearly identified. Caregivers wear coats and labels; care recipients don't. Caregivers know where things are and how they work; care recipients, or patients, expect to be guided. However, these roles are merely functional distinctions and should not overshadow the personalities and cultures of the individuals involved. The activities that take place in the healthcare environment are so neatly prescribed that we can be tempted to come up with a "protocol," a "how to" script to get the job done. Getting the job done is part of it, certainly, but being able to go "off script" and actually communicate with your patient or client is much more rewarding for all parties.

WHO ARE WE?

Introductions can come in many different forms. Usually, we start with a greeting of some type:

SPANISH	ENGLISH
Hola.	Hello.
Buenos días.	Good morning.
Buenas tardes.	Good afternoon.
Buenas noches.	Good evening.
Mucho gusto.	Nice to meet you.
Un placer.	A pleasure.
Encantado/a.	Charmed.
Me alegro de verlo.	I am happy to see you.
¿Cómo le va?	How's it going?
¿Qué tal?	What's new?
¿Cómo está usted?	How are you?
¿En qué lo puedo ayudar?	How may I help you?
¿En qué le puedo servir?	How may I serve you?
¿Cómo andan las cosas?	How are things going?

The above list is by no means exhaustive; however, you can see that the single concept of greeting someone can be expressed through a variety of ways. While you may not be familiar with every possible type of greeting available, you should look to the situation or context in which the language is used to guide you in your understanding.

In addition to the customary greeting, when we meet someone for the first time we try to establish who we are. Here is one possible way to identify yourself:

Me llamo ______________________.	*(your name here)*
Soy especialista en ______________________.	*(your specialty here)*
Trabajo en ______________________.	*(your field or section name here)*
Vengo a ______________________.	*(add infinitive that expresses the task you're about to perform + pronoun referring to the patient or client, maybe preceded by a preposition like "a" or "para" + explanation of the procedure in one or more phrases).*

Next, we determine the identity of the person we have just met. Here is one possible way to identify your patient:

¿Cómo se llama usted?	*(This will be answered with a name.)*
¿Qué le duele?	*(This may be answered with the patient pointing to a body part, or with a rich stream of Spanish.)*

At first glance, the fill-in-the-blank method of communication appears to be quite effective; however, this method is very limited in use. What happens when an individual gives you a response for which you are not prepared?

If you feel more comfortable with the fill-in-the-blanks method as the best form of interaction with your patients or clients, you should seek the assistance of an interpreter at all times. To introduce yourself as an individual, as well as a caregiver, and to understand with certainty the explanations of your patient or client, you need to learn about sentences, word order, nouns, adjectives, articles and pronouns, what they are, and how they're used. This unit will teach you about them and will provide activities for you to practice them.

ASKING QUESTIONS

In Spanish, as with all languages, more than one method is used to form questions.

The speaker can add a tag such as *¿verdad?* or *¿no?* onto the end of statement for which an affirmative response is expected.

SPANISH	ENGLISH
Usted todavía se siente muy débil, ¿no?	You still feel weak, don't you?

The speaker may simply place question marks at the beginning and end of a written statement or use intonation to change a statement into a question.

SPANISH	ENGLISH
El dolor se extiende al cuello.	The pain extends to the neck.
¿El dolor se extiende al cuello?	Does the pain extend to the neck?
Está sangrando mucho la herida.	The wound is bleeding a lot.
¿Está sangrando mucho la herida?	Is the wound bleeding a lot?

Notice that word order is not restricted to placing the subject before the verb.

Alternatively, the speaker may use an interrogative word to introduce questions that direct the listener to answer with a somewhat predictable content. These are the most common interrogative words in Spanish:

SPANISH	ENGLISH	WHAT ANSWER WILL REFER TO
¿qué?	what?	a thing
¿cuál?	which one?	thing/person from a group
¿cuáles?	which ones?	singled out things/people
¿cuánto?	how much?	an amount
¿cuántos?	how many?	a number
¿cuándo?	when?	a time
¿quién?	who?	a person
¿quiénes?	who? (plural)	people
¿cómo?	how?	a way of doing something
¿dónde?	where?	a place
¿a dónde?	where to?	a place
¿por qué?	why?	a reason
¿para qué?	what for?	a purpose

Interrogative words are usually followed by the predicate (main verb) in the question. The subject will often follow the verb. Any direct or indirect object pronoun will be placed before the verb.

SPANISH	ENGLISH
¿Qué tiene usted en la mano?	What do you have in your hand?
¿Cuál de estas medicinas está usted tomando?	Which of these medicines are you taking?
¿Cuáles son las cosas que más le molestan?	What are the things that bother you the most?
¿Cuánto bebe usted?	How much do you drink?
¿Cuántas píldoras hay en el frasco?	¿How many pills are there in the jar?
¿Cuándo puedo quitarme el yeso?	When can I take off the cast?
¿Quién lo atiende a usted?	Who is helping you?
¿Quiénes son los padres del niño?	Who are the parents of the child?
¿Cómo se siente?	How do you feel?
¿Dónde le duele?	Where does it hurt?
¿A dónde llevan al herido? ¿A dónde lo llevan?	Where are they taking the wounded man? Where are they taking him?
¿Por qué quiere lastimarse?	Why do you want to hurt yourself?
¿Para qué sirve esto?	What is this for?

Regardless of the method you choose, remember that Spanish, unlike English, does not require the use of an auxiliary (is, are, do, etc.) to form a question.

¡A PRACTICAR!

1A-PRIN-1

Match the interrogative words in Spanish with the correct translation in English.

1 ¿cuál?	5	**a**	what?
2 ¿cuándo?	2	**b**	when?
3 ¿dónde?	3	**c**	where?
4 ¿por qué?	1	**d**	which one?
5 ¿qué?	6	**e**	who?
6 ¿quién?	4	**f**	why?

1A-PRIN-2

Add the interrogative word needed to complete the questions in the dialogue. Be careful with agreement! Add any prepositions that may be needed to complete the interrogative phrase.

El doctor entra en el cuarto y encuentra a Laura sentada en la camilla.

DOCTOR: Buenas noches, señorita. **(1)** ¿Cómo se llama usted?

LAURA: Laura.

DOCTOR: **(2)** ¿Cómo se siente?

LAURA: Un poco mal, doctor. Me duele todo.

DOCTOR: **(3)** ¿dónde le duele?

LAURA: Aquí (she points to her head) ...en la frente. Creo que me di un golpe.

DOCTOR: Déjeme ver. (Looks at her forehead. Touches it lightly.) **(4)** ¿qué le? pasó esto?

LAURA: Tuve un accidente con el carro. Me mareé y perdí el control.

DOCTOR: **(5)** ¿Porqué? pasó esto?

LAURA: No hace mucho. Acabo de llegar... quizás hace una hora.

DOCTOR: **(6)** ¿dónde iba en el automóvil, para su casa?

LAURA: Venía de una fiesta... Sí, iba para mi casa.

DOCTOR: ¡Qué pena!, ¿no? Su prima llamó y dijo que venía para acá enseguida. Su voz me pareció conocida. **(7)** ¿Cual es su prima?

LAURA: Se llama Carmina Estrada y es doctora. Trabaja en la clínica de La Comunidad.

DOCTOR: ¡Ah, sí! Todos conocemos a la doctora Estrada. No sabía que tuviera una prima.

1A-PRIN-3

Each of the statements below is the answer a patient gave to a particular question. Figure out which of the choices represents the question that precedes the answer.

En la clínica hay mucha gente y todos necesitan la ayuda del intérprete. Hay una familia con varios niños y algunos heridos en un accidente. ¡Todos hablan a la vez!

c **1** Tengo un dolor muy fuerte en esta pierna.
- **a** ¿Cómo es el dolor?
- **b** ¿Cuál es su pierna?
- **c** ¿Dónde le duele?

a **2** Me mandaron de recepción; acabo de llegar.
- **a** ¿Cómo llegó usted hasta aquí?
- **b** ¿Cuál es su problema?
- **c** ¿Dónde estaba usted?

b **3** La enfermera me dijo que perdí el conocimiento.
- **a** ¿Para qué quiere la radiografía?
- **b** ¿Qué le dijo la enfermera?
- **c** ¿Quién habla español?

b **4** No puedo venir a las citas. No tengo automóvil.
- **a** ¿Cómo viene usted a la clínica?
- **b** ¿Por qué no vino usted ayer?
- **c** ¿Qué le pasa a usted?

c **5** El niño está aquí solo.
- **a** ¿Cuál niño está aquí?
- **b** ¿Dónde está el niño?
- **c** ¿Quién está con este niño?

c **6** Después de que se baje la hinchazón.
- **a** ¿Qué le sucedió?
- **b** ¿Por qué no puedo trabajar?
- **c** ¿Cuándo puedo regresar al trabajo?

1A-PRIN-4

Imagine that you're seeing a patient who has been admitted to the emergency department. You need to find out some information and the attending ED doctor doesn't speak Spanish. Write down the questions needed to elicit the information.

1 The patient's name.

2 The reason the patient is in the ED.

3 Who is accompanying the patient home after treatment?

4 Does the patient know that he needs to come back in a week?

1 ¿Cómo se llama usted?

2 ¿Porqué tu aquí?

3 ¿Quien contigo para despues el tratamiento?

4 ¿Sabe usted lo que necesita para volver en una semana?

GENDER

Although we can usually assume that nouns ending in *-a* are feminine and nouns ending in *-o* are masculine, this approach is not always reliable.

Many nouns of Greek origin end in *-a*, but are masculine. Here is a list of the more:

SPANISH	ENGLISH
el clima	climate
el drama	drama
el idioma	language
el mapa	map
el problema	problem
el sistema	system
el tema	topic

Most nouns ending in *-a*, *-d*, *-ción*, *-sión*, *-umbre*, and *-z* are feminine:

SPANISH	ENGLISH
la camilla	stretcher
la casa	house
la sala (de operaciones)	room (operating)
la costumbre	custom
la condición	condition
la habitación	room (patient's)
la decisión	decision
la gravidez, preñez	pregnancy
la luz	light
la niñez	childhood
la vejez	old age
la enfermedad	illness
la felicidad	happiness
la gravedad	seriousness (of an illness)
la personalidad	personality

Most nouns ending in *-o*, *-l*, and *-r* are masculine:

SPANISH	ENGLISH
el baño	bathroom
el teléfono	telephone
el alcohol	alcohol
el colesterol	cholesterol
el ascensor	elevator
el collar	collar
el pulgar	thumb
el sudor	perspiration
el temor	fear

Still, some nouns ending in *-o* and *-l* are feminine. Here are some important exceptions:

SPANISH	ENGLISH
la mano	hand
la piel	skin
la sal	salt
la señal	signal

When infinitives are used as nouns, they are masculine:

SPANISH	ENGLISH
el poder	power
el sangrar	bleeding

Languages, days of the week, rivers, oceans, and mountains are masculine. Notice that in written Spanish days of the week (as well as months of the year) and languages (and nationalities) are not capitalized:

SPANISH	ENGLISH
el español	Spanish
el lunes	Monday
el martes	Tuesday
el miércoles	Wednesday
el jueves	Thursday
el viernes	Friday
el sábado	Saturday
el domingo	Sunday

A few nouns have only one form but require the use of articles to mark the gender.

SPANISH	ENGLISH
el paciente grave	the seriously ill patient (a man)
la paciente embarazada	the pregnant patient (a woman)
el primer cliente	the first client (a man)
la última cliente	the last client (a woman)
el nuevo pediatra	the new pediatrician (a man)
la mejor pediatra	the best pediatrician (a woman)

Some nouns exist in only one gender, but can refer to either men or women.

SPANISH	ENGLISH
un ángel	an angel
una persona encantadora	a charming person
una víctima de las circunstancias	a victim of circumstances

In Spanish, the masculine gender is also the "default" gender. In other words, you must use the masculine forms when you wish to refer to a mixed group, one comprised of both male and female. For example, *los pacientes* can refer to both Mr. and Mrs. García. This means that a noun referring to a group is feminine only if the group is entirely made up of feminine units. For example, *las pacientes* is only used when there are no men in the group of patients.

SPANISH	ENGLISH
Los niños pueden sentirse angustiados.	Children (girls and boys) can feel distressed.
Las niñas pueden sentirse angustiadas.	Girls can feel distressed.

In addition, you can use the masculine form to present a gender-neutral idea.

SPANISH	ENGLISH
Su niño debe aprenderse de memoria la información importante sobre la familia.	Your child (girl or boy) should memorize important information about the family.

NUMBER

All elements of the noun phrase (nouns, pronouns, articles, and adjectives) can appear in either the singular or the plural form. Most nouns form the plural by adding *-s* when the noun ends in a vowel (a, e, i, o, u) and *-es* everywhere else; however, nouns ending in an unstressed vowel with final *-s (la crisis, el lunes)* do not change in form *(las crisis, los lunes).* Also, remember that a final *-z* changes to *-ces* in the plural *(la luz, las luces).* Most adjectives form the plural in the same way as nouns; however, the masculine plural forms of the demonstrative adjectives are an exception. Other elements that do not fit the pattern described above are the plural forms of articles and pronouns, both of which will be discussed later in this chapter.

¡A PRACTICAR!

1A-PRIN-5

Indicate whether the word given below is masculine/singular, feminine/singular, masculine/plural, or feminine/plural.

1	trabajadores	M/S	F/S	**(M/P)**	F/P
2	enfermedad	M/S	**(F/S)**	M/P	F/P
3	peligrosas	M/S	F/S	M/P	**(F/P)**
?4	calentador	M/S	**(F/S)**	M/P	F/P
5	oreja	M/S	**(F/S)**	M/P	F/P
6	azúcares	M/S	F/S	**(M/P)**	F/P
7	temas	M/S	F/S	**(M/P)**	**(F/P)**
8	golpe	**(M/S)**	F/S	M/P	F/P

1A-PRIN-6

Rewrite the list given below to reflect the opposite of the form provided, either the singular or plural. Be sure to include the appropriate article.

1 cortadura profunda

las cortadaras profundas

2 días largos

el día largo

3 problemas graves

el problema grave

4 mano débil

las manos débil

5 paciente estable

los pacientes estables

6 decisiones difíciles

la decision difícil

7 meta posible

las metas posibles

8 personalidad fuerte

laspersonalidades fuertes

WORD ORDER: ADJECTIVES

Where a descriptive adjective will go in the noun phrase (preceding or following the noun) can sometimes be predicted, depending on the type of adjective it is.

When adjectives relate to quantity they precede the noun. The following adjectives belong to that group:

ADJECTIVE	SPANISH	ENGLISH
primer	el primer día	the first day
segundo	la segunda vez	the second time
tercer, etc.	la tercera dosis	the third dose
algún	algún tratamiento	some treatment
ambos	a ambos lados	on both sides
mucho	tiene mucho dolor	has much pain
otro	es otra cosa	it's something else
poco	tiene poca fiebre	has (only) a little fever
tanto	tanto trabajo	so much work
varios	varias experiencias	various experiences

Descriptive adjectives that do not refer to quantities normally follow the noun they modify if the person or thing is not known and must be specifically established. Here we don't know which patient the speaker is referring to unless he or she is described for us.

SPANISH	ENGLISH
El paciente grave estaba en la habitación más fría del hospital.	The seriously ill patient was in the coldest room of the hospital.

If the noun being described is already known, the descriptive adjective precedes the noun.

SPANISH	ENGLISH
El director habló de los graves incidentes causados por la epidemia.	The director spoke of the grave incidents caused by the epidemic.

In the above example, the speaker and his listener know which "grave incidents" are being referred to. Often, the adjective and the noun are already associated with each other, as in "the world-renowned professor Smith." That's why "my best friend" is *mi mejor amiga,* not *mi amiga mejor;* the speaker has already identified her as "best friend."

Sometimes when you change the normal order (the expected order of the elements) of the phrase, the new phrase takes on a new significance, even if the elements of the phrase are the same.

SPANISH	ENGLISH
Un médico bueno no es lo mismo que un buen médico.	A capable doctor is not the same as a kind-hearted doctor.

The following adjectives change meaning when they appear before the noun:

ADJECTIVE	BEFORE THE NOUN	AFTER THE NOUN
antiguo	el antiguo sistema *the previous (former) system*	el sistema antiguo *the old (not new) system*
alto	un alto indicio *a strong indication*	un hombre alto *a tall man*
bueno	un buen médico *a good (capable) doctor*	un médico bueno *a good-hearted (moral) doctor*
cierto	un cierto problema *a certain problem (not determinable)*	un diagnóstico cierto *a true diagnosis*
diferente	en diferentes clínicas *in various (several) clinics*	en clínicas diferentes *in different (distinct) clinics*
grande	un gran hombre *a great man*	un hombre grande *a big (large) man*
medio	media pinta *half a pint*	a temperatura media *at average temperature*
nuevo	el nuevo tratamiento *the new (new to the patient) treatment, different from a previous one*	el tratamiento nuevo *the treatment that just came out, brand new discovery*
pobre	un pobre hombre *a wretch, (luckless) man*	un hombre pobre *a poor man (without money)*
puro	la pura verdad *the honest truth, (nothing but)*	agua pura *pure water*
raro	por una rara casualidad *by sheer coincidence*	una enfermedad rara *a strange sickness*
semejante	semejante problema *such a problem*	un problema semejante *a similar problem*
simple	una simple idea *just a simple idea, (merely) an idea*	una solución simple *an uncomplicated solution*
solo	un solo minuto *only one minute*	un cuarto solo *a single room (alone)*
triste	unas tristes pijamas *some sad-looking (insignificant) pajamas*	una enfermera triste *a sad nurse*
único	su único problema *his only problem*	un problema único *a unique problem*
viejo	un viejo amigo *an old (longtime) friend*	un amigo viejo *an old (aged) friend*

¡A PRACTICAR!

1A-PRIN-7

Ángela is speaking to her great-aunt Beatriz, who is a little hard of hearing. Read what Ángela says to Beatriz and what Beatriz understands. Focus on Beatriz's interpretation of her niece's comment. Check entendió *if Beatriz understood Ángela correctly. If Beatriz misunderstood what Ángela said, even if this could be really true, check* no entendió. *Explain your choice of* entendió *or* no entendió. *You can explain in English.*

Modelo:

A Los pacientes que vienen a la clínica nueva antes iban al hospital.

B Hace tiempo que abrió la clínica, pero es diferente de la que teníamos antes.

entendió _____ *no entendió* __X__

Explanation: The word order of clínica nueva means that the clinic is a brand new clinic, not that it is distinct from another clinic, which existed previously *(diferente de la que teníamos antes).* To say, *esta clínica es diferente de la que teníamos antes,* you say *la nueva clínica,* not *la clínica nueva.*

Ángela y su tía Beatriz hablan sobre la clínica de La Comunidad y se alegran porque ahora la clínica tiene un nuevo director, el doctor Jaime Cuenca.

1

A La clínica de La Comunidad está en una antigua casa de familia.
previous

B Es una casa muy vieja.

entendió __X__ *no entendió* _____

Explanation: Antigua before casa means previous which could mean it is old (vieja)

2

A La cantidad de gente que viene a La Comunidad es un alto indicio de que esta clínica hacía mucha falta aquí.

B La cantidad de gente dice mucho sobre la importancia de la clínica.

entendió __X__ *no entendió* _____

Explanation: They both say it is important based on #

3

A El doctor Cuenca es un buen médico.

B El doctor Cuenca tiene un buen corazón.

entendió _____ *no entendió* __X__

Explanation: B seems to be talking about a corazón buen

4

A El doctor Cuenca me recomendó un tratamiento nuevo.

B Es un tratamiento que acaban de descubrir.

entendió __X__ *no entendió* _____

Explanation: Correct because the nuevo after means new treatment

5

A El nuevo puesto del doctor Cuenca es director de la clínica.

B Él tenía otro puesto antes.

entendió __X__ *no entendió* _____

Explanation: _____

6

A La Comunidad sirve a la gente pobre de esta área. poor

B No hay que pagar mucho en La Comunidad. no fee

entendió X *no entendió* ____

Explanation: ____

7

A Por una rara casualidad la clínica consiguió al doctor Cuenca como director.

B ¡Qué coincidencia!

entendió X *no entendió* ____

Explanation: ____

8

A En la clínica no tratan enfermedades raras; envían a estos pacientes al hospital. strange

B Los enfermos viejos no vienen a la clínica, van al hospital.

entendió ____ *no entendió* X

Explanation: talks about old patients not strange ones

1A-PRIN-8

Use the words from the list to complete the sentences. There will be two words (in addition to any articles you may need to add) in each blank and one word will be used twice.

dolor	magulladora	pura
gran/grande	media	semejante
hombre	nuevo	trabajo
hora	posibilidad	único
verdad	problema	

Juan llega a la clínica quejándose de un dolor en la mano.

CARMINA: Buenos días. ¿Lleva mucho tiempo esperando?

JUAN: No, sólo **(1)** una media hora *(a half an hour)*.

CARMINA: Y usted, ¿cómo se siente hoy?

JUAN: Me duele mucho la mano izquierda.

CARMINA: Veo que tiene **(2)** una magulladora grande *(a large bruise)*. ¿Le duele cuando aprieto aquí?

JUAN: Sí, nunca he tenido **(3)** semejante dolor *(such pain)*.

CARMINA: ¿El dolor se extiende por todo el brazo?

JUAN: No.

CARMINA: Es posible que se haya torcido la muñeca. ¿Es usted alérgico a alguna medicina?

JUAN: **(4)** la pura verdad *(The honest truth)* es que no sé.

CARMINA: Bueno, le voy a poner una tablilla y puede tomar esto si el dolor empeora.

JUAN: Ay, muchas gracias doctora. Ahora me siento como **(5)** un nuevo hombre *(a new man)*. Ahora, mi **(6)** única problema *(only problem)* es encontrar

? **(7)** diferente trabajo *(a different job)*.

or posibilidad

ARTICLES

Articles always agree with the nouns they accompany in gender (masculine or feminine) and number (singular or plural). Definite (the) and indefinite (a, an) articles are similar in English and Spanish and are used in the same way. Which article to use (masculine or feminine) depends on the noun and is something you'll learn as you memorize your vocabulary. Furthermore, whether to use a definite or indefinite article depends on your intent in the sentence, and for this you can guide yourself in Spanish by the same general rules as English.

Definite Articles

GENDER	SINGULAR	PLURAL
Masculine	el	los
Feminine	la	las

Indefinite Articles

GENDER	SINGULAR	PLURAL
Masculine	un	unos
Feminine	una	unas

WHEN TO USE ARTICLES

When a sentence begins with the subject, an article is generally used before the noun to refer to an idea in general or to an abstract notion.

SPANISH	ENGLISH
La ambulancia llega pronto.	The ambulance will arrive soon.
Una ambulancia viene.	An ambulance is on the way.
La gente nunca escucha.	People never listen.

This concept is particularly difficult for English speakers to remember when the subject is some variant of "people." One way of dealing with "people," especially if it is not meant to express the human race in general, is to omit the word entirely and let the plural verb serve as "they," as in the example below.

SPANISH	ENGLISH
Vinieron a verlo todos los días.	They came to see him every day. (People came to see him every day.)

Articles are used to change adjectives into nouns.

SPANISH	ENGLISH
Los nuevos no muestran síntomas de infección.	The new ones don't show signs of infection.
Unos pocos tienen fiebre.	A few have a fever.

When a feminine singular noun *(agua)* starts with *a* stressed *a* or *ha*, the article *la* that would have come in front of the noun is changed to *el*. This only happens in the singular.

SPANISH	ENGLISH
Los pequeños no entienden que el agua está fría.	The little ones don't understand that the water is cold.

When you're speaking about someone, not to him or her, and you wish to refer to him or her by his or her title, *(señor, señora, señorita, doctor,* and *doctora...)*, use the definite article.

SPANISH	ENGLISH
El doctor Ruiz habló en español con los señores García.	Doctor Ruiz spoke Spanish with the Garcías.

Exceptions to this rule are *don* and *doña,* which never use the article. They are somewhat archaic in tone, and not everyone uses them, but when they are used, *don* and *doña* are wonderful expressions of respect, affection, and awareness of the value of the person. They can be used with the person's given name. You will notice when watching *La Comunidad* that Federico addresses Rafa as *don Rafa.*

SPANISH	ENGLISH
Don Miguel, no se preocupe por su señora.	Don't worry about your wife (literally "your lady"), Don Miguel.

The definite article is used before all names of languages, except when the name of the language follows *en, de,* or the verbs *hablar, estudiar, aprender,* or *enseñar.* If there's an adverb between the verbs listed above and the name of the language, the article is used.

SPANISH	ENGLISH
Él habla español.	He speaks Spanish.
Habla bien el español.	He speaks Spanish well.

You should use the definite article in combination with days of the week, dates, seasons, time, and meals. However, the article is omitted when the days of the week are used with *hoy, mañana, ayer, anteayer,* and *pasado mañana.*

SPANISH	ENGLISH
Su próxima cita es el miércoles a las diez de la mañana.	Your next appointment is Wednesday at ten in the morning.
La señora no puede comer el almuerzo porque tiene náusea.	The woman cannot eat lunch because she is nauseated.
Mañana es lunes.	Tomorrow is Monday.

The indefinite articles are omitted after the verb ser when what follows is a noun referring to a profession, religion, nationality, or marital status; however, if the noun is modified, use the article.

SPANISH	ENGLISH
Ella es salvadoreña, también es una enfermera fabulosa.	She is Salvadoran and is also a fabulous nurse.

Indefinite articles are also omitted after *no hay* (in any tense: *no hubo, no habrá...*) when used to indicate *some* or *any.*

SPANISH	ENGLISH
No había medicinas en la farmacia, ni una sola.	There weren't any medicines in the pharmacy, not a single one.

You should omit the indefinite article after *sin* and after *con* when you're talking about a type of object (with an exercise, with a medicine).

SPANISH	ENGLISH
Algunos problemas de salud se pueden resolver sin medicina, pero su enfermedad no se cura con té.	Some health problems can be solved without medical intervention, but your illness can't be cured with a tea.

¡A PRACTICAR!

1A-PRIN-9

Add definite or indefinite articles where needed. Not all blanks require an article.

Duna está cansada. Hoy ha sido un día difícil y ahora ella protesta por las condiciones de trabajo. ¡Y es la una de la tarde solamente!

Las mañanas son **(1)** __los__ peores momentos del día, porque nunca sabemos cuál va a ser **(2)** __el__ programa. Claro que hay **(3)** __un__ horario con citas y trabajos específicos, pero uno nunca sabe **(4)** __la__ verdad hasta que empieza el día. Mira, por ejemplo hoy, en la calle Main acaban de cortar **(5)** __el__ agua, así que **(6)** __la__ gente que vive allí va a llegar tarde para sus citas. **(7)** __las__ cosas que ocurren en una parte de **(8)** __la__ ciudad tienen un impacto en lo que ocurre en **(9)** __la__ otra. Por la tarde creo que va a mejorar **(10)** __el__ ambiente porque vienen muchos **(11)** __los__ niños a visitarme. A mí me gustan mucho **(12)** __los__ niños. **(13)** __los__ primeros vienen ahora y son **(14)** ______ salvadoreños que se mudaron **(15)** __el__ área hace sólo **(16)** __unas__ días. Son unos niños preciosos, saludables, alegres, llenos de preguntas y muy inquietos, pero eso no me molesta, porque me encanta ver que **(17)** __los__ recién llegados tienen buena salud.

1A-PRIN-10

Read the following sentences about the staff and patients of La Comunidad. *Explain in English why the indicated articles are either used or omitted. Then translate the sentence.*

Modelo: El doctor Cuenca llama a su hermana por la mañana.

Explanation: Articles are used to refer to people by their titles. Articles are used with expressions of time.

Translation: *Dr. Cuenca calls his sister in the morning.*

1 La gente llega todas las mañanas a la clínica.

people come every morning to the clinic. 1 refers to idea & 2 expressions of time

2 Jaime Cuenca, el nuevo director, es ______ obstetra.

Jaime Cuenca, the new director, is an obstetrician. Title

3 Laura, la prima de la doctora Estrada, no tiene ______ trabajo.

Laura, cousin of Doctor Estrada, has no job. titles

4 Pasado mañana es ______ martes, 11 de noviembre.

After tomorrow is tuesday, 11th of november. Has reference days of the week & mañana.

DEMONSTRATIVE ADJECTIVES

Demonstrative adjectives are used to indicate nouns.

	SINGULAR	PLURAL
Masculine	este	estos aqui
Feminine	esta	estas
Masculine	ese	esos
Feminine	esa	esas
Masculine	aquel	aquellos
Feminine	aquella	aquellas

Este means "this" and refers to things that are near the speaker. *Ese* and *aquel* both mean "that," but *ese* is used for things that are not very far away from the speaker, while *aquel* is used for things that are far away, both spatially and temporally. Demonstrative adjectives precede the noun and have no accent.

In the absence of a noun, demonstrative adjectives can function as pronouns, and as such they require an accent. The accent distinguishes them in written form from the demonstrative adjectives.

SPANISH	ENGLISH
No me gusta esta opción sino ésa.	I don't like this option; I like that one.

¡A PRACTICAR!

1A-PRIN-11

Fill in the blanks with the correct demonstrative adjective. Keep in mind how far away objects are from the speaker!

Carmina está hablando con Viviana Carrillo, una paciente.

CARMINA: Sra. Carrillo, **(1)** esta medicina que tengo aquí es la que necesita tomar.

VIVIANA: Gracias, doctora. No tengo problemas con **(2)** esta clase de medicina, sino con la otra.

? CARMINA: Y si hace **(3)** ~~estos~~ esos ejercicios que le recomendé, no debe volver a tener los dolores.

VIVIANA: Los prefiero. No me gustan **(4)** ~~estos~~ aquellos ejercicios que me recomendó mi doctor en Venezuela hace años.

CARMINA: Bueno, venga a verme en una semana y ¡asegúrese de traer a **(5)** esos hijos suyos para que los pueda conocer!

1A-PRIN-12

Describe the picture below in a paragraph of at least three sentences using appropriate demonstrative adjectives.

Palabras útiles

sala de espera	escritorio (*desk*)
cuadro (*painting*)	recepción

En esta foto...

POSSESSIVE ADJECTIVES

Possessive adjectives are used in Spanish and English more or less the same way and have similar meanings. They express ownership. Remember, though, that since adjectives in Spanish express agreement, you must make sure that the possessive adjective agrees with the thing possessed! The "short" forms are used before the noun, and the "long" forms are used when the possessive follows the noun, where English would use "of mine, of yours," etc.

Short Form

PERSON	SINGULAR	PLURAL
1st person sing.	mi	mis
2nd person sing.	tu	tus
3rd person sing.	su	sus
1st person pl.	nuestro, nuestra	nuestros, nuestras
2nd person pl.	vuestro, vuestra	vuestros, vuestras
3rd person pl.	su	sus

Here are some examples of how the short form is used:

SPANISH	ENGLISH
Jaime siempre habla con sus amigos por teléfono.	Jaime always speaks with his friends on the phone.
Carmina y Laura van a su casa.	Carmina and Laura go to their house.

Long Form

SPANISH	SINGULAR	PLURAL
1st person sing.	mío, mía	míos, mías
2nd person sing.	tuyo, tuya	tuyos, tuyas
3rd person sing.	suyo, suya	suyos, suyas
1st person pl.	nuestro, nuestra	nuestros, nuestras
2nd person pl.	vuestro, vuestra	vuestros, vuestras
3rd person pl.	suyo, suya	suyos, suyas

Here are a few examples:

SPANISH	ENGLISH
Estos pacientes son míos. Acaban de llegar de Guatemala y por eso necesitan ayuda.	These are my patients. They have just arrived from Guatemala and because of this need help.
Él dice que la idea es solamente un sueño nuestro.	He says that the idea is only a dream of ours.

Since *suyo* can at times be ambiguous, you can use *de él, de ella, de usted, de ellos,* etc. instead of *suyo/a* or *suyos/as.*

SPANISH	ENGLISH
Mi madre trabaja aquí en el hospital pero la madre suya no trabaja. (...pero la de él)	My mother works here in the hospital, but his mother doesn't work.

Vuestro and *vuestra,* singular and plural, are only used in Spain. All Latin Americans and U.S. Spanish speakers originally from Latin American countries use the 3rd person plural forms *(su/sus)* in place of the 2nd person plural.

que : than

que la/el tuya

¡A PRACTICAR!

1A-PRIN-13

Rewrite the sentences so that it is clear who possesses what.

Modelo:
Los libros (de Jaime) están en la oficina.
Sus libros están en la oficina.

1 Los pacientes (de nosotros) esperan en la sala.

Nuestros pacientes esperan en la sala.

2 La clínica favorita (mía) es La Comunidad.

Mi clínica favorita es La Comunidad.

3 La glucosa (de Laura) está un poco baja.

Su glucosa está un poco baja

4 El amigo (de ustedes) está bajo supervisión médica.

Su amigo está bajo supervision medica

5 La paciente (de nosotros) está bajo supervisión médica también.

Nuestra está bajo supervision medica tambien

1A-PRIN-14

Write the sentences following the model being sure to use both the short and long forms of the possessive adjectives. Be creative!

Imagínate que trabajas en otra clínica y que quieres aprender de Jaime lo que él hace en La Comunidad. ¿Cuáles son las diferencias entre las dos clínicas?

Modelo: pacientes, más pobre

Mis pacientes son más pobres que los tuyos.

1 administración, diferente

___

2 clientela, más grande

___

3 presupuesto, más pequeño

___

4 personal, menos diverso

___

5 llamadas telefónicas, menos frecuente

___

1A-PRIN-15

Write a brief paragraph of at least five sentences in which you compare your place of work to La Comunidad*, being sure to use the appropriate demonstrative adjectives.*

___

PRONOUNS

Pronouns, words that can stand in for the entire noun phrase, sometimes reflect the gender and number of the noun they replace. While in English only the pronouns for the third person singular indicate gender (he/she, him/her, his/her), most Spanish pronouns have different forms that reflect number and gender as they function as subjects or objects in a sentence. English has a remarkable tolerance for ungrammatical uses of pronouns.

PERSON	SUBJECT PRONOUNS	DIRECT OBJECT PRONOUNS	INDIRECT OBJECT PRONOUNS
I	yo	me	me
you, informal	tú	te	te
you, formal	usted	lo/la	le
he	él	lo	le
she	ella	la	le
we	nosotros, nosotras	nos	nos
you plural, informal	vosotros, vosotras	os	os
you plural, both informal and formal	ustedes	los, las	les
they	ellos, ellas	los, las	les

Although the direct and indirect object pronouns are included here so you will recognize them, you need now only to focus on the subject pronouns.

The *vosotros* is used in Spain for the informal plural, like a plural of *tú*. These pronouns are also accompanied by specific verbs, those in the *vosotros* form, which are not used at all in Latin America.

SPANISH	ENGLISH
Vosotros podéis ir mañana al laboratorio para que os saquéis una placa del pecho.	You (plural) can go to the lab tomorrow to get a chest x-ray done.

The result is that, to a Spaniard's ear, we are being very formal when we address him and his friends with *ustedes.* Nevertheless, most Spanish speakers are very aware of the regional oddities of other Spanish speakers, very much like speakers of American English are aware of the frequent use of "mate" by Australians or the differences in the pronunciation of words like "schedule" and the spelling of "neighbour and colour" across the Atlantic. The way you pronounce the language, your vocabulary, and choice of structures will signal to a Spaniard that your Spanish comes from Latin America and will cue him to expect the following:

SPANISH	ENGLISH
Ustedes pueden ir mañana al laboratorio para que se saquen una placa del pecho.	You (all) can go to the lab tomorrow to get a chest x-ray done.

¡A PRACTICAR!

1A-PRIN-16

Replace the underlined words with pronouns where needed (sometimes you should not use a pronoun) and rewrite the sentences in a clearer and simpler form. Remember that verbs don't need a subject pronoun for their meaning to be clear. Use the pronouns if the meaning of the verb is ambiguous.

Duna y Carmina hablan sobre Emilia y su familia.

DUNA: Emilia y su familia **(1)** ____________ son de Guatemala, ¿no?

CARMINA: No, me parece que ~~Emilia y su familia~~ **(2)** ellos son de Chiapas. Emilia **(3)** ____________ llegó primero y los padres y hermanos de Emilia **(4)** ____________ llegaron más tarde.

DUNA: ¿Dónde conociste a Emilia?

CARMINA: La conocí **(5)** ella cuando vino con la familia de Emilia **(6)** ____________ a la clínica por primera vez para hacerles los exámenes de rutina.

DUNA: No hace mucho que llegaron, por eso me preocupan los síntomas que veo en Emilia.

CARMINA: Sí, los síntomas que ves en ~~Emilia~~ **(7)** ella son sospechosos. Supongo que hablaste sobre los síntomas con Emilia **(8)** ella.

DUNA: Naturalmente. Emilia, su familia y yo **(9)** nosotros estamos algo preocupados.

CARMINA: Tú, Emilia y su familia **(10)** ustedes pueden contar con mi apoyo.

CONCEPTO IMPORTANTE: AGREEMENT

The *Concepto importante* for *Unidad 1a* centers on the grammatical agreement that occurs within the parts of a noun phrase. A noun phrase is a group of words that function together in the sentence, with a noun as its nucleus. The noun phrase can function as subject, *el esposo de esta señora,* or as object, *un tratamiento intensivo y muy doloroso,* but in all cases the nouns and adjectives within it will agree. In other words, adjectives and articles reflect the noun's gender.

Since *tratamiento,* for example, is a masculine noun and is used here in the singular form, *intensivo* and *doloroso* will also be masculine and singular.

SPANISH	ENGLISH
El esposo de esta señora recibió un tratamiento intensivo y muy doloroso hace unos meses.	The husband of this lady received an intensive and very painful treatment some months ago.

This is extremely important, because your listener will be expecting this coherence within your noun phrases. Incomprehension results if the string breaks, for example, if you say:

El esposo de esta señora recibió un tratamiento intensiva y muy dolorosas hace unas meses.

Your listener will wonder: What happened in the treatment? Who was intensive and painful? What's *unas meses?*

There needs to be agreement, *concordancia* in Spanish, within the noun phrase, as well as between the subject and the predicate of a sentence; this is not a difficult concept, nor is it new for speakers of English.

SPANISH	ENGLISH
Él sabe donde está el paciente.	He knows where the patient is.
También yo sé donde están los pacientes.	I also know where the patients are.

The Difficulty

The problem is not that English sees agreement differently, but that English is highly tolerant of "disagreement." In English we're hardly aware of the existence of gender. Is it "My country, I would do anything for it" or "I would do anything for her"? Speakers of Spanish are intuitively aware that agreement is present and are so fine-tuned to its absence that they perceive the absence of agreement as somehow significant. In other words, if you disregard the gender and number of adjectives accompanying a noun in a phrase, your Spanish-speaking listener will hesitate and try to find meaning in your errors.

When you speak to a Spanish speaker in Spanish you need to be very careful, because *el país* and *la patria* are definitely gendered. If you say, *Es mi país, yo haría cualquier cosa por ella,* your listener will assume that you've changed the topic of conversation in mid-sentence and will wonder who this woman is for whom you'd do anything!

Of course, communication is not such a chamber of horrors, and your listener, hearing your accent, will understand that you are learning the language and will probably come back with "Who is this woman for whom you'd do anything?" or some such phrase, asking you to clarify. Fortunately for us, speech is a complex confluence of meaningful strings, and grammatical structures are only one of many ways to carry meaning. Mistakes in agreement can confuse your listener, but your accent, facial expression, and body language will signal that what you said was probably not what you intended. Where there is an interest in communicating, errors can be made clear, and in time the right message can be conveyed.

Strategies

Try using these simple strategies to help you with **agreement:**

- **Listen** to yourself as you speak! Learn to recognize the grammar points that are the hardest for you and stay aware of them. Question even that which "feels" right if it is the sort of thing you have problems with.
- To help you remember the noun's gender, **learn new nouns with an appropriate article.** The more connections your brain can make with a new item you're trying to store in memory, the easier it will be for you to remember it when you need it. Learn new words in complete phrases, with a gesture or particular use in mind. ("The ER doctor asks the patient: *Mueva la cabeza.*" rather than *mover* = to move.)
- Keep the gender of the nouns that you're using in the sentence in mind **until you finish the sentence.** In the example above, remembering *el país* as a unit may have helped the speaker to avoid using *ella* at the end of the sentence.

¡A PRACTICAR!

1A-PRIN-17

Fill in the blanks with the words needed to complete the sentences correctly. You will need to use more words than just those listed below!

Ashleigh y Duna preparan un cartel (poster) para explicarles a los clientes de la clínica algunos datos sobre el envenenamiento por plomo. Esto es parte del texto:

El plomo es **(1)** un veneno peligroso *(a dangerous poison)* que daña todos los sistemas del cuerpo. **(2)** Muchas casa de Americano *(many American homes)* tienen **(3)** ~~pintura~~ viejo *(old paint)* con plomo. A menudo es la pintura que cubre la madera de las ventanas la que contiene **(4)** muy alto planos *(very high levels)* de plomo y **(5)** un niño pequeño *(a small child)* puede envenenarse fácilmente al masticarla. El plomo puede entrar por **(6)** sus una boca. *(his or her mouth)* o una cortadura. Por esta razón, es importante hacer un análisis de plomo inmediatamente. Mientras espera los resultados del análisis usted debe seguir **(7)** eses recomendaciónes *(these recommendations)*.

1A-PRIN-18

Describe each character by filling in the blanks with the correct form of the words from the lists provided below. Use the words that are provided and add articles, pronouns, and prepositions as necessary. Remember to check for agreement. (Some of the blanks will require more than one word.)

competente	feliz
complicado	lugar
diferente	mucho
inglés	muy

Ya sabemos un poco de la vida de algunos personajes. Por ejemplo, Ángela y Rafa están casados y son **(1)** felizez *(happy)*. Antes vivían en México, pero ahora que viven **(2)** en un diferente lugar *(in a different place)* su relación es **(3)** muy complicado *(very complicated)*. Rafa no se siente **(4)** competente *(capable)* porque no habla bien **(5)** inglés *(English)*; pero en español tenía precisión y vocabulario; era un profesional. Ángela lo anima y le dice que lo quiere **(6)** mucho *(a lot)*.

ambos	joven
enamorado	preocupado

Laura es la prima de Carmina. Carmina está **(7)** preocupada (*worried*) por ella, porque no siempre hace lo que debe y además es diabética. Sin embargo, Laura no le hace caso. Está **(8)** enamorada (*in love*) de Alex aunque pelean mucho. Por eso Carmina siempre está muy molesta con **(9)** ambos joven (*both young people*).

amigo	junto
bueno	mejor
bonito	

Duna y Ashleigh trabajan **(10)** junto (*together*) en la clínica de La Comunidad. Son **(11)** bonitas (*pretty*) y también son **(12)** bueno amigos (*good friends.*) En realidad, Duna es **(13)** su mejor amigo de Ashleigh (*Ashleigh's best friend.*)

cierto	suyo
hombre	asunto
listo	simpático
amigo	

Jaime también tiene amigos, porque es **(14)** un hombre simpático (*a friendly man*) y siempre está **(15)** listo (*ready*) para ayudar a sus amigos, pero hay **(16)** ~~cierto~~ ciertas preguentas (*certain questions*) que le molestan mucho a Jaime. Por ejemplo, todos **(17)** sus amigos (*his friends*) le piden medicinas por teléfono, sin recetas, sin examen médico... Esto lo pone furioso. ¡Qué problema tiene Jaime!

1A-PRIN-19

Use the list of words to construct a complete paragraph that describes a person who may be showing symptoms of the flu. Give six symptoms using the words on the list. Write three sentences minimum.

Palabras útiles

alta	fiebre	peso *(weight)*
apetito	nocturno	sudores *(sweats)*
cansancio	pérdida	sufrir
constante	persistente	tos *(cough)*
escalofríos		

Carmina habla con Jaime sobre Emilia Cortés, una de sus pacientes. Ella describe ciertos síntomas relacionados con la gripe.

—Jaime, me preocupa Emilia Cortés. Ayer vino a verme y tiene todos estos síntomas:

___

___

___

___

___

___

___

___

___

___

¿Qué piensas de su estado? ¿Tendrá gripe?

1A-PRIN-20

After hearing about the risks of working with pesticides, Rafa decides to write an informational article about the problem for La Voz. *Read the article and use this material to write a new paragraph in a more accessible style for your friend Sara.*

Los pesticidas

Los campesinos tienen uno de los trabajos más peligrosos, debido a las largas horas de trabajo y las condiciones bajo las cuales trabajan. Su constante exposición a los químicos agrícolas causa riesgos de salud para ellos y su familia. Estos riesgos se extienden al hogar porque los padres traen los químicos a casa al regresar del trabajo. Por esta exposición a los pesticidas, es más probable que los campesinos y sus hijos desarrollen cierto tipo de leucemia o cáncer. Las leyes actuales no son suficientes para proteger a los campesinos de los posibles efectos de los químicos. Sólo requieren el uso de equipo de protección, entrenamiento y una estación de limpieza con agua limpia. Además muchos rancheros violan las leyes y esto resulta en enfermedades no reportadas. Hay que trabajar para mejorar la situación del campesino.

Querida Sara,

___

___

___

___

___

___

EL VOSEO

Forty percent of Latin Americans in Central America and the Southern Cone (Argentina, Chile, Paraguay, Uruguay, Bolivia) use *vos* as an alternative for *tú.* This is called *el voseo. Vos* is accompanied by specific verb forms and, similar to *vosotros,* is an informal form of address, reserved for the family, close friends, and conversations intended to be funny. Speakers who use *vos* also understand and can use *tú.*

SELF-REFLECTION

1. How do I know the gender of a noun?

If it ends in *-a,* it's usually feminine; if it ends in *-o, -r, -l,* it's probably masculine. Some other endings also indicate one gender or the other, but the best way to know the gender of a noun is to look it up in a dictionary. To remember the gender, memorize every new noun within a phrase. For example, memorize *"Hoy hace mucho calor:* It's very hot today." rather than "*calor:* heat."

2. Can you change the final **-o** *to* **-a**, *or add* **-a** *to a title to make it feminine, like* **doctor, doctora?**

Usually. For example:

MASCULINE	FEMININE
el enfermero	la enfermera
el técnico	la técnica
el farmacéutico	la farmacéutica
el cirujano	la cirujana

Some nouns that refer to humans are identical in form, but show gender in the modifiers. For example:

MASCULINE	FEMININE
el ayudante simpático	la ayudante simpática
el primer estudiante	la primera estudiante
el joven	la joven

Gender is always marked, either in the ending of the word or with words that are completely different. For example:

MASCULINE	FEMININE
el hombre	la mujer
el rey	la reina
el toro	la vaca

3. What's the difference between* mucho *and* muy*? Which one do I use to say that something is "very" serious, for example?

Eso es serio. ¡Es muy serio! Just remember that *"muy"* means "very" while *"mucho"* means "a lot" or "much". For example:

Él trabaja mucho. (mucho + verb)
Él trabaja muy rápidamente. (muy + adverb)
Éste es un trabajo muy importante. (muy + adjective)

FOLLOW-UP TIPS

- Ask people around you for the meaning of new words you hear. —*Usted dijo... ¿Qué significa...?* Try to keep new words within a phrase (*la pierna rota,* not just *"rota"*) when you're learning them.
- Point and ask for the correct term when you need to say something —*¿Cómo se dice...?* Ask for the gender —*¿el... o la...?*
- Try to find time to collect new vocabulary, whether you write it down on the margins of this workbook, or start a "vocabulary sheet" for yourself on a memo pad or your palm pilot.
- Read newspapers and magazines in Spanish when you can. Jot down a few new words and look them up later.
- Listen to Spanish speakers talk to each other!

DO YOU REMEMBER?

You get closer and closer to understanding and speaking Spanish every time you struggle to find meaning in what you hear, to put your thoughts into some form of Spanish. Likewise, you improve as others react to what you say and correct or approve your words.

Aside from all this, as an intermediate learner, you also want to develop the ability to monitor and edit what you say in Spanish on your own. You want to be able to listen to yourself and know when you've made a mistake or what you can say with more clarity or warmth. This is a very high goal, and it will take time, but it's precisely the development of this self-monitor that distinguishes the intermediate learner from the beginner.

Answer the questions based on the explanations found in the *Principios* section of the textbook. If you found any section particularly difficult, go back and try some of the exercises again. There are also links to Spanish language materials on the *Recursos* website.

1 What characteristics of nouns do articles and adjectives reflect?

2 Can we always tell whether a noun is masculine or feminine?

3 If a noun ends in *-s,* what can you assume?

4 If you hear a phrase with an adjective preceding a noun, and that adjective is usually found *after* the noun, what may the speaker be doing?

5 What does "agreement" mean?

6 When a sentence begins with a subject, what comes before the noun?

7 What is the difference between *mucho* and *muy*?

FOOD FOR THOUGHT

The following questions are intended to serve as a springboard for discussion. Think about them as you read the story.

- How can I develop trusting and respectful relationships with my patients and clients?
- How can I recognize and challenge my own assumptions?
- How can I learn to recognize my patients' and clients' strengths and to build on teachable moments?
- How can I become partners with colleagues who are bridges across culture, with other organizations in the community that have similar interests and with members of the community I hope to serve?

NOTES FROM THE FIELD *Wes Wallace*

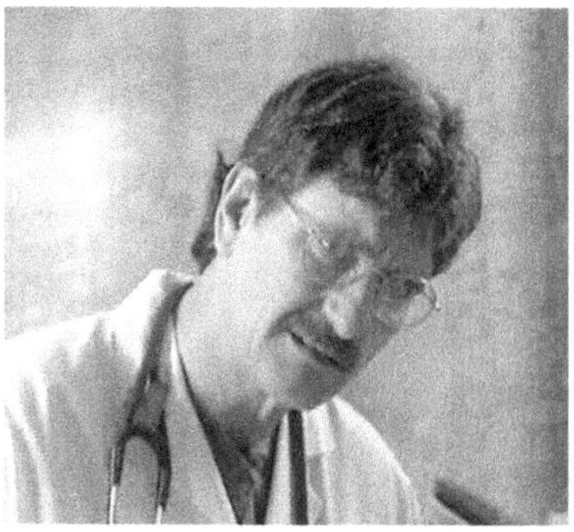

The EMS radio crackled in the Emergency Department "...twenty one year-old male, motor-vehicle crash, combative, speaks only Spanish..."

The gurney sped through the double doors toward the trauma room. A thin brown man struggled against the restraints, his eyes wide with fear and pain. His body was immobilized on a backboard and his head held rigidly by a cervical collar and head blocks. I could only imagine the terror he felt. Half conscious, he'd been dragged from a twisted wreck by strangers yelling at him and to each other in a language he didn't understand. He'd been fastened to a board, while sharp needles were poked into his arms. His pleas had gone unheeded and his questions unanswered. The strange experience continued in the Emergency Department. Strangers in white coats flocked around him, cutting off his clothes and prodding his body.

Finally, I asked everyone to stop for just a moment. I leaned over him so he could see my face and said to him in flawed but understandable Spanish, "I'm Dr. Wallace. You've been in a bad wreck. We're doctors and nurses and we're going to help you. We'll tell you everything we're going to do before we do it."

He visibly relaxed; the look of terror left his face.

DISCUSSION QUESTIONS

Wes describes an all too frequent situation in hospital emergency departments.

1 In addition to speaking Spanish with the patient, what else did Wes do to put him at ease?
Kept him in the loop

2 How do you think Wes felt after seeing the man relax and the "terror leave his face"?
reassured

3 How could Wes advocate for non-English speaking patients in his institution?

4 What types of recommendations might you make where you work? get a translator

LA DIABETES

La diabetes es un problema creciente de salud pública

Más de 18 millones de estadounidenses tienen diabetes. La diabetes, que es ya la sexta causa principal de muerte en Estados Unidos, es responsable de la muerte de más de 200,000 personas cada año. El número de adultos estadounidenses a los que se les ha diagnosticado diabetes, que incluye a mujeres con diabetes gestacional (diabetes que se presenta durante el embarazo), se ha incrementado en un 61% desde 1991 y se calcula que aumente a más del doble para el año 2050.

Las personas con diabetes no producen suficiente insulina o la utilizan inadecuadamente. La insulina es una hormona que permite que la glucosa (el azúcar) sea transportada a las células y se transforme en energía. Cuando la diabetes no es tratada, el azúcar y las grasas permanecen en la sangre y, con el correr del tiempo, dañan varios órganos vitales. La diabetes puede causar enfermedades cardiacas, accidentes cerebrovasculares (derames cerebrales), ceguera, insuficiencia renal, complicaciones durante el embarazo, amputación de las extremidades inferiores, así como fallecimientos relacionados con la gripe y neumonía. Los 5.2 millones de estadounidenses que ignoran que tienen diabetes son particularmente vulnerables a estas complicaciones.

Hay dos tipos principales de diabetes. El tipo 1, que aparece con mayor frecuencia durante la infancia o la adolescencia. La diabetes tipo 2, que está vinculada a la obesidad y a la falta de actividad física, representa entre el 90 y el 95 por ciento de los casos de diabetes y en la mayoría de los casos afecta a personas mayores de 40 años. Sin embargo, ya no se considera una enfermedad que afecta solo a los adultos. El tipo 2 se ve ahora en personas cada vez más jóvenes e incluso en niños y adolescentes.

La diabetes tiene sus efectos mayores en los ancianos, las mujeres y en algunos grupos raciales y étnicos. Uno de cada cinco adultos mayores de 65 años padece de diabetes. Los adultos afro-americanos, hispanos, indios americanos y nativos de Alaska tienen una probabilidad entre dos y tres veces más alta que los adultos blancos de padecer de diabetes.

Además de los millones de estadounidenses con diabetes, se estima que 16 millones de adultos en EE.UU. entre 40 y 74 años de edad tienen prediabetes, es decir, que su nivel de azúcar en la sangre es elevado, pero no lo suficiente como para ser clasificado como diabetes. Las personas con prediabetes tienen un alto riesgo de que esta afección se convierta en diabetes.

La diabetes le cuesta al país cerca de 132,000 millones de dólares al año, 92,000 millones de los cuales por concepto de gastos médicos directos y 40,000 millones por gastos indirectos como consecuencia de la pérdida de productividad. El costo promedio anual por concepto de atención médica de una persona con diabetes ascendió a $13,243 en 2002, en comparación con $2,560 para una persona que no sufre de diabetes. Los gastos por concepto de diabetes representaron el 11% de los gastos del sector salud a nivel nacional durante el año 2002.

CONTESTA LAS SIGUIENTES PREGUNTAS:

1 ¿Sabes que existen dos tipos de diabetes, el tipo I y el tipo II? ¿Cuáles son las principales diferencias entre los dos tipos?

2 La diabetes tipo II es mucho más común hoy día. ¿Cuál crees que es la causa?

Muchas de las complicaciones de la diabetes se pueden prevenir

Si bien la carga que significan las complicaciones de la diabetes es cada vez más alarmante, gran parte de ella podría prevenirse con una detección temprana, mejores servicios de salud y una mejor educación sobre el auto control de la diabetes. Los siguientes son ejemplos de complicaciones relacionadas con la diabetes que podrían ser prevenidas o reducidas.

Enfermedades de los ojos y ceguera. Cada año, entre 12 mil y 24 mil personas pierden la vista en este país a causa de enfermedades de los ojos provocadas por la diabetes. Los exámenes oftalmológicos periódicos así como un tratamiento a tiempo pueden prevenir hasta el 90% de los casos de ceguera causados por la diabetes; sin embargo, sólo al 64.2% de las personas con diabetes se les hizo examen de los ojos con dilatación de pupila en 2002.

Enfermedades renales. Alrededor de 42,813 personas con diabetes sufren de insuficiencia renal cada año y más de 100,000 reciben tratamiento para esta enfermedad. El tratamiento para controlar la presión sanguínea y los niveles de glucosa en la sangre puede reducir en cerca del 50% la tasa de insuficiencia renal relacionada con la diabetes.

Amputaciones. Cerca de 82,000 personas sufren amputación de pierna, pie o dedos del pie cada año como consecuencia de la diabetes. Los programas de atención de los pies en los que se incluyen exámenes periódicos así como la educación del paciente pueden evitar hasta un 85% de estas amputaciones.

Enfermedades cardiovasculares. Las enfermedades cardiacas y los accidentes cerebrovasculares (derrames cerebrales) causan la muerte de cerca del 65% de las personas que sufren de diabetes. Estas muertes podrían reducirse en un 30% mediante mejores tratamientos para controlar la presión sanguínea, la glucosa en la sangre y los niveles de colesterol en la sangre.

Complicaciones del embarazo. Cerca de 18,000 mujeres con diabetes preexistente y alrededor de 135,000 mujeres con diabetes gestacional tienen bebés cada año. Estas mujeres, así como sus hijos, se enfrentan a un riesgo mayor de complicaciones tales como partos de niños sin vida, deformaciones congénitas y una mayor necesidad de realizar cesáreas. Las mujeres que sufren de diabetes gestacional y sus hijos también tienen un mayor riesgo de sufrir de obesidad y de contraer diabetes posteriormente. Estos riesgos pueden reducirse con exámenes de diagnóstico y atención especializada antes, durante y después del embarazo.

Muertes relacionadas con la gripe y neumonía. Cada año, entre 10 mil y 30 mil personas con diabets fallecen a causa de complicaciones de la gripe o la neumonía. Tienen una probabilidad aproximadamente tres veces mayor de perder la vida a causa de estas complicaciones que las personas que no padecen de diabetes; sin embargo, solo un 55% de las personas con diabetes se ponen la vacuna contra la gripe cada año.

To read this article online, go to www.yalebooks.com/salud.

3 Ya sabemos que Laura padece de diabetes, aunque no nos han dicho de cuál de los dos tipos. Según tu opinión, ¿de qué tipo será? ¿Por qué lo crees?

4 Actualmente no existe cura para la diabetes. Por ello, los que padecen esta enfermedad crónica deben cuidarse mucho. Escribe un párrafo con algunas sugerencias para los enfermos de diabetes tipo I o tipo II, el que prefieras.

COMPROBACIÓN

DVD

Las preguntas de Comprobación *están diseñadas para evaluar tu habilidad de usar lo que has aprendido, en situaciones nuevas y diferentes. Aunque el contexto todavía es limitado y las respuestas están restringidas y guiadas, debes interpretar más.*

SECCIÓN A

¿Qué pasa en la Historia*? Escoge las palabras que completan mejor la oración. ¡Cuidado con la gramática!*

1 Ángela y Rafa, dos de los personajes de nuestra historia, están (casado / casados / se casan) y viven ahora en los Estados Unidos porque Ángela tiene (un / una / —) trabajo aquí.

2 Jaime, el director de la clínica, tiene (muchas / muchos / muy grande) problemas con sus amigos y (su / sus) familia porque lo llaman y le piden medicinas por teléfono.

3 Laura y Carmina son (hermanas / primas / tías) pero también son muy diferentes.

4 Carmina es (bonitas y simpáticas / interesante y sincero / seria y responsable) y Laura es (inmaduro y tonto / jóvenes y felices / rebelde y alegre).

5 Duna y Ashleigh son compañeras. Ashleigh está aprendiendo español y Duna es una (buen / buena / buenas) maestra.

SECCIÓN B

Estas oraciones describen el accidente de Laura. Escoge las palabras que completan mejor cada oración.

azúcar	diabetes
baja	diabética
casi	le baja
da cuenta	seria

Laura va por la carretera en su automóvil. Es de noche. Ella es **(1)** diabetica y necesita comer **(2)** azucar, pero no encuentra nada. Ella se **(3)** dacuenta de que su situación es **(4)** seria. **(5)** le baja la glucosa y **(6)** casi choca.

¡A CONVERSAR!

primas
obstetra
Jaime

Carmina laura en Puerto Rico no esopa mexicano periodista

PERSONAJES

DVD

We meet five of the principal characters of the Historia *in* Personajes *in* Unidad 1a. *Discuss these characters with a classmate.*

pharmacéutica esopa de Rafa — obstetra en Puerto Rico

Here are some suggested questions to get you started:

- ¿Quién es ______________________ (Carmina/ Ángela/Rafa/Jaime/Laura)?
- ¿De dónde es?
- ¿Por qué está en los Estados Unidos?

doctora clinica de Comnidad
estudiante in US study english prima de Carmina

¡A RESUMIR!

EPISODIO

Imagine that your classmate has not yet seen episode 1a *of the* Historia. *Recount it, paying particular attention to your use of definite and indefinite articles.*

Modelo: En la primera escena, Ángela y Rafa están preparando la cena. Laura tiene un accidente de carro, y la llevan al hospital.

Continue this conversation with your classmate. Your classmate should ask questions such as those that follow:

- ¿De qué hablan Ángela y Rafa en la primera escena?
- ¿Por qué tiene un accidente Laura?

APLICACIÓN

ESCUCHAR

DVD

As you can see, Laura is both confused and imprecise during her conversation with Dr. Wallace. She is not sure how much pain she is in, for instance, nor does she understand what he is referring to when he asks her to describe her pain using the "pain scale."

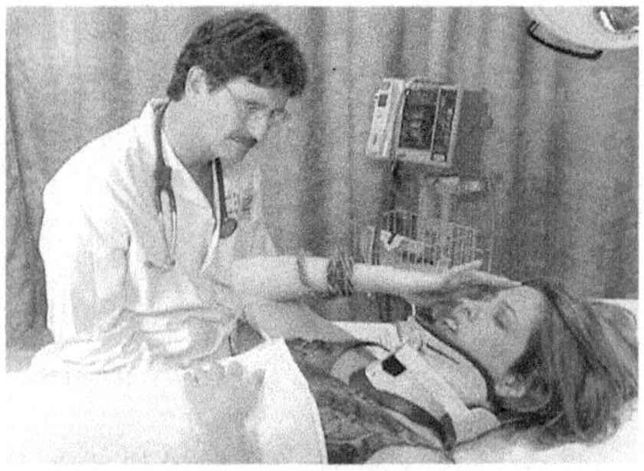

Laura and Dr. Wallace

Role-play:

Continue the conversation between Dr. Wallace and Laura. Have Dr. Wallace explain what the pain scale is to Laura, and how to use it. Once she understands, what will she say?

ANALIZAR

DVD

In this segment, a priest calls Laura after the accident to make sure she is okay.

Laura receives a phone call

Conversation topics:

1 **Complete the dialogue:**
During the phone call, we hear only one side of the conversation. Complete the dialogue. What does the priest say?

2 **Laura refuses to talk to the priest:**
Why do you think Laura does not want to speak to him? Because of her refusal to get on the phone, Carmina has to lie to the priest. What excuse does she give? How does Carmina feel about what she is doing? How can you tell? Have you ever had to tell this type of "white" lie before? Have you ever asked someone else to tell this type of lie for you? If not, would you do so if you were asked?

3 **Alternate outcome:**
Role-play an alternate conversation in which Carmina refuses to lie to the priest. Develop a dialogue between Laura and the priest with a classmate.

EN LA PRÁCTICA

Dr. Wallace examines Laura in the Emergency Room

In this segment Dr. Wallace examines Laura after her car accident. First they decide to communicate in Spanish. Why does Dr. Wallace speak in Spanish? Does Dr. Wallace make any language mistakes during this conversation?

Role-play:

Continue their conversation. Have Laura explain that her accident was likely the result of her diabetes. Dr. Wallace should ask her some questions about her health in general, and also give her some advice on how to live with diabetes. What questions might Laura have for him? Use the sentences below as a conversation starter.

LAURA: Dr. Wallace, yo sé que sufro de diabetes y que es importante cuidarme.

DR. WALLACE: Tiene razón. La diabetes es una enfermedad seria y es importante cuidarse. ¿Cómo se siente en general...?

LENGUA

Ashleigh and Duna speak with a patient from the clinic in this segment. What are this patient's concerns? What does she complain about with regard to her apartment? Have you ever had cause to complain about an apartment, a dorm room, or even a hotel room? Do you think that this woman may have to live in substandard housing because she is an immigrant? Is it easier for landowners and others to exploit immigrants? Discuss these questions with a classmate. Use the sentences below to get started.

Yo creo que la mujer está preocupada porque...
El apartamento tiene muchos problemas como...

MÁS ALLÁ

You have now completed all the grammatical explanations for *Unidad 1a*, but may find that you still don't understand even the simplest of utterances in Spanish even if you understand all the individual words. One way that you, as the speaker, can determine if your listener is understanding your message the way you intended it is to ask, *¿Podría decirme lo que entendió?* (Could you tell me what you understood?), then take note of the listener's response. But what can a listener do to aid in his or her understanding of the message received? Perhaps the problem goes beyond the words being said.

You should take some cues from the speaker's gestures. Spontaneous gestures during speech reveal the speaker's thinking patterns at the time. The speaker intends for the gestures to be meaningful, just as the words are meaningful. For example, cultures express understanding in different ways, but most speakers of English and Spanish have the same gestures for expressing "I don't understand you." We refocus our eyes; we change the position of our head, almost like leaning closer to hear better. This is an example of gestures agreeing with the intended message. What does it signal, therefore, when the gesture you see and the words you hear "say" different things?

In that case, you need to determine separately what the words mean and what the gestures mean. If the two don't agree, the speaker may in fact be intending to express two different messages, even if they're contradictory. In the scene between Ángela and Alex shown on the DVD, Ángela's gestures of concern and discomfort and her words dismissing Alex's concern, *"No, gracias, Alex,"* present contradictory messages, but both the gestures and the words are in agreement with Ángela's thoughts. As a result, the total message is: I'm worried. + This is a serious matter. + Alex, I don't want you involved.

As you progress in your handling of Spanish structures and vocabulary, keep in mind that there's more to language than words.

ENTREVISTA

Read this summary in English of what Ramón Ruiz says in his interview before you watch it on the DVD. Remember that these interviews were conducted to include "authentic language" on the DVD. This means that the interviews are unscripted and at a natural conversational pace. Use the English summary to guide you.

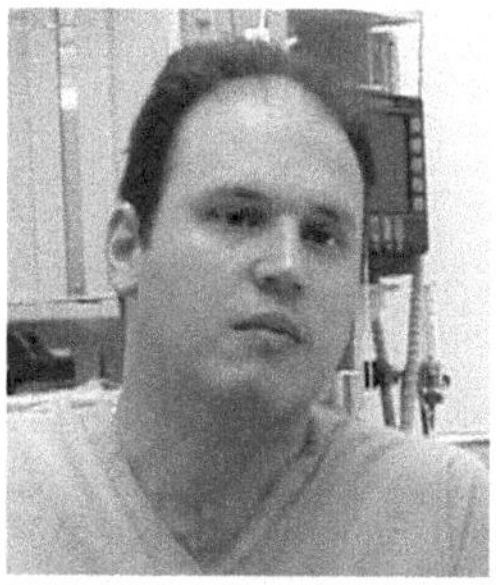

Ramón Ruiz

Dr. Ruiz was born in Pinar del Río, Cuba and immigrated with his parents to Spain, when he was three years old. They were there for one year and came to Miami in 1970. Dr. Ruiz grew up in Miami, went to college in Tallahassee, and went to medical school in Chapel Hill.

The United States is the country Dr. Ruiz knows best, so he feels happy to have the best of two countries. He feels very proud of his homeland and his Cuban culture, and at the same time feels very grateful to an adoptive country that has given him many opportunities to live freely and grow both personally and professionally.

The biggest satisfaction for Dr. Ruiz is to be able to help children with congenital problems and to work with families. When he started off as a surgeon, he thought that surgery was the biggest part of the treatment. Later he realized that the surgical techniques are simply mechanical and are a small part of the total treatment of the patient. What really gives him true satisfaction now is the interaction that he has with the patient and the family, and not necessarily the mechanics of the operation, which is different from when he started, when it was a little the other way around.

In many ways the things that are the hardest are the ones that he likes best. For example, the need that a maxilofacial surgeon has of developing a process of thinking, to resolve complicated geometric problems of soft tissue and bone. He claims that it's not the mechanics of the surgery, but the process of thinking of a case in three dimensions, and creating a treatment plan that is well thought through, that is one of the things that gives him the most satisfaction.

Dr. Ruiz doesn't think that he has typical days. But typically, his day starts off very early. He wakes up very early and gets to the hospital quite early, about six o'clock to visit patients that are interned in the hospital. They do the rounds and solve clinical problems on the floor, the surgery floor. At the beginning of the morning, typically at 7:30, they start with the surgery cases in the operating room of the main building. They operate one or two days a week the whole day. Other days of the week they might operate on a short case, and then they return to the clinic to see post-operative cases. And depending on what week of the month it is, every other week he's on call for traumatic cases during the night.

Watch the interview with Dr. Ramón Ruiz one more time. Listen carefully to what he says, and answer the following questions:

- ¿De dónde es?
- ¿Cuántos años tenía cuando vino a los Estados Unidos con sus padres?
- ¿Qué tipo de médico es?
- ¿Qué es lo que más le gusta de su trabajo?

UNIDAD 1b

NOTE TO THE STUDENT

LOOK AT YOURSELF!

Teachers often talk to each other about their students. If you listened to those conversations, you'd realize that teachers have a way of recognizing students' learning patterns, the "type of learner" that they are. It's too bad that more teachers don't share these observations with their students, because an adult learner has specific strategies that help the learning process along. Are you an auditory, visual, tactile, rhythmic, or environmental learner? Do you remember words by their sounds or do you have to see them on the page before they can make sense? Can you pick out a word from a string of sound, reconstruct what the rest of the message "must have been," and then trust your instincts and respond to the message, even though you don't know exactly what was said? Do you use physical associations or rhymes and sayings to commit information to memory? Do your surroundings best enable you to process new information? Maybe you draw on several different strategies.

You should also consider your thinking style. Are you a reflective, creative, practical, or conceptual thinker? Do you relate new information to past experiences, or do you enjoy manipulating and playing with new information? Do you prefer to have facts and nothing but the facts, without the little extras? Do you need to understand the whole as well as the parts? Perhaps you use a combination of thinking styles. Observe how you interact with language. Knowing how you learn a language is as important as having the right textbooks and ancillary materials.

It is often said that children are better language learners because their brains are hard-wired for this and that the skill is "lost" when we grow up. However, adults also develop strategies to use the mind efficiently, such as categorizing, using hierarchies, abstracting, and simplifying. Knowing what these strategies are can help you develop and take advantage of them. Learning in an organized, efficient way and making the best use of your strengths, requires some self-examination and an honest analysis of how you learn.

YO SOY ASÍ. THAT'S HOW I AM.

Think about the following questions in order to discover what type of learner you are. There are no right or wrong answers to these questions.

1 Consider the physical environment that you prefer for studying. (This includes time of day!) Think about this: do you stand, sit, lie down, or listen to music? Do you isolate yourself in a quiet room?

2 What do you do when you need to commit loads of information to memory?

3 Remember that efficient language learning involves long-term memory. What tricks do you employ to file away information so you can retrieve it easily?

It might be helpful to write down your answers to remind yourself of your particular learning style. Use what you've discovered about yourself to make the time you spend studying more efficient and productive.

VOCABULARIO

Below are the vocabulary words highlighted in this unit. Remember that you can hear these words in action in the *Vocabulario* section of *Unidad 1b* on the *Recursos* webpage. After you've looked at them, write beside each one its English equivalent. If you have any doubt about the words' exact meaning, look them up in a good Spanish-English dictionary. You should have one by now!

Review the words that you wrote in the margins of *Vocabulario 1a*. Look up the meanings of any words you don't know. Remember to use this space to add new and useful words that you find in your study or work, but were not included in *Vocabulario!*

Verbos

enamorarse to fall in love
enfrentar to face/confront
entrar en confianza confide
extrañar to ~~hug~~ miss
huir to flee
mantenerse to maintain
preocuparse por worried
quejarse to complain
revisar to revise
volver a hacer to work

Frases adverbiales y adjetivos

a veces sometimes
cualquier any
diabética diabetic
enamorada de él
grave seriously ill
hace poco recently
recién diagnosticada
recent

Sustantivos

el/la antepasado/a ancestor
el/la compañero/a friend
el/la enfermero/a nurse
el/la trabajador/a social social worker
la guerra war
el papel paper
el prejuicio prejudice
el reto challenge
el tema subject theme

¡A PRACTICAR!

1B-VOC-1

Match the Spanish words with their equivalents in English. If you need help, go to Unidad 1b Vocabulario *on the* Recursos *site.*

1 confiar	8	**a**	to challenge
2 diagnosticar	7	**b**	to complain
3 enamorarse	2	**c**	to diagnose
4 extrañar	3	**d**	to fall in love
5 huir	5	**e**	to flee
6 mantenerse	6	**f**	to keep (oneself)
7 quejarse	4	**g**	to miss
8 retar	11	**h**	to return
9 revisar	1	**i**	to trust
10 trabajar	9	**h**	to review
11 volver	10	**i**	to work

1B-VOC-2

Fill in the right word for each blank. Be careful to make the new word agree with the rest of the sentence, especially the subject of the sentence.

Ashleigh le está dando consejos a una madre sobre el desarrollo de sus hijos.

ASHLEIGH: Señora, no hay que **(1)** preocupese por *(to worry)*. Los niños están saludables y pueden **(2)** se mantenen *(keep)* así si usted les da el cuidado adecuado. Sé que puede ser **(3)** reta *(a challenge)*. encontrar el tiempo suficiente para la familia y el trabajo, pero usted es una buena madre. Lo más importante para un niño pequeño es el amor de la madre, sentirse protegido y acompañado. **(4)** a veces *(Sometimes)*, uno siente que nunca va a ganar **(5)** la guerra *(the war)*, pero tiene que **(6)** confia *(trust)* en sí misma. Además, con su apoyo sus niños pueden **(7)** ________ *(face)* **(8)** cualquier *(any)* cosa.

1B-VOC-3

Doña Esperanza, a patient at the clinic, talks about her life to Duna and Ashleigh. Since Ashleigh had some difficulties understanding the story, Duna translated it into English for her. Rewrite the English version of the story in Spanish to find out exactly what was said.

"My ancestors came to this country to escape the poverty caused by years of war. Sometimes life here can be difficult for us because we must face the prejudices of those people who do not welcome immigrants, but we try not to complain because here we have a future. Still, there are times when we miss the culture and customs of our native homeland."

____

____

____

____

____

____

____

____

____

____

____

____

1B-VOC-4

Read the paragraph and answer the questions in Spanish.

Duna habla sobre su identidad. "Como soy negra, la gente se sorprende cuando hablo español. Pero cuando saben que soy guatemalteca, entran en confianza. Mi marido dice que debería estar orgullosa de ser negra... 'Rather than pretending to be Latina', dice... 'Pretending'! Yo sospecho que tiene algunos prejuicios... ¡Aunque se haya casado con una centroamericana! A veces me siento como el jamón del sándwich: entre culturas... Pero está bien, me gusta... ¡Hay que trabajar con eso!"

1 ¿Qué sorprende a la gente que conoce a Duna?

____

____

2 ¿Qué estrategia le propone a Duna su marido?

____

____

3 ¿Qué piensa Duna de esa estrategia?

____

____

4 ¿Cómo se siente Duna en los Estados Unidos?

____

____

5 ¿Qué significa "hay que trabajar con eso"?

____

____

USEFUL TERMS AND EXPRESSIONS

This section introduces new vocabulary and expressions related to themes found throughout *Unidad 1b* of the DVD.

SUSTANTIVOS

Las condiciones físicas	
las ampollas	blisters
el ataque	attack
el aumento	increase
el bienestar	well being
las cataratas	cataracts
el efecto	effect
el enrojecimiento	redness
el glaucoma	glaucoma
la hipoglucemia	hypoglycemia
las llagas	sores
las manchas	spots
los mareos	dizziness
el medicamento	medicine
la pérdida de peso	weight loss
la placa	plaque
la presión arterial	blood pressure
el riesgo	risk
los temblores	shakes

El cuerpo	
el corazón	heart
los dientes	teeth
las encías	gums
el estómago	stomach
el hígado	liver
los nervios	nerves
el ojo	eye
los órganos	organs
el páncreas	pancreas
el pie	foot
las pupilas	pupils
la retina	retina
el riñón	kidney
las uñas	nails
los vasos sanguíneos	blood vessels
la vejiga	bladder
la vista	vision

El cuidado	
los carbohidratos	carbohydrates
el colesterol	cholesterol
las dentaduras postizas	dentures
el/la dentista	dentist
la diálisis	dialysis
la dilatación	dilation
el frasco	flask/jar
las gotas	drops
la insulina	insulin
el/la oculista	optometrist
la pastilla	pill
la porción	portion
la temperatura ambiente	room temperature
el transplante	transplant

VERBOS	
contribuir	to contribute
convertir(se) en	to convert
debilitar(se)	to weaken
disminuir	to diminish, to decrease
elegir	to choose
funcionar	to function
inyectar(se)	to inject
medir	to measure
merendar	to snack (at night)
morir	to die
pesar	to weigh
prevenir	to prevent
pesar	to weigh
producir	to produce
recetar	to prescribe
recuperar(se)	to recuperate
sostener	to sustain
tapar(se)	to clog
tardar	to be late, to delay
vigilar	to watch

ADJETIVOS Y ADVERBIOS	
cardíaco/a	cardiac
circulatorio/a	circulatory
flojo/a	loose
infectado/a	infected
mensualmente	monthly
nervioso/a	nervous
oscuro/a	dark
pegajoso/a	sticky
renal	renal
secundario/a	secondary
sensible	sensitive

Study the vocabulary before you begin *Principios* because it will be useful when you practice the grammar points of the unit. Remember that this section is not intended to be an exhaustive list of all relevant terms but rather an exposure to some of the basic vocabulary used in health care. The definitions given here are limited, because they are intended for the narrow use of the exercises found in *Principios*. Look the words up in a good Spanish-English dictionary if you want to know other meanings, how to pronounce them, the contexts in which the words can be found, sayings and common expressions using these words, and their derivatives (adjectives from nouns, nouns from verbs, etc.).

PRINCIPIOS

VERBS IN THE PRESENT TENSE

Verbs express action or a state of being and are inflected for person and tense. In other words, verbs indicate *who* or *what* is *doing* or *being* something, as well as when that action or state of being takes place. To determine *who* or *what* and *when*, you need to examine the verb endings. Here are the possible endings and the corresponding subjects for the present tense:

SUBJECT	VERB ENDINGS	SUBJECT	VERB ENDINGS
yo	*-o*	nosotros	*-amos* or *-emos* or *-imos*
tú	*-as* or *-es*	vosotros	*-áis* or *-éis* or *-ís*
usted	*-a* or *-e*	ustedes	*-an* or *-en*
él	*-a* or *-e*	ellos	*-an* or *-en*
ella	*-a* or *-e*	ellas	*-an* or *-en*

Still, how do you determine which ending to use? For this information you look to the infinitive. Every verb in Spanish has one of three endings in the infinitive: *-ar, -er,* or *-ir.* All endings are assigned according to the infinitive of the verb in question. Here is the distribution of present tense endings for the three conjugations as they are used in Latin America:

RECUPERAR	BEBER	SUFRIR
(yo) recuper**o**	(yo) beb**o**	(yo) sufr**o**
(tú) recuper**as**	(tú) beb**es**	(tú) sufr**es**
(Ud., él, ella) recuper**a**	(él, ella, Ud.) beb**e**	(él, ella, Ud.) sufr**e**
(nosotros) recuper**amos**	(nosotros) beb**emos**	(nosotros) sufr**imos**
(Uds., ellos, ellas) recuper**an**	(ellos, ellas, Uds.) beb**en**	(ellos, ellas, Uds.) sufr**en**

Observe how verbs from the *-er* and *-ir* conjugations share a similar pattern, with the exception of the *nosotros* form. This similarity will appear again and again as you progress through the tenses.

Also, note that within the verb endings themselves there are certain "sounds" that you can identify with a particular subject: *-s* for second person singular (*tú*, you [informal]), *-mos* for first person plural (*nosotros,* we), and *-n* for all other plurals (*ustedes, ellos, ellas,* you [plural], they). For example, if a Spanish verb ends in *-mos*, you know that the only subject the sentence can have is some variant of *nosotros* (*Pedro y yo, todos nosotros, nosotros los pacientes*) or some phrase that implies "we," whether or not the subject is stated.

SPANISH	ENGLISH
Necesitamos tomar medicamentos para controlar la diabetes.	We need to take medication to control our diabetes.
Pesamos la comida para saber si tenemos la porción correcta.	We weigh the food to know if we have the correct portion.

It is useful to learn these endings well from the start, because they will reappear in all other tenses. That means that *-s* will always signal *tú, -mos* will always signal *nosotros*, and *-n* will always signal *ustedes, ellos, ellas*, regardless of the verb tense.

Unlike English, Spanish does not require the presence of a subject pronoun to indicate *who* or *what*. Look below at the endings used to indicate the present tense in English.

SUBJECT	VERB ENDINGS	SUBJECT	VERB ENDINGS
I		we	
you (sing.)		you (pl.)	
he	-s	they	
she	-s		

The endings of Spanish verbs, unlike English verb endings, have a distinct ending for each person. As a result, Spanish speakers can do without a subject pronoun, and English speakers cannot. Consequently, in Spanish, subject pronouns are mostly used for emphasis or to highlight contrasts.

SPANISH	ENGLISH
Yo como a la misma hora todos los días, pero tú puedes comer cuando quieras.	I eat at the same time every day, but you can eat whenever you want.

¡A PRACTICAR!

1B-PRIN-1

Circle all of the conjugated verbs in the sentences below in which Carmina is talking to Laura. There are ten verbs.

"Cuidado Laura, la hipoglucemia resulta por muchas razones. Si sufres de mareos, sudores, temblores o confusión significa que el nivel de azúcar sanguíneo está bajo. Veo que no te cuidas bien. Necesitamos trabajar juntas para combatir esta enfermedad. Pienso que consumes demasiado alcohol y que no te preocupas por tu bienestar."

1B-PRIN-2

Find the conjugated verbs in each sentence and determine the subject of each verb.

1 Ashleigh le describe a la señora los efectos de comer demasiado azúcar.

verb(s): describe

subject(s): Ashleigh

2 Vigilo el nivel de azúcar en la sangre.

verb(s): Vigilo

subject(s): I

3 Su páncreas no produce insulina, por eso se inyecta dos veces al día.

verb(s): produce; inyecta

subject(s): pancreas

4 Corres mayor riesgo de sufrir un ataque al corazón.

verb(s): corres

subject(s): you

5 Necesito medir la presión sanguínea por la mañana.

verb(s): necesito

subject(s): I

6 Debes examinarte los pies diariamente para ver si tienen ampollas, llagas, cortaduras o uñas infectadas.

verb(s): Debes, tienen

subject(s): you

7 La diabetes afecta muchas partes del cuerpo como los riñones, el corazón, los ojos, los pies, los dientes y otros órganos.

verb(s): afecta

subject(s): diabetes

8 Las personas que consumen una dieta baja en colesterol reducen su riesgo de tener problemas.

verb(s): consumen

subject(s): las personas

9 Más que cualquier otra comida, los carbohidratos aumentan el nivel de azúcar en la sangre.

verb(s): aumentan

subject(s): carbohidratos

10 A veces los problemas del estómago o de la vejiga resultan porque tienes los nervios dañados.

verb(s): resultan

subject(s): los problemas

11 En la clínica trabajamos con muchos casos como éste.

verb(s): trabajamos

subject(s): nosotros

1B-PRIN-3

Imagine that you are Jaime and that you have to keep track of everyone's schedules at La Comunidad. *Write down what the following people do, using the verbs from the list (and any other regular verbs you know). Be creative!*

Modelo: Jaime (yo): 8:00 ______

A las ocho de la mañana como pan tostado.

Palabras útiles

asistir (a reuniones)	hablar
buscar	leer
comer	limpiar
describir	llegar
discutir	manejar
escribir	revisar

Carmina

7:30 ______

9:00 ______

11:00 ______

Jaime (yo) y Ángela

8:30 ______

9:00 ______

12:30 ______

Duna y Ashleigh

9:00 ______

12:00 ______

3:30 ______

1B-PRIN-4

One of the clinic's patients phones Ángela to discuss insulin treatment for her recently diagnosed diabetes. Use the following words to respond to the patient's questions.

Palabras útiles

el aumento de peso	lentamente
el brazo	el muslo
completo	las pastillas
deber	rápidamente
el estómago	el refrigerador
la hipoglucemia	resultar
la insulina	la temperatura ambiente

1 ¿Cuántas veces al día necesito tomar la insulina?

Necesita tomar la insulina en la mañana y la noche.

2 ¿Dónde me inyecto?

Inyecta en el estómago

3 ¿Cuánto tiempo tarda la insulina en funcionar?

la temperatura ambiente

4 ¿Existen otras formas de insulina?

Sí, hay es dos tipos. Un tipo por la hipoglucemia

5 ¿Dónde guardo el frasco de insulina?

Guarda el frasco en el refrigerador

6 ¿El uso de la insulina produce efectos secundarios?

Posible. Posible el aumento de peso

STEM-CHANGING VERBS

In addition to the endings described above, some verbs undergo a change to the main vowel found in the stem. The stem is the part of the verb found just before the infinitival endings of *-ar*, *-er*, or *-ir*. When you learn a new verb, be sure to check a dictionary, grammar book, or verb wheel to see if it is "stem-changing." If it is, the stem will change in all persons except in the first person plural. In other words, when a verb stem changes in the present tense, the *nosotros* form will not change. The three most common kinds of stem-changing verbs are *-e* > *-ie*, *-e* > *-i*, and *-o* > *-ue*.

Examples of stem-changing verbs, *-e* > *-ie*:

	PENSAR	**EMPEZAR**	**QUERER**	**ENTENDER**	**PREFERIR**
yo	pienso	empiezo	quiero	entiendo	prefiero
tú	piensas	empiezas	quieres	entiendes	prefieres
Ud./él/ella	piensa	empieza	quiere	entiende	prefiere
nosotros	pensamos	empezamos	queremos	entendemos	preferimos
Uds./ellos/ellas	piensan	empiezan	quieren	entienden	prefieren

Examples of stem-changing verbs, *-e* > *-i:*

	PEDIR	**SERVIR**	**REPETIR**	**MEDIR**
yo	pido	sirvo	repito	mido
tú	pides	sirves	repites	mides
Ud./él/ella	pide	sirve	repite	mide
nosotros	pedimos	servimos	repetimos	medimos
Uds./ellos/ellas	piden	sirven	repiten	miden

Note that only *-ir* verbs are present in this category.

Examples of stem-changing verbs, *-o > -ue:*

	ALMORZAR	**ENCONTRAR**	**VOLVER**	**PODER**	**DORMIR**
yo	almuerzo	encuentro	vuelvo	puedo	duermo
tú	almuerzas	encuentras	vuelves	puedes	duermes
Ud./él/ella	almuerza	encuentra	vuelve	puede	duerme
nosotros	almorzamos	encontramos	volvemos	podemos	dormimos
Uds./ellos/ellas	almuerzan	encuentran	vuelven	pueden	duermen

Spanish teachers often use a clever device to remind their students of the vowel change in the stem-changing verbs. They call them "shoe verbs," and lay out the conjugation on the blackboard in the shape of a shoe. The verb forms that have a stem change fit inside the shoe; the verb forms that do not have a stem change are outside the shoe.

CERRAR	
yo cierro	nosotros cerramos
tú cierras	
él cierra	ellos cierran

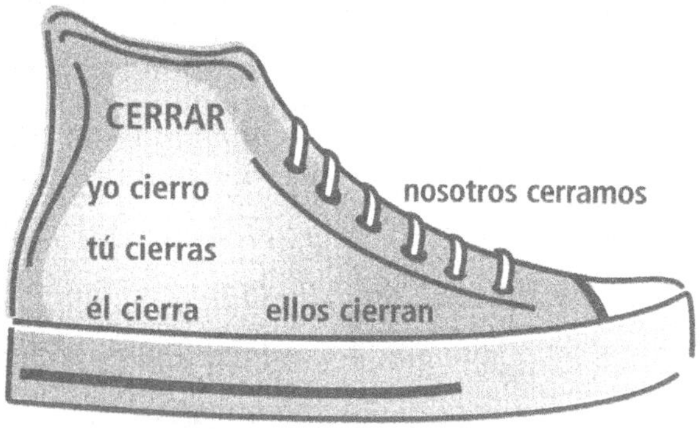

¡A PRACTICAR!

1B-PRIN-5

Write the infinitive for each verb given below and indicate which type of stem-change it undergoes.

1 cuesta costar
-e > -ie -e > -i -o > -ue

2 merendamos merendar
-e > -ie -e > -i -o > -ue

3 convierte convertir
-e > -ie -e > -i -o > -ue

4 duermo dormir
-e > -ie -e > -i -o > -ue

5 pides pedir
-e > -ie -e > -i -o > -ue

6 almuerzan almorzar
-e > -ie -e > -i -o > -ue

7 elegimos elegir to elect to choose
-e > -ie -e > -i -o > -ue

8 cuentas contar
-e > -ie -e > -i -o > -ue

9 pierdo perder
-e > -ie -e > -i -o > -ue

10 recuerdan recordar
-e > -ie -e > -i -o > -ue

1B-PRIN-6

Doña Esperanza describes what she does to take care of her eyes. Write the correct form of the verbs given in parentheses.

Sé que en las personas que tienen diabetes **(1)** pueden *(poder)* ocurrir problemas con la vista. Nosotros **(2)** podemos *(poder)* desarrollar enfermedades como cataratas o glaucoma. Por eso, el médico me **(3)** recomiendo *(recomendar)* visitar al oculista una vez al año. Puesto que yo **(4)** quiero *(querer)* prevenir problemas de los ojos, **(5)** prefiero *(preferir)* seguir sus consejos. Además, mi esposo y yo **(6)** entendemos *(entender)* la importancia de cuidarme bien. Durante el examen el médico me pone gotas y las pupilas se **(7)** vuelve *(volver)* grandes, de esta manera él **(8)** puede *(poder)* ver la retina. Yo **(9)** pienso *(pensar)* que este proceso se llama dilatación. Y yo siempre **(10)** vuelvo *(volver)* a preguntarle: ¿**(11)** encuenta *(encontrar)* usted algo? A lo cual me responde: "Esta vez, no veo ningún problema." Todos mis médicos **(12)** piensan *(pensar)* que es una buena idea hacerme un examen aun cuando no **(13)** muestro *(mostrar)* síntomas. Si tú **(14)** empiezas *(empezar)* a ver manchas oscuras o luces, debes ir al oculista. También, si tú **(15)** sientes *(sentir)* dolor o presión en los ojos yo te **(16)** sugiere *(sugerir)* hacer una cita inmediatamente.

1B-PRIN-7

Imagine that you are a guest in the home of the Salvadoran woman when Ashleigh and Duna arrive. Since you couldn't stay in the room during the visit, your hostess later tells you what went on. Use what you know or have heard about post-traumatic stress syndrome to give your hostess two suggestions that can help her feel more at ease with her memories of the war. Since you're not seeing her as a patient or client, your suggestions are meant as friendly support and encouragement. (You may want to go back and watch this scene again in Unidad 1b *on the DVD before completing this exercise.)*

1 Tus recuerdos son...

2 Te sientes así, pero...

1B-PRIN-8

One of the main obstacles immigrants face is learning a new language. Read the paragraph below in which Rafa describes how he feels about both his Spanish and English language abilities. Then describe your thoughts with regard to your own abilities.

"Igual me siento como un idiota... En español tengo precisión, vocabulario... En inglés me siento como Tarzán... A veces pienso que en este país no sirvo para nada..."

IRREGULAR VERBS

Like English, Spanish has irregular verbs. Still, irregular verbs in the present tense do change in particular patterns.

A number of irregular verbs change only in the first person singular, or the *yo* form. The remaining forms are conjugated in the same manner as the regular present tense.

	VER	PONER	HACER	VALER	CAER	TRAER	SALIR
yo	veo	pongo	hago	valgo	caigo	traigo	salgo
tú	ves	pones	haces	vales	caes	traes	sales
Ud./él/ella	ve	pone	hace	vale	cae	trae	sale
nosotros	vemos	ponemos	hacemos	valemos	caemos	traemos	salimos
Uds./ellos/ellas	ven	ponen	hacen	valen	caen	traen	salen

Above are just a few examples, but there are many more, including, *dar, saber, conocer, nacer, proteger, escoger, caber, satisfacer, distinguir,* and *convencer*. When Spanish-speaking children learn these verbs, they use what they know about language to produce new utterances, with results like *"¡Yo, yo! Yo lo pono."* instead of *"¡Yo, yo! Yo lo pongo."* (Me, me! I put it.) Sooner or later an adult corrects them, saying *"No, pono no, yo lo pongo,"* and the children learn that some words are... well, different. You will have to learn this too. Fortunately, you can do this by consulting a grammar book, a verb wheel, a dictionary or a Spanish-speaking friend, and checking if the *yo* form of the new verb you're learning is different from the others.

Other irregular verbs are stem-changing, but go through a different or an additional change in the first person singular, or the *yo* form:

	TENER	VENIR	DECIR	SEGUIR	ELEGIR
yo	tengo	vengo	digo	sigo	elijo
tú	tienes	vienes	dices	sigues	eliges
Ud./él/ella	tiene	viene	dice	sigue	elige
nosotros	tenemos	venimos	decimos	seguimos	elegimos
Uds./ellos/ellas	tienen	vienen	dicen	siguen	eligen

Here are some examples of similar verbs that fit into the above category: *contener, mantener, obtener, sostener, prevenir,* and *conseguir.*

Still, a few very common verbs seem to have their own way of forming:

	ESTAR	SER	IR	OÍR	HABER
yo	estoy	soy	voy	oigo	he
tú	estás	eres	vas	oyes	has
Ud./él/ella	está	es	va	oye	ha
nosotros	estamos	somos	vamos	oímos	hemos
Uds./ellos/ellas	están	son	van	oyen	han

Haber is of particular interest because it actually has developed two very different uses and, consequently, two separate sets of forms. As an impersonal verb, *haber* has only one available form in the present tense, *hay*. As an auxiliary, used in conjunction with past participles, this verb can be conjugated for every person.

Finally, it is worth mentioning one last group of verbs in which a *-y* is added before the present tense verb endings. These verbs end in *-uir*, but do not contain a *-g* in the stem:

	HUIR	CONTRIBUIR	DISMINUIR
yo	huyo	contribuyo	disminuyo
tú	huyes	contribuyes	disminuyes
Ud./él/ella	huye	contribuye	disminuye
nosotros	huimos	contribuimos	disminuimos
Uds./ellos/ellas	huyen	contribuyen	disminuyen

Once again, observe how the majority of these irregular verbs have either the *-er* or *-ir* infinitive endings.

¡A PRACTICAR!

1B-PRIN-9

Identify the subject (yo, tú, usted/él/ella, nosotros, ustedes/ellos/ellas) and number (singular, plural) of each verb. Translate them after you're finished.

1 caes: you fell
persona tú, **número** 1

2 dan: you gave
persona ustedes, **número** plural

3 diagnostica:
persona él, **número** single

4 eres:
persona tú, **número** single

5 extraño:
persona yo, **número** single

6 hay:
persona el, **número** single

7 huyes:
persona tu, **número** single

8 puede:
persona el, **número** single

9 salimos:
persona nosotros, **número** plural

10 se quejan:
persona ellos, **número** plural

11 soy:
persona yo, **número** single

12 tengo:
persona yo, **número** single

13 terminamos:
persona nosotros, **número** plural

14 va:
persona el, **número** single

15 voy:
persona yo, **número** single

1B-PRIN-10

Carmina speaks about dental health with a group of men who suffer from diabetes. Fill in the blanks with the appropriate forms of the verbs from the list below. Do not repeat any.

caber	ir	tener
contribuir	mantener	traer
dar	poner	ver
haber	saber	ser

¿**(1)** Saben ustedes que los altos niveles de azúcar **(2)** contribuyen a la producción de la placa, esta cosa pegajosa, y pueden dañar la boca, hasta resultar en la pérdida de un diente? Si una persona se mira en el espejo y **(3)** ve enrojecimiento o ampollas en la boca, o si esta persona **(4)** tiene dientes flojos y sensibles o si las dentaduras postizas no **(5)** caben bien en la boca, puede significar que **(6)** hay problemas. Y ustedes me preguntan: ¿cómo **(7)** mantenemos nosotros los dientes y las encías saludables? Lo más importante **(8)** es visitar al dentista. Los dentistas les **(9)** van a revisar toda la boca para ver si existe algún problema. Aquí en mi bolso **(10)** traigo más información sobre esto. Yo les **(11)** doy una copia a cada uno de ustedes y el resto, por si acaso, lo **(12)** pongo encima de la mesa.

1B-PRIN-11

Ashleigh has an appointment today with a patient who was recently diagnosed with diabetes. She needs to practice her Spanish so that she can provide her with some general information about the illness. Don't forget to refer to the **Useful Terms and Expressions** *section for help with vocabulary. You should write at least five sentences. Be creative!*

1B-PRIN-12

Recall the visit that Duna and Ashleigh made to the woman from El Salvador who was suffering from diabetes. In your own words, write what happens during the visit in a paragraph of at least four sentences. Be sure to use plenty of regular and stem-changing verbs in the present tense. If you need help, watch the scene again in Unidad 1b Historia. *(Note: Duna and Ashleigh discuss the woman's diabetes in* En la práctica, Unidad 1b *on the DVD.)*

Cuando Duna y Ashleigh visitan a la mujer salvadoreña...

WHEN TO USE THE PRESENT TENSE

The present indicative in Spanish is used very similarly to the way it is used in English. Consider the following uses of the present tense in Spanish.

To express an event that is happening in the present:

SPANISH	ENGLISH
Ella estudia para ser dentista.	She is studying to be a dentist.

To express the immediacy of an action that is happening before your very eyes, Spanish uses the present progressive to underline its ongoing aspect. We will study the present progressive in *Principios* of *Unidad 2a*.

To express a habitual action, as long as it still holds true:

SPANISH	ENGLISH
Yo me limpio y me examino los pies todos los días.	I clean and examine my feet every day.

To express existing facts or known truths:

SPANISH	ENGLISH
Los vasos sanguíneos se tapan y se debilitan.	The blood vessels become clogged and weaken.

Notice that this is a general statement.

To express the result of a condition, with *si* meaning "if":

SPANISH	ENGLISH
Si se toma los medicamentos, mejora.	If you take the medication, you'll get better.

Unlike Spanish, English uses the future "will" and the verb "to get" with sentences containing the word "if". But be careful with the use of *si*. The present tense is used only when *si* means "if". If *si* means "whether" then the future tense is used in Spanish.

SPANISH	**ENGLISH**
No podemos decir todavía si el paciente mejorará.	We can't yet say whether the patient will get better.

For polite commands:

SPANISH	**ENGLISH**
Me dice si le duele, por favor.	Please, tell me if it hurts.

In place of the simple future tense, except in cases when si means "whether":

SPANISH	**ENGLISH**
El transplante es mañana.	The transplant is tomorrow.
Instead of:	Instead of:
El transplante será mañana.	The transplant will be tomorrow.

The present tense sounds much stronger and more definitive than the simple future tense because the message indicates the certainty of the action.

¡A PRACTICAR!

1B-PRIN-13

Match the statements on the left with the use of the present tense on the right.

1 Con una dieta balanceada no puede sentirse mejor.

2 La cita con la oculista es esta tarde.

3 Si no se disminuye el nivel de azúcar, no mejora.

4 Le escribo una receta para as pastillas de insulina.

5 Me pongo inyecciones para controlar la diabetes todos los días.

6 Me cuenta su rutina diaria, por favor.

__6__ **a** for polite commands

__2__ **b** in place of a future tense

__5__ **c** to express a habitual action that is still true

__X 3__ **d** to express a known fact or truth

__4__ **e** to express a present event

__3__ **f** to express the result of a condition

1B-PRIN-14

For each of the uses of the present tense in Spanish, write two sentences that exemplify its functions. You can use any context you wish, i.e. La Comunidad, la diabetes, la nutrición, *or* tu trabajo.

To express an event that is happening in the present:

1 Monto ~~la~~ una bicicleta ir a la escula.

2 Como ~~la~~ una manzana.

To express a habitual action, as long as it still holds true:

3 Todos los días como cena con mi novio.

4 ~~Todos los días~~ yo duermo ocho horas a noche.

To express a known fact or truth:

5 Come verduras puede tener un salud bueno

6 Tome aqua es buen para tú cuerpo porque hidrate.

To express the result of a condition with *si* (meaning "if"):

7 Si no duerme ocho horas a noche, no mejora.

8 Si ejercise con otra persona, mejora.

For polite commands:

9 Pasala el aqua, por favor.

10 Comes las verduras, por favor.

In place of the future tense:

11 Mi clase de chemica es esta tarde.

12 Corro esta tarde

CONCEPTO IMPORTANTE: "to be"

In this lesson we're going to study the Spanish equivalents of the English verb "to be."

The Difficulty

"To be" in English can be translated as *ser, estar, tener, haber* or *hacer* depending on the context. In fact, English uses the verb "to be" for many expressions for which Spanish has specific verbs. So you see, the alternatives aren't just *ser* or *estar*. For that reason, it's better not to think of the entire sentence first in English and then translate it word by word into Spanish. The likelihood of error using this slot-machine method of translation is much higher than if you looked at the context and then decided what you're trying to say. Think: *What is the message?* and then go directly to the appropriate Spanish structure.

Ser

There are some contexts that exclusively require *ser*.

We find *ser* in sentences that are balanced with two arms, one on either side, each with the same grammatical value. The subject and what we say about it are the same. In this type of construction, *ser* functions like an equal sign.

CONSTRUCTION TYPE	SPANISH	ENGLISH
Two nouns:	La doctora es pediatra.	The doctor is a pediatrician.
A noun and a pronoun:	Yo soy el doctor Wallace.	I am Dr. Wallace.
A noun and a clause:	Esta habitación es la que usted busca.	This room is the one you are looking for.
Two pronouns:	Eso no es mío.	That isn't mine.
Two clauses:	Lo que ella dice es lo que hace.	What she says is what she does.
Two adverbs (adverb and adverbial clause):	Mañana es cuando lo vamos a examinar.	Tomorrow is when we're going to examine you.

To express time in general in Spanish, we also use *ser*.

SPANISH	ENGLISH
Es la una.	It's one o'clock.
Son las tres.	It's three o'clock
¿Qué hora es?	What time is it?
Es tarde.	It's late.

Take another look at the examples provided for *ser* when it is used to communicate the current time. You can see that several of them also represent constructions in which *ser* joins like elements, such as two nouns.

Estar

There are some contexts that exclusively require *estar*.

To express that something is in a place, we normally use *estar*, especially when the thing or person we're referring to is known or specific.

SPANISH	ENGLISH
La clínica está en un área que empieza a desarrollarse.	The clinic is in an area that is starting to grow.
El doctor Ruiz está de guardia.	Dr. Ruiz is on call.

Certain expressions also are limited to *estar*.

SPANISH	ENGLISH
Estoy contento.	I'm happy. (Note: "Feliz" is an inner quality of life. *Soy feliz*. I'm a happy person. Don't use *alegre* with *estar* as it means "joyful" and refers to outward appearances.)
Estoy de acuerdo.	I agree.
Estoy de buen/mal humor.	I'm in a good/bad mood.
Estoy de pie/sentado.	I'm standing/sitting.
Estoy de vacaciones/de viaje/ de visita.	I'm on vacation/traveling/visiting.
Estoy en contra de...	I'm against...

Ser and/or *Estar* With Adjectives

Unlike in the previous contexts, which require either ser or *estar*, there are other contexts in which you must choose between *ser* and *estar*. Whether to use *ser* or *estar* to express that something "is" (subject + *ser/estar* + predicate adjective) depends on your perception of the situation. If you are expressing an expected or objective situation, you should use *ser*. If you are expressing a momentary or subjective situation, you should use *estar.*

The norm can vary depending on the speaker and the culture, however. A patient who says, *"Mi esposa es muy bonita. Es pálida y serena."* considers paleness and serenity the norm of beauty and is describing his wife as a beautiful pale and serene woman. That is how he objectively defines her. If the normally hyperactive daughter of the same patient came in to see you seriously dehydrated, you might say, *"Su hija está enferma. Está pálida y serena."* meaning that the child is pale and quiet just today, not always.

This is your subjective point of view. You have not changed the quality of paleness or serenity. Your choice of *estar* is not determined by the adjectives. Your perspective determines the verb you choose. The child is not her usual self. This is a momentary situation; therefore you must use *estar* if you want to express this. Let's examine this difference between the use of *ser* and *estar* a bit more closely.

Little Sara is three months old and a little underweight for her age but is otherwise developing normally. You say to her mother, *"Sara es buena. Es un poco flaquita."* very proud of yourself for having remembered the diminutive of *flaca*, thin, in order to soften the message that Sara is a little underweight. To your surprise, the mother acts distressed and worried. *"¿Qué puedo hacer, doctor?* No quiero que se me muera." (What can I do, doctor? I don't want my little girl to die.) "Oops!" you think, or something to that effect.

Sara es buena means Sara is good (a good girl) and *Es un poco flaquita* means that she is a somewhat skinny, or a delicate child. Your message implies that Sara is little and will always stay that way, because that's how she is. If you change both verbs to forms of *estar*, (you'll need to change the adjective *buena* to the adverb *bien*) you say, *"Sara está bien pero está un poco flaquita."* meaning that she is doing fine but right now she is a little skinny (emphasizing the moment). Magically, the mother smiles! You think to yourself, "Sara appears a little low on the charts NOW, but she is otherwise in good health. This implies now, so I have to use *estar*!"

Fortunately, some situations are unquestionable; you know that the man *"está enfermo"* if he catches a cold because a momentary condition is implied. On the other hand, if a child is advanced —tall and skilled for his age— we say that *"el niño está muy desarrollado."* meaning that this child has developed beyond what would be expected of the norm. This is your subjective description of the child.

As a result of these two opposing perspectives, some adjectives take on different meanings when they're used with one or the other of these verbs.

ADJETIVO	SIGNIFICADO CON ESTAR	SIGNIFICADO CON SER
aburrido	bored, disinterested	boring, uninteresting
bueno	tasty, attractive	healthy, good for you
ciego	distracted, ignorant	blind
listo	ready	clever
maduro	ripe	mature
mudo	dumbfounded	mute
rico	delicious	rich
sordo	unheeding	deaf
verde	unripe	green
vivo	alive	lively, bright

Both *ser* and *estar* are also used in combination with compound verbs, but we will cover those constructions in subsequent units.

Expressions with *Tener* and *Hacer*

You must memorize certain expressions that require either *tener* or *hacer*. The use of either verb in such expressions might seem odd to you, but you must remember that the way in which speakers of Spanish view the world and the way in which you view it are not necessarily one and the same.

Tener can be translated as "to be" in the following expressions:

SPANISH	ENGLISH
Tengo frío.	I am cold.
Tenemos calor.	We are hot.
Tienen hambre.	They are hungry.
Tiene cuidado.	He/She is careful.
Tengo 21 años.	I am 21 years old.
Tenemos miedo.	We are afraid.
Tienes sueño.	You are sleepy.
Tienen razón.	They are correct.
Tiene suerte.	He/She is lucky.
Tengo éxito.	I am successful.
Tienes prisa.	You are in a hurry.
Tienen sed.	They are thirsty.

Hacer can be translated as "to be" in the following expressions:

SPANISH	ENGLISH
Hace frío.	It's cold.
Hace calor.	It's hot.
Hace sol.	It's sunny.
Hace buen/mal tiempo.	It's nice/bad weather.
Hace viento.	It's windy.
¿Qué tiempo hace?	How's the weather?

Hay

Hay is used to express "there is" or "there are" in Spanish.

SPANISH	ENGLISH
Hay muchos pacientes esperando en la sala.	There are a lot of patients waiting in the room.

Hay is a form of *haber* which is easy to use, because it has only one form for each tense.

SPANISH	ENGLISH
Hay mucho trabajo hoy.	There's a lot of work today. *(present tense)*
Había muchos pacientes aquí ayer.	There were a lot of patients here yesterday. *(imperfect)*
Hubo varias operaciones esa noche.	There were several operations that night. *(preterit)*
Habrá espacio en la clínica mañana.	Tomorrow there will be space at the clinic. *(future tense)*

This verb is impersonal because there is no subject implied; we don't know who is doing the action, and it isn't relevant.

Are There Other Ways in Which Spanish Expresses the English Verb "to be"?

As you must have surmised by now, the expression of the English concept of "to be" cannot be covered by just *ser* and *estar*. The Spanish language makes use of a wide variety of constructions to convey this notion. Take note of the examples below.

SPANISH	ENGLISH
Llego tarde.	I am late.
Después de media hora nace el niño.	After a half hour, the child is born.
Me alegro.	I am glad.
Está cantando.	He is singing.

Strategies

Try using these simple strategies to help you distinguish between *ser* and *estar*:

- Focus on what you're going to say about something before you choose *ser* or *estar*.
- Consider whether the situation you're describing is momentary. If it is, remember to use *estar* with an adjective.
- Ask yourself the intention of your description: are you defining or describing? Remember to use *ser* to define.
- Review your list of memorized phrases that use *ser* or *estar*.

¡A PRACTICAR!

1B-PRIN-15

Match the statements on the left with the use of the present tense on the right.

1 ¿De dónde es usted?
2 ¿Estás lista para ir de visita?
3 ¿Qué tomas cuando tienes sed?
4 Entre mis antepasados hay indios garífunas y esclavos africanos.
5 Es una paciente nueva en la clínica.
6 No necesitamos abrigo porque hace buen tiempo hoy.
7 Son las diez de la mañana y llegamos tarde.
8 Soy salvadoreña.
9 Tenemos prisa porque tenemos que hacer varias visitas.
10 Tienes razón.
11 Toda mi familia está en El Salvador.

4 **a** Among my ancestors there are Garifuna Indians and African slaves.
2 **b** Are you ready to go visiting?
8 **c** I am Salvadoran.
7 **d** It is ten in the morning, and we are late.
11 **e** My entire family is in El Salvador.
5 **f** She is a new patient at the clinic.
9 **g** We are in a hurry because we have to make several visits.
6 **h** We don't need a coat because the weather is nice today.
3 **i** What do you drink when you are thirsty?
1 **j** Where are you from?
10 **k** You are right.

1B-PRIN-16

In your own words (in English), explain difficulties you find in distinguishing between the Spanish verbs meaning "to be." What are the differences between them?

just Knowing when to use each on the spot

1B-PRIN-17

Look at the following pictures and describe them, using the hints provided and using either ser *or* estar.

1 Esta manzana no ________ ________ (*unripe*); ¡me la voy a comer ahora!

2 ¡Qué ________ ________ este pastel!

3 ______ ______ ______________; ______ hora de cenar.

4 Este farmacéutico nunca ________ ________ porque siempre tiene que preparar tantas recetas.

1B-PRIN-18

Imagine that Ashleigh is speaking with the diabetic woman from El Salvador. First rewrite the sentences in Spanish. Then organize the sentences in the form of a coherent dialogue between Ashleigh and her patient.

a Good, because it is important to have support at home.
b How many people are in your family?
c How old are the children?
d I am happy to know that you are in good hands.
e Is there someone who can help you with your injections?
f My husband is there to help.
g There are three children and four adults.
h They are very young.

1 ________________________________

2 ________________________________

3 ________________________________

4 ________________________________

5 ________________________________

6 ________________________________

7 ________________________________

8 ________________________________

1B-PRIN-19

Read the dialogue and complete the sentences using the verbs in the list. Verbs can be used more than once.

compartir	hacer	saber
dar	pensar	ser
deber	poder	tener
decir	ponerse	
estar	querer	

Dos clientes de la clínica La Comunidad, Rebeca y Cheryl, están esperando a Jaime en la sala de espera. Mientras tanto, ellas hablan sobres sus hijos.

CHERYL: Cuántos años (1) tiene ______ su hijo?

REBECA: (2) Tienen ______ dos, Raúl y Federico. (3) Son ______ gemelos *(twins)* y (4) tenemos ______ tres años.

CHERYL: ¡Dios mío! ¡Gemelos de tres años! Usted (5) tienes ______ ser una santa. ¿Cómo se las arregla usted *(how do you manage)* con esos niños? Yo, con mi Miguelito de dos años y medio me (6) soy ______ volviendo loca.

REBECA: Ah, no (7) estoy ______ tan difícil. A esta edad (8) dicen ______ muchas preguntas, (9) quieren ______ explorarlo todo, pero también (10) ______ mucho uno con el otro. Además, cuando la cosa (11) es ______ muy difícil, yo se los (12) dice ______ al padre. Mi esposo (13) es ______ un ángel.

CHERYL: Yo no (14) ______ dejarle a Miguelito a su padre, porque él no (15) quiere ______ nada de niños.

REBECA: Ah, mi esposo tampoco, pero eso no (16) es ______ un problema. Él siempre (17) ______ que lo único que (18) ______ que hacer es mirarlos y ellos se portan bien. Yo (19) ______ que él (20) ______ mucho más estricto que yo y los niños no se aprovechan de él como se aprovechan de mí que soy mucho más paciente y buena gente que él.

1B-PRIN-20

Go to Unidad 1b Historia *and watch again the scene between Alex and Laura. Imagine that you are watching the scene as a psychology experiment, unseen by either of them. Write a paragraph of at least five lines in Spanish in which you analyze their relationship. Explain their behavior and the results you think it will have, being sure to use several examples of* ser, estar, *and other verbs in the present tense.*

Alex y Laura hacen una pareja...

SELF-REFLECTION

1. *How do you know that a verb is irregular?*

Assume that a verb is regular when you first meet it. Listen for changes in the vowel of the stem as speakers around you use it. Look up the infinitive in a good dictionary and read the examples given for other meanings or phrases in which the verb appears. There are also excellent books of verbs and good, inexpensive verb wheels that list irregular verbs in all tenses. Most grammar books used for teaching Spanish to speakers of other languages have lists of irregular verbs in the appendix.

2. *What's the easiest way to remember how a verb changes forms?*

Memorize them! You'll know your most efficient way of memorizing lists, but to speak fluently you'll need to be able to produce the correct verb form in a conversation when it is needed. You improve your chances of getting it right by studying language in context. Write a paragraph, a dialogue, or a story using the verb forms you want to memorize. Ask a Spanish-speaking colleague to correct spelling and grammatical errors. Working with the forms and relating them both to other items of language and to a meaningful context help memory and recall. If you're a visual learner, write the verb forms in a shape that reminds you of something concrete —like a shoe!

FOLLOW-UP TIPS

DVD

- Go back over the two episodes of *Historia* that you have seen so far and listen to what the characters say. How do they use verbs?
- Try to get used to thinking about what you're going to say before you decide how to say it. Take a step back from the English in your head, back to the underlying message.
- Consider the context in which the conversation you're having is taking place. What is needed here? Have you been in this situation before? Can you remember what was said then?

DO YOU REMEMBER?

Answer the questions based on the explanations found in *Principios Unidad 1b* of the textbook. If you found any section particularly difficult, go back and try some of the exercises again. There are also links to Spanish language materials on the *Recursos* website.

1 What do you listen for to determine the subject of a verb?

2 If a verb ends in *-s,* who is the speaker talking to?

3 If you want to talk about a group that includes yourself, how should your verbs end?

4 What are the three types of stem-changes that a verb can undergo?

5 How do you say "there is"?

6 What's the importance of "now" in the distinction between *ser* and *estar*?

7 How do you know that a verb is irregular?

8 Do you remember the uses of the present tense in Spanish?

FOOD FOR THOUGHT

The following questions are intended to serve as a springboard for discussion. Think about them as you read the story.

- How can I develop trusting and respectful relationships with my patients and clients?
- How can I recognize and challenge my own assumptions?
- How can I learn to recognize my patients' and clients' strengths and to build on teachable moments?
- How can I become partners with colleagues who are bridges across culture, with other organizations in the community that have similar interests and with members of the community I hope to serve?

NOTES FROM THE FIELD

Chris Harlan is a public health nurse. At the time of this story, she was working with migrant farm workers in Newton Grove, North Carolina.

Years ago I was asked to visit a young woman whose boyfriend was a migrant farm worker. She was about 17 years old and had experienced several miscarriages. She recently had surgery to correct an anomaly with her uterus. Her physician stressed the importance of waiting at least a year before becoming pregnant again in order for the uterus to heal properly. I was asked to talk with her about the reasons for the surgery and the things she could do to have a healthy baby in the future.

Our conversation was going well. As we talked, I realized how extremely important it was for her to have a baby, and also how important it was to her relationship with the boyfriend with whom she was traveling.

I needed to find a way to encourage her to wait before becoming pregnant again. It was important that her boyfriend finds a different job so they would not have to travel during the pregnancy. I knew I was asking her to make significant changes in her life and expectations for motherhood. Finally, to reassure her, I said, "You know, I was 32 when I had my first baby."

As soon as I spoke, the expression on her face changed. The trust and rapport I had built during the two hours of our visit went flying out the window. How could I expect her to see that waiting was something positive? It was as if I had asked her to wait until she was nearly old enough to be a grandmother before having her first child!

DISCUSSION QUESTIONS

Now that you have read Chris's story, think about her interaction with her patient.

1 What cultural assumption did Chris make that influenced her patient interaction?

2 What could Chris have said or done next to regain the trust *(confianza)* of the young woman?

MANJARES

Comida y familia

¿QUIERE que los hábitos alimenticios de sus hijos sean más saludables? Entonces revise su propia dieta. Según un estudio realizado por la Universidad de Londres con niños de dos a seis años, cuantas más frutas y verduras consuman papá y mamá, mayor será la probabilidad de que sus hijos las consuman también. Los que prueban antes en su vida estos alimentos tienden a elegirlos por su propia cuenta con mayor frecuencia. Los pequeños que reciben pecho comen frutas y verduras más a menudo que aquellos que son alimentados con biberón. ¿La razón? La leche materna tiene el sabor de los alimentos que consume la madre.

Hablando de leche, investigadores de la Facultad Baylor de Medicina y de la Universidad Penn State hallaron que las madres de las niñas que consumían los niveles de calcio recomendados eran a su vez grandes consumidoras de leche. JANICE LEARY

CONTESTA LAS SIGUIENTES PREGUNTAS:

1 ¿Te preocupa la nutrición? ¿Intentas seguir una dieta equilibrada?

2 ¿Hay algún alimento que consumas simplemente porque es saludable? ¿Evitas ciertas comidas porque son poco saludables?

3 ¿Tiene mucho color tu dieta? ¿Cómo era tu dieta de niño? ¿Comías de todo o no?

Sí, tengo mucho color me dieta, y cuando yo era un nino.

COMPROBACIÓN

DVD *Las preguntas de* Comprobación *están diseñadas para evaluar tu habilidad de usar lo que has aprendido, en situaciones nuevas y diferentes. Aunque el contexto todavía es limitado y las respuestas están restringidas y guiadas, debes interpretar más.*

SECCIÓN A

¿Qué pasa en la Historia*? Escoge las palabras que completan mejor la oración. ¡Cuidado con la gramática!*

1 Nuestra historia continúa con Ángela, Rafa, Carmina y Laura. Ángela se preocupa porque (en contra / enciende / encuentra) que faltan narcóticos de la farmacia. Como farmacéutica, su responsabilidad (es / está / se) tener en orden el inventario, por eso ahora (es / está / se) muy nerviosa.

2 Rafa trata de tranquilizarla, pero ella dice que no (pide / pone / puede) quitarse el problema de la cabeza.

3 Mientras tanto, Carmina trata de ayudar a su prima Laura, que (tenga / tiene / tuve) problemas de salud y hasta sufrió un accidente de noche en la carretera.

4 Laura (es / está / se) diabética pero no se (carga / cuida / toma) porque bebe mucho, fuma y no (va / viene / vuelve) al médico con regularidad para hacerse los exámenes que necesita.

SECCIÓN B

Estas oraciones describen a Duna. Escoge las palabras que completan mejor cada oración.

a veces	prejuicio
cualquier	recién
enfrentan	reto
entrar	tiene
huyendo	todas

Duna es una trabajadora social que trabaja con Ashleigh, la enfermera de La Comunidad. Las dos van a hacer una visita a una señora diabética que ha sido **(1)** ______________ diagnosticada y necesita ayuda. **(2)** ______________ lo único que los pacientes necesitan es un poco de apoyo. Estar enfermo ya es un problema, y estar enfermo en un país extranjero es un **(3)** ______________ todavía mayor. Para Duna es muy fácil **(4)** ______________ en confianza con los pacientes que hablan español, porque ella sabe muy bien lo que ellos **(5)** ______________. Duna es cariñosa y alegre y puede hablar tranquilamente con **(6)** ______________ persona.

¡A CONVERSAR!

PERSONAJES

DVD *Ashleigh and Duna introduce themselves in Personajes in this unit. Discuss these characters with a classmate.*

Here are some suggested questions to get you started:

Ashleigh and Duna

- ¿Quién es ______________ (Ashleigh (Duna)?
- ¿Cómo es ella?
- ¿Qué hace en la clínica?
- ¿Qué relación existe entre ellas?

enfermera
US
clinic

trabajor de social
guat
hospital

¡A RESUMIR!

EPISODIO

Imagine that you and a classmate need to tell a third classmate who didn't do his homework what happened in the second episode. Summarize it for him, being sure to mention the case of the missing drugs, Ángela's concern about the extra key to the drug cabinet, Ashleigh and Duna's visit to the diabetic patient, Carmina's boyfriend Abe, and Alex and Laura's relationship. Use the following sentences as conversation starters.

Al principio, Jaime y Ángela hablan de los narcóticos que faltan...

Ángela piensa que no es solamente un error de contabilidad...

APLICACIÓN

CONVERSAR

DVD

After watching this segment, answer the following questions posed by Rafa:

Rafa

Mexico ~~Arizona~~ Mexicano

muy a gusto

1 ¿De dónde eres? (Continúa discutiendo esta pregunta, agregando varios detalles, por ejemplo: ¿Cómo es este lugar? ¿Por cuánto tiempo has vivido allí? ¿Hay hispanohablantes que viven allí?)

2 ¿Cómo te sientes al hablar otro idioma?

3 ¿Cómo es un día normal en tu trabajo (o si no tienes un trabajo, en tu vida)?

Expansión:

¿Por qué nos propone estas preguntas Rafa? ¿Por qué le importa a él este tipo de preguntas?

ANALIZAR

DVD

Duna establishes a connection with a patient from the clinic in this scene, by talking with her about their shared experiences. After watching this segment, answer the following questions:

Duna and the Salvadoran patient

- ¿Qué recuerda Duna sobre su niñez?
  sus padres nerviosos
- ¿Qué recuerda la paciente sobre la guerra?
  explosiones, la sangre,
- ¿Qué hace en la clínica?
- La paciente parece muy tranquila mientras habla de cosas traumáticas. ¿Cómo demuestra su tristeza a Duna?

What questions do you have about the war in El Salvador? Do some research on-line about the history of El Salvador, and discuss what you learn with a classmate.

EN LA PRÁCTICA

Duna and Ashleigh

DVD *In this segment Duna and Ashleigh speak with a patient from the clinic. Because Ashleigh is still learning Spanish, she makes several mistakes, most of which Duna corrects. Which error does Duna correct? Can you identify any errors that Duna does not correct? What do you think of the way the patient reacts to Ashleigh's use of Spanish? Have you ever been in Ashleigh's position?*

Expansión:

Continue this interview with two classmates. (If there are only two of you, you can do the role-play without one of the characters.) Use the following sentences as a springboard to get you started.

ASHLEIGH: ¿Comió usted algo después del desayuno...?

LENGUA

DVD *Eres miembro del equipo de emergencia que llega al lugar del accidente que tuvo Laura. Recibes información de los testigos. Debes escribir 6 ó 7 oraciones, incluyendo información sobre lo siguiente:*

- Descripción del lugar, la hora y la situación
- Descripción de la conductora (Laura)
- Descripción del automóvil
- Tu opinión sobre la conductora y el accidente

MÁS ALLÁ

It's amazing how brief the spoken part of a message has to be when we're talking to someone who "speaks the same language" we do. By that we mean someone who shares the same experiences, worldview, and immediate context and who is thinking along the same lines as we are at that moment. You probably know couples who have been together so long that they finish each other's sentences or don't even have to speak to communicate very complex thoughts accurately. Think of how many movies have memorable scenes where the dialogue is hardly an indication of what is *really* going on.

The reverse can happen when you are not a member of the group. You can't read the unspoken signs. You don't know the implications of the choices the speaker is making in vocabulary and structures, in gestures and silences. You can't fill in the blanks that the speaker is leaving, while the speaker assumes that you can "get the drift." And the worst thing is that everyone does this to a degree; we all assume that our listener can meet us half way!

No matter how fluent you are in a language, the potential for losing your way in a conversation is very real if you aren't careful to check at regular intervals, to make sure that what you are understanding is what the speaker intended. If you're speaking with someone from another culture who is in any way under stress or distracted by worries or the newness of the surroundings, you should check even more often to make sure that the communicative link between you is still strong and that you're still on common ground. Not only will you feel more confident in your role as a healthcare professional, but also so will your patients.

The next time you need to perform a comprehension check, consider trying one of the following:

SPANISH	ENGLISH
Usted quiere decir que... *(and repeat what you understood the speaker to say)*	You mean... *or* You want to say that...
Antes de continuar quiero estar seguro de que nos entendemos.	Before continuing I want to be sure that we understand each other.
Por favor, dígame si estoy en lo correcto. *(Follow this with your version of what the speaker said to you.)*	Please, tell me if I am right [in what I'm saying].

ENTREVISTA

DVD

Read this summary in English of what Jesús Brañas says in his interview before you watch it on the DVD. Remember that these interviews were conducted to include "authentic language" on the DVD. This means that the interviews are unscripted and at a natural conversational pace. Use the English summary to guide you.

Jesús Brañas

Jesús begins the interview by introducing himself and saying that he's not Jaime. He says that although Jaime is Puerto Rican, "I am not a *'balsero'*, I'm Cuban." He expresses his pride in being Cuban, Latino, and from the Caribbean. Although Jesús claims that he and Jaime are very different, he says that like Jaime, he is also very much a perfectionist, that he likes things to turn out well, and that sometimes he gets involved in things that no one has asked him to do. "I'm a family man," he continues, "but I'm not as square as Jaime, no, I'm more sporty..."

When asked about Jaime's personal life, Jesús laughs and says that to tell that would require another chapter, a XXX one! Then he says he's just kidding; although Jaime does have a personal life, the film focuses on his professional life because he has attained goals in his life through his studies, sacrifices, and because he has a sense of the community.

Jesús continues that he is from Havana, Cuba, and that he was born many years ago —not as many as Jaime, he jokes, but around that. He remembers that he wanted to act ever since he was five years old and that from that time on he was always singing and dancing. His parents told him that was fine but that since artists died of hunger he had better study something else. "And so I became a dentist," Jesús says, adding that he studied dentistry in the University of Havana and practiced there until he left Cuba in 1983 for Venezuela. He spent eight years in Venezuela and is happy that it's been 12 years already that he's been a proud American citizen. Jesús lives in Miami and enjoys his life there.

Last night Jesús says that he went salsa dancing because a Puerto Rican friend of his told him about a salsa place. He said that all had a great time and that everyone danced, even the producers. He ends by commenting on the producers' dancing talents, "Ah, there are so many little salsa classes that should be given there, but it was a good time."

Watch the interview with Jesús Brañas (Jaime) one more time, and then discuss the following issues with a classmate:

- ¿Qué dice el actor sobre su propia identidad?
- ¿De dónde es él?
- ¿Qué opinaron sus padres sobre su deseo de ser actor?
- ¿En qué se parecen Jesús y Jaime, según él?
- ¿Cómo es el personaje de Jaime?
- ¿Qué dice el actor sobre su vida artística y profesional?
- ¿Qué hicieron los actores la noche anterior?

Do an on-line search of Jesús Brañas to see if you can discover what he is doing now.

UNIDAD 2a

NOTE TO THE STUDENT

Have you ever stopped to consider how the way in which you view the world affects the way you speak? Language and culture are interconnected, not independent of one another. Meaning and understanding are derived from many sources, such as existing beliefs and practices, and knowledge of these factors is imperative if you truly wish to communicate effectively. Such an understanding will help you to gain a patient's or client's trust and reduces the possibility that you will fail to provide the appropriate treatment or services.

WHAT IS DISEASE?

Our understanding of the causes of illness is reflected in cultural traditions and beliefs. Americans place a very high value on the biomedical model and germ theory, for instance. We describe the germ that causes the illness, and we seek medications that will treat or kill the germ, thus leading to wellness. In other cultures, the cause and cure of illness will be explained in relation to spiritual beliefs or social relationships gone wrong. Many of our patients are willing to take drugs to cure tuberculosis, for example, knowing that a particular germ caused the TB, but they may also look for causation on other levels and seek remedies that draw on spiritual and/or religious beliefs.

It is important to ask your patients and clients what they believe caused the illness and what they believe will cure it. As you suggest your own theory and prescribe treatment, ask if they are taking any other medications or teas or if they are being treated by a family member, *curandero, espiritista*, or other type of traditional healer.

WHAT OTHER TREATMENT OPTIONS ARE THERE?

Here is a sample of some common herbs and their uses:

SPANISH	ENGLISH	USE
Ajo	Garlic	Hypertension, antibiotic, cough syrup
Canela	Cinnamon	Antispasmodic, gastric symptoms
Cápsulas de víbora de cascabel pura	Mexican rattlesnake powder (capsules)	Cleansing the blood of toxins/impurities, leukemia
Gobernadora	Chaparral	Arthritis, tea for cancer, venereal disease, tuberculosis, cramps, *pasmo*
Manzanilla	Chamomile	Nausea, colic, anxiety, problems with menstruation, as an eyewash
Orégano	Oregano	Expectorant
Pasionaria	Passion flower	Anxiety, hypertension
Salvia	Sage	Diabetes, hair loss
Tilia, Tilo	Linden flowers	Sedative, diabetes, hypertension
Tronadora	Trumpet flowers	Adult onset diabetes, gastric symptoms, chickenpox
Yerbabuena	Peppermint	Hypertension, *susto*
Zábila	Aloe vera	External cuts and burns, internally as a purgative or immune stimulant

These are just a few examples of the many plants available. Although some plants cannot be obtained in the United States, in Mexico the herbs can be bought in the open markets. Just remember to ask about possible *remedios caseros* (home remedies) to avoid any adverse drug interactions and to recognize harmful remedies. If you are unfamiliar with the herb in any way, ask your patient to bring in a sample for testing.

VOCABULARIO

Below are the words that are highlighted in *Unidad 2a Vocabulario*, which can be viewed at the *Recursos* website. After you have looked at them, write its English equivalent beside each one. If you have any doubt about a word's exact meaning, look it up in a good Spanish-English dictionary.

Review the words that you have written on the margins of *Vocabulario* so far. Look up the meanings of any words you don't know.

Remember to use this space to add new and useful words that you find in your study or work, but were not included in *Vocabulario*!

Verbos

acercarse

bajar la presión

dar resultados

dejar que

doler

hacer los ejercicios

hacer una cita

parecer

recordar a

relajarse

respirar

tocar

Adverbios y adjetivos

cómodo

tocado

tranquilo

últimamente

Sustantivos

la ambulancia

el apetito

el aspecto

la bala

las heridas

el omóplato

los pandilleros

los problemas de pandillas

el pulmón

la yerbabuena

¡A PRACTICAR!

2A-VOC-1

Match the picture with the sentence that most accurately describes the scene. Review Unidad 2a Historia if you need some help remembering the story.

1 _____ El hombre se acerca y la invita a bailar.

2 _____ Los pandilleros se van y él se tranquiliza un poco.

3 _____ Toca al hombre para revisarle las heridas.

4 _____ A él le duelen las piernas.

5 _____ Le parece una buena idea tomar la yerbabuena además de hacer los ejercicios.

a

b

c

d

e

2A-VOC-2

Match the Spanish sentences below with the appropriate English translation.

Después de escuchar los disparos, Carmina sale afuera para ayudar al hombre herido.

1 A lo mejor la bala no te tocó el pulmón.

2 Bueno, tranquilo, la ambulancia está por llegar.

3 Deja que te ponga más cómodo.

4 Intenta no moverte, te ha entrado en el omóplato.

5 Parece que la herida no es muy grave.

6 ¿Recuerdas lo que pasó?

7 ¿Te duele mucho aquí?

8 Veo que puedes respirar bien.

__6__ **a** Do you remember what happened?

__7__ **b** Does it hurt much here?

__8__ **c** I see that you are able to breathe fine.

__5__ **d** It seems that the wound is not very serious.

__3__ **e** Let me make you more comfortable.

__2__ **f** Okay, stay calm; the ambulance is about to arrive.

__1__ **g** The bullet probably didn't touch your lung.

__4__ **h** Try not to move; it has penetrated your shoulder blade.

2A-VOC-3

Write the sentences that complete the dialogue, using the words from Vocabulario, *and others that you know. Be careful with agreement!*

El hombre con quien Carmina habla en La Pueblita nos cuenta cómo se cuida.

Hola, soy paciente de la clínica y la doctora Carmina me dice que **(1)** tengo la presión ~~arterial~~ alta *(I have high blood pressure).* Por eso, **(2)** [hago] ejercicios *(I exercise)* todos los días. Junto con los ejercicios, **(3)** bebo ~~que~~ té de yerbabuena [para] relajarme *(I drink peppermint tea to relax).* Parece que todo va bien porque **(4)** ~~últimamente~~ tengo [más] apetito ~~mas~~ *(lately I have more of an appetite).* También, me siento más tranquilo. La doctora dice que **(5)** las resultas son buenos [los resultados] *(the results are good)* y que debo **(6)** hacer ~~una~~ [otra] cita en dos semanas *(make another appointment in two weeks).*

2A-VOC-4

Review Unidad 2a Historia *and watch the last scene after everyone leaves La Pueblita and hears the gunshot. Imagine that Rafa wants to write an article to tell the community about the events that occurred. Write a paragraph of at least four sentences in Spanish explaining what happened. Write from his point of view and use the present tense to make the story more effective.*

¿UNA NOCHE DE SALSA?

USEFUL TERMS AND EXPRESSIONS

This section introduces new vocabulary and expressions related to themes found throughout *Historia 2a* of the DVD.

SUSTANTIVOS

El ejercicio

la actividad física	physical activity
la articulación	joint
la barra	bar
el calentamiento	warm-up
el enfriamiento	cool down
el latido del corazón	heartbeat
los músculos	muscles
el peso	weight
el relajamiento	relaxation
la rutina	routine

La dieta / La nutrición

los alimentos	food
el almuerzo	lunch
el calcio	calcium
las calorías	calories
la cantidad	quantity
la cena	dinner
el contenido	content
el desayuno	breakfast
la fibra	fiber
el flúor	fluoride
las grasas	fats
la merienda	snack
el sabor	taste
el sodio	sodium

En la farmacia

el ácido	acid
el biberón	bottle (for baby)
la cataplasma	poultice
el chupete	pacifier
el envase	package
las etiquetas	labels
la marca	brand name
la mezcla	mixture
las tabletas	tablets, pills

La salud

la autoestima	self-esteem
las bolitas	tiny balls
el cerebro	brain
el comportamiento	behavior
el derrame cerebral	stroke, brain hemorrhage
los lunares	moles
las masas	masses
la molestia	discomfort
la próstata	prostate
la regla	period
los remedios	remedies
los senos	breasts
el útero	uterus

VERBOS	
adelgazar	to grow thin
andar en bicicleta	to ride a bicycle
asar	to roast
aumentar	to increase
cansar(se)	to tire
colar	to strain
digerir	to digest
eliminar	to eliminate
engordar	to gain weight
estirar(se)	to stretch
exponer	to expose
fatigar(se)	to wear out
fortalecer	to strengthen
freír	to fry
hervir	to boil
hornear	to bake
padecer de	to suffer from
pegar(se)	to stick
picotear	to snack
remojar	to soak
repetir	to have seconds
separar(se)	to separate
sufrir	to suffer

ADJETIVOS	
adecuado/a	adequate
enlatado/a	canned
excesivo/a	excessive
inactivo/a	inactive
moderado/a	moderate

Study the vocabulary before you begin *Principios* because it will be useful when practicing the grammar points of the unit. Remember that this section is not intended to be an exhaustive list of all relevant terms but rather an exposure to some of the basic vocabulary used in healthcare. The definitions given here are limited to the way the words are used in the exercises found in *Principios*. Look the words up in a good Spanish-English dictionary if you want to know other meanings, the way to pronounce them, the contexts in which the words can be found, sayings and common expressions using these words, and their derivatives (adjectives from nouns, nouns from verbs, etc.).

PRINCIPIOS

ADVERBS

Adverbs are used to answer the questions *when*, *where*, *how*, and *how much*. We use adverbs to transform meanings of verbs, adjectives, and other adverbs. As in English, adverbial concepts can be expressed by a single word or by a phrase. Such devices enable us as speakers to communicate in a more precise or expressive manner because we are able to paint a clearer picture of the events we are trying to describe. Take a look at how the sentence below evolves as adverbs are added.

SPANISH	ENGLISH
La gente corre.	The people run.
La gente corre rápidamente.	The people run quickly.
La gente corre rápidamente afuera.	The people run quickly outside.

Which sentence would you prefer to use to describe the final scene outside of La Pueblita?

With the addition of adverbs, the story becomes more interesting and is more likely to engage the listener. As an intermediate learner, you are at the stage where you must begin to create more precise and expressive strings of language. The basic construction of "subject + verb + object" should no longer be sufficient for you. From this point forward, you should stay away from the basic utterance and attempt to add at least one adverb to every sentence you write and speak. Practice is the best way to make the use of adverbs automatic. Here are a few common adverbs to help you get started.

Many adverbs use adjectives as their base. For the majority, you just add *-mente*, the counterpart to the English *-ly*, to the feminine form of the adjective. If the adjective is neutral and ends in *-e*, simply add *-mente* to the adjective.

excesivo/a > excesiva**mente**	excessively
fuerte > fuerte**mente**	strongly
tranquilo/a > tranquila**mente**	calmly
último/a > última**mente**	lately

Other adverbs are distinct words. This is only a partial list.

SPANISH	ENGLISH	SPANISH	ENGLISH
a menudo	often	hoy	today
a veces	sometimes	mal	poorly/badly
allí	there	mañana	tomorrow
anoche	last night	mucho	a lot
anteayer	the day before yesterday	poco	a little
aquí	here	pronto	soon
ayer	yesterday	siempre	always
bien	well	tarde	late
de vez en cuando	once in a while	temprano	early

Placement of adverbs depends on your own style of writing. Generally, adverbs may precede or follow the verb, adjective, or adverb that they describe. If you use two adverbs of the *-mente* type together, add the suffix to the second adverb only. However, you will still need to change the first adjective to its feminine form, if it has one.

Δ to feminine

SPANISH	ENGLISH
El farmacéutico cuenta las píldoras lenta y cuidadosamente.	The pharmacist counts the pills slowly and carefully.

In addition to adverbs, Spanish makes use of a variety of verbal forms that take on adverbial qualities. We will study some of these verbal forms in the sections that follow.

¡A PRACTICAR!

2A-PRIN-1

Circle all of the adverbs in the sentences below; a patient is talking to Carmina. There are eleven adverbs in all.

Es que últimamente he estado bastante bien porque me mantengo muy activo físicamente. Hago diariamente la rutina de ejercicios que usted me recomendó anteayer. Empiezo temprano por la mañana con un período de calentamiento, y después ando en bicicleta por treinta minutos al día. También me reviso el peso regularmente.

2A-PRIN-2

Ashleigh is practicing her Spanish and wants to learn how to describe to her patients some symptoms of the illnesses below. Help her out by filling in the blank with the appropriate form of the adverb.

1 La osteoporosis:
Los huesos se rompen fácilmente *(fácil)*.

2 Un ataque al cerebro:
No habla claramente *(claro)*.

3 La enfermedad cardíaca:
(Probable) Probablemente siente molestia o malestar en el pecho.

4 Inflamación de la próstata:
Orina frecuentemente *(frecuente)* por la noche.

5 La hipertensión:
(Normal) normalmente uno no tiene síntomas.

6 La diabetes:
Los riñones no pueden limpiar adecuadamente *(adecuado)* la sangre.

7 El cáncer de los senos:
Hay que examinarlos *(cuidadoso)* cuidadosamente, buscando masas o bolitas.

8 Periodontitis:
(Lento) lentamente los dientes se separan de las encías y pueden caerse.

2A-PRIN-3

Carmina tells Duna all about what happened the previous evening; Duna was unable to attend because she did not have a babysitter for her son. Help Carmina tell the story by filling in the blanks with the appropriate adverb from the list below. Not all adverbs will be used.

afuera	ayer	muy
a menudo	de repente	poco
a veces	entonces	pronto
allí	hoy	siempre
anoche	mal	tarde
anteayer	mañana	temprano

"Déjame contarte el relato de lo que pasó **(1)** ayer anoche. Pues, vamos nosotros al club, Laura, Abe y yo. Bueno, tú ya sabes eso porque **(2)** a menudo estamos **(3)** allí. **(4)** Poco después de llegar nosotros, entran Ashleigh, Rafa, y Ángela. **(5)** Pronto Laura empieza a aburrirse y decide bailar con un hombre. **(6)** de repente, Alex llega y ve a Laura bailando con éste, y a partir de ese momento las cosas se ponen **(7)** ________. Alex y el hombre se pelean, Laura y Alex se pelean, y el pobre de Abe en medio de todo. Por fin, los hombres, unos pandilleros creo, se van. **(8)** ________ escuchamos un disparo que viene de **(9)** ________. Salgo para enterarme de la situación y encuentro a uno de los pandilleros tirado en el suelo. Por supuesto, nos vamos **(10)** ________ para no encontrarnos con más problemas."

2A-PRIN-4

Think about your personal health habits and use the adverbs given below, or any others that you can think of, to describe what things you do and when and how you do them. Write at least five sentences.

a menudo	de vez en cuando
a veces	diariamente
afuera	frecuentemente
bien	hoy
cuidadosamente	mal
mañana	mensualmente
mucho	muy
poco	pronto
semanalmente	siempre
tarde	temprano

A menudo corro.

En la mañana siempre desayuno.

THE PRESENT PARTICIPLE

In Spanish, the present participle is commonly formed by adding *-ando* or *-iendo* to the stem of the infinitive. Which ending is selected is determined by the ending of the infinitive. Generally, if the infinitive ends in *-ar*, add *-ando*. If the infinitive ends in *-er* or *-ir*, add *-iendo*. You will also be pleased to know that these endings do not change for gender and number.

The three basic conjugations for the present participle are:

-AR	**-ER**	**-IR**
cans**ar** > cans**ando**	manten**er** > manten**iendo**	sufr**ir** > sufr**iendo**

Some stem-changing verbs undergo additional changes to form of the present participle. Still, they do follow a pattern, and the majority of these verbs end in *-ir*.

Those *-ir* verbs that have a stem change from *-e-* > *-ie-* or *-e-* > *-i-* in the present tense will stem change from *-e-* > *-i-* in the present participle form.

PRESENT TENSE	**-e- > -ie-**	**-e- > -i-**
	pr**e**venir > previ**e**ne	rep**e**tir > rep**i**te
PRESENT PARTICIPLE	**-e- > -i-**	**-e- > -i-**
	pr**e**venir > prev**i**niendo	rep**e**tir > rep**i**tiendo

If, as a result of the stem-change, *-iendo* is preceded by an *-i*, the first *-i* is dropped. Verbs ending in *-eír* fall into this category.

fre**ír** > fr**i**endo	re**í**r > r**i**endo	sonre**ír** > sonr**ie**ndo

Those *-ir* verbs that stem change from *-o-* to *-ue-* in the present tense will stem change from *-o-* to *-u-*. (NOTE: *Poder* is the only exception because it changes from *-o-* to *-u-* even though it ends in *-er*.)

PRESENT TENSE	**-o- to -ue-**
	m**o**rir > m**ue**re
PRESENT PARTICIPLE	**-o- to –u**
	m**o**rir > m**u**riendo

While most verbs fit into the patterns described above, exceptions occur in verbs that belong to either the *-er* or *-ir* verb conjugations that normally take *-iendo*.

With these verbs, the change actually occurs to the ending used to form the present participle and is a direct result of sound changes. Here the *-i-* of *-iendo* changes to *-y-*. This change takes place because either there is no verb stem to which to add the ending or these verb stems end in a vowel. It is important to understand that the verbs that fall under this category are not stem-changing verbs.

caer > ca**y**endo	disminuir > disminu**y**endo	leer > le**y**endo
creer > cre**y**endo	ir > **y**endo	oír > o**y**endo

While conjugating verbs may seem overwhelming when trying to determine what form to use, just remember to look for the patterns. As adult learners, we learn best through associations, and these patterns will become more and more apparent as you progress. If you go back to *Unidad 1b* and compare the way the present tense is formed, including all of the exceptions, with how the present participle is formed, you can see the patterns.

¡A PRACTICAR!

2A-PRIN-5

Choose the correct form of the present participles for the verbs given below.

c **1** contribuir:
a contribuendo **b** contribuiendo
c contribuyendo

b **2** digerir:
a digerando **b** digeriendo
c digiriendo

c **3** doler:
a doliendo **b** dueliando
c dueliendo

c **4** empezar:
a empeciendo **b** empezando
c empiezando

c **5** escoger:
a escogiando **b** escogiendo
c escojiendo

c **6** freír:
a freiendo **b** freyendo
c friendo

a **7** funcionar:
a funcionando **b** funcionendo
c funcioniendo

c **8** medir:
a mediendo **b** midiando
c midiendo

a **9** padecer:
a padeciendo **b** padezcando
c padieciendo

c **10** suceder:
a sucedendo **b** sucediando
c sucediendo

2A-PRIN-6

Provide the correct form of the present participle and meaning for the verbs below.

1 aumentar:
Forma: ______
Significado: ______

2 consumir:
Forma: consumiendo
Significado: ~~to consume~~ consuming

3 dormir:
Forma: ______
Significado: ______

4 estimular:
Forma: ______
Significado: ______

5 leer:
Forma: leyendo
Significado: reading

6 prevenir:
Forma: ______
Significado: ______

7 producir:
Forma: ______
Significado: ______

8 sostener:
Forma: ______
Significado: ______

WHEN TO USE THE PRESENT PARTICIPLE

We know that the Spanish forms of *-ando* and *-iendo*, as well as their offshoots, are equivalent to the English form of *-ing* when translated literally. However, we must not get ahead of ourselves and assume that these forms are also identical in use. They are not. Let us take a closer look at English in order to better understand the differences.

In English the *-ing* form can be used in three ways: 1) as a gerund or verbal noun; 2) as a verbal adjective; 3) as an adverb. It just so happens that the same form covers three very different functions. Spanish, however, represents these three functions in three very different ways. Herein lies the difficulty for a native speaker of English. You must be careful not to associate the *-ando* and *-iendo* forms of Spanish with the nominal or adjectival functions of their English counterpart. Instead, Spanish makes use of the infinitive or a relative clause. Compare the two sets of examples given below.

ENGLISH	SPANISH
As a noun:	**As a noun:**
Riding a bicycle is a healthy activity.	El andar en bicicleta es una actividad saludable.
I like doing exercises.	Me gusta hacer ejercicio.
I will go after relaxing a while.	Voy después de relajarme un poco.
As an adjective:	**As an adjective:**
Meat is a type of food containing many proteins.	La carne es un alimento que contiene muchas proteínas.
Sugar is a fattening food.	El azúcar es una comida que engorda.

In other words, the present participle in Spanish cannot function as a noun or as an adjective. Now that we know how not to use the present participle in Spanish, the question is, when do we use it?

As in English, the present participle in Spanish is used:

- By itself to express the means by which something is done:

SPANISH	ENGLISH
Eliminando la grasa de la dieta, puedes bajar de peso.	By eliminating fat from your diet, you can lose weight.

- As an adverb in conjunction with verbs of motion, perception, representation, and repetition:

SPANISH	ENGLISH
Todos los días sale desayunando aprisa.	Every day he leaves eating his breakfast in a hurry.
Siempre te veo repitiendo.	I always see you having seconds.
Me imagino trabajando muy duro.	I imagine myself working very hard.
Sigo haciendo ejercicios todos los días.	I continue exercising every day.

- In conjunction with *estar* to form the present progressive tense.

¡A PRACTICAR!

2A-PRIN-7

Duna often counsels troubled teens on the dangers of becoming involved with gangs. Select the correct translations of the sentences provided below.

1 I miss talking to my friends everyday.

a Extraño hablando con mis amigos todos los días.

b Extraño hablar con mis amigos todos los días.

2 Sometimes I spend the entire day sleeping.

a A veces paso dormir todo el día.

b A veces paso todo el día durmiendo.

3 The people running the programs are very experienced.

a La gente que dirige los programas tiene mucha experiencia.

b La gente dirigiendo los programas tiene mucha experiencia.

4 Does doing harm to your parents make you feel good?

a ¿Hacerles daño a tus padres te hace sentir bien?

b ¿Haciéndoles daño a tus padres te hace sentir bien?

2A-PRIN-8

Read the following sentences about gang violence in the community. Explain in English why the present participle is or is not used in Spanish. Then translate the sentence.

Modelo:

No entienden la importancia de recibir una buena educación.

Explanation: Present participles are not used as nouns.

Translation: They do not understand the importance of receiving a good education.

1 **Trabajando** con los jóvenes, podemos ayudar la comunidad.

Explanation: ______________________________

____

____

____

____

Translation: ______________________________

____

____

2 Siguen **aumentando** los incidentes relacionados con la violencia.

Explanation: ______________________________

____

____

____

____

Translation: ______________________________

____

____

____

3 Ser parte de una pandilla les hace sentir fuertes.

Explanation: ______________________________

____

____

____

____

____

Translation: ______________________________

____

____

____

____

4 Los pandilleros van **destruyendo** la propiedad de la gente inocente.

Explanation: ______________________________

____

____

____

____

____

Translation: ______________________________

____

____

____

____

2A-PRIN-9

Look at the sentences that follow and determine whether they would be rewritten in Spanish using the present participle. Then rewrite them.

1 I usually prefer dancing to watching television.

Sí ________ **No** ___✓___

____

____

____

2 I often get my exercise by walking up and down the stairs.

Sí ___✓___ **No** ________

____

____

____

3 Quitting smoking is not easy for me.

Sí ___✗___ **No** ___✓___

____

____

____

4 I always stretch before doing any exercise.

Sí ________ **No** ___✓___

____

____

____

5 A diet high in fat is a contributing factor for heart disease.

Sí ________ **No** ___✓___

____

____

____

enojar: to anger

THE PRESENT PROGRESSIVE

To form the present progressive, combine the present tense of *estar* with a present participle. Because these two elements work together as a compound tense, nothing can be placed between them.

estoy		
estás		cansando
está	+	manteniendo
estamos		sufriendo
están		

This construction is used in Spanish to indicate that an action is occurring at the moment of the utterance. By using this compound construction, the speaker wishes to emphasize the fact that the statement and the action are simultaneous. The speaker is emphasizing the notion of "in progress". English uses this construction in a similar manner.

Even though any tense of *estar* can combine with the present participle, here we are treating only the present progressive, because it occurs most frequently. Native speakers often opt for other more appropriate constructions when their point of reference is something other than the present, a point that will be revisited throughout the textbook.

* Agrees in gender o/a & os/as

abrir: abierto

cansar: to get tired
embarazar: to inseminate
resolver: to solve

¡A PRACTICAR!

2A-PRIN-10

Jaime is hungry and wants to go eat lunch, but he cannot find anyone to accompany him. Help him out by filling in the blanks with the correct form of the present progressive for the verb.

JAIME: ¡Qué día más ocupado **(1)** estoy tieniendo *(tener)*! Ni siquiera he podido encontrar tiempo para almorzar. Voy a ver si alguien quiere acompañarme. Hola, Duna y Ashleigh, ¿qué **(2)** están haciendo *(hacer)*? ¿Tienen ganas de ir a comer conmigo?

DUNA: Lo siento, Jaime, no puedo. Un cliente me **(3)** está esperando *(esperar)* en la recepción.

ASHLEIGH: Tampoco puedo ir contigo porque **(4)** ~~estás~~ estoy analizando *(analizar)* los resultados de una prueba de sangre para Carmina.

JAIME: Está bien, ¿saben dónde está ella?

ASHLEIGH: **(5)** Está hablando *(hablar)* con Laura sobre lo de anoche.

JAIME: ¿Y Ángela?

ASHLEIGH: En la farmacia, **(6)** está recontando *(recontar)* los narcóticos de nuevo.

JAIME: ¿Y Alex? durmiendo

DUNA: A lo mejor ya **(7)** está dormiendo *(dormir)* porque fue a casa temprano por un dolor de cabeza.

JAIME: Bueno, entiendo. Ustedes me **(8)** estan deciendo *(decir)* que tengo que almorzar solo.

estan diciendo

2A-PRIN-11

Every day so much goes on in the clinic. Look at the picture below and describe what's happening today. Write at least five different sentences using the present progressive.

PAST PARTICIPLES

In general, infinitives ending in *-ar* add *-ado* to their verb stem, and infinitives ending in *-er* or *-ir* add *-ido* to form the past participle. Does this pattern remind you of something else you just studied? If not, look at the section on present participles found in this unit.

Below are the basic conjugations for the regular forms of the past participle.

-AR	**-ER**	**-IR**
toc**ar** > toca**do**	parec**er** > parec**ido**	her**ir** > her**ido**

This second list covers some of the most common irregular forms of the past participle. The best way to tackle these is to memorize them.

abrir > abierto	morir > muerto
cubrir > cubierto	poner > puesto
decir > dicho	romper > roto
descubrir > descubierto	ver > visto
escribir > escrito	volver > vuelto
hacer > hecho	

Finally, a few verbs that require the addition of an accent mark to the past participle ending. Notice that they belong to the *-er* verb group.

traer > traído	caer > caído	creer > creído

traído caído creído

¡A PRACTICAR!

2A-PRIN-12

Match the infinitive with the correct past participle.

1 componer	6	**a** padecido
2 decaer	4	**b** escrito
3 envolver	7	**c** recetado
4 escribir	1	**d** compuesto
5 hacer	9	**e** retenido
6 padecer	2	**f** decaído
7 recetar	3	**g** envuelto
8 reducir	5	**h** hecho
9 retener	8	**i** reducido
10 romper	10	**j** roto

2A-PRIN-13

Provide the correct form of the past participles for the infinitives below. Then write what each signifies.

1 prescribir:

Forma: ~~prescribo~~ prescrito

Significado: prescribed

2 ver:

Forma: Visto

Significado: seen

3 tapar:

Forma: tapado

Significado: Stuffed

4 hinchar

Forma: hinchado

Significado: ______

5 mantener mantenido

Forma: ~~mantienido~~

Significado: ______

6 sentir:

Forma: sentido

Significado: ______

7 morir:

Forma: muerto

Significado: ______

8 vomitar:

Forma: vomitado

Significado: ______

WHEN TO USE THE PAST PARTICIPLE

Conveniently, the functions of the past participle in Spanish parallel those of English. Basically, past participles have three functions:

- By themselves, past participles work the same way as adjectives; they describe nouns and reflect both gender and number:

SPANISH	ENGLISH
un nivel **moderado** de ejercicio	a **moderate** level of exercise
una cantidad **adecuada** de comida	an **adequate** quantity of food

For the most part, verbs have only one past participle. In rare cases, a verb has two separate forms. One is used for the adjectival function and the other is used in the compound construction and has a verbal meaning.

INFINITIVE	ADJECTIVAL PARTICIPLE	VERBAL PARTICIPLE
despertar	despierto	despertado
elegir	electo	elegido
freír	frito	freído
incluir	incluso	incluido

As with all other structures, through language practice you will come to learn which verbs have two forms of past participles. You can always check your dictionary or ask someone who speaks Spanish.

- Past participles can join with *haber* to indicate the perfect tenses. Whether a perfect tense indicates present, past, future, conditional, or subjunctive, its counterpart is determined by the form of *haber*. What is the purpose of the perfect tenses? Their function is twofold: 1) to let us know that an action or state is completed or achieved; 2) to tell us when the result of the action or state was, is, or will be evident. In this capacity, it is the function of the past participle to indicate the completion of an action or the achievement of a state.
- Past participles can join with *ser* to refer to the passive voice.

¡A PRACTICAR!

2A-PRIN-14

The clinic has a dietician who comes to meet with patients once a week. Read the paragraph below from one of her pamphlets and circle the past participles. There are five past participles in the pamphlet.

Para todos nosotros es importante comer una dieta balanceada. Se deben leer las etiquetas de los envases de comida y buscar los datos sobre nutrición para saber si la comida contiene la cantidad adecuada de los nutrientes requeridos. Es necesario no comer demasiada comida dulce, salada o con grasa. De hecho es mejor evitar ciertas comidas azucaradas como las pasas, o las que se pegan en las superficies de los dientes, porque pueden causar caries. En vez de picotear todo el día, uno debe hacer tres comidas al día y dos meriendas saludables. Así también evitamos la obesidad. La comida y la merienda deben incluir alimentos variados de los grupos alimenticios básicos. Nunca es tarde para empezar a comer correctamente.

2A-PRIN-15

Here are some tips from the dentist who volunteers each week at the clinic. Write the noun that each past participle modifies. Then translate the sentence.

1 Es importante recibir la cantidad **recomendada** de flúor.

Sustantivo: la cantidad

Traducción: ______________________________

____

2 Usted debe tener el agua **analizada** para verificar su contenido.

Sustantivo: ______________________________

Traducción: ______________________________

____

3 A veces el flúor es un gel **pintado** sobre los dientes.

Sustantivo: ______________________________

Traducción: ______________________________

____

4 También hay un suplemento **producido** en forma de tabletas o gotas.

Sustantivo: ______________________________

Traducción: ______________________________

____

5 Unos gérmenes invisibles **llamados** bacterias convierten el azúcar en ácidos.

Sustantivo: ______________________________

Traducción: ______________________________

____

6 Por eso, es necesario prevenir las caries **causadas** por el biberón.

Sustantivo: ______________________________

Traducción: ______________________________

____

7 Es importante no darle al bebé un chupete **remojado** en miel o azúcar.

Sustantivo: ______________________________

Traducción: ______________________________

____

8 Los dientes quedan **expuestos** a líquidos azucarados.

Sustantivo: ______________________________

Traducción: ______________________________

____

2A-PRIN-16

Ashleigh and Duna visit with one of the elderly patients of the clinic to see how she is doing. During the visit they discover that she is not eating very well for various reasons. Rewrite the paragraph below in English to discover how they advise her.

Si usted no puede ir al mercado o cocinar debe contactar los programas ofrecidos por grupos de la comunidad o por organizaciones dedicadas al servicio de la gente mayor. Muchas veces tienen un servicio de comida distribuida a domicilio. Si le hace falta dinero, puede comprar las marcas genéricas que venden en el mercado. También puede buscar productos enlatados porque usted puede guardar este tipo de comida por más tiempo. Y como último, mi manera preferida de ahorrar dinero es usar cupones.

____

____

____

____

____

____

____

____

____

____

____

____

____

____

2A-PRIN-17

Think about your own profession or your future profession. What are some important recommendations that you can give to your patients or clients? Write at least five using past participles as adjectives.

Palabras útiles

abrir	desear	preparar
adecuar	encontrar	prescribir
causar	escribir	recomendar
contener	mencionar	requerir
descubrir	preferir	sugerir

Modelo: Hay que venir con una actitud abierta.

____

____

____

____

____

____

____

____

____

____

____

____

____

____

____

____

____

____

THE PRESENT PERFECT

To form the present perfect, you must combine the present tense of haber —*he, has, ha, hemos, han*— with the past participle of the main verb. When joined with *haber,* past participles take on verbal qualities and always end in *-o*; therefore, these endings do not change for gender and number. Observe that the two forms are always used together and are never separated.

TOCAR	MANTENER	SUFRIR
he tocado	he mantenido	he sufrido
has tocado	has mantenido	has sufrido
ha tocado	ha mantenido	ha sufrido
hemos tocado	hemos mantenido	hemos sufrido
han tocado	han mantenido	han sufrido

Students learning to use the perfect tenses often confuse the verb *haber* with *tener*. Why does this confusion occur? Actually, the answer is very logical. Both verbs translate into English as "to have". Where English makes use of one verb, Spanish makes use of two. Since *tener* is the first verb you learn as meaning to "to have," you are most familiar with it. Consequently, you tend to use it whenever the meaning "to have" is indicated. (Native speakers of Spanish encounter a somewhat similar situation when learning to distinguish between the English verbs "to make" or "to do". Both concepts are encompassed in the single verb *hacer*.) One way to help distinguish between *tener* and *haber* is to equate *tener* with the meaning "to physically possess."

- indirect object pronoun in front of conjugated verb
- conj. haber to match who you are talking to/about

¡A PRACTICAR!

2A-PRIN-18

Write the correct form of the present perfect for the verbs listed below.

1 (Yo / no hacer) ______________________

2 (Todos nosotros / llegar) ______________

3 (La doctora Estrada / examinar) ________

____

4 (Tú / decir) ________________________

5 (Alex / sufrir) ______________________

6 (Ustedes / almorzar) _________________

7 (Mis colegas / ir) ____________________

8 (El tratamiento / ser) _________________

5 Los ejercicios / servir / para fortalecer los músculos.

____

____

6 Yo / terminar / la rutina con un período de enfriamiento.

____

____

7 Nosotros / trabajar / mucho para adelgazar.

____

____

2A-PRIN-19

Use the cues provided to form complete sentences.

1 ¿Tú / ir /a hablar con la dietista esta semana?

____

____

2 Mi hermano / estar / en el hospital tres veces.

____

____

3 Mis amigos y yo / prometer / comer regularmente.

____

____

4 El terapista físico / poner / una barra para que me sirva de apoyo.

____

____

2A-PRIN-20

A mother arrives with her sick child and Ashleigh needs to find out some information. Write down the questions needed to elicit the information. Use the present perfect.

1 What's the problem?

____

____

2 How long?

____

____

3 Is this the first time?

____

____

4 Is there evidence of any serious illness in the family?

____

____

WHEN TO USE THE PRESENT PERFECT

In Spanish, the present perfect is equivalent to the English use of "have/has" + the past participle. For a guide of when to use the present perfect, take a look at the examples provided below.

SPANISH	ENGLISH
¿Has encontrado una rutina adecuada?	Have you found an adequate routine?
Hoy he hecho mucho ejercicio.	I have done a lot of exercise today.
Este año ha venido mucha gente a la clínica.	Many people have come to the clinic this year.
Este mes no he engordado mucho.	I have not gained much weight this month.
Los niños han visitado al doctor tres veces este mes.	The children have visited the doctor three times this month.
El doctor ha estado llamándote todo el día.	The doctor has been calling you all day.
Hemos esperado por dos horas.	We have waited for two hours.

A closer examination of the above sentences reveals clues that can guide us in our decision to use the present perfect. Adverbs and adverbial phrases such as *hoy, ahora, ya, este año, este mes, todo el día*, and *por dos horas* all indicate a period of time up to and including the moment of speech. That is to say, the *when* of the result of the action or state can be further described and/or stressed by your choice of adverb or adverbial phrase. In the above examples, the result of the action exists at least up until the present, the specific point in time indicated; however, the actual time frame for each result varies.

* preterit does not require a compound tense

¡A PRACTICAR!

2A-PRIN-21

Carmina and her patient discuss his hypertension. Use the verbs provided to write the questions that would elicit the responses given below. Remember to use the present perfect.

Modelo:

Sí, mi padre también tiene la presión alta.

(padecer): ¿____________________?

Pregunta: *¿Su padre ha padecido de presión alta?*

1 No, no tengo molestias en la cabeza. Ni ahora, ni nunca.

(sufrir): ¿____________________

____________________?

2 No. No tengo ningún problema con la vista.

(tener): ¿____________________

____________________?

3 Sí, siempre hay días difíciles en el trabajo. A veces me siento muy agobiado.

(haber): ¿____________________

____________________?

4 Tomo té de yerbabuena y hago ejercicio.

(hacer): ¿____________________

____________________?

5 Sí, las dos cosas funcionan muy bien.

(ser): ¿____________________

____________________?

6 Sí, aquí tengo una muestra del té.

(traer): ¿____________________

____________________?

2A-PRIN-22

Again, think about your own profession or your future profession. What are some general questions that you should ask your patients or clients? Write at least five, using the present perfect.

POR AND *PARA*

Por and *para* are two of many prepositions found in the Spanish language. Consistently, these two prepositions have proven to be difficult for all students, so our best advice here is to be patient and give yourself time to master their uses. Once again, the fact that English often uses one word whereas Spanish uses two makes their mastery all that more challenging. The most frequent English translation for these two prepositions is *for*. As a result, students tend to pick whichever preposition sounds right at the time of the utterance. Unfortunately, this approach will not always lead to the appropriate choice. The best way to distinguish between *por* and *para* is to memorize when to use them. Then, when trying to determine which preposition to use, avoid the English translation of *for* by applying the more specific meaning to the context.

Por

Here are some of the most common uses of *por*:

- To refer to an exchange:

SPANISH	ENGLISH
En La Pueblita uno puede comprar algo de beber por dos dólares.	In La Pueblita one can buy something to drink for two dollars.

- Expressions:

SPANISH	ENGLISH
Por la mañana Jaime trabaja en la clínica.	During the morning, Jaime works at the clinic.
¿Laura, **por qué** bailas con aquel hombre?	Laura, why are you dancing with that man?
Por lo general, prefiero no freír la comida.	In general, I prefer not to fry the food.
Por fin, ha llegado la ambulancia.	At last, the ambulance has arrived.

- To indicate duration:

SPANISH	ENGLISH
Pobre Jaime, ha estado en esa reunión por dos horas.	Poor Jaime, he has been in that meeting for two hours.

- To express motive:

SPANISH	ENGLISH
Laura necesita dejar de beber por la diabetes.	Laura needs to stop drinking because of her diabetes.

- To express "means by":

SPANISH	ENGLISH
Normalmente, mandan los resultados por correo.	Normally, they send the results by mail.

- To express movement through:

SPANISH	ENGLISH
Todas las tardes a Otelo le gusta dar un paseo por el barrio.	Every afternoon Otelo likes to take a walk through the neighborhood.

- To express favor:

SPANISH	ENGLISH
Las enfermeras están por el cambio.	The nurses are in favor of the change.

- As the equivalent of *per* in English:

SPANISH	ENGLISH
Hay cien píldoras por frasco.	There are 100 pills per bottle.

Try not to become too overwhelmed by the list. ***E***ventually, ***e***veryone ***d***evelops ***m***any ***m***ethods for ***m***emorizing the ***f***unctions of ***p***or. Or, you can turn to mnemonic methods like the one used in the previous sentence to guide you.

Eventually	E:	Exchange
Everyone	E:	Expressions
Develops	D:	Duration
Many	M:	Motive
Methods	M:	Means by
Memorizing	M:	Movement through
Functions	F:	Favor
Por	P:	Per

Para

Here are some of the most common uses for *para*.

- To express an opinion:

SPANISH	ENGLISH
Para mí, es importante reducir el nivel de colesterol.	For me, it is important to reduce my level of cholesterol.

- To compare:

SPANISH	ENGLISH
Para ser un hombre tan joven, Alex tiene mucho dolor.	For such a young man, Alex has a lot of pain.

- To indicate a destination or recipient:

SPANISH	ENGLISH
Ashleigh y Duna van para la casa de una paciente de la clínica.	Ashleigh and Duna are going to the house of one of the patients from the clinic.
Ángela está llenando la receta para el hombre.	Angela is filling the prescription for the man.

■ To mean "in order to":

SPANISH	ENGLISH
El paciente de Carmina toma medicina para controlar la presión.	Carmina's patient takes medicine in order to control his pressure.

■ To refer to a future time:

SPANISH	ENGLISH
El hombre hace una cita con Carmina para mañana.	The man makes an appointment with Carmina for tomorrow.

■ To refer to an item's use:

SPANISH	ENGLISH
La yerbabuena es para bajarme la presión.	The peppermint is for lowering my pressure.

Remember that through practice you will learn when to use this preposition. ***O**ne **c**an **d**evelop an **i**nstinctive **f**eel for **u**sing **p**ara.* Sometimes it is useful to find a tool, like the one below, to help you with the process.

One	O:	Opinion
Can	C:	Comparison
Develop	D:	Destination
Instinctive	I:	In Order to
Feel	F:	Future Time
Using	U:	Use
Para	P:	*Para*

On the other hand, by memorizing the rules guiding the use of one of the prepositions, you could employ the process of elimination. Such a strategy would require that you learn every rule that pertains to the chosen preposition. However, this method will help you to choose between *por* and *para* only when you are aware that one of the two must be used.

¡A PRACTICAR!

2A-PRIN-23

All of the people working at the clinic are very busy. Below are just some examples of their conversations. Choose between por *and* para *to complete their sentences.*

1 (***Por / para***) comprobar la infección, necesito hacer un análisis de orina.

2 Los resultados van a estar listos (***por / para***) el próximo viernes.

3 Tengo buenas noticias (***por / para***) ti.

4 La insulina es (***por / para***) controlar la diabetes.

5 ¿(***Por / para***) qué no esperas en mi oficina?

6 Emilia está en los Estados Unidos (***por / para***) su esposo.

7 Normalmente no trabajo (***por / para***) la tarde.

8 Ahora mismo salgo (***por / para***) el gimnasio.

9 He estado llamándote (***por / para***) dos horas.

10 (***Por / para***) ser director, ellos piensan que puedo darles una receta sin examinarse.

2A-PRIN-24

Jaime has his hands full with a patient. Help him out by filling in the blanks with either por *or* para. *Then explain why you chose that particular preposition.*

1 La prueba de Papanicolaou sirve ________ detectar el cáncer del útero.

Razón: ____________________

____

2 La mamografía le puede resultar incómoda ________ pocos minutos.

Razón: ____________________

____

3 Mandamos las muestras ________ el laboratorio.

Razón: ____________________

____

4 El embarazo puede ser difícil ________ los fibromas.

Razón: ____________________

____

5 La ecografía sirve ________ ver si hay quistes.

Razón: ____________________

____

6 Necesito un análisis de sangre ________ estar seguro.

Razón: ____________________

____

7 ¿ ________ cuánto tiempo dura la regla?

Razón: ____________________

____

2A-PRIN-25

Duna has just returned from a conference on gang violence. To find out about the information she gathered, combine phrases from the column A with phrases from column B to form meaningful sentences.

A		B
1 Algunos se hacen miembros...		**a** ...los miembros de la pandilla.
2 Lo hacen todo...		**b** ...media hora todos los días.
3 Los miembros dejan señales de su presencia...		**c** ...su comportamiento violento.
4 Muchos jóvenes se hacen parte de una pandilla...	**por / para**	**d** ...todas partes de su territorio.
5 A veces terminan en la cárcel...		**e** ...problemas con la familia, la escuela, o su autoestima.
6 Uno debe hablarle a su niño al menos...		**f** ...recibir protección.

1 ______

2 ______

3 ______

4 ______

5 ______

6 ______

2A-PRIN-26

Look at the discharge sheet below. Use por *and* para *to explain it to the patient.*

Patient:	María Luisa López
Discharge to:	Home Facility
Prescription:	Motrin every 6 hours as needed for pain.
Special Instructions:	Call to report fever, bleeding, or abdominal pain. No driving for 2 weeks. Call tomorrow for an appointment in 2 weeks.

1 ______

2 ______

3 ______

4 ______

5 ______

6 ______

2A-PRIN-27

One of the clinic's patients seeks some advice from la abuela *of the neighborhood. Listen to the advice that she offers, and answer the questions that follow. Then write your reactions to the content, using* por *and* para *in your response. Keep in mind how these two prepositions are used.*

Por lo general si tiene un bebé que no duerme bien y llora constantemente, debe comprar la planta llamada yerbabuena. No cuesta mucho dinero comprarla. Debe usted hervirla por unos minutos, y después, colarla. Ahora la mezcla necesita enfriarse un poco. Después de esperar que se enfríe puede poner la mezcla en el biberón del bebé, no importa la cantidad. Yo siempre añado azúcar para mejorar el sabor. La cantidad de azúcar depende de la edad del niño, y para los recién nacidos recomendamos añadir muy poco azúcar. El niño puede tomar cuanto quiera. Como resultado, el niño se siente y duerme mejor.

Here are some ideas to consider:

1 What is the purpose of the treatment?

2 Is this a common treatment?

3 How is the treatment administered?

4 Do you agree with the advice?

1 ______________________________

____

____

____

____

____

2 ______________________________

____

____

____

____

____

3 ______________________________

____

____

____

____

____

4 ______________________________

____

____

____

____

____

CONCEPTO IMPORTANTE: THE PRESENT PROGRESSIVE

The *Concepto importante* for *Unidad 2a* examines when to use the compound construction known as the present progressive. In particular, the use of the present progressive is compared to that of the present tense. At first glance, this construction appears to be simple, one that does not require any special attention. Its components are not at all complicated, so one can very easily memorize their forms. Unfortunately, the ease of forming the present progressive creates a false sense of confidence that inspires us to extend this construction to any and every situation in which the English translation would require *-ing*.

What We Know

In *Unidad 1b Principios*, we studied the different uses of the present tense. We learned to use this tense when expressing an event happening in the present, asking questions, expressing a result when combined with *si*, expressing polite commands, expressing a future action, and expressing the past when used as a tool to narrate. We also know that the present tense of *estar* is combined with the present participle to indicate that an action is in progress at the moment of speech. Therefore, even though this compound tense stresses that the statement and the action are simultaneous, it is still connected to the simple present tense. Finally, we know that in English we translate the ending of the Spanish present participle as *-ing*.

The Difficulty

When we learn a new construction, we tend to use it everywhere. This tendency becomes even more apparent when how this new construction is formed is relatively easy to grasp, as is the case with the present progressive. To further complicate matters, we incorrectly assume that the present tense and the present progressive are interchangeable because they share the word "present" in their name. To the contrary, the present progressive has a very restricted role in the Spanish language, one exclusive to the present tense.

SPANISH	ENGLISH
¿Cómo se siente hoy?	How are you feeling today?
¿Qué está haciendo con esa almohada?	What are you doing with that pillow?

In the first sentence, the present tense is used as a tool for general reference to the present. The second example, however, emphasizes the ongoing action as it is witnessed. You might say that the present progressive is more closely connected to the "true" present. Consequently, this construction cannot be extended to other contexts in which the more neutral present is found.

The above explanation seems logical enough; however, native speakers of English still encounter problems when trying to come to terms with when to use the present progressive. This confusion arises from the fact that in English the counterpart to the Spanish present participle can be extended to contexts in which Spanish would require a different form. Look at the examples given below.

FUNCTIONS	ENGLISH	SPANISH
To express a future event	I am working with them tomorrow.	Yo trabajo con ellos mañana.
In combination with "if" to express an expected result	If you are following the directions, it should work.	Si sigues las instrucciones debe de funcionar.
To express the present progressive	At this moment, the children are sleeping.	En este momento, los niños están durmiendo.

The three sets of sentences given above show that English employs the *-ing* form to convey the immediate future, an expected result, and the present progressive, whereas in Spanish two different constructions must be used, either the present tense or the present progressive. Since non-native speakers often identify the *-ing* form of English with the *-ando* and *-iendo* forms of Spanish, they tend to assign the same functions to each. Consequently, when communicating in Spanish, the speakers use the present progressive in contexts reserved exclusively for the present.

Strategies

Try these simple strategies to help you with the **present progressive:**

- Understand that the fact that the same type of form exists across languages does not mean that these forms will be identical in function.
- Be aware of the habits that you have formed by speaking English.
- Consider the type of action you wish to express, an action "in progress" or one more neutral.
- Remember to use the present progressive only to denote an action "in progress".

¡A PRACTICAR!

2A-PRIN-28

Determine which tense would be used to translate the following sentences into Spanish.

1 Right now I am examining a patient.

Pres. ________ ***Pres. prog.*** ________

2 We are visiting that family next week.

Pres. ________ ***Pres. prog.*** ________

3 You should call me if you are experiencing any pain.

Pres. ________ ***Pres. prog.*** ________

4 The medication is helping to reduce the fever.

Pres. ________ ***Pres. prog.*** ________

2A-PRIN-29

Examine the following paragraph. Then identify the constructions in italic and explain why they were used.

Me siento **mucho mejor,** ***tengo*** **más apetito... además,** ***estoy haciendo*** **los ejercicios que usted me recomendó. Mañana** ***hablo*** **con la dietista para encontrar la dieta más adecuada para mí... pues, últimamente** ***estoy pensando*** **en mi familia y** ***pienso*** **regresar a casa.**

1 ________________________________

____

____

2 ________________________________

____

____

3 ________________________________

____

____

4 ________________________________

____

____

5 ________________________________

____

____

6 ________________________________

____

____

____

2A-PRIN-30

Listen in on the following conversation between a doctor and his patient and rewrite in Spanish what is said.

PACIENTE: I am taking antibiotic injections to treat the infection.

DOCTOR: Are they helping to reduce the symptoms?

PACIENTE: Yes. Also, I am receiving treatment from an herbalist. Actually, I am going to see her after I leave the clinic.

DOCTOR: I can see that the medicines are working and that you are getting better.

2A-PRIN-31

Here is a scene from the Historia 2a. *Imagine that you are there and describe in Spanish the events that are taking place. Write at least five sentences.*

SELF-REFLECTION

1. How do I recognize adverbs and participles?

As is the case with most words, you need to examine the endings. In Spanish, most adverbs of manner end in *-mente*. However, some adverbial forms simply must be memorized. You can also look to see where the word is placed in the sentence, as well as examine the context. Think about the word's relationship to other words in the sentence. Is it used to describe verbs, adjectives, or adverbs? Does the word or phrase answer the question *when, where, how,* or *how much*? If so, then you are most likely dealing with an adverb or words that function as an adverb. If the word answers the above questions, but ends in *-ando, -iendo,* or *-yendo,* then you have encountered a present participle. Recognizing past participles entails a bit more work. Still, if you come across the forms *-ado/a* or *-ido/a* you most likely have found a past participle. Just make sure that word is modifying another element present in the sentence. As for those irregular forms of the past participle, they must be memorized.

2. What do I need to remember when forming the present progressive and the present perfect?

It is important to keep in mind that both are compound tenses; therefore they consist of two elements. *Estar* in conjunction with the present participle forms the present progressive. *Haber* in conjunction with the past participle forms the present perfect. Both types of participles always end in *-o* when used to form the compound tenses. Finally, never separate the two components because only when they work together are they considered to be a tense.

3. What is the best strategy for learning to distinguish between **por** *and* **para***?*

Only time will tell which strategy will work best for you. One suggestion is to not think of the two prepositions as equivalents to the English preposition *for*. Instead, consider the more precise alternate meanings and make your decision accordingly.

FOLLOW-UP TIPS

- In conversation and when reading, begin to notice the individual elements of the sentence. Study how the various elements interact with one another.
- Examine your own speech and writing. Ask yourself if you are truly communicating an accurate picture of the events. Could you be more descriptive? Are you provoking the desired reaction? Are you painting a vivid enough picture for the listener?
- Whatever you do, learn how structures are used in Spanish. Do not rely on direct translations from English. Memorize expressions or whole sentences and attempt to use at least one in your next conversation.

DO YOU REMEMBER?

Answer the questions based on the explanations found in *Principios Unidad 2a* of the textbook. If you found any section particularly difficult, go back and try some of the exercises again. There are also links to Spanish language materials on the *Recursos* website.

1 What do adverbs describe?

2 Does the present participle reflect the gender and number?

3 Can you use the present participle in Spanish in the same way as it is used in English?

4 How do you form the past participle?

5 What do you use to form the present perfect tense?

6 Is the present perfect used to relate any kind of past action?

7 What two prepositions in Spanish can be translated as "for" in English?

8 Do you remember the differences between the use of the present and present progressive tenses in Spanish?

FOOD FOR THOUGHT

The following questions are intended to serve as a springboard for discussion. Think about them as you read the story.

- How can I develop trusting and respectful relationships with my patients and clients?
- How can I recognize and challenge my own assumptions?
- How can I learn to recognize my patients' and clients' strengths and to build on teachable moments?
- How can I become partners with colleagues who are bridges across culture, with other organizations in the community that have similar interests and with members of the community I hope to serve?

NOTES FROM THE FIELD

Deborah Bender is an associate professor of Public Health who has conducted research in Bolivia.

In Bolivia, I worked with a group of colleagues to provide education about family planning. We were concerned whether to include husbands in the sessions. At that time, the issue was particularly sensitive. It was the early 1990s and only recently had family planning been openly permitted in the country. One physician, with years of experience, suggested that the men wouldn't be interested in coming. He alleged that the men were more interested in birthing their cattle than in what happened to their wives —cattle brought income; women didn't!

It was a moment when I, the *gringa*, chose to be very quiet. After all, I was the outsider. But the insensitivity of the remark caught the attention of the women health professionals in the group.

We decided to take the empirical approach. We invited both men and women to the family planning sessions.

Several days later *Doctora* Aurora came to find me saying that a couple had asked to learn about family planning. I went with her to listen. As the couple sat on folding chairs in the sparsely furnished exam room, *Doctora* Aurora explained several available methods. When she finished, the husband quietly commented, "You know, we men need to know these things. Today, it is too expensive to have many children. And, who will take care of the children if something happens to their mother?"

For all the lofty discussions we had had as health care professionals, I was struck by the simplicity of the man's comment. "We need to know these things."

DISCUSSION QUESTIONS

As an outsider, Deborah found herself in a difficult position.

1 What do you think about her decision as a *gringa* to be "very quiet"?

2 What do you think of the way the women health professionals responded to the opinion of their male colleague?

3 What about the comment of the husband "...we men need to know these things. Today, it is too expensive." Were you surprised by his attitude?

4 Have you ever been in a situation with a patient/client when you realized that because of your own assumptions you had missed a teachable moment? What happened? What did you learn?

FAMILIA SANA

Muy a PECHO

Los hispanos se toman muy en serio los asuntos del corazón, excepto cuando se trata de su salud. "Pensamos que no debemos preocuparnos, pero es un mito que los hispanos tengamos menos problemas cardiacos que otros grupos étnicos", dice la doctora Gladys Velarde, directora del Programa Strong Women's Heart, del Centro Médico de la Universidad de Rochester. Todos los años, más del 30% de las muertes de hispanos en este país se debe a males cardiacos y apoplejías. Velarde señala que las mujeres hispanas desarrollan factores de riesgo relacionados con el corazón antes que las mujeres blancas, no hispanas. Aquí le decimos cómo proteger a su familia:

No espere a sentirse mal: "Podría tener colesterol alto o hipertensión sin sufrir síntomas, y todo eso causa problemas cardiacos", dice Velarde. Asegúrese de que su familia se haga frecuentes exámenes médicos.

Conozca sus números: Controle su colesterol; las LAD tienen que ser de 50 o más, las LBD, de menos de 100, y los triglicéridos de menos de 150. Su presión arterial debe ser 120/80, y la glucosa en la sangre debe ser normal. Si fuera necesario disminuir sus niveles, su médico podría recomendarle un cambio de dieta, ejercicio o tal vez algún medicamento.

Reconozca el problema: Cuando un hombre sufre un ataque al corazón, en general experimenta un gran dolor en el pecho, dificultad para respirar, sudoración o náuseas. Además de esos síntomas, las mujeres pueden sentir sudor frío, mareo o una fatiga repentina al realizar sus actividades cotidianas. Si presenta cualquiera de estos síntomas, no pierda tiempo, dice la doctora Velarde. "Llame al 911. Aun si resulta que no era nada, es mejor prevenir que lamentar".

N. KALISH

¿SABÍA QUE...?

Los hispanos son 36% menos propensos que los blancos no hispanos a tener un buen control del colesterol.

Fuente: Colegio de Médicos de Estados Unidos

To read this article online, go to www.yalebooks.com/salud.

CONTESTA LAS SIGUIENTES PREGUNTAS:

1 ¿Crees que es importante hacerse revisiones médicas con frecuencia? ¿Vas al médico con regularidad?

2 ¿Cuáles son los síntomas de un ataque al corazón según el sexo del que lo sufre?

3 ¿Qué quiere decir "Más vale prevenir que lamentar"? ¿Cómo lo decimos en inglés?

COMPROBACIÓN

DVD *Las preguntas de* Comprobación *están diseñadas para evaluar tu habilidad de usar lo que has aprendido, en situaciones nuevas y diferentes. Aunque el contexto todavía es limitado y las respuestas están restringidas y guiadas, debes interpretar más.*

SECCIÓN A

¿Qué pasa en la Historia*? Escoge las palabras que completan mejor la oración. ¡Cuidado con la gramática!*

1 ¡En este episodio han (ocurrida / ocurridos / ocurrido) tantas cosas que es difícil contarlas todas! El personaje principal ha (estado / sido / tenido) Alex, que tuvo una pelea con unos individuos que nadie conocía.

2 Como todos los compañeros en La Comunidad son muy amigos, les gusta salir juntos a las noches de salsa que (está teniendo / hay / son) en un bar del área. Rafa es a quien más le gusta bailar y estas fiestas lo (ayudado / ayudan / está ayudando) a sentirse más a gusto lejos de su tierra.

3 Pero esta noche (están viniendo / venido / vienen) al bar unos hombres extraños, que se meten en líos con Ashleigh y con Alex. Finalmente, uno de ellos (está sufriendo / sufre / sufrido) una herida de bala.

4 Mientras tanto, hemos (vemos / viendo / visto) a Alex tomarse unas pastillas en el baño mientras los mexicanos están (peleados / pelean / peleando) en el estacionamiento.

SECCIÓN B

Estas oraciones describen el tiroteo que tiene lugar afuera de La Pueblita. Escoge las palabras que completan mejor cada oración.

apetito	recomendado
duele	relájese
herido	respirar
hiriendo	siente
pulmón	tocado

Los clientes de La Pueblita oyen un tiro y salen corriendo. Carmina se acerca al **(1)** ______________ y le pide a los demás que se retiren, para que él pueda **(2)** ______________. Carmina determina que la bala no ha **(3)** ______________ ningún órgano importante. El herido respira bien y Carmina supone que su **(4)** ______________ está bien. El joven dice que le **(5)** ______________ mucho, pero sólo cuando se ríe.

¡A CONVERSAR!

PERSONAJES

DVD

We meet one of Carmina's patients in this segment of Personajes. *Discuss the following questions with a classmate:*

- ¿De qué padece este paciente?
- ¿Cómo trata su enfermedad?
- Qué más te gustaría saber de este paciente?

Role-play a dialogue between this patient and Carmina. Have Carmina use the strategy explained in the **Más allá** *section of the textbook to make sure she understands what her patient tells her. Use the following sentence as a way to get started.*

Señor, quiero estar segura de que lo entiendo. Usted me dice que...

¡A RESUMIR!

EPISODIO

Imagine that you and your partner work for a periodical that prints synopses of all the programs on the local television station. You have been assigned to summarize the third episode of La Comunidad, *which is airing weekly on your local station. In five sentences, summarize what happens in this episode.*

Expansión:

- *Discuss with your partner the following questions:*
- *What does the episode reveal about Alex?*
- *Has your opinion of him changed? If so, how?*

APLICACIÓN

ESCUCHAR

DVD

In this segment Carmina attempts to talk to Alex about what happened the night before, in La Pueblita. While Alex does not really want to discuss his problems with her, she does manage to get some information out of him. What does he say? What more would you like to know? If you were Carmina, what questions would you ask Alex?

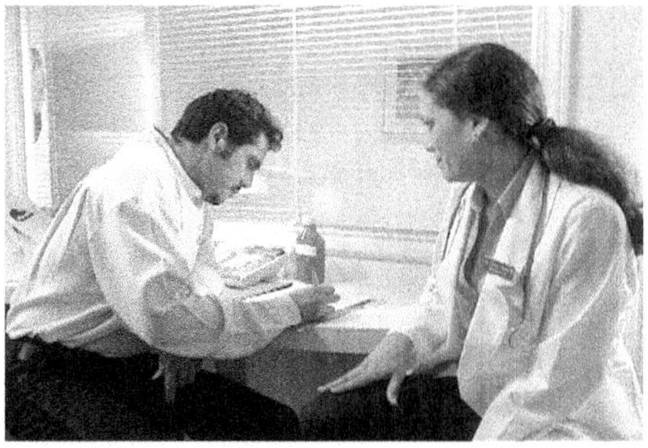

Carmina and Alex

Expansión:

Continue this conversation between Carmina and Alex with a classmate. Use the following sentence as a springboard to your conversation:

Alex, ¿tomaste algo para el dolor...?

ANALIZAR

DVD

This segment focuses on a conversation between Carmina and Laura at La Pueblita. Watch the conversation, and discuss the following questions with a classmate:

Carmina and Laura

- ¿Qué le molesta a Laura?
- ¿Qué trata de hacer Carmina con Laura?
- ¿Cuál es el problema que causa la discusión?
- Si tú fueras Carmina, ¿qué más le dirías a Laura? Cómo reaccionaría Laura?

Expansión:

Role-play an expanded dialogue between Carmina and Laura, using their conversation in La Pueblita as a starting off point.

EN LA PRÁCTICA

Carmina's patient

Para conversar:

DVD

Lo que cree un paciente sobre las causas de su enfermedad puede ser muy diferente de lo que te enseñaron en tu entrenamiento profesional. ¿Qué le puede decir Carmina al paciente en cuanto a las causas de su hipertensión?

Representa tus ideas con un compañero de clase.

LENGUA

DVD

1 Ashleigh:
Ashleigh está tratando de aprender español y también trata de entender mejor a la comunidad hispanohablante. Tú debes ayudarla, describiendo para ella la escena que acabas de ver. Escribe un párrafo de siete u ocho oraciones.

2 El joven herido:
El joven herido, Maximiliano, se recupera y quiere regresar a México. Ayuda a Ashleigh a escribir una carta oficial para un médico mexicano. Puedes empezar con el ejemplo abajo:

Estimado Doctor,

Mi nombre es Ashleigh Simms. Soy enfermera y atendí a Maximiliano en La Pueblita...

____

____

____

____

MÁS ALLÁ

Have you ever had a conversation with someone and you could not recall the exact word to express your thought? You try inserting whatever comes to mind but are still unable to make your message clear. Then your listener joins in and attempts to fill in the blank, only to cause you to respond with, "not exactly" or "yeah, that's it". Sometimes it even gets to the point where you toss and turn all night in search of this evasive word so that you can clarify your intended meaning during your next encounter with whomever you were speaking. Why is it that a word can bring so much turmoil into our lives? Well, sometimes just any old word will not do.

Words can be specialized or change meaning within contexts, between dialects, and between languages. Consequently, you must know both how you intend for the word to be understood, as well as how the listener will understand it, if you wish to avoid any miscommunication. This is especially important when the entire message depends on the use of the correct word. As members of the healthcare profession, you would not want to mistake the word *coger* for *agarrar* when dealing with patients or clients from Latin America.

For a language student, such errors are common because you have yet to master the grammar, let alone the vocabulary and all of its nuances. In fact, you witness this type of miscommunication in two scenes shown on the DVD in which Ashleigh is speaking with a diabetic patient. The first example appears in *Unidad 1a, Historia, ¿La diabetes corre en su familia?... ¿Qué corre?* The second is in *Unidad 1b, En la práctica,* when Ashleigh responds, *Las cucarachas no muerden*. In both situations, Ashleigh is unaware of the specialized meanings of the two words between languages. She assumes that her understanding of the two words is the same as that of the woman. Fortunately, Duna is there to clarify things.

As you gain more exposure to the Spanish language, you too will learn what words are used where, when, how, and why. Have patience with the process and try not to become frustrated. Often, facial cues and gestures will guide you through such situations. In the meantime, you can make use of the many other tools available to you, such as a dictionary, an interpreter, another human being, gestures, pictures, or circumlocution. Another piece of advice is to avoid using idioms or expressions that might take on a very different meaning when translated into Spanish. Just remember that it is always best to double-check with your audience to make sure that you are speaking the same language.

ENTREVISTA

DVD *Read this summary in English of what Isaura Rodríguez says in her interview before you watch it on the DVD. Remember that these interviews were conducted to include "authentic language" on the DVD. This means that the interviews are unscripted and at a natural conversational pace. Use the English summary to guide you.*

Isaura Rodríguez

How did I get to the United States? It was many years ago, against my will, because I didn't want to come here. I had a good job in Mexico, I worked for the state government, and I had my family, mainly, my roots, and... I had everything there, in my country. But I had to come here, and then I began to have kids, and always I was thinking about returning to my country. I thought that when my kids grew up they would go to high school and that I could go back to my country with them speaking two languages and having better opportunities. Then they could study in a Mexican university and would be some fabulous professional people. But my dream went nowhere. When they began to grow up, the first finished high school and had to begin to study at college while they others finished high school, and then they didn't have the same dreams that I did. And my dreams began to disappear little by little. And well, now that my children have grown, I have grandchildren and I have to stay here. I adore my grandchildren. I couldn't live without them. So, it was in this way that I came here, and here I stay.

How do I feel about speaking a different language, having a different language, having different beliefs and values in a foreign country? That's a good question. I try to maintain my roots, I try to keep my culture alive, I try to share it with my children and with everyone I can, I try to share it with the community. It's a beautiful culture. I feel proud of being what I am. I have tried to make my children proud to be who they are. And it's difficult because when I came here without speaking English it was really tough and I had to learn it in order to get ahead for my children and to get ahead for myself, always fighting to be able to help others. It's something very tough but good; we do everything possible to keep our culture alive.

A typical day in my job? I guess I'll begin with my house. I run around in the morning, I help my kids to get ready for school, I help to make breakfast, to make lunch for my husband, I run to the clinic. I get there, and from the moment we open we're always attending to people who are waiting for us for whatever reason. Later we have the day's itinerary, we attend to all the people who come, now we're providing transportation because we don't have anyone who can help us with that, so I have to run around looking for some of the patients, bring them to the clinic, attend to them, and return them to their houses. Sometimes it's a hard job and the days are very long, but I enjoy it because I love my job. Then the day ends; it's supposed to end around 5 o'clock, but for my supervisor and me it sometimes ends around 7 or 8 at night.

Isaura Rodríguez speaks to us about her personal experiences in this interview. Watch the interview for a second time, and then discuss the following questions with a classmate:

- ¿Cómo llegó ella a los Estados Unidos? ¿Por qué decidió quedarse?
- ¿Cómo se siente al ser de otra cultura y hablar español en los Estados Unidos?
- ¿Cómo es un día típico en su trabajo?

UNIDAD 2b

NOTE TO THE STUDENT

WHERE TO FROM HERE?

Now that you've been in the course for a while, you're starting to feel more comfortable with the language. What you learned as a beginner is becoming more reliable and new vocabulary and structures are starting to fall into place. It's time to look around!

WORKING WITH AN INTERPRETER

When you communicate with a patient or client, establishing a climate of trust is high on your list of priorities. The patient who *knows* what is going on, who has the answer to "what is going to happen to me?" is more likely to trust you, and if the patient or client you're working with does not speak English well, an interpreter is your best ally.

Clearly the ideal situation is for the care provider and the patient or client to speak in private and with complete understanding. Your skill in Spanish may allow this to happen in most cases. When you notice that communication may have deteriorated, or when the content of your message is critical (as in requesting consent for a complicated procedure), you should call in an interpreter, if for no other reason than to make sure that you and your patient or client are indeed "at the same place."

If your place of work offers the services of interpreters, learn to make the most of this. Interpreters can: 1) facilitate communication between caregiver and recipient, 2) advocate for the care recipient, and 3) mentor the caregiver.

WHERE DO WE STAND?

When you want to communicate with a patient or client, you should always face that person, whether or not an interpreter is present. Maintain eye contact with your patient or client. The interpreter will take a position from where he or she can see your face and your patient's to avoid missing any clues that facial expression or body language may provide; however, you should maintain the appearance of a two-way conversation with the "real" recipient of your care, whether you're sitting or standing. Think of the interpreter as a voice.

WHAT WILL THE INTERPRETER SAY?

Every interpreter has a personal style of communicating, but many use the "first person" form of delivery. This means that you will say in English, "I want to explain this procedure to you," and the interpreter will say, *Yo quiero explicarle a usted este procedimiento*, rather than, *El doctor quiere explicarle a usted este procedimiento.* This style or method is difficult for some patients to understand, so it is best if you allow the interpreter time to explain to the patient or client what the "first person" delivery involves and anything else that the interpreter feels will expedite communication. In some cases, especially if the care recipient is under stress or emotionally unstable in any way, the use of the first person might be confusing. Negotiate this with the interpreter *before* the meeting with your patient or client.

It will save you time if you can establish your patient's background as much as possible on your own before the interpreter arrives. You can do much with the Spanish you know, and in this course you have been practicing how to recognize signs that your listener does not understand what you're saying or is misinterpreting your words. You should therefore know what from your conversation so far is definitely clear and what needs to be checked out.

When the interpreter arrives, fill him or her in. It is easier for the interpreter to interpret when he knows what to expect.

During the consultation with the patient or client, do not say to the interpreter "tell her that..." or "ask him if..." You ask and you tell. The interpreter will translate what you say. If your explanations are clear, detailed, complete, and if you allow the care recipient to ask questions and find a "comfort zone," just like you would when providing care to an English speaker, the interpreter will not need to do anything other than translate back and forth. On the other hand, the interpreter is more likely than you to notice signs of misunderstanding or doubt in the care recipient. If this happens, the interpreter will let you know that there are signs that the communication has deteriorated. At this point, allow the interpreter to advocate. The interpreter will say something like, "Do you mind if I explain what... is?" or, "Can I ask the patient whether he knows what... is?" The interpreter and the patient will discuss what you have communicated until the interpreter is confident that the patient and you are on the same page. Answer any questions the interpreter may put to you and allow time for the interpreter to pass this information on to your patient.

During the consultation, remember to ask your patient or client every now and then, "Can you explain to me what I just explained to you?" or, "I'm going to ask you a question to make sure that you understand completely what I explained" and proceed to ask a specific question that will tell you that your message was understood completely and clearly. If you do these things regularly and your interpreter brings back an answer that is acceptable to you, you won't have to sit and wait for the interpreter and the patient to discuss what you have been talking about until everyone is informed.

THE INTERPRETER AS MENTOR

Most interpreters are very aware of the satisfaction that care recipients feel when a care provider tries to speak their language and of how good this is for the health of the patients. They will help you communicate in Spanish directly with your patients or clients if you ask them.

If the interpreter is able to help you, try to communicate in Spanish and ask for assistance when you need a word or aren't sure of what structure to use. Duna does this for Ashleigh when they visit the diabetic patient, for example. Remember to negotiate this mentoring away from the patient before the consultation and to accept the interpreter's judgment of your language skills. If the interpreter feels that you are not ready for this type of interaction yet, wait until you're further along in *¡A su salud!*

WHAT TO SAY AND WHAT NOT TO SAY

Do not say in front of interpreters anything that you don't want translated.

Assume that the patient will understand everything! Some patients do understand much more English than they can speak, just as you understand more Spanish than you can speak.

When you are working with a care recipient and you discover that you need an interpreter, you can say something like, *Quiero estar seguro* (or *segura) de que nos entendemos completamente. Así que voy a llamar a un intérprete*. "I want to make sure that we understand each other completely. So, I'm going to call an interpreter." You can make a sign with your hand for the patient or client to wait for you, or you can make a "talking on the telephone" sign while you're explaining what you're going to do. You can even say, *Vuelvo en seguida*. "I'll be right back."

VOCABULARIO

Below are the words that you will see in *Unidad 2b Vocabulario* at the *Recursos* website. After you have looked at them, write beside each one its English equivalent. If you have any doubt about the words' exact meaning, look them up in a good Spanish-English dictionary.

Review the words that you have written on the margins of *Vocabulario* so far. Look up the meanings of any words you don't know. Remember to use this space to add new and useful words that you find in your study or work, but were not included in *Vocabulario*!

Verbos

arriesgar

cuidarse

dar miedo

dejar de

desayunar

embarazar(se)

hacer daño

ir

sospechar de él

Adverbios y adjetivos

a lo mejor

como si

cuanto antes

de todos modos

demasiado

embarazada

todavía no

última

Sustantivos

la cerradura

los detalles

el embarazo

el embarazo de riesgo

el farmacéutico

los mareos

la muestra

la prueba

la regla

¡A PRACTICAR!

2B-VOC-1

Match the Spanish words with their English equivalents. If you need help, go to Unidad 2b Vocabulario *at the* Recursos *website.*

1 arriesgar	____	**a**	to cause fear
2 comprobar	____	**b**	to go
3 cuidarse	____	**c**	to harm
4 dar miedo	____	**d**	to have breakfast
5 dejar de	____	**e**	to make pregnant
6 desayunar	____	**f**	to risk
7 embarazar	____	**g**	to stop (doing something)
8 hacer daño	____	**h**	to suspect
9 ir	____	**i**	to take care of oneself
10 sospechar	____	**j**	to test, make sure

2B-VOC-2

Fill in each blank with the correct word. Be careful with agreement between the new word and the rest of the sentence. If you need help, review Unidad 2b Vocabulario, *or review the first exercise in this section.*

La clínica tiene muchos folletos para la comunidad que contienen información sobre la salud. Éste trata sobre el embarazo.

¿Está usted **(1)** ____________ *(pregnant)*? Si usted ha sido diagnosticada con alguna enfermedad como la diabetes, es importante **(2)** ____________ *(take care of yourself)* bien durante el **(3)** ____________ *(pregnancy)*. Si **(4)** ____________ *(still)* no ha visitado al médico es necesario **(5)** ____________ *(to make an appointment)* **(6)** ____________ *(as soon as possible)* para no **(7)** ____________ *(to risk)* su salud y la de su bebé.

2B-VOC-3

Look at the photos below. Use the vocabulary provided to write one or two sentences that describe each scene. You can choose to follow the storyline or to use your imagination. Be sure to incorporate grammar that you have studied up to this point.

1 la farmacéutica
la cerradura
sospechar

2 el embarazo de riesgo
dar miedo
demasiado

3 a lo mejor
los mareos
cuidarse

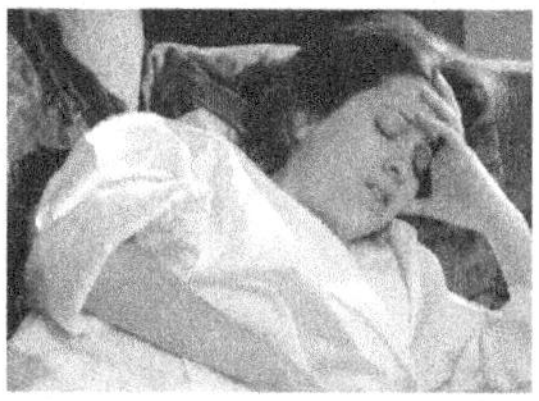

4 la regla
la prueba
ir

2B-VOC-4

Laura just found out that she is pregnant, and she is feeling scared and confused. Help her to write today's diary entry. Below are some ideas just to get you started.

_________ de _________

Esta vida mía es tan loca. No vas a creer lo que me ha pasado hoy.

USEFUL TERMS AND EXPRESSIONS

This section introduces new vocabulary and expressions related to themes found throughout *Historia 2b* of the DVD.

SUSTANTIVOS

Los especialistas	
el/la audiólogo/a	audiologist
el capellán	chaplain
el/la consejero/a	counselor
el/la neonatólogo/a	neonatologist
La salud	
el abuso	abuse
el ácido fólico	folic acid
el acosador	assaulter
la alimentación	food/feeding
el apoyo	support
los asuntos	matters
el comportamiento	behavior
el consejo	advice
el coraje, el enojo	anger
el cuidado	care
el desarrollo	development
la leche	milk
los moretones	bruises
el nacimiento	birth
los oídos	(inner) ears
el parto	delivery
las señales	signals
los sentimientos	feelings
el temor	fear
la víctima	victim
las vitaminas	vitamins
Palabras adicionales	
el arma	weapon
el asiento	seat
las costumbres	habits
la cuna	crib
la declaración	statement
el derecho	right
las escaleras	stairs
las máquinas	machines
los quehaceres	chores
la toalla	towel

VERBOS

amenazar	to threaten
castigar	to punish
colocar	to place
compartir	to share
dar a luz	to give birth
demostrar	to demonstrate
echar	to toss
empujar	to push (something)
exhibir	to exhibit
exigir	to demand
experimentar	to experience
golpear	to hit
mentir	to lie
meter(se)	to get involved
mostrar	to show
nacer	to be born
obligar	to obligate
oler	to smell
pedir prestado	to borrow
presionar	to press; put pressure on
privar	to deprive
prometer	to promise
pujar	to push (during birth)
quedar(se)	to remain
reconocer	to recognize
reír(se)	to laugh
respetar	to respect
vigilar	to watch over

ADJETIVOS Y ADVERBIOS

avergonzado/a	ashamed, embarrassed
boca arriba	face up
prometer	to promise
culpable	guilty
desconocido/a	unknown
humillado/a	humiliated
orgulloso/a	proud
prematuro/a	premature
religioso/a	religious
respiratorio/a	respiratory
seguro/a	safe
tibio/a	warm
transmitido/a	transmitted

Study the vocabulary before you begin *Principios* because it will be useful when practicing the grammar points of the unit. Remember that this section is not intended to be an exhaustive list of all relevant terms but rather an exposure to some of the basic vocabulary used in healthcare. The definitions given here are limited to the way the words are used in the exercises found in *Principios*. Look up the words in a good Spanish-English dictionary if you want to know other meanings, how to pronounce them, the contexts in which the words can be found, sayings and common expressions using these words, and their derivatives (adjectives from nouns, nouns from verbs, etc.).

PRINCIPIOS

PRETERIT

The preterit is one of the simple verb forms used to refer to a past action or state. Memorization is an effective method for learning how to form the preterit because there are so many irregulars. However, you should be able to manage them if you group the verbs together according to their patterns.

Here is the distribution of preterit endings for the three types of infinitives:

	LIMPIAR	MOVER	SALIR
yo	limpi**é**	mov**í**	sal**í**
tú	limpi**aste**	mov**iste**	sal**iste**
él/ ella/ usted	limpi**ó**	mov**ió**	sal**ió**
nosotros	limpi**amos**	mov**imos**	sal**imos**
ellos/ ellas/ ustedes	limpi**aron**	mov**ieron**	sal**ieron**

As with the present tense, the *-er* and *-ir* verbs follow a similar pattern in the preterit.

¡A PRACTICAR!

2B-PRIN-1

Conjugate the infinitives below in the preterit. Then write down their meaning.

1 beber (yo)

Pretérito: ____________________

Significado: ____________________

2 comer (nosotros)

Pretérito: ____________________

Significado: ____________________

3 consumir (ellas)

Pretérito: ____________________

Significado: ____________________

4 dejar (Laura)

Pretérito: ____________________

Significado: ____________________

5 nacer (el bebé)

Pretérito: ____________________

Significado: ____________________

6 permitir (el médico)

Pretérito: ____________________

Significado: ____________________

7 presionar (ellos)

Pretérito: ____________________

Significado: ____________________

8 recomendar (tú)

Pretérito: ____________________

Significado: ____________________

9 reconocer (nosotros)

Pretérito: ____________________

Significado: ____________________

10 respetar (yo)

Pretérito: ____________________

Significado: ____________________

11 sufrir (las víctimas)

Pretérito: ____________________

Significado: ____________________

12 pensar (tú)

Pretérito: ____________________

Significado: ____________________

2B-PRIN-2

Bianca's baby was born prematurely. A lot of people worked together to take care of her child. Explain what each one did by completing the sentences below in a logical manner. Use the words provided to help you.

administrar los primeros cuidados
ofrecer apoyo religioso
trabajar con los problemas de alimentación
examinar los oídos del bebé
revisar las máquinas respiratorias

1 El audiólogo ____________________

2 El trabajador social ____________________

3 El terapeuta ocupacional ____________________

4 El capellán ____________________

5 El terapeuta respiratorio ____________________

6 El neonatólogo ____________________

2B-PRIN-3

Read the following paragraph in which a patient describes her marital situation to Duna. Then, using the preterit, describe what happened from Duna's point of view. Write at least four sentences.

Primero me grita porque, según él, la casa está sucia. Después me aprieta el brazo y amenaza con darme bofetadas. Sale con otra mujer y al llegar a casa me exige sexo. Al terminar, me empuja por las escaleras y me muestra un arma para controlarme.

1 ______________________________

2 ______________________________

3 ______________________________

4 ______________________________

2B-PRIN-4

Duna and Ashleigh discuss a suspected case of child abuse. Use the cues provided to respond to the questions below.

1 DUNA: ¿Exhibieron los niños señales de abuso?
ASHLEIGH: Sí, ______________________________

2 DUNA: ¿El médico identificó el tipo de abuso?
ASHLEIGH: No, ______________________________

3 DUNA: ¿Alguien golpeó a la niña?
ASHLEIGH: Sí, ______________________________

4 DUNA: ¿Le encontraste moretones al niño?
ASHLEIGH: No, ______________________________

5 DUNA: ¿Demostró algún comportamiento nervioso o agresivo?
ASHLEIGH: Sí, ______________________________

6 DUNA: ¿Expresaron sentimientos de temor hacia los padres?
ASHLEIGH: Sí, ______________________________

7 DUNA: ¿Respondió el niño con emoción?
ASHLEIGH: Sí, ______________________________

2B-PRIN-5

One of your patients, a six-year-old boy, is the subject of a custody dispute. His father suspects that his mother's new boyfriend abused him during his last visit to see his mother. What questions can you ask the father about the incident in question to determine if abuse did occur? Use the verbs provided below to create five questions in the preterit.

cambiar	ocurrir	lastimar
hablar	suceder	

1 ______________________________

2 ______________________________

3 ______________________________

4 ______________________________

5 ______________________________

STEM-CHANGING VERBS IN THE PRETERIT

Some of the verbs that undergo stem changes in the present tense also undergo stem changes in the preterit; therefore, recognizing these verbs shouldn't prove to be too difficult since you are already familiar with their patterns. If you need a quick review, go back to *Unidad 1b*.

- *-ir* verbs that stem change from *-e-* > *-i-* or *-e-* > *-ie-* in the present tense will stem change from *-e-* > *-i-* in the third person singular *(él, ella)* and plural *(ellos, ellas)* as well as in the *usted/ustedes* forms of the preterit tense. Also, notice how the distribution of endings for these verbs is the same as that of the regular verbs.

MENTIR	**PEDIR**	**REPETIR**	**SENTIR**	**SERVIR**
mentí	pedí	repetí	sentí	serví
mentiste	pediste	repetiste	sentiste	serviste
mintió	pidió	repitió	sintió	sirvió
mentimos	pedimos	repetimos	sentimos	servimos
mintieron	pidieron	repitieron	sintieron	sirvieron

SEGUIR	**PREFERIR**	**REÍRSE**	**VESTIRSE**	**DIVERTIRSE**
seguí	preferí	me reí	me vestí	me divertí
seguiste	preferiste	te reíste	te vestiste	te divertiste
siguió	prefirió	se rió	se vistió	se divirtió
seguimos	preferimos	nos reímos	nos vestimos	nos divertimos
siguieron	prefirieron	se rieron	se vistieron	se divirtieron

- Those *-ir* verbs that have a stem change from *-o-* to *-ue-* in the present tense will stem change from *-o-* to *-u-* in the preterit tense. As in the previous example, this change will occur only in the third person singular *(él, ella)* and plural *(ellos, ellas)* as well as in the *usted/ustedes* forms. Again, notice how the distribution of endings for these verbs is the same as that of the regular verbs.

DORMIR	**MORIR**
dormí	morí
dormiste	moriste
durmió	murió
dormimos	morimos
durmieron	murieron

¡A PRACTICAR!

2B-PRIN-6

Circle the verbs in the preterit. Then give the infinitive for each. There are five verbs total.

Los padres mintieron con respecto a su situación familiar. Prefirieron no discutirla con desconocidos, lo que no le sirvió de nada al niño. Desafortunadamente, los médicos consiguieron pruebas del abuso demasiado tarde y el niño murió por las heridas.

1 ______________________

____

____

2 ______________________

____

____

3 ______________________

____

____

4 ______________________

____

____

5 ______________________

____

____

2B-PRIN-7

Jaime examines one of his patients. Fill in the blanks with the correct form of the verb in preterit. Some verbs must be used more than once.

conseguir	seguir
dormir	sentir
pedir	

JAIME: Buenos días señora García. ¿Cómo se siente hoy?

LA SEÑORA: Pues, estoy muy cansada. Anoche no **(1)** ______________ bien. Ahora entiendo cómo se **(2)** ______________ mi madre después de ayudarme una noche con el bebé.

JAIME: ¿**(3)** ______________ usted mis consejos?

LA SEÑORA: Sí, le **(4)** ______________ ayuda a mi esposo, pero le es difícil porque tiene que trabajar todo el tiempo. Me **(5)** ______________ terrible por tener que exigirle tanto. También mi esposo le **(6)** ______________ prestado el coche a su hermano.

JAIME: Excelente ¿**(7)** ______________ ustedes las vitaminas?

LA SEÑORA: Sí, nosotros las **(8)** ______________ ______________ ayer.

JAIME: Muy bien. Bueno, vamos a ver cómo está el bebé.

VERBS WITH SPELLING CHANGES

Two types of spelling changes exist in the preterit tense. Some verbs only change in the first person singular (*yo*) and others change in both the third person singular (*él, ella*) and plural (*ellos, ellas*), and in the *usted/ustedes* forms. It is easy to remember to make most of these spelling changes because of the rules of pronunciation: *tocé* would not conserve the hard "c" of the original word *tocar*, necessitating a change to *toqué*.

The spelling changes described below are restricted to the first person singular (*yo*) of the preterit tense and only affect those verbs pertaining to the *-ar* conjugation. Observe how the distribution of endings remains the same as that of the regular preterit.

■ Examples of *-c-* changing to *-qu-*:

BUSCAR	TOCAR	PRACTICAR
bus**qu**é	to**qu**é	practi**qu**é
buscaste	tocaste	practicaste
buscó	tocó	practicó
buscamos	tocamos	practicamos
buscaron	tocaron	practicaron

■ Examples of *-g-* changing to *-gu-*:

JUGAR	LLEGAR	PAGAR
ju**gu**é	lle**gu**é	pa**gu**é
jugaste	llegaste	pagaste
jugó	llegó	pagó
jugamos	llegamos	pagamos
jugaron	llegaron	pagaron

- Examples of *-z-* changing to *-c-*:

COMENZAR	EMPEZAR	ALMORZAR
comen**cé**	empe**cé**	almor**cé**
comenzaste	empezaste	almorzaste
comenzó	empezó	almorzó
comenzamos	empezamos	almorzamos
comenzaron	empezaron	almorzaron

- Observe how the distribution of endings for this group remains the same as that of the regular preterit; however, the *-i* is changed to *-y* for both the third person singular and plural.

CAER	CONTRIBUIR	DISTRIBUIR
caí	contribuí	distribuí
caíste	contribuiste	distribuiste
ca**yó**	contribu**yó**	distribu**y**ó
caímos	contribuimos	distribuimos
ca**y**eron	contribu**y**eron	distribu**y**eron

¡A PRACTICAR!

2B-PRIN-8

Choose the correct form of the verb for the subject provided.

1 ustedes	____ **a** contribuiste	____ **b** contribuyeron	____ **c** contribuyó
2 yo	____ **a** buscamos	____ **b** buscó	____ **c** busqué
3 ellos	____ **a** llegaron	____ **b** llegaste	____ **c** llegó
4 nosotros	____ **a** empecé	____ **b** empezamos	____ **c** empezó
5 yo	____ **a** pagaron	____ **b** pagó	____ **c** pagué
6 ella	____ **a** me caí	____ **b** nos caímos	____ **c** se cayó
7 tú	____ **a** almorcé	____ **b** almorzamos	____ **c** almorzaste
8 yo	____ **a** tocaron	____ **b** tocó	____ **c** toqué

2B-PRIN-9

Rewrite the sentences below in the preterit.

1 El bebé llega temprano.

____

2 La leche materna contribuye al buen desarrollo mental del bebé.

____

3 Comienzo a darle la fórmula a los seis meses.

____

4 Busco un asiento de bebé seguro para el coche.

____

5 Distribuyen cupones en el Departamento de Salud.

____

6 No castigo físicamente a los niños.

____

2B-PRIN-10

María found out several months ago that she was pregnant. Now she is making a list of everything she and her family have done to prepare for the baby. Use one verb and phrase provided below to complete each item in the list. Write complete sentences using the preterit tense.

buscar	un buen médico
colocar	a comer mejor
comenzar	de El Salvador para ayudar
empezar	la cuna en el cuarto del bebé
fregar	a pensar en nombres
llegar	la casa entera

1 Yo ______________________________

2 Mi esposo ______________________________

3 Mis padres ______________________________

4 Mi madre ______________________________

5 Mi esposo y yo ______________________________

6 Yo ______________________________

IRREGULAR PRETERIT FORMS

A few verbs have developed what appear on the surface to be unpredictable patterns of conjugation. Nevertheless, they do follow a pattern of some sort. In addition, it is important to note that the distribution of endings for the preterit of these verbs differs from that discussed in the previous sections.

Verbs that have a stem change for every person:

- Examples of *-uv-* verbs:

TENER	ESTAR	ANDAR
tuve	estuve	anduve
tuviste	estuviste	anduviste
tuvo	estuvo	anduvo
tuvimos	estuvimos	anduvimos
tuvieron	estuvieron	anduvieron

- Examples of *-u-* verbs:

PODER	SABER	PONER
pude	supe	puse
pudiste	supiste	pusiste
pudo	supo	puso
pudimos	supimos	pusimos
pudieron	supieron	pusieron

- Examples of *-i-* verbs and *-j-* verbs:

QUERER	VENIR	HACER
quise	vine	hice
quisiste	viniste	hiciste
quiso	vino	hizo
quisimos	vinimos	hicimos
tuvieron	vinieron	hicieron

DAR	DECIR	TRAER
di	dije	traje
diste	dijiste	trajiste
dio	dijo	trajo
dimos	dijimos	trajimos
dieron	dijeron	trajeron

- Very irregular forms:

SER	IR
fui	fui
fuiste	fuiste
fue	fue
fuimos	fuimos
fueron	fueron

Be aware that *ser* and *ir* have the same form in the preterite tense. Once you get used to this, it should not be confusing. You can always discern which verb is being used based on context.

puso/pusc : to get + adj. tired sick temporary

to become

hacerse + profesion : to become permanet

volverse loco to become/go crazy

¡A PRACTICAR!

2B-PRIN-11

Choose the correct stem change in the preterit for the infinitives listed below.

1 decir ___ **a** -uv- ___ **b** -u- ___ **c** -i- ___ **d** -j-
2 estar ___ **a** -uv- ___ **b** -u- ___ **c** -i- ___ **d** -j-
3 hacer ___ **a** -uv- ___ **b** -u- ___ **c** -i- ___ **d** -j-
4 poder ___ **a** -uv- ___ **b** -u- ___ **c** -i- ___ **d** -j-
5 poner ___ **a** -uv- ___ **b** -u- ___ **c** -i- ___ **d** -j-
6 querer ___ **a** -uv- ___ **b** -u- ___ **c** -i- ___ **d** -j-
7 saber ___ **a** -uv- ___ **b** -u- ___ **c** -i- ___ **d** -j-
8 tener ___ **a** -uv- ___ **b** -u- ___ **c** -i- ___ **d** -j-
9 traer ___ **a** -uv- ___ **b** -u- ___ **c** -i- ___ **d** -j-
10 venir ___ **a** -uv- ___ **b** -u- ___ **c** -i- ___ **d** -j-

2B-PRIN-12

Susana describes her pregnancy. Use the cues provided below to write complete sentences in the preterit.

1 Yo / estar cansada por nueve meses.

____

2 Mi esposo / ser una gran ayuda durante el embarazo.

____

3 Él / hacer todos los quehaceres por nueve meses.

____

4 Yo no / poder comer ciertos tipos de comida por mucho tiempo.

____

5 Mis amigos / traer muchos regalos para el bebé cuando nació.

____

6 En el octavo mes yo / tener que quedarme en la cama.

____

7 Mis padres / venir para celebrar el nacimiento.

____

8 Mi pobre madre / no querer regresar a casa y se quedó con nosotros.

____

2B-PR IN-13

Duna is talking with some friends who suspect that a child is being abused. Write the questions that would elicit the answers provided.

Modelo: Venimos a reportar el posible abuso de un niño.

¿Por qué vinieron?

1 ¿______________________________?

Supe del abuso ayer.

2 ¿______________________________?

No, Carlos no les dijo nada a los padres.

3 ¿______________________________?

No, no fui a la policía porque no estoy segura.

4 ¿______________________________?

No hicimos nada.

5 ¿______________________________?

No, no trajimos ninguna prueba del abuso.

IMPERFECT

The imperfect is the other simple verb form used to refer to a past action or state. Here are the endings for the three conjugations:

SACAR	CAER	PREFERIR
sac**aba**	ca**ía**	prefer**ía**
sac**abas**	ca**ías**	prefer**ías**
sac**aba**	ca**ía**	prefer**ía**
sac**ábamos**	ca**íamos**	prefer**íamo**
sac**aban**	ca**ían**	prefer**ían**

Do you recognize any patterns? Remember to continue to create categories and associations to help you manage the various tenses and their forms as you progress with your studies. Your ability to quickly recognize or produce a particular form will increase your level of confidence, and enable you to focus more on how the language functions rather than get bogged down with how the elements are formed.

Irregular Forms of the Imperfect

Now some good news: only three verbs are irregular in the imperfect. This will give you more time to commit the preterit to memory. Note, however, that a pattern appears to exist: *ir* and *ser* are also irregular in the present and in the preterit.

IR	SER	VER
iba	era	veía
ibas	eras	veías
iba	era	veía
íbamos	éramos	veíamos
iban	eran	veían

¡A PRACTICAR!

2B-PRIN-14

Choose the correct subject for the verb provided.

1 contribuía	___ **a** ellos	___ **b** nosotros	___ **c** yo
2 daba	___ **a** la enfermera	___ **b** los hombres	___ **c** mi esposo y yo
3 decían	___ **a** ella	___ **b** tú	___ **c** ustedes
4 contaba	___ **a** ellos	___ **b** la víctima	___ **c** tú
5 llegábamos	___ **a** nosotros	___ **b** usted	___ **c** yo
6 mostrabas	___ **a** él	___ **b** tú	___ **c** yo
7 queríamos	___ **a** el paciente	___ **b** la familia	___ **c** nosotros
8 tenían	___ **a** la clínica	___ **b** las mujeres	___ **c** usted

2B-PRIN-15

Below are verbs in the preterit tense. Rewrite them in the imperfect. Then write the subject of each verb.

1 asistieron

Imperfecto: ___________; ***Sujeto:*** ___________

2 caminé

Imperfecto: ___________; ***Sujeto:*** ___________

3 diste

Imperfecto: ___________; ***Sujeto:*** ___________

4 encontró

Imperfecto: ___________; ***Sujeto:*** ___________

5 hablamos

Imperfecto: ___________; ***Sujeto:*** ___________

6 hice

Imperfecto: ___________; ***Sujeto:*** ___________

7 puso

Imperfecto: ___________; ***Sujeto:*** ___________

8 salieron

Imperfecto: ___________; ***Sujeto:*** ___________

9 tocó

Imperfecto: ___________; ***Sujeto:*** ___________

10 trabajaste

Imperfecto: ___________; ***Sujeto:*** ___________

11 viste

Imperfecto: ___________; ***Sujeto:*** ___________

2B-PRIN-16

Mrs. Gonzalez tells her neighbor about life with her ex-husband. Fill in the blanks with the correct form of the verb in the imperfect.

Cuando yo **(1)** ______________ *(vivir)* con él, siempre me **(2)** ______________ *(privar)* de dinero. Mi esposo no me **(3)** ______________ *(dejar)* ir sola a ningún lugar. Él me **(4)** ______________ *(controlar)* en todo lo que yo **(5)** ______________ *(hacer)*. Incluso, nosotros **(6)** ______________ *(ir)* juntos al mercado. La familia no se **(7)** ______________ *(meter)* en nuestro asunto. Según ellos, nosotros **(8)** ______________ *(ser)* felices y todos los matrimonios **(9)** ______________ *(ser)* así.

2B-PRIN-18

Did you use to have a routine that you followed every day, week, or month? Provide at least five examples of a routine you used to have.

1 ______________________________

____

2 ______________________________

____

3 ______________________________

____

4 ______________________________

____

5 ______________________________

____

2B-PRIN-17

Throughout her pregnancy, Teresa followed a very strict routine. Look at the sample calendar below and write in Spanish what she did every day. Remember to use the imperfect.

	lunes	martes	miércoles	jueves	viernes	sábado	domingo
8:00	vitaminas	vitaminas	vitaminas	vitaminas	vitaminas	vitaminas	vitaminas
9:00	ejercicio		ejercicio		ejercicio		
10:00		médico				trabajo	trabajo
11:00							
12:00	almuerzo	almuerzo	almuerzo	almuerzo	almuerzo	almuerzo	almuerzo
1:00							
2:00	siesta	siesta	siesta	siesta	siesta	siesta	siesta

1 Los lunes ______________________________

2 ______________________________

3 ______________________________

4 ______________________________

5 ______________________________

6 ______________________________

7 ______________________________

EXPRESSIONS OF TIME

In *Unidad 2a* you learned that the functions of the present perfect in Spanish parallel those of the present perfect in English. Nevertheless, some expressions require the use of the present perfect in English but not in Spanish. These constructions revolve around specific units of time and indicate an action that began in the past but has not yet been completed. It is precisely this notion of incompletion that prohibits the Spanish language from using the present perfect. Instead, Spanish relies on the simple present or the present progressive in conjunction with a unit of time and an adverbial phrase to convey this concept. Here are the four basic patterns:

- *Hace* + unit of time + *que* + verb in the simple present or present progressive:

SPANISH	ENGLISH
Hace unos minutos que estoy aquí.	I have been here for a few minutes.

- Verb in the simple present or present progressive + *desde hace* + unit of time:

SPANISH	ENGLISH
Ella duerme desde hace tres horas.	She has been sleeping for three hours.

- Verb in the simple present or present progressive + *desde* + date:

SPANISH	ENGLISH
Vivo sola desde el 5 de mayo.	I have been living alone since May 5th.

- The simple present of *llevar* + unit of time + present participle:

SPANISH	ENGLISH
Llevamos meses hablando con la consejera.	We have been talking to the counselor for months.

If you stop and think back on the previous chapters, you should be able to list other instances in which a Spanish tense has a much more restricted use than its English counterpart, such as the use of the present progressive or the verb "to be."

present participle/progressive

algunos días : few days

don't do what you would do in English

¡A PRACTICAR!

2A-PRIN-19

Below are some of the comments heard on a daily basis at the clinic. Rewrite the following sentences in Spanish. Use at least two different ways.

1 She has been pushing for an hour.

a ______________________________

b ______________________________

2 I have been experiencing pain for a few days.

a ______________________________

b ______________________________

3 I have been diabetic for years.

a ______________________________

b ______________________________

4 We have been waiting for hours.

a ______________________________

b ______________________________

2A-PRIN-20

Rafa interviews one of the migrant workers, a friend of Federico's. Rewrite the sentences below in English to find out what he said.

1 Estoy aquí desde septiembre.

____

2 Llevo unos meses compartiendo una casa con gente desconocida.

____

3 Hace unas semanas que trabajo para esta compañía de construcción.

____

4 Le mando dinero a la familia desde hace una semana.

____

CONJUNCTIONS

Up until this point in the textbook, we have been concentrating on how to express a single conceptor idea through the use of a subject, the adjectives that describe the subject, a verb, and the adverbs that describe the verb. However, as speakers of a language, we know that oral and written communication can be much more complex than that. We often combine more than one idea in a single utterance to avoid speaking and writing in a choppy and repetitious manner. One way in which we combine ideas within a single sentence is through the use of conjunctions.

Conjunctions create a link between words or groups of words. The type of conjunction you use depends on what is to be linked, but equally important is the relationship between the elements you are joining together. The two basic types of conjunctions are coordinating and subordinating.

- Coordinating conjunctions can be found in several contexts. They are used to join like elements, such as nouns, adjectives, adverbs, infinitives, or independent clauses (groups of words that can function alone as complete thoughts), to show that the two are of equal importance. Some examples of this type are *y, o, pero, sino, así que,* and *sino que.*

SPANISH	ENGLISH
Necesitas llamar a la policía y hacerte un examen médico.	You need to call the police and have a medical exam.
Hablé con su amigo, pero no dijo nada.	I spoke with his friend, but he said nothing.
Juan no es agresivo, sino tímido.	Juan is not aggressive but shy.

Note that both *y* and *o* undergo spelling changes when they precede a word beginning with the same vowel *(*or *hi* or *ho).*

SPANISH	ENGLISH
Ella vino a mí e inició todo.	She came to me and initiated everything.
Es preferible que la revise Andrés u Octavio.	It's preferable that either Andrés or Octavio check it.

You are probably most comfortable with this type of conjunction because it can be extended to a variety of contexts. As a result of this false sense of security, learners tend to overuse it, often creating run-on sentences or misrepresenting the relationship between the elements being linked. This misuse is most evident when a coordinating conjunction is used to join clauses. In many instances, the more appropriate choice is the subordinating conjunction because it can better define the relationship between the two elements.

- Subordinating conjunctions are much more restricted in their application, at least with respect to the context in which they are found. These conjunctions are used only to link clauses that reflect an unequal relationship. In other words, one clause is dependent upon the other for meaning and does not form a complete thought when examined separately. Subordinating conjunctions always precede the dependent clause, which usually indicates a cause, purpose, time, contrast, or condition associated with the main idea of the sentence. Below is a list of some of the most common conjunctions of this type:

a condición de que	toqué	mientras que
a fin de que	con tal de que	no obstante
a menos que	cuando	para que
a no ser que	de manera que	porque
a pesar de que	de modo que	puesto que
ahora que	desde que	salvo que
antes de que	después de que	si
apenas	donde	sin que
aun cuando	en caso de que	siquiera
aun si	en cuanto	tan pronto como
aunque	hasta que	ya que

Now that you know where and why you use subordinating conjunctions, you need to determine *when* to use them. The conjunctions listed above can be divided into three categories:

1 those that are always followed by the indicative

2 those that are always followed by the subjunctive

3 those that can be followed by either the indicative or the subjunctive, depending on the intended meaning.

For our purposes here, we will examine those subordinating conjunctions that fall under categories 1 and 3, focusing on their respective meanings when coupled with a verb in the indicative. Don't worry—we will revisit subordinating conjunctions again when we discuss the subjunctive in *Unidad* 4b.

Here is a partial list of the subordinate conjunctions that are or can be followed by the indicative, as well as their respective meanings. The "(i)" following the conjunction signifies that this conjunction is only used with the indicative, never the subjunctive.

	SPANISH	ENGLISH
To indicate cause:	como	since
	de manera que	in a way that
	de modo que	in a way that
	donde	where
	porque (i)	because
	puesto que (i)	since
	según	according to
	ya que (i)	since

	SPANISH	ENGLISH
To indicate time:	ahora que (i)	since
	apenas	as soon as
	cuando	when
	desde que (i)	since
	después de que	after
	en cuanto	as soon as
	hasta que	until
	mientras	while
	tan pronto como	as soon as
To indicate a contrast:	aunque	although
	no obstante	in spite of
	a pesar de que	in spite of the fact

A closer examination of the above conjunctions reveals that when used in combination with the indicative, these refer to facts or the habitual certainty of an action. Take a look at the examples provided below:

SPANISH	ENGLISH
Como Carmina es mi prima, tengo que aguantarle su consejo.	Since Carmina is my cousin, I have to endure her advice.
Tan pronto como supe las noticias, se las conté.	As soon as I found out the news, I told him.
Tomo las vitaminas prenatales, aunque no me gustan.	I take the prenatal vitamins, even though I don't like them.

Also worth mentioning are correlative conjunctions. These consist of more than one word and are separated by other elements of the sentence. Below are a few examples of this type:

o ... o	either ... or
ni ... ni	neither ... nor
no sólo ... sino también	not only ... but also
tan ... que	so ... that

SPANISH	ENGLISH
No sólo me grita, sino también me pega.	Not only does she shout at me, but she also hits me.

¡A PRACTICAR!

2B-PRIN-21

Duna is preparing a pamphlet on sexual abuse. Match the sentence in Spanish with the correct translation in English.

1 A pesar de que usted se siente culpable, no es la verdad. ____

2 Aunque es su esposo, no tiene derecho a violarla. ____

3 Cuando una mujer sale sola por la noche, se pone en riesgo de ser una víctima. ____

4 Cuando uno es víctima del acoso sexual, reacciona emocionalmente de muchas maneras. ____

5 La niña se siente avergonzada porque fue víctima de acoso sexual. ____

a Even though he is your husband, he does not have the right to violate you.

b In spite of the fact that you feel at fault, it is not true.

c The girl feels ashamed because she was a victim of sexual assault.

d When a woman goes out alone at night, she puts herself at risk of being a victim.

e When one is a victim of sexual assault, one reacts emotionally in many ways.

2B-PRIN-22

The sentences below describe the relationship between Carmina and Laura. Use the appropriate conjunction to combine the two clauses to make complete sentences.

aunque	mientras
de manera que	porque
después de que	tan pronto como

1 Carmina hace de mamá de su prima / se preocupa mucho por ella.

____

____

2 A veces Laura se comporta / se causa daño físico.

____

____

3 Laura fuma y bebe / no debe hacerlo.

____

____

4 Carmina espera a Laura / ésta tiene la cita con Jaime.

____

____

5 Todos los días duerme una siesta / llega a casa.

____

____

6 Laura siempre se siente mejor / habla con Carmina.

____

____

____

CONCEPTO IMPORTANTE: PRETERIT VS. IMPERFECT

In Spanish, both the preterit and the imperfect refer to a past action or state, with each one representing a different way of looking at it. Interestingly, understanding the difference between preterit and imperfect is not difficult for students, but producing it is.

What We Know

Popular explanations for the preterit and imperfect assign the following functions to the two tenses:

PRETERIT	IMPERFECT
To report actions completed at a given point in the past.	To describe repeated or continuous actions, states or events in the past.
To narrate past events, a series of events.	To express an action occurring at the same time as another event or action.
To indicate specialized meanings when combined with certain verbs.	To refer to the simple past (he worked), past progressive (was working), and "used to" (used to work) without reference to the beginning or the end of the action.
	To tell time.
	To describe a physical, mental, and emotional state.
	To describe the background and set the stage for another action.

The Difficulty

Mastering when to use the preterit and imperfect is especially difficult for speakers of the English language for several reasons. First, the functions as presented above lead students to incorrectly believe that the imperfect occurs more frequently than the preterit, especially because more functions are attributed to the imperfect. Consequently, when forced to hazard a guess, students are likely to opt for the imperfect over the preterit. Second, it is very difficult to use the above criteria because of the ambiguity when applied to specific contexts; such ambiguity often leads to overlap, contradiction, and confusion. For example, when a doctor wishes to say "He was tired all week," should this condition be equated with the continuous function of the imperfect or to one of the descriptive functions of the imperfect? All seem plausible. Unfortunately, none of the proposed options are correct because the doctor would be instructed to use the preterit, as in *Estuvo cansado toda la semana.* Nevertheless, you will try to fit your sentence into one of the prescribed categories simply because they exist. Third, the categories depicted above appear to have been arbitrarily assigned, as they are inconsistent with respect to the types of functions attributed to the two tenses.

Unfortunately, there are no shortcuts when it comes to understanding how to choose between the preterit and the imperfect. To begin to differentiate between the two tenses, you need to steer clear of neatly prescribed categories, however helpful to the beginning student, and understand that the speaker, not some artificial context, determines which tense to use. In other words, both tenses can be found in identical contexts; however, the choice of tense depends on the speaker's perspective of the past action or state conveyed. True, certain contexts have become associated with a particular tense. Such associations, however, can be attributed to or have been influenced by accepted cultural norms. Furthermore, it is important to move beyond the notion that the preterit refers to a completed action, especially because all past actions are over and done with and, therefore, completed. That is to say, both the preterit and imperfect are used to describe the same completed past tense; they just focus on different parts of the action or state.

The preterit is used to focus on either the beginning or the end point of an action, state, or idea; and the imperfect focuses on the middle point of an action, state, or idea already begun and in effect. You don't know which part you wish to emphasize unless you know where you are going with your thought. Sometimes you are so busy conjugating in your head and trying to focus on isolated elements that you forget to think ahead, look at the whole picture, and then break it down. Understandably, you will need practice in order to develop an awareness of these distinctions, especially since the English language does not always make them so clear. You should try to start to familiarize yourself with these possible perspectives by examining how you use the past tenses in English. What are you are trying to convey? Do you wish to focus on a particular phase of the event or idea, or do you wish to approach it as a whole?

Strategies

Try these simple strategies to help you discern between the preterit and the imperfect:

- Remember that both the preterit and the imperfect are tools that can be used to recall an identical past event or idea.
- Understand that traditional explanations are there to guide you and that they are designed to be as concise as possible. Consequently, such explanations cannot account for every possible situation.
- Remember that the preterit and the imperfect refer to different phases of a past event or idea.
- Be aware of the intent of your message and do not simply choose the tense that first comes to mind.

¡A PRACTICAR!

2B-PRIN-23

Determine which tense would be used to translate the following sentences into Spanish.

1 I always took good care of myself.

_____ ***Preterit*** _____ ***Imperfect***

2 I stopped smoking.

_____ ***Preterit*** _____ ***Imperfect***

3 I ate at the same time every day.

_____ ***Preterit*** _____ ***Imperfect***

4 I was pregnant for 9 months.

_____ ***Preterit*** _____ ***Imperfect***

5 I loved to snack while I was pregnant.

_____ ***Preterit*** _____ ***Imperfect***

2B-PRIN-24

A proud mother remembers the birth of her child. Circle the tense that best completes the story.

Cuando (**estuve / estaba**) embarazada yo (**tomé / tomaba**) ácido fólico todos los días. El médico me (**dijo / decía**) que (fue / era) necesario cuidarme bien y tomar las vitaminas. Esto fue lo que (**ayudó / ayudaba**) a prevenirle defectos de nacimiento a mi bebé. También (**mantuve / mantenía**) una dieta saludable. Por la mañana (**bebí / bebía**) dos vasos de leche porque (**necesité / necesitaba**) calcio para mi bebé. Juan (**nació / nacía**) el 11 de noviembre. Ese día (**fue / era**) el mejor de mi vida. Mi esposo y yo (**estuvimos / estábamos**) muy orgullosos de nuestro primer hijo.

2B-PRIN-25

Examine the following paragraph. Then identify the constructions in bold and explain why they were used.

Una noche mis amigas y yo **salimos** a un bar donde se **bailaba** salsa. **Pasamos** toda la noche bebiendo y divirtiéndonos con la gente. De hecho, **conocí** a un hombre muy guapo. **Era** de Bolivia y **se llamaba** Alejandro. Al terminar la noche, Alejandro me **invitó** a su casa. Puesto que no lo **conocía** muy bien le **di** las gracias y me **fui** para mi casa con mis amigas.

1 ______________________________

____

2 ______________________________

____

3 ______________________________

____

4 ______________________________

____

5 ______________________________

____

6 ______________________________

____

7 ______________________________

____

8 ______________________________

____

9 ______________________________

____

10 ______________________________

____

2B-PRIN-26

Ashleigh is practicing her Spanish. Below are some common questions asked when someone is in trouble. Help her to rewrite them in Spanish.

1 How did you know that something bad was happening to you?

____

____

2 When did it begin?

____

____

3 What were the symptoms?

____

____

4 Did you get help?

____

____

5 What were you doing before everything started?

____

____

6 What did you do after it stopped?

____

____

2B-PRIN-27

Duna wants to share the experiences of a Lithuanian immigrant with some of her Hispanic clients. Help her translate the following into Spanish.

I came to the United State because I wanted to find a better life for my children and to escape the abuse I suffered. When I arrived, I had no money, no job, and I was scared. I did not know what I was going to do. There was no one to take care of my children while I looked for work. One day at church I met this woman who told me about a job in a factory. The next day I went to speak with the boss, and I got it.

____

____

____

____

____

____

____

____

____

____

2B-PRIN-28

Every day is a busy day at the clinic. Look at the picture below and use the preterit and the imperfect to describe the scene. Write at least six sentences.

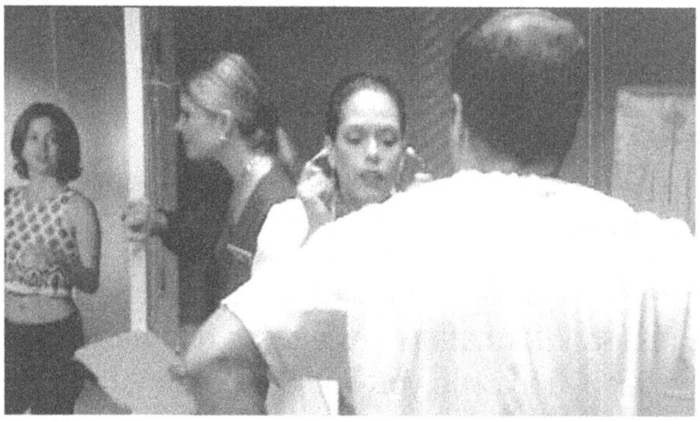

____

____

____

____

____

____

SELF-REFLECTION

1. What is the best strategy for committing the preterit forms of the verbs to memory?

Whether you try flash cards, songs, rhymes, your best bet for managing the various forms of the preterit would be to group them together according to their patterns of conjugation. Once you are familiar with the basic pattern of one member of the group, you will have no problem applying it to the others. Therefore, as long as you know which verbs belong to what group, all you need to do is transfer the corresponding endings, stem changes, or spelling changes.

2. Why does the English language permit the use of the present perfect in certain expressions of time while the Spanish language does not?

In Spanish, the present perfect is somewhat more restricted in its use than its English counterpart. Consequently, the present perfect in Spanish can refer only to an action completed in the recent past, with the resultant state showing ties to the present. Time expressions, on the hand, revolve around specific units of time and indicate an action that began in the past but has not yet been completed. It is precisely this notion of incompletion that prohibits the Spanish language from using the present perfect.

3. What do I need to consider when using conjunctions?

Conjunctions enable speakers to create complex thoughts and utterances by linking words or groups of words. The elements being joined will determine the type of conjunction used. Coordinating conjunctions serve to unite similar elements, and subordinating conjunctions unite dissimilar elements. Not only do you have to consider which conjunction to use, but depending on the particular conjunction, you will also have to determine the appropriate tenses.

FOLLOW-UP TIPS

- Every time you learn a new verb, be certain to check its infinitive type. You should also look to see if it has a stem change or if it undergoes a spelling change. Once you have the relevant information, group this verb with those of an identical pattern.
- Reflect on you own communicative skills. Are you actively trying to incorporate more expressive and complex constructions into you repertoire, or are you playing it safe by sticking to familiar territory?
- Remember to develop learning strategies that work best for you. Not everyone acquires and retains information in the same manner. If you are most comfortable with succinct grammar explanations and you find that this method best works for you, then do not feel compelled to alter your ways.

DO YOU REMEMBER?

Answer the questions based on the explanations found in *Principios Unidad 2b* of the textbook. If you found any section particularly difficult, go back and try some of the exercises again. There are also links to Spanish language materials on the *Recursos* website.

1 What are the endings for the regular preterit verbs?

2 Give examples of two spelling changes that occur in the preterit.

3 Which two verbs have the same exact form in the preterit?

4 How many irregular verbs are there for the imperfect? List them.

5 What type of action do the expressions of time indicate?

6 What happens to *y* and *o* when they precede a word that begins with either *i* or *o*, or *hi* or *ho*?

7 How many subordinating conjunctions can be used only with the indicative?

8 What phases of an action, event, or idea are expressed through the imperfect?

FOOD FOR THOUGHT

The following questions are intended to serve as a springboard for discussion. Think about them as you read the story.

- How can I develop trusting and respectful relationships with my patients and clients?
- How can I recognize and challenge my own assumptions?
- How can I learn to recognize my patients' and clients' strengths and to build on teachable moments?
- How can I become partners with colleagues who are bridges across culture, with other organizations in the community that have similar interests and with members of the community I hope to serve?

NOTES FROM THE FIELD

Randy Latta is a dentist working with a rural mobile dental program.

I was impressed that *Papá* brought little Luisa to the clinic, because usually mothers or aunts or grandmothers bring the children when they are sick. As he spoke to his daughter in rapid-clipped Spanish, I hoped he would be patient with my fledgling attempts to explain his daughter's condition to him. After the exam, I bravely began to explain... when *Papá* interrupted me saying in English, "That's okay, doc, I speak Spanish to Luisa because she was learning so much English that she was forgetting her Spanish! I want her to always remember her heritage." I was relieved... and respected *Papá* for his wisdom.

DISCUSSION QUESTIONS

During a dental encounter with a father and his young daughter, Randy makes several observations.

1 What does Randy's story reveal about his assumptions?

2 Based on what *Papá* says to Randy, what can you infer about the values and strengths of his family?

¿Cómo se manifiesta el abuso o maltrato?

Muchas latinas viven situaciones de abuso emocional, físico y sexual además de otras formas de dominio en sus relaciones de pareja. Esto ocurre en relaciones entre parejas de diferentes o del mismo sexo. Pero muchas veces no están seguras si son o no víctimas de violencia doméstica y no saben qué hacer.

Si piensa que para ser abusada le tienen que haber dado golpes, causado moretones u otras heridas, sepa que el abuso también se presenta de otras maneras.

¿Cómo se manifiesta el abuso o maltrato?

Abuso Verbal o Emocional

- ☐ ¿Vive usted o ha vivido con alguien que frecuentemente la ofende, le grita, la insulta y la humilla? O tal vez ¿le critica constantemente sus habilidades como pareja o madre?
- ☐ ¿Se pone demasiado celoso?
- ☐ ¿No la deja ver a su familia o a sus amistades, controla el teléfono, lee su correspondencia?
- ☐ ¿La ha amenazado con quitarle los hijos si no hace lo que él/ella pide?
- ☐ ¿La ha amenazado con lastimarla o lastimar a sus niños/as, las mascotas, o sus familiares?
- ☐ ¿La ha amenazado con llamar al Servicio de Inmigración e informarles sobre su estado legal para que la deporten?
- ☐ ¿Le niega el acceso a los bienes de la familia tales como el automóvil, las cuentas bancarias, o controla todas las finanzas de la familia y la obliga a rendirle cuentas de todo sus gastos?
- ☐ ¿Le destruye las cosas?

Abuso Físico o Sexual

- ☐ ¿En vez de discutir la situación, su pareja pierde la paciencia la empuja, le jala el pelo, o la golpea?
- ☐ ¿La ha forzado a tener relaciones sexuales cuando usted está cansada, enferma, o sencillamente no tiene deseos?
- ☐ ¿La ha forzado a participar en actos sexuales que usted no desea?

Estas son algunas de las conductas que el agresor usa para poder controlarla. Si le ha sucedido alguna de estas cosas, puede ser que la estén abusando o maltratando. Pero recuerde que no está sola. Lamentablemente hay muchas mujeres en circunstancias parecidas a la suya.

Lo bueno es que tiene alternativas y hay quien la pueda ayudar.

¿Qué puede hacer si ha sido maltratada?

Usted no es la causa del abuso y no merece ser maltratada. Todos tenemos derecho a vivir una vida sin violencia.

Llame a un programa local contra la violencia doméstica. Usted podrá hablar sobre:

- ☐ su situación
- ☐ un plan de seguridad para usted y sus niños/as
- ☐ un plan para alejarse de la persona violenta
- ☐ un lugar seguro, refugio o albergue para usted y sus niños/as
- ☐ algunos programas para hombres o mujeres que quieren mejorar sus vidas
- ☐ referencias a programas que le pueden ayudar con ropas o comidas
- ☐ cómo obtener una orden de protección y otros servicios legales

Las personas que trabajan en estos programas entienden su situación, frecuentemente hablan su idioma, conocen los valores culturales y espirituales

CONTESTA LAS SIGUIENTES PREGUNTAS:

1 ¿Se limita el maltrato a los casos de abuso físico? ¿Qué otros tipos de maltrato existen?

2 ¿Puedes dar algunos ejemplos de abuso verbal y emocional? ¿Algunos de estos ejemplos te hacen pensar en Alex? ¿Crees que Alex sería capaz de abusar de Laura?

de las mujeres latinas y saben cómo orientarlas. Además estas personas conocen las leyes del estado donde usted vive y conocen las nuevas leyes de inmigración y cómo ayudarlas a resolver su estado legal.

Estos programas le ayudarán a buscar alternativas que estén a su alcance, y esto se hace en total confidencialidad.

Llame la Línea Nacional de Emergencia de La Violencia Doméstica.

Hablarán con usted, le ayudarán a encontrar refugio o un programa local contra la violencia doméstica.

Llame al 911

Si está en peligro, no espere.

Busque ayuda legal

Puede obtener una orden de protección e información sobre las leyes de inmigración.

Prepare un plan de seguridad

Antes que ocurra otro acto de violencia, haga planes para estar segura dónde va a ir y cómo va a llegar en caso de emergencia. No le cuente a su pareja lo que está planeando. Deje lo siguiente en la casa de una amiga o vecina:

- ☐ Una bolsa con ropa para usted y sus niños/as
- ☐ Documentos importantes (copias de pasaportes, tarjetas o permisos de inmigración, actas de nacimiento, actas de matrimonio, reportes de la policía y reportes médicos. Incluya documentos de sus hijos y, si es posible, de su esposo.)
- ☐ Un juego extra de llaves y moneda suelta para llamar por teléfono

La violencia en la relación de pareja es un crimen y un problema que afecta a muchas mujeres y a sus niños/as. Las mujeres a veces no se atreven a buscar ayuda por temor a lo desconocido, al agresor, porque no tienen dónde ir y por miedo de tener que criar a los niños/as solas.

No arriesgue su vida ni la de sus niños/as.

Usted NO MERECE ser maltratada por nadie, no importa quien sea.

Sabemos que tomar la decisión de cambiar su vida no es fácil pues las experiencias nuevas siempre provocan mucha incertidumbre. Pero teniendo la información y el apoyo necesario, se puede lograr vivir en paz.

Cómo Conseguir Ayuda

Hay muchos lugares que ofrecen ayuda las 24 horas del día, refugios de emergencia, ayuda legal e información sobre cuáles son las opciones seguras para usted y sus hijos/as. Para más información y asistencia, llame a:

Línea Nacional de Emergencia de la Violencia Doméstica

1-800-799-7233
1-800-787-3224 TTY

Este folleto es parte de una serie creada por la Alianza Latina Nacional para Erradicar la Violencia Doméstica. Para obtener copias de este folleto, vaya a www.dvalianza.org o mande un mensaje por correo electrónico a information@dvalianza.org

This project was supported by Grant No. 2001-WT-BX-K004 awarded by the Office on Violence Against Women, Office of Justice Programs, U.S. Department of Justice. Points of view in this document are those of the author and do not necessarily represent the official position or policies of the U.S. Department of Justice.

011006

To read this article online, go to www.yalebooks.com/salud.

3 ¿Qué puede hacer una víctima de maltrato?

4 Describe la escena que tuvo lugar en el club La Pueblita. Recuerda que debes utilizar el imperfecto y el pretérito en tu descripción.

COMPROBACIÓN

DVD *Las preguntas de* Comprobación *están diseñadas para evaluar tu habilidad de usar lo que has aprendido, en situaciones nuevas y diferentes. Aunque el contexto todavía es limitado y las respuestas están restringidas y guiadas, debes interpretar más.*

SECCIÓN A

¿Qué pasa en la Historia*? Escoge las palabras que completan mejor la oración. ¡Cuidado con la gramática!*

1 ¡Laura está embarazada! Carmina le había aconsejado a Laura que fuera a la clínica a hacerse un examen y ella (estuvo / fue / iba). Entonces se enteró de que (estaba / estuvo / iba) a tener un bebé, pero esa noticia no la alegró mucho.

2 Carmina le (decía / dicho / dijo) que se tranquilizara, porque aquello no (era / estaba / fue) el fin del mundo. ¡Pobre Laura! Con esta noticia se le (venía / viene / vino) el mundo abajo. ¡Tanta responsabilidad!

3 (Ahora / Antes / Ayer) ella tiene mucho miedo porque tendrá que darle la noticia a Alex, el padre del bebé. Pero recientemente los dos (tendieron / tenían / tuvieron) una pelea muy seria. ¿Cómo irá a reaccionar Alex?

4 Nosotros sabemos que (aún / durante / mientras) todos se divertían en La Pueblita, Alex estaba en el baño tomándose unas píldoras. Debe estar muy enfermo.

SECCIÓN B

Estas oraciones describen la relación entre Carmina y Laura. Escoge las palabras que completan mejor cada oración.

a lo mejor	miedo
como si	para que
daño	por supuesto
creía	primo
dejar de	sobrino

Carmina quería mucho a Laura y ya estaba ilusionada por el embarazo de Laura y su nuevo **(1)** ____________. Claro que ella sabía que Laura tenía mucho **(2)** ____________ e iba a necesitar todo su apoyo, pero esto no era un problema para Carmina. Ella siempre había tratado a Laura **(3)** ____________ fuera una hija. Carmina sabía que la relación entre Laura y Alex era bastante inestable. Pero **(4)** ____________ que este hijo los ayudaría a ver las cosas más claras. Por ahora lo más importante para Carmina era ayudar a Laura a evitar los hábitos que pudieran hacerles **(5)** ____________ a ella y al bebé, **(6)** ____________ ambos, la madre y el niño, gocen de buena salud.

¡A CONVERSAR!

PERSONAJES

DVD *Imagine that Laura has heard what Alex says about her when he introduces himself to us. How would she react?*

Role-play a conversation between Alex and Laura based on what Alex has said about her, and taking into account their somewhat volatile personalities. Use the opening below as a guide.

ALEX: Laura, tú sabes muy bien que es verdad lo que dije...

¡A RESUMIR!

EPISODIO

Imagine that your instructor has asked you to report what happened in this episode to the class. Prepare your report by taking turns talking about what happened in the past. Pay attention to use of the preterit and imperfect. Remember to use the preterit when giving a series of past (completed) events, and the imperfect for descriptions and conditions in the past. Use the sentences below as a way to get started.

En este episodio, Laura descubrió que...
Jaime y Ángela discutieron...

APLICACIÓN

CONVERSAR

DVD

Answer the following questions with a classmate:

1. ¿Qué prefieres hacer tú cuando estás cansado/a, ir a una fiesta o quedarte en casa?
2. A ti, ¿te gusta bailar?
3. ¿Qué pasó en La Pueblita? ¿Cómo estará el herido?

Duna, Ángela, Carmina and Alex discuss what happened the previous night in La Pueblita

ANALIZAR

DVD

Watch this segment, and answer the following questions:

- ¿Cómo actúa Carmina? ¿Como amiga? ¿Como doctora? ¿Como hermana mayor?
- ¿Qué hábitos tiene Laura que ponen en riesgo su embarazo?
- ¿Cuál es el consejo más beneficioso que Carmina le da a Laura en este caso?

Carmina and Laura talk about Laura's pregnancy

EN LA PRÁCTICA

Laura has her first appointment with Jaime

DVD

What do they discuss? Does Jaime seem concerned? What does he ask Laura?

Discuss the following with a classmate:

Al final de la escena Laura dice que aunque Alex y ella discuten a menudo, "él nunca me pega." Imagínate que Laura es tu paciente. ¿Qué le respondes tú a esto? ¿Tienes más preguntas o consejos para ella? Representa una conversación entre Laura y Jaime basada en tus ideas.

LENGUA

DVD

Discuss the following with a classmate:

1 Alex y Duna:

Duna no estaba en La Pueblita, pero a ella le interesa mucho el incidente. Alex le da su versión. Representa una conversación entre Alex y Duna en la que él se explica, y Duna le hace preguntas. Aunque Duna ya sabe más sobre lo que pasó, todavía tiene preguntas.

2 Duna y Laura:

Después, Duna decide hablar con Laura también. Representa una conversación entre ellas, dándole a Laura la oportunidad de dar su versión de la historia.

MÁS ALLÁ

Imagine that you are listening to someone talk on the phone. You have no idea what the person on the other end is saying because you are not participating in the conversation. You hear the words, "She's pregnant. I'm so sorry." Your mind starts to consider all the possibilities of who could be pregnant and why is it such a bad thing. Is it a good friend, you wonder? What happened? Unfortunately, you only have your own thoughts to guide you because you are missing a part of the message. Eventually, you find out that it was the neighbor's dog and that they were going to have to give up the puppies. You let out a sigh of relief because you now understand the problem. There would have been no confusion or misunderstanding if only you had known from the beginning what was being discussed. Communication is a two-way street. You need to be aware of the entire message if you want the conversation to be meaningful for all parties involved.

In all languages, the actual message as perceived by the speaker or listener is determined by a combination a several elements, both verbal and non-verbal. As you continue to study the Spanish language, you will begin to notice that many of the grammar choices that you as the speaker must make involve more than deciding on a time reference point, such as present, past, and future. In addition, each decision revolves around a certain perspective or viewpoint and context. Therefore, not only do you need to determine the substance of the message but also how you wish the listener to understand what it is you're trying to say. What aspect of the message is highlighted? Where is the focus of the message —the beginning, the middle, or the end? What is the tone? Where is the intonation? What are the facial cues? All of these components make up the whole message, and you must learn to consider each and every one when trying to create mutual understanding.

ENTREVISTA

DVD

José Viller

Read this summary in English of what José Viller says in his interview before you watch it on the DVD. Remember that these interviews were conducted to include "authentic language" on the DVD. This means that the interviews are unscripted and at a natural conversational pace. Use the English summary to guide you.

I have four children: Remén, Omar, Fabiola, Lupita, and... that's all. I was going to say "and ..." but that's all!

[Federico is] a very nice character, very human... he has a lot... he still has the ability to give a lot because in spite of the fact that he's sick and in spite of the fact that he received the news of the disease he's still optimistic. He still has the desire to live, he works, he's enthusiastic, he's happy, he gets along with everyone, he earns people's affection and he loves everyone. Federico is a very nice character. When I am acting as him he fills me with tears, with sadness because he has a disease from which possibly, he may not survive. And in that instant I am thinking that I won't make it and for that reason I love Federico. He has a lot in common with me: he's very human, and he's simple. The most important thing is that he's a person who comes to work, he enjoys his work, company, he enjoys everything that he does and sees: the sun, the moon, the air, all that he sees and perceives. And he tries to share it with everyone. Federico is a nice character.

You all are great people, very nice. Even though I don't speak English, I perceive those good vibes from every one of you, that sympathy, from everyone. You're a marvelous family. I hope God gives me the chance, and that you give me the call to work with you again!

Watch the video of the interview with José Viller once more, and then discuss the following questions with a classmate:

Lee las preguntas de abajo antes de ver la entrevista, y contéstalas con un compañero/a de clase después de ver la entrevista una o dos veces.

- ¿Qué dice José sobre su propia vida?
- ¿Qué dice sobre el personaje de Federico?
- ¿Qué tienen José y Federico en común?
- ¿Qué dice de la gente que trabaja con él en La Comunidad?

UNIDAD 3a

NOTE TO THE STUDENT

WHAT'S HAPPENING TO MY SPANISH?

You have arrived at the point in your studies where many students start to feel as if they are moving backwards, rather than full steam ahead, with respect to their language abilities. Just remember that although your progress may not be as apparent as you would like, it does not mean that you are making no progress.

WHY DOES THIS HAPPEN?

Up until now you have mainly been concentrating upon committing forms to memory. Grammar has not been much of an issue because you have been able to rely heavily on your English knowledge and skills; for example, most languages share the basic elements with which you're familiar, e.g., nouns, adjectives, verbs, present and past tenses, etc.

In addition, with the exception of *ser/estar* and the preterit and the imperfect, learning grammar has been restricted to concepts that you have mastered in the English language. For the most part, the functions of these elements between the two languages have been similar. When functions did differ, it was usually because Spanish used the constructions in a more restricted manner.

To this point, English has served you well as a base, but as you begin to examine the nuances and more difficult aspects of the Spanish language, you need to get away from learning Spanish through English. You cannot always rely on English as your guide, because it is at this point where learning Spanish truly means learning a new language, something that is *different* from English. Just as doctors go on to their residencies so that they can specialize, you too must go on to specialize your Spanish.

WHAT'S NEXT?

You will begin to encounter more and more elements, constructions, and uses that are not only different from what you're used to, but that also simply do not exist in English. So, if you've depended on trying to find comfortable English parallels to aid your learning of Spanish, you've developed a habit that must now be broken in order for you to advance to the next level. Don't try to learn Spanish through English, but you must now proceed as if you don't have any English parallels or guides.

THE ROLE OF FORMAL GRAMMAR

When learning a new language, a discussion of grammar is unavoidable, especially since you must try to find common ground on which to build, as well a way in which to categorize the various elements. Remember that the function of these categories is no different from that of the categories you have already used to memorize irregular verb forms, adjectives, etc.; the purpose of these categories is to group like things together and to create meaningful associations. The difficulty here is that you must now learn that in some areas the Spanish language moves beyond English with respect to form and function. Therefore, it is important to be careful to not apply the categories you use for English to Spanish categories. To put it simply, your English will no longer inform your Spanish. For example, how English defines an indirect object may not the same as how Spanish does. True, it can be helpful to draw on your knowledge of formal grammar, however you must remember that your definitions are not necessarily appropriate when applied to Spanish. Still, if you feel that you need to revisit these more complex categories in English before you can begin to tackle those in Spanish, it is time to dust off that Freshman English grammar book.

IT'S IN THE DETAILS

Whatever you do, don't get discouraged. Your progress is better than you think. Although your improvement might not be as visible as before, you are learning a great deal. You are focusing on the details and learning to fine-tune your communicative abilities. In fact, now you are becoming increasingly aware of the errors you make and your utterances are a result of a conscious decision. You will find yourself often stopping in mid-sentence to correct an error. Just remember, they say that once you begin to dream in Spanish that you are almost there.

VOCABULARIO

Below are the vocabulary words highlighted in this unit. Remember that you can hear these words in action in the *Vocabulario* section of *Unidad 3a* on the *Recursos* webpage. After you have looked at them, write beside each one its English equivalent. If you have any doubt about the words' exact meaning, look them up in a good Spanish-English dictionary.

Review the words that you have written on the margins of *Vocabulario* so far. Look up the meanings of any words you don't know.

Remember to use this space to add new and useful words that you find in your study or work, but were not included in *Vocabulario*!

Verbos

asustar

atender

caerse

cuidarse

heredar

llegar

mejorar

romper

soñar

tragar

transmitir

Adverbios y expresiones preposicionales

insalubres

por lo de

positivo/a

recién llegados

sanitario/a

Sustantivos

la confianza

la enfermedad

el nivel

la pena

lo peor

el ratito

los servicios

las vacunas

los cuatro vientos

el VIH

las viviendas

¡A PRACTICAR!

3A-VOC-1

Choose the appropriate meaning in English for the word in bold. Pay attention to the context in which the word is found.

1 Todos los **recién** nacidos deben recibir una serie de vacunas.

_____ **a** freshly
_____ **b** newly
_____ **c** only

2 Es importante trabajar con personas que son de **confianza**.

_____ **a** confidence
_____ **b** reliable
_____ **c** trusting

3 El paciente **llegó** temprano para su cita en la clínica.

_____ **a** arrived
_____ **b** reached
_____ **c** sufficed

4 Les da mucha **pena** a los inmigrantes pensar en la familia que han dejado.

_____ **a** punishment
_____ **b** shame
_____ **c** sorrow

5 Ashleigh y Duna **atienden** a muchos pacientes en su propia casa.

_____ **a** bear in mind
_____ **b** pay attention to
_____ **c** take care of

6 Los médicos de la Comunidad se preocupan mucho por el **nivel** de cuidado que recibe su clientela.

_____ **a** height
_____ **b** level
_____ **c** standard

3A-VOC-2

Fill in the correct word for each blank. Be careful with agreement between the new word and the rest of the sentence. If you need help, review Unidad 3a Vocabulario.

Milagros habla por teléfono con su esposo sobre la visita de Ashleigh y Duna.

Sí, sí se fueron hace **(1)** ______________________ *(a little while)*... No, no hay ningún problema aquí. Todo está muy bien. Sólo vinieron para hablarme de algunos de los **(2)** ______________________ *(services)* de la clínica. Hablamos de la familia en México y de cómo **(3)** ______________________ *(I dream)* con tener a mi familia cerca. ¿Cuándo vienes para la casa?... No, no me **(4)** ______________________ *(it frightens)* estar sola. Sólo me da **(5)** ______________________ *(sorrow)* no verte en todo el día... Sí, **(6)** ______________________ *(recently)* comí unas empanadas.

3A-VOC-3

Complete the sentences below in a logical manner. If you need help, use the vocabulary from this section or previous sections studied.

1 Rafa cuenta a los cuatro vientos que los patrones ____________________

____

____

2 Carmina sueña con ____________________

____

____

3 Cuando Alex llega a la clínica __________

____

____

4 Ashleigh no tiene mucha confianza _____

____

____

____

5 Laura se asusta porque _______________

____

____

6 Carmina explica que las vacunas _______

____

____

____

7 Alex traga muchas pastillas porque _____

____

____

____

8 La diabetes es una enfermedad que _____

____

____

____

3A-VOC-4

After her visit with Duna and Ashleigh, Milagros decides to send her family a brief letter. Help her to write the letter. Below are some ideas just to get you started.

________ *de* ________

Queridos padres,

Los extraño mucho. Acá todo es diferente.

____

____

____

____

____

____

____

____

____

____

____

____

____

____

____

____

____

Un millón de besos,

Milagros

USEFUL TERMS AND EXPRESSIONS

This section introduces new vocabulary and expressions related to themes found throughout *Historia* 3a of the DVD.

SUSTANTIVOS

La salud

las alergias	allergies
el algodón	cotton
el aliento	breath
las caries	cavities
las células rojas	red blood cells
el cepillo de dientes	toothbrush
la cesárea	cesarean
la comezón	itching
el cordón	umbilical cord
la curita, la tirita	band aid
el enjuague bucal	mouthwash
las erupciones	rashes
los espasmos	spasms
el excremento	stool
el/la foniatra	speech pathologist
el habla	speech
el hilo dental	dental floss
el maltrato	poor treatment
los mocos	mucus
la molestia	bother, pain
el paladar	palate
las paperas	mumps
la pasta dental	toothpaste
la piel	skin
el protector bucal	mouthpiece
la quijada	jaw
el sarampión	measles
el sarro	tartar
los selladores dentales	sealants
los sonidos	sounds
el suplemento	supplement
la temperatura	temperature
el tétanos	tetanus
el tirón	tug
la tos	cough
el tratamiento	treatment
la varicela	chicken pox

Palabras adicionales

la carta de incapacidad	work excuse
la cuenta	bill
la fuente	source
el interés	interest
el biberón, la mamadera	baby's bottle

el negocio	business
la noticia	news
el orgullo	pride
el pañal	diaper
los ruidos	noises
el seguro	insurance
la tarjeta	card
VERBOS	
aconsejar	to advise
acordar(se)	to remember
añadir	to add
callar(se)	to quiet
casar(se)	to marry
chequear, revisar	to check, examine
chuparse el dedo	to suck the thumb
contar	to tell, to count
dar el pecho	to breastfeed
dar(se) vuelta	to turn
dar(se) prisa	to hurry
demostrar	to demonstrate
desaparecer	to disappear
desarrollar	to develop

desprender(se)	to detach
divertir(se)	to have a good time
enojar(se)	to get angry
estornudar	to sneeze
implantar	to implant
llenar(se)	to fill
mirar	to look at
olvidar(se)	to forget
parecer(se)	to resemble
provocar	to provoke
quitar(se)	to remove, to take away
sentar(se)	to sit
suavizar(se)	to soften
subir	to climb, go up
sugerir	to suggest
ADJETIVOS Y ADVERBIOS	
gratis	free
mojado/a	wet
perjudicial	dangerous
permanente	permanent

Study the vocabulary before you begin *Principios* because it will be useful when practicing the grammar points of the unit. Remember that this section is not intended to be an exhaustive list of all relevant terms, but rather provides exposure to some of the basic vocabulary used in healthcare. The definitions given here are limited, because they are intended for the narrow use of the exercises found in *Principios*. Look the words up in a good Spanish-English dictionary if you want to know other meanings, how to pronounce them, the contexts in which the words can be found, sayings and common expressions using these words, and their derivatives (adjectives from nouns, nouns from verbs, etc.).

PRINCIPIOS

PRONOUNS

A pronoun is a word that stands for one or more nouns, such as people, places, things, concepts, and thoughts. They are normally used to refer to someone or something that has already been mentioned. Without pronouns we would be forced to repeat the same nouns over and over. Imagine how monotonous communication would be.

Similar to nouns, pronouns can function as subjects and objects of other words. As is common in the Spanish language, pronouns reflect person, number, and sometimes gender. In this section, we will examine the direct object, the indirect object, prepositional, reflexive, reciprocal, and the indefinite pronouns. Subject pronouns were already discussed in *Unidad 1b*.

DIRECT OBJECT PRONOUNS

Direct object pronouns represent the noun immediately governed by the verb. They answer the question *Who? or What?,* but be careful not to confuse direct objects with subjects.

SPANISH	ENGLISH
¿Llamaste a los padres del niño? Sí, **los** llamé.	Did you call the child's parents? Yes, I called **them**.
¿Tiene usted seguro? No, no **lo** tengo.	Do you have insurance? No, I do not have **it** (any)?
¿Tomaste las radiografías? Sí, **las** tomé.	Did you take the x-rays? Yes, I took **them**.
¿Cuándo recibió usted los resultados? **Los** recibí ayer.	When did you receive the results? I received **them** yesterday.
En cuanto a la muestra de sangre, **la** mando para el laboratorio.	As for the blood sample, I send **it** to the laboratory.

Normally, the direct object pronoun replaces the noun it represents. The only exception is when the noun precedes the verb; the last sentence above demonstrates this. For the most part, Spanish uses direct object pronouns in the same way as English. In fact, if you examine all of the sentences found above, you see that the only difference between the two languages is in the placement of the direct object pronoun within a sentence. Spanish places the object pronoun before the conjugated verb and English places it after. We will examine placement of all object pronouns in greater detail in the *Concepto importante* section of this unit.

Below are the direct object pronouns, as they exist in Spanish:

SUBJECT	DIRECT OBJECT PRONOUN		SUBJECT	DIRECT OBJECT PRONOUN	
yo	me	*me*	nosotros	nos	*us*
tú	te	*you*			
usted, él, ella	lo, la	*you, him, her, it*	ustedes, ellos, ellas	los, las	*you, them*

Both the third person singular *(usted, él, ella)* and plural *(ustedes, ellos, ellas)* pronouns vary according to gender.

Understanding when to use direct object pronouns is seldom tricky for native speakers of English; however, it is worth mentioning four very common errors:

- Students sometimes use the direct object pronoun as the subject of a verb. The pronouns *lo* and *la* are translated into English as "him," "you," "it," and "her." Notice that one of the possible meanings in English is the neutral form "it." In English, "it" can represent either the direct object pronoun or the subject pronoun. Spanish, however, usually conveys this notion of a neutral subject through the absence of a subject pronoun altogether.

SPANISH	ENGLISH
Llueve por la mañana.	**It rains** in the morning.
Hace frío en el invierno.	**It is** cold in winter.
Es importante comer bien.	**It is** important to eat well.

As a result, a student mistakenly will turn to the pronoun *lo* or *la* when he wishes to express in Spanish the concept of "it" as a subject.

- Students sometimes confuse the personal *a*, with the prepositional *a*, which often results in the incorrect use of the indirect object pronoun over the direct object pronoun. Don't forget that in Spanish a direct object must be preceded by *a* when it represents a specific person or group of people.

	SPANISH	ENGLISH
Direct Object	Quiero mucho **a** mis hijos.	I love my children very much.
Object Pronoun	**Los** quiero. **Les** quiero.	I love **them** very much.
Direct Object	Las vacunas protegen **a** mis niños de enfermedades infantiles.	Vaccines protect my children from childhood illnesses.
Object Pronoun	Las vacunas **los** protegen de enfermedades infantiles. Las vacunas **les** protegen de enfermedades infantiles.	Vaccines protect **them** from childhood illnesses.

- Some Spanish verbs correspond with English verbs that require a preposition. Through habit native speakers of English will often transfer the use of the preposition to the Spanish language, forgetting that the prepositional meaning is inherent in the verb itself. As a result, sentences such as *Esperábamos para los resultados* or *He buscado para trabajo* begin to appear, instead of *Esperábamos los resultados / Los esperábamos* or *He buscado trabajo / Lo he buscado.*
- Students sometimes feel compelled to use direct object pronouns with certain verbs of movement such as *ir, venir,* or *salir.* However, the basic nature of these verbs does not permit this type of construction, not even in English.

SPANISH	ENGLISH
¿Fue Miguel a la reunión? Sí, fue.	Did Miguel go to the meeting? Yes, he went.
¿Salieron para el hospital? Sí, salieron hace una hora.	Did they leave for the hospital? Yes, they left an hour ago.

So, why does this happen? Again, English is the culprit. If you reexamine the English examples given above you see that there is more than one way to answer the question. Compare the sentences found below.

Did Miguel go to the meeting? Yes, he went.	Did Miguel go to the meeting? Yes, he went to **it**.
Did they leave for the hospital? Yes, they left an hour ago.	Did they leave for the hospital? Yes, they left for **it** an hour ago.

Take note of the presence of "it" in the second set of sentences. Since the Spanish language does not make use of a neutral form to represent this same notion, students opt to extend the direct object pronoun to these contexts, ignoring the fact that they are dealing with a prepositional phrase. Remember that similar form and function in one instance does not necessarily mean similar form and function in every instance.

¡A PRACTICAR!

3A-PRIN-1

Read the following sentences in Spanish and determine which ones can be rewritten with a direct object pronoun.

1 Ella ha tenido una cesárea.

Sí _____ ***No*** _____

2 Hicieron una prueba de sangre.

Sí _____ ***No*** _____

3 El foniatra trabaja con los niños con problemas del habla.

Sí _____ ***No*** _____

4 Ellos han ido al dentista dos veces este año.

Sí _____ ***No*** _____

5 ¿Duerme bien la niña?

Sí _____ ***No*** _____

6 El niño toma leche de biberón.

Sí _____ ***No*** _____

7 Necesitan algunas vacunas antes de empezar la escuela.

Sí _____ ***No*** _____

8 Los miembros de la familia López visitan al médico cuando están enfermos.

Sí _____ ***No*** _____

3A-PRIN-1

Read the following sentences in Spanish and determine which ones can be rewritten with a direct object pronoun.

1 Veo **manchas** en los dientes.

____

2 El dentista llama **a los padres** para hablar del tratamiento.

____

3 Usted se puede cepillar **los dientes** con una cepillo suave.

____

4 Uso **una pequeña cantidad de pasta dental.**

____

5 Mis hijos comen **frutas y vegetales** en vez de dulces.

____

6 No pongo **jugo** en su biberón.

____

7 Mis niños miran **a su papá** con temor cuando tienen que ir al dentista.

____

8 Los niños toman un **suplemento de flúor**.

____

9 Los selladores dentales previenen **caries** en los dientes permanentes.

____

10 El uso del hilo dental disminuye **el riesgo de enfermedades de las encías**.

____

3A-PRIN-3

A migrant worker arrives at the clinic after being hurt. Use the cues provided to answer the questions below. Replace the direct object with the correct direct object pronoun.

1 ¿Quién lo trajo aquí? (a usted)

Un compañero ______________________

____

2 ¿Recibió usted la herida en el trabajo?

Sí, ______________________

____

3 ¿Tiene usted problemas con la vista?

____

____

4 ¿Tiene usted alergias?

No, ______________________

____

5 ¿Toma sus medicamentos todos los días?

No, ______________________

____

6 ¿Tiene usted el comprobante de su seguro?

No, ______________________

____

7 ¿Ha traído la tarjeta de Medicaid?

Sí, ______________________

____

8 ¿Necesita una carta de incapacidad para el supervisor?

Sí, ______________________

____

3A-PRIN-4

Mrs. Sánchez tells her neighbor about her son's accident. Rewrite the paragraph below and remove all unnecessary redundancy by substituting the redundant direct object with the appropriate direct object pronoun.

A mi hijo le encanta jugar al béisbol. Un día mi hijo jugaba al béisbol cuando de repente recibió un golpe en la boca y se le desprendió un diente. Inmediatamente, coloqué el diente en un vaso de leche y llamé a la dentista. Visitamos a la dentista esa misma tarde. Examinó la herida. Limpió la herida e implantó el diente de nuevo. Después de visitar a la dentista, fuimos a comprar un protector bucal. Y desde entonces mi hijo usa este protector bucal cuando practica deportes.

____

____

____

____

____

____

____

____

____

3A-PRIN-5

You need to do a preliminary hearing exam on a six-month old child. Use the words listed below to create six questions. Then, answer each question based on your knowledge of the appropriate behavior for a child of this age. Remember to use the direct object pronoun in your response.

demostrar	a las personas cuando hablan
imitar	instrucciones
mirar	interés en sonidos
mover	palabras simples
reconocer	los nombres de objetos comunes
seguir	los ojos en la dirección del sonido

1 ¿____?

____

____

2 ¿____?

____

____

3 ¿____?

____

____

4 ¿____?

____

____

5 ¿____?

____

____

6 ¿____?

____

____

INDIRECT OBJECT PRONOUNS

In Spanish, the indirect object pronoun references the person or thing incidental to the main action.

SPANISH	ENGLISH
La recepcionista **me** dio una cita para el viernes.	The receptionist gave **me** an appointment for Friday.
Laura **les** contó las noticias.	Laura told **them** the news.
Nos mandó la cuenta.	He sent **us** the bill.
El doctor **le** recetó un antibiótico.	The doctor prescribed **him** an antibiotic.

In the above examples, the indirect object is connected to the verb, but is not controlled by it. Its presence is dependent upon the result or effect of the action. Once again, in Spanish the pronoun precedes the verb.

- Here are the Spanish indirect object pronouns:

SUBJECT	DIRECT OBJECT PRONOUN		SUBJECT	DIRECT OBJECT PRONOUN	
yo	me	*me*	nosotros	nos	*us*
tú	te	*you*			
usted, él, ella	lo, (se)	*you, him, her, it*	ustedes, ellos, ellas	les, (se)	*you, them*

Observe that the *yo, tú,* and *nosotros* forms are identical to those of the direct object pronouns. On the surface, the two sets of pronouns only vary with respect to both the third person singular *(usted, él, ella)* and plural *(ustedes, ellos, ellas)*. Not only are they different, but they also do not reflect gender. In addition, indirect object pronouns have a second form available for the third person singular and plural; *se* is used whenever a third person indirect object pronoun is found in combination with a third person direct object pronoun.

Le añaden flúor.	OR	**Se lo** añaden.
Les buscaron ayuda.	OR	**Se la** buscaron.

- A common misconception is that the Spanish indirect object pronoun functions in an identical manner to that of English. This is not exactly true. English restricts the use of the indirect object pronoun to contexts in which the primary meaning is either giving-to or doing-for someone or something, as well as doing-to someone. Spanish, on the other hand, extends the use of the indirect object pronoun also to include contexts with the meaning doing-to and giving-up something. The English prepositions commonly associated with all possible contexts are: "to", "for", "from", "on", "in", and "of".

Examine the following sentences:

SPANISH	ENGLISH
Ella **me** dio una inyección.	She gave an injection **to me**.
Él **nos** preparó la cena.	He prepared dinner **for us**.
Le quitaron la mamadera.	They took the bottle **from him (her)**.
¿La picadura?, **le** pusimos hielo.	The bite? We put ice **on it**.
¿Los ojos?, **les** pones gotas.	The eyes? You put drops **in them**.
Les tienen miedo.	They are afraid **of them**.
Ella **le** tomó la temperatura.	She took **his (her, your)** temperature.

While Spanish employs an indirect object in each sentence above, only the first two English examples can be rewritten to include an indirect object pronoun, "She gave me an injection" and "He prepared us dinner". The remaining sentences require the use of either a prepositional phrase or a possessive.

Therefore, Spanish often employs an indirect object pronoun where English makes use of a prepositional phrase. Still, you need to be careful because this does not mean that Spanish indirect object pronouns are always interchangeable with the prepositions or possessives listed in English above; they are only found when the person or thing is perceived as gaining or losing something as a result of the action and the primary meaning is either giving up, giving to, doing to, or doing for.

- Some verbs are usually found in conjunction with indirect object pronouns because the primary meaning of giving up, giving to, doing to, or doing for is inherent in the verb itself.

SPANISH	ENGLISH	SPANISH	ENGLISH
caer bien	get along with / to suit	gustar	to like
caer mal	to not get along with / to not suit	hacer falta	to be necessary
disgustar	to disgust	importar	to be important
doler	to hurt	interesar	to interest
encantar	to love	molestar	to bother
faltar	to lack	quedar	to remain

While some appear to be obvious candidates for the use of the indirect object pronoun, others have consistently caused problems for students because they function in a manner opposite to their English counterparts. Remember that English translations are approximations, not exact equivalents.

SPANISH	ENGLISH
Les hace falta dinero.	Money is necessary **to them**. *(They need money.)*

¡A PRACTICAR!

3A-PRIN-6

Indicate which sentences can use an indirect object pronoun when translated into Spanish.

1 You should take all of your medicine.

Sí _____ ***No*** _____

2 My arm hurts because of the shot.

Sí _____ ***No*** _____

3 He needs to go to the clinic.

Sí _____ ***No*** _____

4 My stomach is bothering me because I ate too much.

Sí _____ ***No*** _____

5 I brought a list of his current medications for the doctor.

Sí _____ ***No*** _____

6 They asked the man for help.

Sí _____ ***No*** _____

7 We left for the hospital after we heard about the accident.

Sí _____ ***No*** _____

8 I want to examine his eyes.

Sí _____ ***No*** _____

3A-PRIN-7

Fill in the blanks with the appropriate indirect object pronoun.

1 __________ dan **al niño** tres dosis de la vacuna contra el tétano y la difteria.

2 Con el sarampión __________ salen erupciones **a la piel**.

3 El médico __________ dice **a nosotros** que llamemos si hay cualquier problema.

4 Mis vecinos __________ recomendaron **a mí** la clínica.

5 Tenemos que ir al doctor si no __________ baja la temperatura **al bebé**.

6 Debes decir __________ **a mí** si __________ duele **a ti**.

7 Algunas vacunas pueden provocar __________ reacciones alérgicas **a los niños**.

3A-PRIN-8

Rafa has been investigating Mr. Hugo Anderson. Based on what you know from the DVD, answer the questions below.

1 ¿Qué le molesta a Rafa sobre el señor Anderson?

2 ¿Por qué le da miedo a Ángela el trabajo que hace Rafa?

3 ¿Qué les hace a los inmigrantes el señor Anderson?

3A-PRIN-9

Milagros tells her husband Eliodoro about Ashleigh and Duna's visit. What do you think she tells him? Write a dialogue of at least five sentences. Remember to use indirect object pronouns.

PREPOSITIONAL PRONOUNS

As the name suggests, these pronouns always follow a preposition.

SPANISH	ENGLISH
Encontré un buen dentista **para ustedes.**	I found a good dentist **for you.**
Voy **por ellos.**	I am going **for them** *(on their behalf).*

Below are the forms of the prepositional pronouns in Spanish:

SUBJECT	DIRECT OBJECT PRONOUN	SUBJECT	DIRECT OBJECT PRONOUN
yo	mí	nosotros	nosotros, nosotras
tú	ti		
usted, él, ella	usted, él, ella, sí	ustedes, ellos, ellas	ustedes, ellos, ellas, sí

Understanding when to use these constructions does not pose much of a problem for the native speakers of English; however, there is a tendency toward overuse.

If you look back over the previous section in which indirect object pronouns were discussed, you see that English can use a prepositional construction where Spanish usually requires an indirect object pronoun. In Spanish, however, the indirect object pronoun can be accompanied by the preposition a coupled with an object of a preposition. As a consequence, students may erroneously equate the functions of the English prepositional phrase with those of the Spanish prepositional phrase, especially because the two constructions so closely resemble one another with respect to both form and position. In turn, students will replace the indirect object pronoun with the prepositional pronoun construction.

SPANISH	ENGLISH
Ella **me** dio una inyección **a mí**.	She gave an injection **to me**.
Él **nos** preparó la cena **a nosotros**.	He prepared dinner **for us**.
Le quitaron la mamadera **a él**.	They took the bottle **from him**.
¿La picadura?, **le** pusimos hielo.	The bite? We put ice **on it**.
¿Los ojos?, **les** pones gotas.	The eyes? You put drops **in them**.
Les tienen miedo **a ellos**.	They are afraid **of them**.
Ella **le** tomó la temperatura **a él**.	She took **his** temperature.

Just remember that when a verb is present in the sentence, "*a* + pronoun" can never replace the indirect object. It can, however, accompany the indirect object pronoun serving either to clarify ambiguities caused by the third person singular and plural forms or as emphasis for any of the forms.

¡A PRACTICAR!

1A-PRIN-10

Match the object of a preposition with the correct translation in English.

1 a él	_____	**a** her
2 a ella	_____	**b** him
3 a ellos	_____	**c** himself
4 a mí	_____	**d** me
5 a nosotros	_____	**e** them
6 a sí	_____	**f** us
7 a ti	_____	**g** you *(pl.)*
8 a usted	_____	**h** you *(sing., formal)*
9 a ustedes	_____	**i** you *(sing., informal)*

3A-PRIN-11

Provide the object of a preposition that corresponds with the indirect object pronoun in each sentence.

1 Le interesa el negocio de Hugo Anderson.

_____ **a** a él

_____ **b** a mí

_____ **c** a nosotros

2 Nos habla del maltrato hacia los inmigrantes

_____ **a** a nosotros

_____ **b** a ti

_____ **c** a ustedes

3 Les disgusta lo que hace este hombre.

_____ **a** a ella

_____ **b** a ellos

_____ **c** a usted

4 ¿Qué te parece la columna de Rafa?

_____ **a** a mí

_____ **b** a ti

_____ **c** a usted

5 Me preocupan las condiciones de las viviendas.

_____ **a** a mí

_____ **b** a ti

_____ **c** a usted

6 Necesita darles mejores servicios.

_____ **a** a ella

_____ **b** a ellas

_____ **c** a usted

REFLEXIVE PRONOUNS

Reflexive pronouns are used to show that the subjects have acted directly on themselves or done something directly to or for themselves, not to someone or something else. Therefore, both subject and reflexive pronouns represent the same person.

SPANISH	ENGLISH
El patrón **se llama** Anderson.	**The boss calls himself** Anderson. *(The boss's name is Anderson.)*
Después de trabajar, **me baño**.	After working, **I bathe myself**.

Take a look at the reflexive pronouns found in Spanish.

SUBJECT	DIRECT OBJECT PRONOUN		SUBJECT	DIRECT OBJECT PRONOUN	
yo	me	*myself*	nosotros	nos	*ourselves*
tú	te	*yourself*			
usted, él, ella	se	*yourself, himself herself, oneself*	ustedes, ellos, ellas	se	*yourselves, themselves*

Similar to direct object and indirect object pronouns, reflexive pronouns are placed before the conjugated verb. In addition, the *yo*, *tú*, and *nosotros* forms are identical to those of the direct and indirect object pronouns. Unlike the other types of object pronouns, both the third person singular and plural share the same form.

- Reflexive constructions in Spanish function similarly to those in English; however, there are instances in which English will omit the reflexive pronoun or make use of some other element such as "get", "up", "down", or "away".

SPANISH	ENGLISH
Los pacientes **se sentaron** en la sala de espera.	The patients **sat down** in the waiting room.
Toda la familia **se enfermó**.	The entire family **got sick**.

The fact that English does omit the reflexive pronoun in so many instances tends to create some difficulties for students because they are more inclined to equate the English notion with that of the non-reflexive form of the Spanish verb. Such difficulties are compounded even further since many verbs in Spanish can be used either reflexively or non-reflexively.

SPANISH	ENGLISH
El niño fue a la clínica porque **se lastimó** el brazo.	The child went to the clinic because he **hurt** his arm.
El hombre **lastimó** a la mujer.	The man **hurt** the woman.

- Also problematic is the fact that many reflexive verbs in Spanish are not overtly reflexive in English. Often they are expressed through possessive constructions, especially when pertaining to the human body.

SPANISH	ENGLISH
Me preocupo por la salud de ellos.	**I worry** about their health.
Me cepillo los dientes dos veces al día.	**I brush** my teeth two times a day.

Notice that in the last example the definite article is used instead of the possessive adjective when a person does something to or for himself.

The key is to remember that reflexive pronouns are used to show that the subjects have acted directly on themselves or done something directly to or for themselves. You can always check with a dictionary or your instructor to find out if a verb should be used reflexively.

¡A PRACTICAR!

3A-PRIN-12

Provide the appropriate form of the verb in the present tense for each subject. Then, write down the meaning.

1 (yo) inyectarse

Presente: ____________________

Significado: ____________________

2 (tú) cuidarse

Presente: ____________________

Significado: ____________________

3 (ellos) sentirse

Presente: ____________________

Significado: ____________________

4 (nosotros) ponerse

Presente: ____________________

Significado: ____________________

5 (ella) romperse

Presente: ____________________

Significado: ____________________

6 (él) caerse

Presente: ____________________

Significado: ____________________

7 (ustedes) irse

Presente: ____________________

Significado: ____________________

8 (ellos) quejarse

Presente: ____________________

Significado: ____________________

9 (ella) divertirse

Presente: ____________________

Significado: ____________________

10 (ellos) darse cuenta de

Presente: ____________________

Significado: ____________________

3A-PRIN-13

Complete the sentences with the correct forms of the verb in the present and preterit.

Modelo:

(levantarse): Normalmente ____________ a las siete, pero ayer ____________ a las seis.

Normalmente ***me levanto*** a las siete, pero ayer ***me levanté*** a las seis.

1 ***(acostarse)***: Normalmente Rafa y Ángela ____________ a las once, pero ayer ____________ a las diez.

2 ***(dormirse)***: Normalmente Carmina ____________ rápidamente, pero el otro día no ____________ tan fácilmente.

3 ***(extenderse)***: Normalmente el dolor no ____________ a la pierna, pero anteayer ____________ hasta el pie.

4 ***(cansarse)***: Normalmente nosotros no ____________ de hacer ejercicio, pero ayer ____________ después de unos minutos.

5 ***(enfermarse)***: Normalmente yo no ____________, pero la semana pasada ____________.

3A-PRIN-14

Translate the sentences below into Spanish.

1 The mother worried because her child cried all of the time.

____
____
____

2 Every year the children get sick from the flu.

____
____
____

3 I was in a hurry to get home to my sick child.

____
____
____

4 Finally, the baby quieted down and fell asleep.

____
____
____

5 Did you become aware of any swelling or redness?

____
____
____

6 Did you remember to give her the medicine this morning?

____
____
____

3A-PRIN-15

Ashleigh and Duna went to the hospital to help Federico. Answer the questions below according to the information provided by the Historia *section of the DVD.*

1 ¿Dónde se cayó?

____
____
____
____
____

2 ¿Se rompió algo?

____
____
____
____
____

3 ¿Quién se asustó?

____
____
____
____
____

4 ¿Por qué se fueron todos del hospital?

____
____
____
____
____

3A-PRIN-16

Laura needs to take a closer look at her life. Use the verbs below to tell her what she does too much or does not do enough of.

divertirse
divertirse
divertirse
darse cuenta de
acordarse

1 ______________________________

2 ______________________________

3 ______________________________

4 ______________________________

5 ______________________________

3A-PRIN-17

Consider your life and your present routine. Does it differ from your earlier routines, when you were younger? Write five sentences in which you compare your present routine to that of your past. Be sure to use both the present and imperfect tenses.

Modelo:

Ahora me cepillo los dientes dos veces al día, pero antes no me cepillaba los dientes nunca.

1 ______________________________

2 ______________________________

3 ______________________________

4 ______________________________

5 ______________________________

RECIPROCAL PRONOUNS

Latin American Spanish makes use of two reciprocal pronouns: *nos* and *se*.

SPANISH	ENGLISH
Nos vemos en una semana.	We'll see **each other** in a week.
Rafa y Ángela **se** quieren mucho.	Rafa and Ángela love **each other** a lot.

Like English, Spanish uses these forms to denote "each other" or "one another". As such, they only occur in the plural.

SUBJECT	RECIPROCAL PRONOUN
nosotros	nos
ustedes, ellos, ellas	se

Although it seems that you would confuse the reciprocal pronouns with the reflexive pronouns, context will help you to distinguish between the two.

SPANISH	ENGLISH
Duna y Ashleigh son buenas amigas. **Se ven** en el trabajo.	Duna and Ashleigh are good friends. They **see each other** at work.
Cuando ellos **se ven** en el espejo, no ven nada.	When they **see themselves** in the mirror, they don't see anything.

¡A PRACTICAR!

3A-PRIN-18

Indicate which sentences are reflexive and which are reciprocal.

1 Mi familia y yo nos ayudamos en tiempos difíciles.

Reflexivo: ____

Recíproco: ____

2 Laura y Alex se pelean de vez en cuando.

Reflexivo: ____

Recíproco: ____

3 Los niños se llaman Gabriela y William.

Reflexivo: ____

Recíproco: ____

4 Los trabajadores se hablan durante el descanso.

Reflexivo: ____

Recíproco: ____

5 Mi esposo y yo nos preocupamos por nuestros hijos.

Reflexivo: ____

Recíproco: ____

3A-PRIN-19

Translate the following sentences into Spanish.

1 Carmina and Laura take care of each other.

____

____

____

____

2 Rafa and Ángela love each other very much.

____

____

____

____

3 We all met each other at the clinic.

____

____

____

____

4 Duna and Ashleigh respect each other.

____

____

____

____

5 Federico and his family do not speak to each other.

____

____

____

____

INDEFINITE PRONOUNS

Indefinite pronouns do not refer to a specific person, place, thing, or idea. They can function as a subject, direct object, or indirect object. Some forms are invariable and others can reflect gender and number. You will come to learn these words through language practice.

Here is a partial list of the indefinite pronouns used in Spanish:

algo	*something*	nadie	*no one*
alguien	*someone*	ninguno/a/s	*none*
alguno/a/s	*some*	otro	*another*
ambos/as	*both*	todo/a/s	*all*
cada uno	*each one*	uno	*one*
nada	*nothing*		

¡A PRACTICAR!

3A-PRIN-20

The paragraph below contains important information about vaccinations. Fill in the blank with the appropriate indefinite pronoun. Be careful with agreement.

No hay **(1)** ________________ *(nothing)* más importante que la salud. **(2)** ________________ *(Everyone)* deben vacunarse. **(3)** ________________ *(No one)* puede asistir a la escuela sin recibir sus vacunas. **(4)** ________________ *(Some)* causan reacciones adversas, pero la mayoría de ellas no es muy seria. Es necesario mantener un historial de las vacunas que ha recibido **(5)** ________________ *(each one)* de sus hijos.

3A-PRIN-21

Help Ashleigh translate the following paragraph into Spanish.

Everyone thinks that the first visit to the dentist is scary, but with your help it can be something positive. One needs to explain to the child that someone is going to examine and clean the child's teeth. It is important to assure the child that nothing bad is going to happen.

____

____

____

____

____

____

____

____

____

____

____

3A-PRIN-22

Look at the picture below. Use the indefinite pronouns to describe what is happening or not happening. Write at least five sentences.

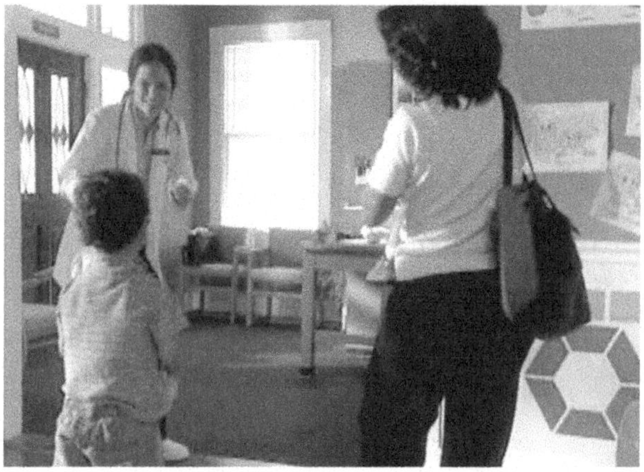

____

____

____

____

____

____

____

____

____

____

____

____

RELATIVE CLAUSES

Relative clauses are those that provide additional information about a noun or a pronoun by either defining or describing it. Such clauses are introduced by relative pronouns, words used to relate one concept to another concept in the sentence.

Relative pronouns in Spanish are:

como	*the manner in which*	el cual, la cual, los cuales, las cuales	*who, whom, which*
cuando	*in which, when*	el que, la que, los que, las que	*who, whom, which*
cuyo/a/s	*whose*	que	*who, that, which*
donde	*on which, where*	quien, quienes	*who, whom*

SPANISH	ENGLISH
Se cepilló los dientes **como** le enseñé a hacerlo.	He brushed his teeth **the way** I taught him to do it.
Recuerdo el día **cuando** me rompí el pie.	I remember the day **when** I broke my foot.

For the most part, *como, cuando, cuyo,* and *donde* are self explanatory; nevertheless, remember that *cuyo* functions as an adjective and must agree with what it modifies (this will follow *cuyo*). Owing to an overlap in meaning, most students struggle with *que, el cual, el que, quien,* and their variations. Once again context is the determining factor: defining vs. describing.

- *Que:*

  Que is the most common relative pronoun and it is used both to define and describe a noun or pronoun. *Que* can refer to a person with the meaning "who" or to a thing with the meaning "that" or "which". However, when *que* follows a preposition it can only refer to a thing.

SPANISH	ENGLISH
La bacteria es algo **que** destruye los dientes.	Bacteria is something **that** destroys teeth.
El hombre **que** trabaja para la clínica ha tenido un accidente.	The man **who** works for the clinic has had an accident.
Es el grupo al **que** pertenezco.	This is the group to **which** I belong.

- *El que* and its variations:

  The use of *el que* helps to make a stronger connection between clause and noun or pronoun. When the clause serves to describe the noun or pronoun and it is not essential to the complete and meaningful thought, *el que* can be used to refer to a person with the meaning "who" or "whom" and to a thing with the meaning "which". Basically, *el que* and *el cual* are interchangeable relative pronouns; however, the preference is for *el que*.

SPANISH	ENGLISH
La prueba, **la que** hice hace una semana, no indicó nada.	The test, **which** I did a week ago, didn't indicate anything.

- *El cual* and its variations:

  As with *el que,* the use of *el cual* helps to make the connection between clause and noun or pronoun stronger. When the clause serves to describe the noun or pronoun and it is not essential to the complete and meaningful thought, *el cual* can be used to refer to a person with the meaning "who" or "whom" and to a thing with the meaning "which". This construction is usually restricted to formal speech and writing.

SPANISH	ENGLISH
La medicina, **la cual** no quería, ayudó a mejorarme.	The medicine, **which** I did not want, helped make me better.

- *Quien* and *quienes:*

  When the clause serves to describe the noun or pronoun and it is not essential to the complete and meaningful thought, *quien* can be used only to refer to a person with the meaning "who". However, this use has become more and more infrequent in spoken Spanish because most native speakers show a preference for *que. Quien* is also used to refer to people when preceded by a preposition. In this function, *quien* takes on the meaning of "whom".

SPANISH	ENGLISH
Laura, **quien** es prima de Carmina, está embarazada.	Laura, **who** is Carmina's cousin, is pregnant.
Laura no sabe **a quien** pedirle ayuda.	Laura doesn't know **whom** to ask for help.

- *Lo que* and *lo cual:*

  Whenever you need to refer to an event, an idea or there is no noun or pronoun present, use *lo que* or *lo cual.*

SPANISH	ENGLISH
Lo que más me preocupa es la fiebre.	**What** worries me most is the fever.

Keep in mind that although we often omit the relative pronouns in English; Spanish does not permit this. Relative pronouns may seem complicated, but only because we often use short or incomplete sentences when communicating orally. When you have time to organize your thoughts, try incorporating these pronouns to help vary your style. You can always express something in a different way.

¡A PRACTICAR!

3A-PRIN-23

Study the following sentences and write below each one the word or words to which the relative pronouns refer.

1 A veces existen condiciones **que** causan reacciones adversas.

____

____

2 Si tiene una fiebre puede darle aspirina, **la cua**l ayuda a bajarle la temperatura.

____

____

3 Usted debe mantener un historial donde puede anotar las vacunas **que** han recibido sus hijos.

____

____

4 Las vacunas pueden producir algunos efectos secundarios, **los cuales** normalmente no son muy serios.

____

____

5 Iban a una clínica **en la que** el cuidado era gratis.

____

____

6 La enfermera, **la que** me da las inyecciones, es muy amable.

____

____

7 Las vacunas nos protegen de muchas enfermedades **cuyos** efectos pueden ser graves.

____

____

8 Ellos pueden contraer enfermedades de los niños con **quienes** juegan.

____

____

3A-PRIN-24

Complete the paragraph below with the appropriate relative pronoun. Be careful with agreement.

El tétano es una enfermedad **(1)** __________ ataca primero los músculos de la quijada. Es causado por gérmenes comunes, **(2)** __________ se encuentran en lugares sucios o insalubres. También produce espasmos **(3)** __________ pueden afectar la respiración. Las personas a **(4)** __________ les dan la vacuna pueden sufrir fiebre, dolor e irritabilidad. La varicela normalmente no tiene síntomas muy perjudiciales, **(5)** __________ son erupción en la piel, comezón y fiebre. El sarampión es una enfermedad **(6)** __________ síntomas son erupción en la piel, fiebre y tos. Además, las personas **(7)** __________ tienen esta enfermedad pueden sufrir problemas del oído.

3A-PRIN-25

Ashleigh is talking with a mother who just gave birth to a premature infant. Help her to explain the effects of bilirubin by translating the paragraph into Spanish.

A baby whose liver is premature can suffer from too much bilirubin, which is having too many old red blood cells. This is something that causes the skin to turn yellow and makes the baby sleepy. We know that all of the old red blood cells have disappeared by the change in color of his/her poop, which turns from green to yellow.

1A-PRIN-26

Choose one of the illnesses from below and use your best Spanish to explain to your patients what it is and how it works.

el polio
la difteria
la tos ferina
Hib

THE FUTURE TENSE

Spanish has one simple future tense. To form the future, you add the appropriate endings to the infinitive form of the verb. The endings for the three verb types are the same, and all endings, with the exception of the nosotros forms, have an accent.

	DAR	**PERDER**	**IR**
(yo)	da**ré**	perde**ré**	i**ré**
(tú)	da**rás**	perde**rás**	i**rás**
(usted, él, ella)	da**rá**	perde**rá**	i**rá**
(nosotros)	dar**emos**	perder**emos**	ir**emos**
(ustedes, ellos, ellas)	da**rán**	perde**rán**	i**rán**

A few verbs do not form the future by adding the endings to the infinitive. Instead they have an irregular stem. Still, the endings are the same as for the regular verbs. The most frequently used verbs and their stems are:

caber	*cabr-*	querer	*querr-*
decir	*dir-*	saber	*sabr-*
haber	*habr-*	salir	*saldr-*
hacer	*har-*	tener	*tendr-*
poder	*podr-*	valer	*valdr-*
poner	*pondr-*	venir	*vendr-*

¡A PRACTICAR!

3A-PRIN-27

Provide the correct form of the verb for the subject listed. Then, give the meaning.

1 (yo): decir

Futuro: ______________________

Significado: ______________________

2 (el bebé): llorar

Futuro: ______________________

Significado: ______________________

3 (tú): ver

Futuro: ______________________

Significado: ______________________

4 (nosotros): cambiar

Futuro: ______________________

Significado: ______________________

5 (ellos): hacer

Futuro: ______________________

Significado: ______________________

6 (ustedes): estar

Futuro: ______________________

Significado: ______________________

7 (ella): dar

Futuro: ______________________

Significado: ______________________

8 (usted): saber

Futuro: ______________________

Significado: ______________________

3A-PRIN-28

Fill in the blank with the appropriate form of the verb in the simple future.

1 Yo ______________ *(dar)* el pecho porque la leche materna protege a mi hijo contra infecciones.

2 Yo sé que el bebé ______________ *(comer)* por lo menos ocho veces al día.

3 Mi esposo y yo no ______________ *(dormir)* mucho durante los primeros meses.

4 Los cólicos no ______________ *(durar)* toda su vida.

5 Cuidar de su boca le ______________ *(ayudar)* a mantener el buen aliento.

6 Mis padres ______________ *(venir)* a verlo en unas semanas.

7 Probablemente, yo ______________ *(estar)* cansada el resto de mi vida.

3A-PRIN-29

Milagros is curious about breastfeeding and childcare. Tell her what to expect by creating five sentences in the simple future. Use the words listed below to help you. Remember that you might have to add additional ones.

caerse	el cordón	sentir
chupar	llenarse	suavizarse
empezar	los senos	tener
dolor	sensibilidad	un tirón

1 ____________________

2 ____________________

3 ____________________

4 ____________________

5 ____________________

3A-PRIN-30

Consider your own profession or future profession. Provide examples of five of the most important questions you are asked at your place of work. Use the future!

1 ____________________

2 ____________________

3 ____________________

4 ____________________

5 ____________________

WHEN TO USE THE SIMPLE FUTURE

The Spanish language makes use of three different constructions to express future actions: present tense, "go-futures", and future tense.

- **Present Tense:**

We already learned in *Unidad 1b* that the present tense is one way to talk about immediate future actions. By using the present tense, you as the speaker convey your message with a greater degree of certainty. Adverbs of time often accompany the present tense when used in this function.

SPANISH	ENGLISH
Lo hago mañana.	I will do it tomorrow.

- **"Go-Futures":**

A second way to express an immediate future action is to use a "go-future". English employs a similar construction. To form this type of future you use a form of *ir* + *a* + infinitive.

SPANISH	ENGLISH
Lo voy a hacer mañana.	I am going to do it tomorrow.

- **Future Tense:**

While its purpose is to indicate any event in the future, this tense is also used to discuss the remote future, predictions and probability. Only the future tense can be used to convey the three aforementioned notions. It translates into English as "will", "probably", or "must".

SPANISH	ENGLISH
Algún día seré dentista.	One day I will be a dentist.
La situación del inmigrante mejorará con el tiempo.	The immigrant's situation will get better in time.
Tendrá una infección del oído.	She probably has an ear infection.
¿Dónde estará el médico?	Where might the doctor be?

¡A PRACTICAR!

3A-PRIN-31

Determine which type of future is indicated by each sentence.

1 Si tiene mocos y estornuda, ¿estará enfermo?

_____ **a** Futuro remoto

_____ **b** Predicción

_____ **c** Probabilidad

2 Después de encontrar un trabajo, cambiaremos de casa.

_____ **a** Futuro remoto

_____ **b** Predicción

_____ **c** Probabilidad

3 Mis padres creen que tendré cuatro hijos como lo hicieron ellos.

_____ **a** Futuro remoto

_____ **b** Predicción

_____ **c** Probabilidad

4 Los científicos encontrarán una cura para el cáncer del seno.

_____ **a** Futuro remoto

_____ **b** Predicción

_____ **c** Probabilidad

5 El niño llora. ¿Tendrá hambre?

_____ **a** Futuro remoto

_____ **b** Predicción

_____ **c** Probabilidad

3A-PRIN-32

Think about your profession or future profession. What changes are on the horizon? Use the verbs below to provide examples of the different uses for the simple future as they pertain to you.

1 ser

Futuro: ______________________________

____

Predicción: ______________________________

____

Probabilidad: ______________________________

____

____

2 tener

Futuro: ______________________________

____

Predicción: ______________________________

____

Probabilidad: ______________________________

____

____

3 poder

Futuro: ______________________________

____

Predicción: ______________________________

____

Probabilidad: ______________________________

____

____

CONCEPTO IMPORTANTE: PRONOUN PLACEMENT

Verbs often have more than one object pronoun. While English speakers typically understand the difference between direct and indirect object pronouns, they often become lost when trying to place them in Spanish. They sometimes wish that they could freeze time in a conversation in order to untangle the pronouns and think, "Wait, did she just say she gave it to him, or that he gave it to her?" Since subject pronouns are often omitted in Spanish, English speakers must learn to wait until they hear the verb (which frequently follows a string of object pronouns) in order to know who is performing the action. This section is intended to help you understand why you find this confusing and to give you some strategies to help eliminate this confusion so you can understand and use object pronouns with ease.

What We Know

Two object pronouns can be present in a single sentence. If a sentence does contain two object pronouns, these pronouns will always appear in the following order: reflexive, indirect, and direct. The mnemonic RID might help you to remember the order.

SPANISH	ENGLISH
Me los cepillo.	I brush them.
Nos las dieron.	They gave them to us.

When a third person indirect object pronoun precedes a third person direct object pronoun, *se* is the indirect object pronoun that must be used. Remember that two object pronouns beginning with the letter "l" may never exist side by side. The first must always change to *se*. Take another look at the example provided in the section in which indirect object pronouns were discussed.

Le añaden flúor.	*OR*	**Se lo** añaden.
Les buscaron ayuda.	*OR*	**Se la** buscaron.
Les dieron las vacunas.	*OR*	**Se las** dieron.

Furthermore, we know that the object pronouns can be placed before the conjugated verb of the sentence; however, other options do exist. Object pronouns can also be attached to the present participle, the infinitive, and affirmative commands. Placement of object pronouns in conjunction with commands will be treated at greater length in *Unidad 3b*.

SPANISH	ENGLISH
Necesita dárselas. *OR* Se las necesita dar.	She needs to give them to him. She needs to give them to him.
Está dándonoslas. *OR* Nos las está dando.	She is giving them to us. She is giving them to us.

In both examples above, an accent mark is added to the construction with the object pronouns; however, the rules for placing the accent mark within the two constructions differ. In the case of the infinitive, you must have two object pronouns attached to it in order to use an accent. When two object pronouns are present, you count back three syllables and place the accent there. As for the present participle, count back four syllables before placing the accent if you add two object pronouns. If you add only one object pronoun to the end of a present participle, count back three syllables and place the accent there. (An easy way to remember this is that the accent is used to conserve the stress of the original word before pronouns were attached to it. Put the accent where the stress falls in that original word.) Also, notice that the object pronouns are never separated, unless they pertain to two different verbs.

SPANISH	ENGLISH
Te aconsejo pedirlo.	I advise you to ask for it.
Le hizo recontarlos.	He made her recount them.

The Difficulty

Imagine that someone comes up to you and says, "Him it give." You smile politely and wonder, "What did she mean? Who gave what to whom?" This is essentially the problem English speakers face when confronted with object pronouns in Spanish: the sentence order seems to indicate the opposite of what is actually meant. It takes a while for the brain to untangle the order and to figure out, in fact, who did do what to whom.

As native a speaker of English, you are accustomed to presenting object pronouns in a specific order, as well as to placing them in a specific location. In fact, you are even familiar with the order of first using the indirect object pronoun and second using the direct object pronoun. For example, the English sentence "He sent us the bill" demonstrates this verb + indirect object + direct object construction. So, then why do students struggle so much with this concept?

- One answer is that the conjugation of the verb determines the subject in Spanish. Since many verbs in English have the same conjugation (I go, you go, we go, they go), we are accustomed to paying attention to the first pronoun we see as a clue to the subject of the verb. Spanish often omits subject pronouns, meaning that the first pronoun we hear is usually an object pronoun.
- Second, Spanish normally places these pronouns in a position completely opposite to that of English. In Spanish, the object pronouns can and often do precede the conjugated verb, but in English they cannot. In English these pronouns must follow the conjugated verb.

SPANISH	ENGLISH
Usted se la escribe a ella.	You write it to her.
Me lo quiere pedir.	He wants to order it for me.
¿El diagnóstico? Sí, se lo he dicho.	The diagnosis? Yes, I have told it to her.

- Finally, English speakers of Spanish tend to get confused because of the long list of possibilities that the pronouns *le*, *les*, and *se* have. *Le* can mean "to him, to her, or to you" while *les* can mean "to them or to you all." The list for *se* is even longer, with the possible meanings "to him, to her, to you, to them, or to you all." This is why *le*, *les*, and *se* are frequently qualified by *a él, a ustedes*, etc. With time you will learn to sort out all of these meanings and won't be so panicked every time you hear one of these pronouns used in a sentence.

  Don't worry, when your ear becomes accustomed to the right sound of pronouns, you will be able to choose the correct forms and order more easily. Practice will enable you to better discern between the object and reflexive pronouns.

Strategies

Try these simple strategies to aid you with the use and placement of object pronouns:

- You can always place the object pronouns before the main conjugated verb of the sentence.
- Remember that object pronouns can only be attached to infinitives, present participles, and affirmative commands.
- Memorize the order in which object pronouns appear when found together: reflexive, indirect, and direct.
- Be careful when drawing parallels between Spanish and English; understand that sometimes languages are just different.

¡A PRACTICAR!

3A-PRIN-33

Choose the most appropriate response for each question asked.

1 ¿Le compraste las vitaminas?

_____ **a** Sí, le las compré.
_____ **b** Sí, se la compré.
_____ **c** Sí, se las compré.

2 ¿Nos dieron una cita para el viernes?

_____ **a** Sí, nos la dieron.
_____ **b** Sí, nos las dieron.
_____ **c** Sí, nos lo dieron.

3 ¿Te explicó el problema?

_____ **a** Sí, me la explicó.
_____ **b** Sí, me lo explicó.
_____ **c** Sí, te lo explicó.

4 ¿Les trajeron los resultados?

_____ **a** Sí, los les trajeron.
_____ **b** Sí, se lo trajeron.
_____ **c** Sí, se los trajeron.

5 ¿Me lo quieres dar?

_____ **a** Sí, lo te quiero dar.
_____ **b** Sí, quiero dártelo.
_____ **c** Sí, te quiero darlo.

6 ¿Me las estás buscando?

_____ **a** Sí, estoy buscándosela.
_____ **c** Sí, estoy buscandotela.
_____ **d** Sí, estoy buscándotelas.

7 ¿Vas a pedírselo?

_____ **a** Sí, le lo voy a pedir.
_____ **b** Sí, le voy a pedirlo.
_____ **c** Sí, se lo voy a pedir.

3A-PRIN-34

Someone is injured on the job. Respond to the questions below using both direct and indirect object pronouns.

1 ¿Le puso usted unas toallas limpias a la cortada?

Sí, ______________________________

2 ¿La enfermera le puso a usted una inyección contra el tétano?

Sí, ______________________________

3 ¿Le dio el supervisor un descanso al trabajador herido?

Sí, ______________________________

4 ¿Te pusiste una curita?

No, ______________________________

5 ¿Me puedes recetar una crema antibiótica?

Sí, ______________________________

3A-PRIN-35

Using the vocabulary provided below, create a brief handout about vaccinations for the patients of La Comunidad. *You may also wish to incorporate other vocabulary that you have learned up to this point.*

asustar	cuidarse	transmitir
la enfermedad	las vacunas	atender
heredar	la confianza	los servicios

____
____
____
____

SELF-REFLECTION

1. How can I eliminate monotony and redundancy from my speech and writing?

Spanish has a variety of elements available that enable the speaker to communicate in a more efficient, yet expressive, manner. Direct, indirect, reflexive, prepositional, indefinite, and relative pronouns are some ways in which the speaker can communicate in a more coherent manner by relating one element of an utterance to another. You need to be aware of how and when to use each one in order to take your abilities to the next level.

2. What is the main difference between object pronouns and relative pronouns?

lObject pronouns represent a person, thing, or an idea. They are normally used to refer to someone or something that has already been mentioned. Relative pronouns also refer to something that has already been mentioned in the sentence; however, they do not replace it. Instead, relative pronouns serve to connect additional information to a noun or a pronoun by either defining or describing it.

3. Why are there three ways to express the future in the Spanish language?

When a particular construction is viewed as being too general to properly express the meaning intended, the speaker often turns to elements perceived to represent a similar yet more specific perspective. This is the way the present tense along with time expressions and the go-futures came to represent the immediate future. Both construction types create a closer connection between the action and the time when the action will be completed.

FOLLOW-UP TIPS

- Remember that it is important to think ahead and consider the entire utterance or idea that yo wish to convey. When you try a piecemeal approach to language, you are more likely to commit errors. You might produce the correct forms in isolation; however, your execution will most likely suffer.
- Examine your own communication abilities. Must you rely on short, choppy sentences to express yourself? Do you incorporate a lot of unnecessary repetition? Consider the elements described in this unit that you could use to help eliminate monotony and redundancy from your speech and writing.
- By now you should have a number of linguistic tools at your disposal. It is time to try to experiment with language. See how many different ways you can come up with to express the same concept.

DO YOU REMEMBER?

Answer the questions based on the explanations found in *Principios Unidad 3a* of the textbook. If you found any section particularly difficult, go back and try some of the easier exercises again. There are also links to Spanish language materials on the *Recursos* website.

1 Which forms of the direct object pronoun reflect gender and number?

2 Give examples of two spelling changes that occur in the preterit.

3 How do you say "I like to eat healthy food"?

4 Which prepositional construction is only found with in conjunction with the indirect object pronoun?

5 For which type of verb do the object pronoun and the verb reflect the same subject?

6 How does the reciprocal pronoun translate into English?

7 Which is the most common relative pronoun?

8 What are the endings for the simple future tense?

9 What types of future does the simple future express?

10 What is the order of object pronouns?

11 Which is the most common relative pronoun?

12 Where are object pronouns found?

13 What are the possible meanings for the object pronoun *se*?

FOOD FOR THOUGHT

The following questions are intended to serve as a springboard for discussion. Think about them as you read the story.

- How can I develop trusting and respectful relationships with my patients and clients?
- How can I recognize and challenge my own assumptions?
- How can I learn to recognize my patients' and clients' strengths and to build on teachable moments?
- How can I become partners with colleagues who are bridges across culture, with other organizations in the community that have similar interests and with members of the community I hope to serve?

NOTES FROM THE FIELD

Chris McQuiston is an associate professor of nursing who conducts participatory research with the Latino community.

Recently, clinics in several counties in North Carolina reported newly diagnosed cases of rubella. It was apparent that the Latino community was predominately affected by this epidemic. Unfortunately, one Latina with the virus was pregnant. Many health care providers and administrators assumed that Latinos were not immunized because they were "non-compliant." They soon learned that in several Latin American countries the standard for vaccination requires that children should be immunized against measles, but not against rubella. Additional confusion resulted from the realization that in the U.S., the MMR vaccination packages the three vaccines: measles, mumps, and rubella.

Once the differences were sorted out, outreach workers spread the word and Latino families willingly came to health departments, clinics and health fairs asking for the immunization. Health care providers and clinic administrators learned a lesson about practices in other countries and realized that they had leapt to the wrong conclusion about non-compliance and rubella.

DISCUSSION QUESTIONS

As health care professionals we don't often recognize that standards we accept as universally important may not be the standards of the countries from which many immigrants come.

1 Think about the situation described by Chris. How might this story have been different if health care providers had understood that many immigrants are not immunized against rubella in their home countries?

2 What could be done to avoid outbreaks of rubella in your community?

3 The term "non-compliant" suggests that the provider always knows what is best and understands the situation. Can you think of situations in your practice where "non-compliance" might really reflect a difference in cultural beliefs or values?

FAMILIA SANA

Una inyección de salud

SI ALGUIEN le dijera que darle a su hijo un breve y algo doloroso pellizco ahora podría salvarle la vida más adelante, usted comenzaría a pellizcarlo, ¿verdad? Aún así, más de 20% de los padres no vacunan a sus hijos contra enfermedades peligrosas como es debido, pues creen erróneamente que las vacunas pueden causar daño. Aquí le mostramos cómo distinguir entre los mitos y las realidades de la inmunización, según la doctora Flavia Mercado, para que le dé a sus hijos la protección que merecen.

Mito: Mis hijos no necesitan vacunas hasta que vayan a la escuela.

Realidad: Los recién nacidos deben recibir su primera vacuna contra la hepatitis B antes de ser dados de alta del hospital. Con el fin de que su sistema inmunológico se desarrolle por completo, su hijo debe recibir varias rondas más de vacunas antes y después de entrar a la escuela ¿Qué sucede si ya se le pasaron esas primeras vacunas? "Comience ahora mismo", dice la doctora Mercado.

Mito: Una vacuna puede hacer que uno contraiga la enfermedad contra la cual protege.

Realidad: Aunque las vacunas están hechas de partes de microbios, éstos han sido destruidos o debilitados para que ya no puedan causar enfermedades. "Estudio tras estudio ha demostrado que las vacunas son seguras y efectivas", dice la doctora Mercado. Los efectos secundarios, si los hay, generalmente son leves y pueden incluir una fiebre baja, o hinchazón o dolor en el sitio donde se aplicó la inyección.

Mito: Si otros niños reciben vacunas, mi hijo no las necesita.

Realidad: ¡Erróneo! Mucha gente no se vacuna, y si se enferma, lo mismo puede pasarle a su hijo.

NANCY KALISH

Incluso **los adolescentes necesitan** recibir algunas **vacunas para aumentar su inmunidad** contra ciertas enfermedades, como difteria y meningitis.

To read this article online, go to www.yalebooks.com/salud.

CONTESTA LAS SIGUIENTES PREGUNTAS:

1 ¿Crees que debe ser obligatorio que los niños demuestren que tienen puestas todas las vacunas recomendadas antes de asistir a la escuela? ¿Sabías que los padres pueden negarse a ponérselas a sus hijos?

2 ¿Cuáles son los efectos secundarios de las inmunizaciones mencionados en la lectura?

3 ¿Hay vacunas recomendadas para los adolescentes y/o los estudiantes universitarios? ¿Por qué?

4 ¿Qué opinas de las vacunas opcionales? Por ejemplo, ¿tienes puesta la vacuna contra la gripe?

COMPROBACIÓN

DVD *Las preguntas de* Comprobación *están diseñadas para evaluar tu habilidad de usar lo que has aprendido, en situaciones nuevas y diferentes. Aunque el contexto todavía es limitado y las respuestas están restringidas y guiadas, debes interpretar más.*

SECCIÓN A

¿Qué pasa en la Historia? *Escoge las palabras que completan mejor la oración. ¡Cuidado con la gramática!*

1 Rafa escribió una columna de salud en *La Voz* sobre las viviendas insalubres porque él (ellas / las / se) ha estado investigando.

2 Descubrió que las viviendas pertenecen a un tal "Hugo Anderson", (cual / porque / quien) les pide un dineral a los inmigrantes (cuales / los cuales / que) viven en ellas, pero no (ellas / las / se) mantiene en buen estado.

3 Ángela se preocupa porque sabe que Rafa puede actuar impulsivamente, pero él sabe que, si sigue investigando, (encontrará / encuentra / encuentre) la evidencia que busca y (podrá / pueda / puede) conseguir resultados.

4 Lo que Rafa quiere es mejorar el nivel sanitario de los inmigrantes que (vive / viven / vivir) en estas viviendas, llamar la atención de las autoridades y terminar con los malos servicios.

5 Ángela teme que todo lo que Rafa hace constituye un (reto / riesgo / risco) para él porque habla mal el inglés y no se puede defender muy bien.

SECCIÓN B

Estas oraciones describen la visita que hace Federico al hospital, después de su caída en el trabajo. Escoge las palabras que completan mejor cada oración.

a los cuatro vientos	negativa
atienden	pena
confianza	por lo
con	positivo
encontrarán	rompí
lo peor	urgencia

Mientras tanto, Federico tuvo que ir al hospital por un accidente de trabajo. "Seguramente **(1)** ________________ que soy VIH **(2)** ________________, " pensó él y llamó a la clínica de La Comunidad. Duna y Ashleigh se preocuparon mucho **(3)** ________________ del VIH y fueron a buscarlo con **(4)** ________________. pero Federico no estaba tan mal. A las dos les dio mucha **(5)** ________________ con él y se lo llevaron a la clínica de La Comunidad. No estaba muy enfermo. **(6)** ________________ que tenía era una gran tristeza.

¡A CONVERSAR!

PERSONAJES

DVD

We meet Federico in Personajes *in this unit. While he speaks of his family in Mexico, and indicates that he continues to send them money, he also tells us that he is no longer in contact with them. He explains that he has been diagnosed with HIV, and that he is too embarrassed to tell them.*

Federico

Role-play a conversation between Federico and his wife, a conversation that will take place after some years without any contact. What questions will his wife have? How will Federico explain himself and answer her questions? What questions will he have for her?

¡A RESUMIR!

EPISODIO

Imagine that one of your classmates hasn't yet seen the episodio. Summarize the episode for your classmate, who will ask you questions based on what happened in the last episode of the Historia. Use the model questions below as a guide.

CLASSMATE: ¿Qué pasó cuando Laura le dio la noticia a Alex?
YOU: Alex se enojó.

Your questions should also cover the following material:

- Will Laura be able to make the necessary changes in her life? (*¿Podrá dejar de fumar? ¿Dejar de tomar?*)
- Ángela asks Federico to install a new lock in the pharmacy. Why does Alex look so surprised and concerned?
- Who is Hugo Anderson? Why is Rafa investigating him?

APLICACIÓN

ESCUCHAR

DVD *During their conversation, Milagros tells Ashleigh that she feels very lonely. Why? What reasons does she give? Do you think that family connections are more important, or stronger, in the Hispanic culture?*

Ashleigh visits Milagros in her apartment

Role-play two conversations between Milagros and her mother. In the first conversation, Milagros talks to her mother about her pregnancy and the fact that she has little support here in the United States. Use the following sentences as a way to start the conversation.

MADRE: Milita, ¿cómo estás?
MILAGROS: Mamá, todo está bien. ¡Pronto serás abuela otra vez! Pero es difícil estar embarazada aquí sin tu apoyo.

Imagine that Milagros has had her baby and calls her mother to convey the happy news. Use the following sentences as a model.

MADRE: ¿Ya llegó el bebé?
MILAGROS: LA bebé, mamá, ¡es niña!

ANALIZAR

DVD Watch this segment, keeping the following questions in mind:

Jaime receives a phone call

- ¿Quién llama? ¿Cómo lo sabes?
- ¿Puedes imaginar cuál es la pregunta o pedido de esta persona que hace que Jaime reaccione con frustración?

1 *Role-play a similar scene with a classmate.* ¿Quién llama? ¿Qué quiere?

2 *While in the U.S. patients need a doctor's prescription for a wide variety of medicines, in many countries the pharmacist can dispense medicines after a consultation with the patient. With this in mind, how would you respond to a phone call like the one Jaime received? Role-play a new scene, with your changes.*

EN LA PRÁCTICA

Carmina speaks with a mother about immunization

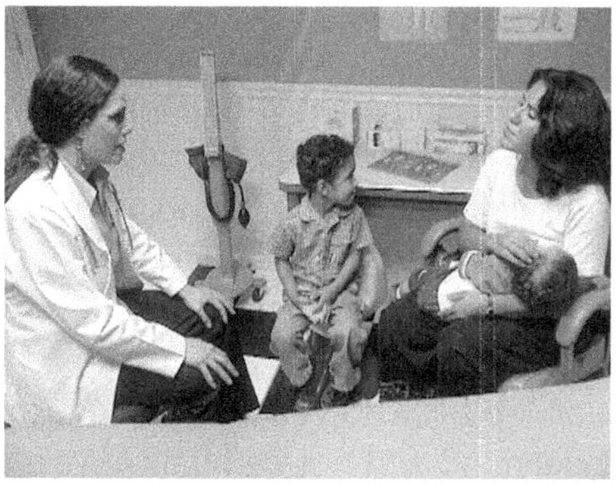

DVD

Perhaps you already know that national standards of health vary from one country to another.

Investigate the recommended childhood vaccinations in the U.S., and role-play a conversation between Carmina and the mother from this segment. While Carmina should explain which immunizations are recommended and why, the mother will clearly have questions about possible side effects (efectos secundarios) and any dangers associated with these immunizations. The sentence below can get you started.

CARMINA: Señora, a su hijo todavía le falta una vacuna...

LENGUA

DVD

In this segment, Laura makes three promises:

1 *to stop smoking* (dejar de fumar)

2 *to stop drinking* (dejar de beber)

3 *to give Alex the news about her pregnancy* (darle la noticia al padre)

a *Role-play a conversation between Laura and Carmina in which Laura asks Carmina's help in keeping these promises.*

b *As you saw in this unit's episode, Alex does not react well to the news. Is this entirely his fault? Do you think Laura might have better prepared him for such important news?*

Role-play a conversation between Laura and Alex, one in which she does a better job preparing him for the news. How does he react this time?

c Jaime quiere escribir un artículo en *La Voz* para aconsejar a las jóvenes embarazadas. Imagina que eres Jaime y escribe dos ó tres párrafos sobre la historia de Laura —sin dar su nombre. Debes incluir consejos que toquen los siguientes temas:

- no beber en exceso
- no fumar
- hacerse exámenes médicos con regularidad
- mejorar las relaciones de familia
- planificar el futuro (¿regresar a Republica Dominicana?, ¿casarse con Alex?, etc.)

MÁS ALLÁ

What visual images come to mind when you read or hear the words "Novocain", "UV light" and "drill"? What do you think comes to mind when a small child hears those very same words? Children probably have a very different understanding of the words, if they have one at all. So how do you make it so a child will understand and not be afraid? We rely on such techniques as humor, the use of specialized grammar, or even word association with familiar objects to achieve this goal. In dentistry, for example, when working with children it is common practice to refer to "Novocain" as "sleepy juice", "UV light" as "a flashlight", and "a drill" as "Mr. Whistle".

When communicating with children, we often change the style of language that we use. We try to speak in a less formal and non-threatening manner because, as a result of our life experiences and stage of physical development, adult language is different from child language. This is true for all cultures. Keep this in mind if you are working with children. Even though the children probably know more Spanish than you do, they are still children.

Like English, Spanish makes use of special vocabulary or constructions when dealing with children; for example, words such as *un chichón* (a booboo), *hacer pipí* (to go peepee), and *hacer pupú* (to go poopoo) are used instead of the more formal counterpart. Sometimes, the diminutive *ito / ita* is added to the end of a word to mean "little". As you continue to study Spanish, keep in mind your audience and the tools that will help facilitate effective communication with them, especially if you plan to or currently work with children.

ENTREVISTA

DVD

Read this summary in English of what Rocío Quiñones says in her interview before you watch it on the DVD. Remember that these interviews were conducted to include "authentic language" on the DVD. This means that the interviews are unscripted and at a natural conversational pace. Use the English summary to guide you.

Rocío Quiñones

How did I get interested in the field that I now work in? Well, my father is a doctor and there was always an emphasis in the health field in my house... There was always an understanding that we would go to college, and the joke in my house is that we'll all be doctors but that we get to decide what kind! My older brother is a doctor and when he entered medicine I was still in college. I began to research [the field] and was thinking that the best would be to go into medicine, but always in the back of my mind was dentistry. And then [my father] sent me to speak with Dr. John Perry, who is a good friend of our family's now, so that I could look into that possibility. And that's how I became interested little by little in it. I also though that in dentistry, unlike medicine, as a woman I would have a little more flexibility in having a family and things like that. I would still have an academic life like I could have in medicine but sometimes there's more flexibility in dentistry. And that's how I ended up taking the MCAT and the DAT. I did well on the MCAT but I did stupendously well on the DAT and I told myself, "Well, that's what I'm going to try." At first I wanted to do music, but my father always pushed me towards the health field, and I'm very happy that he pushed me into this area.

I don't think... a typical day... I don't think that I have a typical day, but now in these two years that I'm here doing this fellowship there are certain things that I could generalize about. For example, on Mondays I work in private practice in this... here in Woodcroft very near here. And on Tuesdays, Wednesdays, Thursdays and Fridays I'm in class or doing research. Sometimes I teach medical students about pediatric dentistry. There's a lot of variety and that's part of the reason that I'm still studying and why I eventually want a career that's at least somewhat academic —because of the variety of activities that you can do.

How did I arrive in the United States? I was born in Columbus when my father was studying medicine. He was doing his residency in pathology. And I grew up there until when I was three years old we returned to El Salvador. We were going to live there forever. But the war began in the 1970s and my father, as the minister of health, decided, well, he didn't decide, we had to leave. And we ended up in Mexico for a while and after a while we went to the border [of the U.S.] and I began school in El Paso. We couldn't return to El Salvador because the war continued until 1991. At this time Canada opened its doors to immigrants that were coming from El Salvador. We ended up going to Ontario for four years and then to Manitoba for eleven years until I decided to enter dentistry and came to North Carolina to do my residency.

Watch the interview with Rocío Quiñones once more, and answer the following questions:

- ¿Cómo se interesó en la odontología?
- ¿Cómo es un día típico en su vida profesional?
- ¿Cómo llegó a los Estados Unidos?

UNIDAD 3b

NOTE TO THE STUDENT

There has been a serious accident and the emergency room doctor must now speak with the victim's family. Unfortunately, the doctor only speaks English and the family only speaks Spanish. As the doctor enters the waiting room he is met by a large group of people all speaking at once in a language unfamiliar to him. He can tell by the expressions on their faces that they are worried for their loved one and are in desperate need of information. Calmly and slowly he tries to explain how the child is doing. The crowd listens intently, but he can tell by the confused look on their faces that his message has not been understood. Again, the crowd responds with a barrage of what can only be determined to be questions. The doctor directs the two people closest to him to calm down with a motion of his hand; he then pats them on the shoulder, smiles, and gives them thumbs up. Hysteria changes to glee as smiles appear on the faces of everyone involved. Thankfully, the message has been received. The question is *how*. What happened that caused the crowd to react the way it did? What guided the doctor in his actions?

BODY LANGUAGE

Remember that communication involves much more than the spoken and written word. Have you ever watched a movie or a television program with the sound turned down? Or, have you ever held a conversation in a crowded public place? In many instances, you find that you can grasp the gist of what is going on, even though you have no idea of all that is being said.

How is it possible that you can guess or predict the events that have taken or will take place? The answer is that we can send messages to one another simply by using our bodies. Think about all of the non-verbal ways, other than writing, in which you communicate on a daily basis. You might point, roll your eyes, raise your eyebrows, shrug your shoulders, wave, yawn, smile, frown, hug, hold hands, etc. All of these actions communicate a particular idea to the individual or group of individuals participating in the conversation. Our understanding of these gestures and facial expressions help to guide our responses, especially when part or the entire spoken message has been lost.

DOES BODY LANGUAGE VARY ACROSS CULTURES?

Not all gestures and expressions are universal. Just as native speakers of English have come to associate a particular notion with a particular gesture or expression, so too have native speakers of Spanish. For example, native speakers of English learn to convey respect by making eye contact, yet to someone raised in the Hispanic cultures, eye contact is sometimes perceived as disrespectful. Another example of this type is pointing. U.S. culture teaches us to point with our index finger; however, many Hispanic cultures deem this to be disrespectful and prefer to use the entire hand when pointing. Thus, there is ample opportunity for misunderstanding simply through the use of gestures and facial expressions. Even the notion of personal space varies from culture to culture.

HOW CAN I AVOID MISUNDERSTANDINGS?

The best way to avoid misunderstandings is to participate actively in the conversation. In other words, not only must you be an active speaker, but also an active listener. Only you are aware of the reaction you are expecting. If the listener's reaction contradicts or does not match your expectations, you might need to clarify your message. One way to avoid miscommunication is to always use a combination of devices, such as language, gestures, and expressions, to convey your thoughts so that you can ensure accuracy. A second way to do this is to have the person explain the message, as he or she understood it. Finally, you can always restate your message using different words, gestures, and expressions. Along these same lines, when communicating with native speakers of Spanish, observe which gestures and expressions are used in a particular context. Pay attention to the non-verbal cues that accompany the spoken words so that you learn how to appropriately use them. Most of all, remember that you don't always have to use words or sounds to talk to others.

VOCABULARIO

Below are the vocabulary words highlighted in this unit. Remember that you can hear these words in action in the *Vocabulario* section of *Unidad 3b* on the *Recursos* webpage. After you have looked at them, write beside each one its English equivalent. If you have any doubt about the word's exact meaning, look it up in a good Spanish-English dictionary.

Review the words that you have written on the margins of *Vocabulario* so far. Look up the meanings of any words you don't know.

Remember to use this space to add new and useful words that you find in your study or work, but were not included in *Vocabulario*!

Verbos

ahorrar
apresurarse
aprovecharse de
arruinar
compartir
conseguir
contagiar
contratar
dedicarse a
equivocar
ir mal
pelear

Adverbios y expresiones

además
al fin y al cabo
compartiendo
contagiado
en camino
la menor
mal

Sustantivos

la culpa
la etapa
la idea
el jefe
las jeringas
el portador
la sangre
el SIDA
un tal

¡A PRACTICAR!

3B-VOC-1

Match the picture with the sentence that most accurately describes the scene.

1 _____ El quiere conseguir un trabajo en la clínica.

2 _____ Le va mal porque sufre tanto dolor.

3 _____ Las dos comparten una casa.

4 _____ Se apresura en encontrar información sobre un tal Anderson.

5 _____ En el camino a casa ven a su amiga.

6 _____ Van a tomarle una muestra de sangre.

a

b

c

d

e

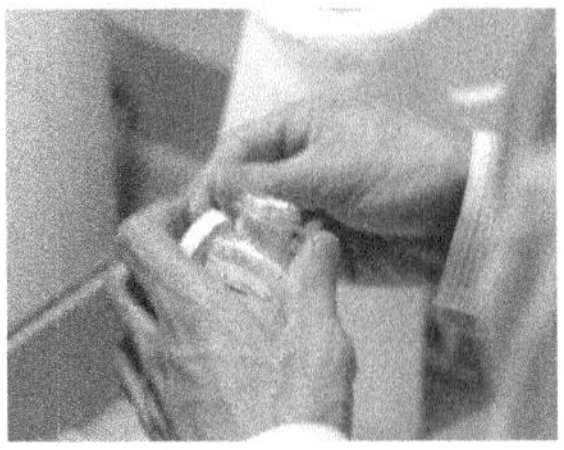

f

3B-VOC-2

Fill in the correct word for each blank. Be careful with agreement between the new word and the rest of the sentence. If you need help, review Unidad 3b Vocabulario, *or go back to the first exercise in this section.*

Rafa entrevista a unos hispanos que viven en los apartamentos del señor Hugo Anderson.

RAFA: ¿Y tú crees que el señor Anderson **(1)** ______________________ *(takes advantage of)* la situación del inmigrante?

HOMBRE: ¡Por supuesto! Él sabe que para nosotros es difícil **(2)** ______________ *(to obtain)* casa en este pueblo y nos cobra tanto que no podemos **(3)** ______________ *(save)* ni un peso. Por eso, **(4)** ______________ *(we share)* viviendas. La mayoría de la gente no tiene **(5)** ______________________ *(the least idea)* de lo difícil que es para nosotros. **(6)** ______________ *(Besides)* a mucha gente no le importa. **(7)** ______________ *(In short)*, nos **(8)** ______________ *(they blame)* y dicen que **(9)** ______________ *(we ruin)* las casas nosotros mismos.

3B-VOC-3

Take a look at the photos below. Use the vocabulary provided to write one or two sentences that describe each scene. You can choose to follow the story line or to use your imagination. Be sure to incorporate grammar that you have studied up to this point.

1 dedicarse a
el jefe
aprovecharse de

2 pelear
la culpa
equivocar

3 ahorrar
compartir
la idea

4 el SIDA
las jeringas
contagiar

1 ______________________________

____

____

2 ______________________________

____

____

3 ______________________________

____

____

4 ______________________________

____

____

3B-VOC-4

Using some of the vocabulary provided below, create a brief handout about AIDS for the patients of La Comunidad. *You may also incorporate other vocabulary that you have learned up to this point.*

contagiar	compartir
contratar	conseguir
además	el SIDA
las jeringas	la sangre
el portador	la idea

____

____

____

____

____

____

____

____

____

____

____

____

____

____

____

____

____

____

____

____

USEFUL TERMS AND EXPRESSIONS

This section introduces new vocabulary and expressions related to themes found throughout *Historia 3b* of the DVD.

SUSTANTIVOS

El cuerpo

el área genital	genital area
los ganglios linfáticos	lymph nodes
la lengua	tongue
el pecho	chest
el pene	penis
los pulmones	lungs
el tórax	thorax
la vagina	vagina
las vías urinarias	urinary tracts

Los fluidos

el esputo	spit, sputum
las heces	feces
la orina	urine
el postema, el pus	pus
el semen	semen
el sudor	sweat, perspiration
el vómito	vomit

Las condiciones físicas

el aborto	abortion
la dosificación, la dosis	dosage
la esterilidad	sterility
el flujo, la secreción	discharge
la gripe	flu
la inflamación	inflammation
la irritación	irritation
la mejoría	improvement
la neumonía	pneumonia
la recuperación	recovery
la sensación de ardor	burning sensation

En la farmacia

las agujas	needles
los condones	condoms
el control de natalidad	birth control
el jarabe para la tos	cough syrup
la máscara	mask
los guantes	gloves
el pañuelo de papel	tissue
el sabor	flavor
el tejido	fabric, textile

Palabras adicionales	
el archivo	file
la beca	grant
la billetera	wallet
los boletines	bulletins
la bolsa	bag
el/la colega	colleague
el cura	priest
los formularios	forms
los sueños	dreams
el/la viudo/a	widow
el voluntario	volunteer
VERBOS	
agrandar(se)	to get bigger
aislar(se)	to isolate
alcanzar	to reach
amamantar	to breast-feed
botar	to throw (away), to expel
caber	to fit
calmar(se)	to calm down
colgar	to hang (up)
comportar(se)	to behave
comprobar	to verify, to prove
cubrir	to cover
donar	to donate
evitar	to avoid
gozar	to enjoy
ingresar	to become a member
inhalar	to inhale
marcar	to mark, to dial
orinar	to urinate
rellenar	to fill (out)
rezar	to pray
sacar	to take out, to stick out
toser	to cough
ventilar	to ventilate
ADJETIVOS Y ADVERBIOS	
a corto plazo	short-term
anticonceptivo/a	contraceptive
espeso/a	thick, dense
nocturno/a	nocturnal
respiratorio/s	respiratory

Study the vocabulary before you begin *Principios* because it will be useful when practicing the grammar points of the unit. Remember that this section is not intended to be an exhaustive list of all relevant terms, but rather is an exposure to some of the basic vocabulary used in healthcare. The definitions given here are limited, because they are intended for the narrow use of the exercises found in *Principios*. Look the words up in a good Spanish-English dictionary if you want to know other meanings, how to pronounce them, the contexts in which the words can be found, sayings and common expressions using these words, and their derivatives (adjectives from nouns, nouns from verbs, etc.).

PRINCIPIOS

Giving orders is one of the most important linguistic tasks facing any health professional. It is also one of the most delicate: if you fail to communicate what your patient or client needs to do, the consequences could be serious. While potentially difficult even when dealing with English-speakers, the situation becomes even more critical when communicating with your non-English speaking patients or clients. Consider for a moment the following example: A Spanish speaking patient is told to take some medicine once a day. Her physician, in well-intended Spanglish, carefully writes out the instructions for her: "*Tome* once *a día,*" but the woman understands *Once veces al día*, takes the medicine eleven times, and ends up in the hospital with a severe reaction.[1]

While certainly one of the more difficult linguistic tasks facing students, forming commands in Spanish isn't as terrible as it might initially seem. There are, in fact, several ways in which to give a command or to make a request. You saw in *Unidad 1b* how the present tense could be used to make a polite request.

SPANISH	ENGLISH
¿Me traes el archivo?	Will you bring me the file?
¿Me dice donde le duele?	Tell me where it hurts.

A second construction, known as the conditional, can also be used to make a polite request. However, sometimes you need to be more direct when asking someone to do something; in fact, you need to tell him. To accomplish this, Spanish has specific forms available known as commands. The purpose of a command is to directly tell someone to do something. Direct commands are divided into three types: formal *(usted* and *ustedes)*, informal *(tú)*, and *nosotros*. The type of command is determined by the person or group of persons addressed. In other words, the person or group of persons being addressed also determines the subject.

1 The authors of *¡A su salud!* attempted to track down the source of this oft-cited example (which also appeared on an episode of television's *ER*) but couldn't find it. With luck it is an urban legend; regardless it serves to explain the importance of communicating one's commands clearly.

FORMAL COMMANDS

Formal commands are used when the subject is either *usted* or *ustedes*. Notice that there is a singular and a plural form for the formal commands. Here is the distribution of endings for each verb type:

	-AR	-ER	-IR
usted	-e	-a	-a
ustedes	-en	-an	-an

The endings listed above come from the present subjunctive. Once again you see that the *-er* and *-ir* verb conjugations follow the same pattern.

- The stem of the *yo* form of the verb in the present indicative is used as the base for formal commands. Go back to *Unidad 1b* if you feel you need a review of the present tense verb forms. Here are some examples of the *usted* and *ustedes* commands, as they exist in Spanish:

	-AR	-ER	-IR
usted	tom**e**	com**a**	escrib**a**
	apriet**e**	pong**a**	pid**a**
	cuent**e**	vuelv**a**	duerm**a**
ustedes	tom**en**	com**an**	escrib**an**
	apriet**en**	pong**an**	pid**an**
	cuent**en**	vuelv**an**	duerm**an**

These endings are the same whether the command is affirmative or negative. Negative refers to the addition of *no* or its equivalent to a sentence.

SPANISH	ENGLISH
Tome la medicina con comida.	Take the medicine with food.
No tome la medicina sin comida.	Don't take the medicine without food.
Nunca tome la medicina sin comida.	Never take the medicine without food.

- In addition, some verbs will undergo spelling changes to the stem before adding the appropriate *usted* and *ustedes* endings. You saw most of these spelling changes before when you studied the preterit in *Unidad 2b*. However, take note that none of these forms requires an accent mark. It might help to remember the spelling changes if you keep in mind that they exist for reasons of pronunciation. *Sece*, for example, would not conserve the hard "c" of the verb *secar*, whereas *seque* does. Here are some examples of the spelling changes that occur.

Examples of *-car* changing to *-qu* before *-e*:

SACAR	SECAR	MARCAR
saque	seque	marque
saquen	sequen	marquen

Examples of *-gar* changing to *-c* before *-e*:

TRAGAR	COLGAR	PAGAR
trague	cuelgue	pague
traguen	cuelguen	paguen

Examples of *-zar* changing to *-c* before *-e*:

EMPEZAR	CRUZAR	ADELGAZAR
empiece	cruce	adelgace
empiecen	crucen	adelgacen

- **Irregular Formal Commands:**

Some verbs reflect changes that seem illogical and not based on any overt patterns. Nevertheless, there is a pattern; all of these forms come from the present subjunctive. Below are the most common irregular verbs:

	SER	IR	SABER
usted	sea	vaya	sepa
ustedes	sean	vayan	sepan

	ESTAR	DAR
usted	esté	dé
ustedes	estén	den

Verbs like *ser, ir,* and *estar* change their form entirely. Others such as *estar* and *dar* add an accent (the accent on *dé* is added to distinguish it from the preposition *de*). Do these verbs seem familiar to you? Notice how the same verbs appear to be irregular in all tenses.

¡A PRACTICAR!

3B-PRIN-1

Give the infinitive form for each formal command listed. Then indicate the type of spelling change that took place.

1 elijan:

Infinitive: ______________________

Spelling Change: ______________________

2 comiencen:

Infinitive: ______________________

Spelling Change: ______________________

3 distribuya:

Infinitive: ______________________

Spelling Change: ______________________

4 llegue:

Infinitive: ______________________

Spelling Change: ______________________

5 coloquen:

Infinitive: ______________________

Spelling Change: ______________________

6 gocen:

Infinitive: ______________________

Spelling Change: ______________________

7 incluya:

Infinitive: ______________________

Spelling Change: ______________________

8 alcance:

Infinitive: ______________________

Spelling Change: ______________________

9 recoja:

Infinitive: ______________________

Spelling Change: ______________________

10 cuelguen:

Infinitive: ______________________

Spelling Change: ______________________

3B-PRIN-2

Provide the correct form of the formal command for the verbs listed below.

1 no usar (usted)

____

2 comprar (ustedes)

____

3 tener (usted)

____

4 leer (usted)

____

5 no aceptar (usted)

____

6 poner (ustedes)

____

7 quitar (usted)

____

8 guardar (ustedes)

____

9 seguir (ustedes)

____

10 no consumir (ustedes)

____

3B-PRIN-3

After his accident, Federico makes an appointment with Carmina for a checkup. Fill in the blanks with the correct form of the formal command.

CARMINA: Bueno, **(1)** ______________ *(inhalar)*, por favor. Todo me parece muy bien. ¿Ha tenido problemas respiratorios o con la visión?

FEDERICO: No, doctora, me siento bien.

CARMINA: Me alegro, Federico. Pues, no encuentro ningún problema, pero es mejor no tomar riesgos. Por ahora, no **(2)** ______________ *(volver)* al trabajo por unos días. **(3)** ______________ *(recordar)* tomar la medicina prescrita. **(4)** ______________ *(Dormir)* y **(5)** ______________ *(descansar)* lo suficiente. **(6)** ______________ *(Hacer)* los ejercicios recomendados. **(7)** ______________ *(Comer)* alimentos saludables. Y sobre todo, **(8)** ______________ *(tomar)* tiempo para sí mismo y no se **(9)** ______________ *(olvidar)* de sus necesidades.

FEDERICO: Por supuesto. Muchas gracias por todo, doctora.

3B-PRIN-4

One of the patients at the clinic is infected with TB and wants to know what he should do to protect the people around him. Translate the sentences below into Spanish to help Ashleigh instruct him on the best ways to protect his family.

1 Avoid close contact with the members of your family.

____

____

2 Sleep in a separate room.

____

____

3 Cover your mouth with a tissue when you cough.

____

____

4 Place the tissue in a bag and throw it away.

____

____

5 Ventilate your room and house frequently.

____

____

6 Take all of your medicine.

____

____

3B-PRIN-5

Reflect on your own career or your future career. You most likely are or will be giving instructions everyday. What are some of the most common instructions that you give on a typical day? Provide at least six.

1 ______________________________

____

2 ______________________________

____

3 ______________________________

____

4 ______________________________

____

5 ______________________________

____

6 ______________________________

____

INFORMAL COMMANDS

Informal commands are used when the subject is either *tú* or *vosotros*. In this unit we will only examine the forms used to express *tú* since *vosotros* is restricted to Spanish from Spain. Consequently, informal commands will only be used when the subject is singular. Unlike formal commands, informal commands use different forms depending on whether the command is affirmative or negative.

■ Regular Affirmative Informal Commands:

Here is the distribution of endings for regular affirmative *tú* commands:

	-AR	-ER	-IR
tú	-a	-e	-e

Observe that these endings are identical to those of the third person singular of the present indicative. In fact, the verb stems are also identical.

	-AR	-ER	-IR
Present Indicative	limpia	corre	comparte
	aprieta	lee	repite
	cuenta	mueve	duerme
Informal Command	limpia	corre	comparte
	aprieta	lee	repite
	cuenta	mueve	duerme

Although both forms are exactly alike, there is no confusion between the two. Context enables the speaker and listener to establish the intended meaning of the verb form. Take a look at the examples provided below:

	SPANISH	ENGLISH
Informal Command	Hola Carlos, saca la lengua por favor.	Hello, Carlos. Stick out your tongue please.
Present Indicative	El doctor entra y Carlos saca la lengua para él.	The doctor enters, and Carlos sticks out his tongue for him.

Cues within the two sentences allow the speaker and listener to know who is being addressed, as well as what is being discussed. Other factors such as the purpose and place of the conversation help to guide both speaker and listener. Thus, the two functions are never confused.

- **Irregular Forms in the Affirmative:**

Some of the most frequently used verbs have an irregular form when used in an affirmative expression. As you have probably already surmised, these verbs often have irregular forms and do in the commands as well.

tener — *ten*	salir — *sal*	decir — *di*
venir — *ven*	hacer — *haz*	ser — *sé*
poner — *pon*	ir — *ve*	

It is easiest to learn the irregulars through memorization. You are best served by grouping them together according to the patterns they exhibit, for example, the three letter forms ending in *-n*, those forms comprised of three letters not ending in *-n*, and those forms consisting of two letters.

- **Negative Commands:**

Contrary to the affirmative informal commands, negative informal commands and formal commands follow a similar pattern of formation because the endings used here also come from the present subjunctive. Here is the distribution of endings for each verb type:

	-AR	**-ER**	**-IR**
negative tú	-es	-as	-as

As with the formal commands, negative informal commands add the endings listed above to the stem of the *yo* form of the verb in the present tense. Remember that to form negative commands you simply need to use *no* or one of its equivalents in connection with the main verb. Here are some examples of the negative *tú* commands:

	-AR	**-ER**	**-IR**
negative tú	no tom**es**	no com**as**	no escrib**as**
	no apriet**es**	no pong**as**	no pid**as**
	no cuent**es**	no vuelv**as**	no duerm**as**

In addition, some verbs will undergo spelling changes to the stem before adding the appropriate *tú* endings. You have already seen most of these spelling changes before when you studied the preterit in *Unidad 2b* and the formal commands in the previous section. Here is a quick reminder of some of the spelling changes that occur with the negative *tú* commands.

Examples of *-car* changing to *-qu* before *-e*:

SACAR	SECAR	MARCAR
no saques	no seques	no marques

Examples of *-gar* changing to *-gu* before *-e*:

TRAGAR	COLGAR	PAGAR
no tragues	no cuelgues	no pagues

Examples of *-zar* changing to *-c* before *-e*:

EMPEZAR	CRUZAR	ADELGAZAR
no empieces	no cruces	no adelgaces

- **Irregular Negative Informal Commands:**

The irregular verbs for the negative informal commands are the same as those for the formal commands. Here are the most common irregular verbs:

	SER	IR	SABER
tú	no seas	no vayas	no sepas

	ESTAR	DAR
tú	no estés	no des

¡A PRACTICAR!

3B-PRIN-6

Jaime is giving "the talk" to Ricardito, his nephew. Read the paragraph below and circle all of the informal command forms. There are 10 total.

Sólo los condones pueden ayudar a prevenir el embarazo y las enfermedades venéreas. Compra tus propios condones. Usa condones de látex y no compres los de tejido animal. Siempre ten los condones a mano, en tu bolsa o en tu billetera. No te pongas nunca condones viejos o dañados. No uses nunca el mismo condón más de una vez. Lee bien la etiqueta y sigue las instrucciones. No tomes alcohol ni drogas antes de tener relaciones sexuales. Sé responsable.

3B-PRIN-7

One of the pamphlets on AIDS awareness came back from the printer with a few mistakes. Help the clinic fix the errors by providing the opposite command form for the one found below.

1 No reconozcas los síntomas.

____

2 Si estás infectada con el VIH, amamanta al bebé.

____

3 Dona sangre, plasma y órganos.

____

4 No uses tu propio cepillo de dientes.

____

5 No dejes de fumar ni usar drogas.

____

6 Comparte jeringas y agujas.

____

7 No hagas regularmente ejercicios físicos.

____

8 Ponte crema con petrolato.

____

9 No limites el número de parejas sexuales.

____

10 No tengas en cuenta que la píldora anticonceptiva no previene la transmisión del VIH.

____

3B-PRIN-8

Duna spends much of her time counseling and offering advice to others. Today she is meeting with a group of teenagers and all of them have questions that need answers. Help lighten her workload by reading the questions below and dispensing advice based on what you have read.

1 ¿Qué hago si resulta que estoy infectado con el VIH?

____

____

2 Si estoy embarazada y quiero un aborto, ¿dónde puedo conseguirlo?

____

____

3 ¿Cómo puedo mantenerme saludable por más tiempo?

____

____

4 ¿Cómo puedo saber si tengo tuberculosis?

____

____

5 ¿Cómo puedo acordarme de cuándo tomar la medicina?

____

____

6 ¿Qué hago si veo sangre o pus en la orina?

____

____

7 ¿Qué hago si se me olvida tomar la medicina un día?

____

____

8 ¿Cómo puedo curarme de una infección de las vías urinarias?

____

____

3B-PRIN-9

Read the paragraph below. Counsel your friend on how he should change his habits in order to better protect himself from sexually transmitted diseases.

"Este año he tenido como seis parejas diferentes. A dos de ellas, las conocí en un bar. Sólo pasé una noche con cada una. No me acuerdo si usamos condones porque aquellas noches había tomado bastante cerveza. Por el momento, ando con una sola mujer. Estamos pensando en casarnos."

1 ______________________________

2 ______________________________

3 ______________________________

4 ______________________________

5 ______________________________

6 ______________________________

3B-PRIN-10

Study the picture below. What do you think Rafa and Ángela are arguing about? Create a dialogue of at least five sentences.

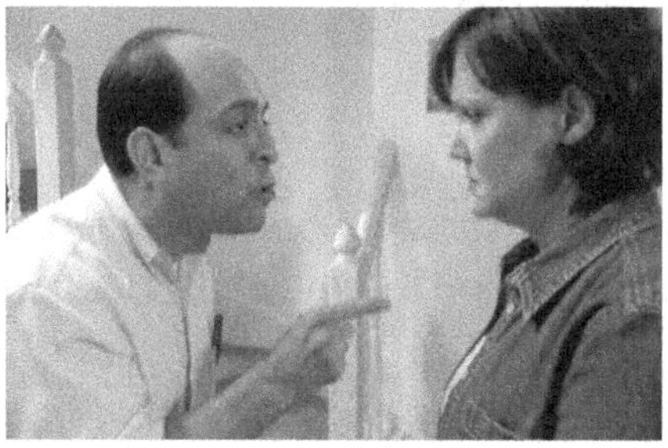

____

____

____

____

____

____

____

NOSOTROS COMMANDS

Nosotros commands are equivalent to the English "let's." A speaker who wants to be included or involved in the order or request uses this type of command. The present subjunctive provides the basis for the form.

Below is the distribution of endings:

	-AR	-ER	-IR
nosotros	-emos	-amos	-amos

Like the formal and negative informal commands, most *nosotros* commands add the endings listed above to the stem of the *yo* form of the verb in the present tense. Although the *nosotros* commands appear to follow in the footsteps of formal and negative informal commands, there are some differences. With respect to *nosotros* commands, you must pay close attention to the stem changing verbs. Some will not exhibit the stem change.

- All of the verbs that do stem change belong to the *-ir* conjugation. Stem changing verbs that pertain to the *-ar* and *-er* verb conjugations do not.

  -ir verbs that stem change from *-e-* to *-ie-* or from *-e-* to *-i-* will stem change from *-e-* to *-i-* in the *nosotros* command.

SEGUIR	SENTIR	PEDIR
sigamos	sintamos	pidamos

  -ir verbs that stem change from *-o-* to *-ue-* will stem change from *-o-* to *-u-* in the *nosotros* command.

DORMIR	MORIR
durmamos	muramos

- In addition, some *nosotros* commands will undergo the same spelling changes as the formal and negative informal commands. Here is a quick reminder of the spelling changes that occur:

  Examples of *-car* changing to *-qu* before *-e*:

SACAR	SECAR	MARCAR
saquemos	sequemos	marquemos

  Examples of *-gar* changing to *-gu* before *-e*:

TRAGAR	LLEGAR	PAGAR
traguemos	lleguemos	paguemos

Examples of *-zar* changing to *-c* before *-e*:

REZAR	CRUZAR	ALCANZAR
recemos	crucemos	alcancemos

- **Irregular *Nosotros* Commands:**

The irregular verbs for the *nosotros* commands are the same as those for the formal commands and the negative informal commands. Here are the most common irregular verbs:

	SER	IR	SABER
nosotros	seamos	vayamos	sepamos

	ESTAR	DAR
nosotros	estemos	demos

- With the exception of the verb *ir*, all of the endings are the same whether the command is affirmative or negative. Here are some examples of the *nosotros* commands, as they exist in Spanish:

	-AR	-ER	-IR
Affirmative	llam**emos**	pong**amos**	escrib**amos**
	compr**emos**	hag**amos**	salg**amos**
Negative	no llam**emos**	no pong**amos**	no escrib**amos**
	no compr**emos**	no hag**amos**	no salg**amos**

The forms for *ir* are the following:

	SPANISH	ENGLISH
Affirmative	Vamos	Let's go
Negative	No vayamos	Let's not go

Spanish turns to the present indicative to form the affirmative *nosotros* command of *ir*.

¡A PRACTICAR!

3B-PRIN-11

Conjugate the infinitives below to reflect the forms of the nosotros command. Then write down their meaning.

1 exigir
Forma: ______________________
Significado: ______________________

2 mirar
Forma: ______________________
Significado: ______________________

3 no hacer
Forma: ______________________
Significado: ______________________

4 disminuir
Forma: ______________________
Significado: ______________________

5 consultar
Forma: ______________________
Significado: ______________________

6 ir
Forma: ______________________
Significado: ______________________

7 limpiar
Forma: ______________________
Significado: ______________________

8 no castigar
Forma: ______________________
Significado: ______________________

9 medir
Forma: ______________________
Significado: ______________________

10 seguir
Forma: ______________________
Significado: ______________________

3B-PRIN-12

Before one of the weekly staff meetings, Jaime puts together a list of goals for La Comunidad. *Rewrite them to form* nosotros *commands.*

1 Debemos rellenar estos formularios.

____

2 Necesitamos revisar el presupuesto.

____

3 Tenemos que construir nuevos edificios.

____

4 Debemos solicitar una beca del gobierno.

____

5 Necesitamos encontrar maneras para alcanzar a más gente.

____

6 Tenemos que contratar a Federico.

____

3B-PRIN-13

Carmina is discussing the condition of one of her patient's with the patient's husband. She doesn't want to be over-confident so she makes some rather general statements using the nosotros commands. Translate what she says into Spanish.

1 Let's say that everything is going as expected.

____

2 Let's make an appointment for a month from now.

____

3 Let's see if there is any improvement before we change the medication.

____

4 Let's increase the dosage.

____

5 Let's pray for a quick recovery.

____

COMMANDS AND OBJECT AND REFLEXIVE PRONOUN PLACEMENT

In *Unidad 3a* we examined the placement of object pronouns within a sentence. You learned that there were three possible positions for the object pronoun:

1 Before the conjugated verb

2 Attached to the end of an infinitive

3 Attached to the end of a present participle

However, there exists a fourth possibility. When used in conjunction with an affirmative command, object pronouns must be attached to the end of the verb form.

	USTED	USTEDES	TÚ	NOSOTROS
Affirmative	siénte**se**	siénten**se**	siénta**te**	sentémo**nos**
	cuénte**la**	cuénten**lo**	cuénta**la**	contémos**la**
	díga**selo**	dígan**selo**	dí**selo**	digámo**selo**
Negative	no **se** siente	no **se** sienten	no **te** sientes	no **nos** sentemos
	no **la** cuente	no **la** cuenten	no **la** cuentes	no **la** contemos
	no **se lo** diga	no **se lo** digan	no **se lo** digas	no **se lo** digamos

In the examples provided above, the affirmative *nosotros* commands lose the final *-s* when the reflexive object pronoun is added, as in *sentémonos*. The final *-s* of the *nosotros* command is also dropped when the indirect object pronoun se is attached to the end of the affirmative command form.

In addition, observe the pattern of accentuation for the affirmative commands in combination with object pronouns. You place the accent mark three syllables back when one object pronoun is added to the end of the verb and four syllables back when two pronouns are added. (Remember, this is done to conserve the stress of the original word.) The only exception to this rule occurs when the verb form is comprised of one syllable. In such cases, you need be concerned with the accent mark only when two object pronouns are added; then count back to the third syllable.

Also, note that the subject pronoun follows the verb when used in affirmative and negative commands.

	USTED	USTEDES	TÚ	NOSOTROS
Affirmative	Vaya **usted**.	Vayan **ustedes**.	Ve **tú**.	Vamos **nosotros**.
Negative	No vaya **usted**.	No vayan **ustedes**.	No vayas **tú**.	No vayamos **nosotros**.

¡A PRACTICAR!

3B-PRIN-14

Place the object pronouns in the appropriate position, according to whether the command is affirmative or negative. Don't forget to **add the accent mark** *when necessary.*

1 No ______ digas ______ a nadie que soy portador de VIH. *(le)*

2 Por favor, ______ sienten ______ aquí. *(se)*

3 Ashleigh, ______ da ______ la receta, por favor. *(le)*

4 ______ pon ______ esta crema por la mañana y antes de acostarte. *(te)*

5 No ______ preocupe ______ usted, su esposo va a estar bien. *(se)*

6 ______ acostemos ______ temprano esta noche. *(nos)*

7 ______ cuiden ______ bien, niños. *(se)*

8 No ______ sientas ______ mal. *(te)*

9 Ay mi amor, ______ relaja ______ un poquito antes de empezar a trabajar. *(te)*

10 Recuerde, ______ proteja ______ contra las enfermedades venéreas. *(se)*

3B-PRIN-15

Provide the opposite command form for the one given below.

1 Muéstramelo.

____

2 No se lo pongan.

____

3 Empecémoslo.

____

4 No la traiga.

____

5 No me la pidas.

____

6 Quítatelo.

____

7 Díganosla.

____

8 Protéjanse.

____

9 No se lo tengas.

____

10 No nos reunamos.

____

3B-PRIN-16

Based on your knowledge of HIV, answer the questions using the appropriate command and object pronouns. Pay attention to the subject of the verb so that you can answer appropriately.

1 Si soy portadora de VIH, ¿debo darle el pecho a mi bebé?

____

____

____

2 ¿Cómo podemos saber con certeza que estamos infectados con el virus?

____

____

____

3 ¿Necesitamos vacunarnos para prevenir infecciones como la neumonía o la gripe?

____

____

____

4 ¿Debo lavarme las manos y otras partes del cuerpo inmediatamente después de tener contacto con la sangre u otros fluidos corporales tales como orina, semen, heces o vómito?

____

____

____

5 ¿Debemos utilizar guantes al estar en contacto con fluidos que contengan el virus?

____

____

____

3B-PRIN-17

Suppose you are Alex's friend and he just told you about how he reacted to Laura's pregnancy. What would you advise him to do next? Give Alex at least six suggestions.

Palabras útiles

calmarse	explicarle
decirle	irse
enojarse	pedirle disculpas

1 ______________________________

____

____

____

2 ______________________________

____

____

____

3 ______________________________

____

____

____

4 ______________________________

____

____

____

5 ______________________________

____

____

____

6 ______________________________

____

____

____

THE CONDITIONAL

Spanish has one way to express the conditional. To form the conditional, you add the appropriate endings to the infinitive form of the verb. The endings for the three verb types are the same.

	DAR	**PERDER**	**IR**
yo	dar**ía**	perder**ía**	ir**ía**
tú	dar**ías**	perder**ías**	ir**ías**
usted, él, ella	dar**ía**	perder**ía**	ir**ía**
nosotros	dar**íamos**	perder**íamos**	ir**íamos**
ustedes, ellos, ellas	dar**ían**	perder**ían**	**irían**

The conditional is formed in the same way as the simple future tense. A few verbs do not form the conditional by adding the endings to the infinitive. Instead they have an irregular stem. Still, the endings are the same as for the regular verbs. The most frequently used verbs and their stems are:

caber	*cabr-*	querer	*querr-*
decir	*dir-*	saber	*sabr-*
haber	*habr-*	salir	*saldr-*
hacer	*har-*	tener	*tendr-*
poder	*podr-*	valer	*valdr-*
poner	*pondr*	venir	*vendr-*

Note that both the conditional and the simple future share the same irregular verbs.

¡A PRACTICAR!

3B-PRIN-18

Provide the subject pronouns and the meaning for each verb found below.

1 contribuirían

Sujeto: ______________________

Significado: ______________________

2 usarías

Sujeto: ______________________

Significado: ______________________

3 daríamos

Sujeto: ______________________

Significado: ______________________

4 diría

Sujeto: ______________________

Significado: ______________________

5 encontraríamos

Sujeto: ______________________

Significado: ______________________

6 hablaría

Sujeto: ______________________

Significado: ______________________

7 pagarías

Sujeto: ______________________

Significado: ______________________

8 apoyarían

Sujeto: ______________________

Significado: ______________________

3B-PRIN-19

Duna and Ashleigh are trying to explain to Emilia's family the tests they need to undergo to see if anyone in the family has been infected with tuberculosis. Ashleigh keeps forgetting words, so Duna helps her out by providing the words she needs. Use the words Duna provides to create complete and logical sentences in the conditional.

Modelo:

ASHLEIGH: La prueba... si usted...

DUNA: (tuberculina) (indicar) (está infectado)

ASHLEIGH: *La prueba de la tuberculina indicaría si usted está infectada.*

1 ASHLEIGH: Emilia, si usted está... que hacerse radiografía....

DUNA: (infectado) (tener) (tórax)

ASHLEIGH: ______________________

____

____

____

____

2 ASHLEIGH: La fotografía, o placa, ... si... hubieran causado... daño...

DUNA: (mostrar) (bacterias) (algún) (pulmones)

ASHLEIGH: ______________________

____

____

____

____

3 ASHLEIGH: El esputo ... que una persona infectada... al toser.

DUNA: (ser) (líquido) (espeso) (botar)

ASHLEIGH: ______________________________

____

____

____

4 ASHLEIGH: Un examen de esputo... si hubiera...

DUNA: (comprobar) (bacterias) (tuberculosis)

ASHLEIGH: ______________________________

____

____

____

3B-PRIN-20

Below is a photo of an accident. Think about what you would or wouldn't do if you were there at the scene. Give at least five examples and remember to use the conditional.

1 ______________________________

____

____

____

2 ______________________________

____

____

____

3 ______________________________

____

____

____

4 ______________________________

____

____

____

5 ______________________________

____

____

____

WHEN TO USE THE CONDITIONAL

Like English, the Spanish language employs the conditional to convey four basic notions: to make a polite request, to express the future from a past perspective, to express probability, and to create conditional sentences.

■ To Make a Polite Request:

Another way to ask someone to do something is to use the conditional.

SPANISH	ENGLISH
¿Me echaría una mano?	Would you give me a hand?
Me gustaría hablar con el doctor.	I would like to speak with the doctor.
¿Podría usted ayudarme?	Would you (be able to) help me?

Of course, this type of request is less direct than a command. Here the conditional is used to soften the request.

■ To Refer to a Future from a Past Perspective:

By using the conditional this way, your intent is to express "would." This use parallels that of the English conditional.

SPANISH	ENGLISH
Juan me dijo que empezaría el tratamiento en un mes.	Juan told me that he would begin treatment in one month.

Be careful not to confuse the "would" indicated by the conditional with that of the imperfect. While the distinction can be blurred in English, it is very clear in Spanish as demonstrated through the use of two different forms.

	SPANISH	ENGLISH
Conditional	Antes de tener sexo con otra persona, aprendería algo de su historia sexual.	Before having sex with another person, I would learn something about his/her sexual history.
Imperfect	Antes de tener sexo con otra persona, aprendía algo de su historia sexual.	Before having sex with another person, I would (used to) learn about his/her sexual history.

- **To Express Probability:**

In this capacity, the conditional is used to make certain assumptions about a past action or state.

SPANISH	ENGLISH
Sufrirían de SIDA.	They were probably suffering from AIDS.
Ya experimentarían síntomas.	They probably were already experiencing symptoms.

- **To Create Conditional Sentences Using "if-clauses":**

This type of sentence requires the presence of *si* and the past (or imperfect) subjunctive. See *Unidad 4b* for a detailed explanation of the past subjunctive. Again, the meaning of the conditional is "would," and it is found in the dependent clause (the one not containing *si*). English also uses the conditional to convey this notion.

SPANISH	ENGLISH
Si yo fuera ella, dejaría de fumar.	If I were she, I would stop smoking.
Si usted tuviera una infección, le dolería mientras orina.	If you had an infection, it would hurt while urinating.

¡A PRACTICAR!

3B-PRIN-21

Match the sentence in Spanish with the correct translation.

1 ¿Esperarías hasta que estuvieras lista para tener relaciones sexuales?
2 ¿Podrías mantener a un niño tú solo?
3 Si se besaran con la boca cerrada no se infectarían.
4 Probablemente ellos no usarían control de natalidad.
5 Si yo fuera ella, haría una cita con el médico.
6 Yo hablaría con mis hijos si tuviera tiempo.

___ **a** I would speak with my children if I had time.
___ **b** If I were she, I would make an appointment with the doctor.
___ **c** If you kissed each other with your mouths closed you would not get infected.
___ **d** They probably would not use birth control.
___ **e** Would you be able to take care of a child on your own?
___ **f** Would you wait until you were ready to have sexual relations?

3B-PRIN-22

Ashleigh has been very busy all day. Below is a sample of some of her conversations. Read the sentences below. Explain which type of conditional each one represents. Then, translate each one into English.

1 Yo consultaría con un médico si notara flujo anormal del pene (o la vagina).
Tipo de condicional: ______________________ ***Traducción:*** ______________________
____

2 Según lo que dijo el médico, sin recibir tratamiento, la gonorrea podría causar esterilidad, artritis y problemas cardiacos.
Tipo de condicional: ______________________ ***Traducción:*** ______________________
____

3 Me imagino que ellos estarían muy contentos al saber que los resultados fueron negativos.
Tipo de condicional: ______________________ ***Traducción:*** ______________________
____

4 ¿Me dirías cuantas parejas has tenido?
Tipo de condicional: ______________________ ***Traducción:*** ______________________
____

5 La enfermera me explicó que tendría una sensación de ardor al orinar.
Tipo de condicional: ______________________ ***Traducción:*** ______________________
____

6 La irritación, la inflamación o la sensibilidad en el área genital son algunos de los síntomas que experimentaría si tuviera una enfermedad venérea.
Tipo de condicional: ______________________ ***Traducción:*** ______________________
____

3B-PRIN-23

Emilia might have tuberculosis, but she is afraid to be tested. Carmina explains to her the importance of having the test done. Read the paragraph below and rewrite it, substituting the conditional wherever possible. Be careful —the conditional cannot be used in every instance.

"Un resultado positivo en la prueba de tuberculina señala que el paciente ha estado en contacto con la enfermedad y tiene bacterias inactivas en el sistema. Decimos que este paciente está infectado aunque no muestre síntomas de la enfermedad y ni siquiera sepa él mismo que está infectado. Si toma las medicinas adecuadas todos los días, mantiene el cuerpo fuerte y es capaz de defenderse de la infección, la tuberculosis no se desarrollará. En un paciente fuerte que está bajo tratamiento, las defensas del cuerpo controlan las bacterias inactivas, aislándolas del resto del sistema. Las bacterias pueden permanecer vivas, pero inactivas, dentro de un cuerpo por años. Cuando el paciente descubre que está infectado, debe prevenir la enfermedad. Mientras estén inactivas las bacterias que causan la tuberculosis, no pueden hacerle daño al paciente ni contagiar a otros."

____

____

____

____

____

____

____

____

____

3B-PRIN-24

What would you do or how would you feel in the following situations? Use the conditional to complete the thoughts below in a logical manner. Provide at least two possibilities for each.

1 Si supiera que mi hijo de 16 años va a ser padre...

a ____

____

b ____

____

2 Si mi pareja me dijera que tiene una enfermedad venérea...

a ____

____

b ____

____

3 Si mi mejor amigo me dijera que sufre de HIV...

a ____

____

b ____

____

4 Si el doctor me informara que tengo tuberculosis...

a ____

____

b ____

____

CONCEPTO IMPORTANTE: FORMAL VS. INFORMAL SPEECH

One of the first things students of Spanish learn is that Spanish uses different forms of address. In other words, we speak differently in linguistic terms to children, friends, and family members than we do to patients, strangers, or elders. While the difference between *tú* and *usted* is very easy to grasp intellectually, actually conjugating verbs appropriately is often another matter. English speakers of Spanish often give themselves mental tongue-lashings after speaking informally to people with whom they should have used *usted*. Take heart: most Spanish speakers are aware that this distinction does not come naturally to English speakers and are not offended when the wrong form is used!

What We Know

As you know, the Spanish language has two forms of address: formal and informal. Unlike English, Spanish distinguishes between formal and informal subjects. In other words, some subjects require the *usted* form and others require the *tú* form. The *usted* form is used to distance yourself from the other party or parties with whom you are communicating; therefore, if you are in a position of authority over someone or if someone has authority over you, the *usted* form would be the most appropriate choice. Another reason for the use of the formal is as an expression of respect; for example, you would use this form when speaking with someone noticeably older than you. Finally, you might opt to use the *usted* when you are communicating with people with whom you are unfamiliar or during first encounters.

SPANISH	ENGLISH
Buenas tardes señor. Por favor, pase usted.	Good afternoon, sir. Please, come in.
Dígame doctor, ¿fueron positivos los resultados de las pruebas?	Tell me, doctor, were the test results positive?
Es un placer conocerla. Espere un momento y busco a su hermano.	A pleasure to meet you. Wait a moment and I will look for your brother.

The *tú* form, on the other hand, represents familiarity and is normally used when communication occurs between friends or when the social status of the parties involved is equal. Informal forms of address are also common between members of the immediate family, as native speakers of English understand the family unit. Finally, adults make use of the *tú* form when addressing children.

SPANISH	ENGLISH
Alex, tómate unas aspirinas para el dolor. –Ya me tomé cuatro, Ángela.	Alex, take some aspirins for the pain. –I already took four, Angela.
Rafa, mi amor, ten cuidado con el señor Anderson.	Rafa, my love, be careful with Mr. Anderson.
Hola, Pepito, déjame escuchar tu pecho.	Hello, Pepito. Let me listen to your chest.

The Difficulty

Understanding why a particular form of address is used is not a difficult concept for language students; however, putting what one has learned into practice is a horse of a different color. Even after overcoming the experience of choosing a verb conjugation —any verb conjugation!— in a conversation, only to discover that the choice was incorrect, many learners still have trouble knowing when to use the formal and when to use the informal. Most of the difficulty is encountered when trying to apply the guidelines provided in the previous section to specific contexts. Sometimes contexts will overlap, and which form should be used is unclear. A closer examination of some of the relationships between the people who work at the clinic will help to clarify the difference in use.

- First, there is the relationship between Jaime and Federico. Federico works part-time for the clinic and Jaime is its director; therefore, you would expect Federico to use *usted* whenever addressing Jaime. Jaime, on the other hand, is Federico's boss. The two work together, but are not friends. Furthermore, Federico is an older gentleman. Consequently, Jaime employs *usted* when speaking with Federico. This example fits well into the categories provided.
- Now let's take a look at the relationship between Duna and Federico. Since the two are friends, you might expect them to use the *tú* command when speaking with one another; however, this is not the case. Both employ the *usted* command. First, Duna and Federico are not close friends. Second, Federico is noticeably older than Duna. Third, they are members of the opposite sex. All of these factors combined demonstrate that the formal command is the most appropriate choice.
- Finally, let's examine the relationship between Alex and Ángela. The two are colleagues, but Ángela is actually Alex's boss. Consequently, you might expect them to use the *usted* command when addressing one another. However, they are friends and see each other in social situations. As a direct result, the informal *tú* command is appropriate.

True, some contexts will be more problematic. Just remember to examine the roles of everyone participating in the conversation. If someone has more than one role, choose the one most relevant to the context at hand. Another method is to use the *usted* command to start out with and follow up with an invitation to use the informal command if you feel the situation merits familiarity. You also can listen for cues from the individual with whom you are speaking.

Strategies

Try these simple strategies to help you better understand how to use formal and informal commands:

- Remember to make the listener aware of the fact that you are giving a command. Use hand signals and/or pauses as guides for the listener.
- Before attempting to use a command, consider your role in the conversation, as well as the role of the listener. Remember that formal commands are used to distance yourself from the listener.
- Listen to the person or groups of people with whom you are speaking. Try to pick up clues as to how they view your status through the use of informal and formal commands.
- Be aware that in Latin American Spanish there is only one type of command used to speak to more than one person: *ustedes*, the plural form of the formal command.

¡A PRACTICAR!

3B-PRIN-25

Select the appropriate command form you would use when speaking to the individuals or groups of individuals listed below.

____ **1** el cura de la iglesia local

a tú **b** usted **c** ustedes

____ **2** un buen colega de trabajo

a tú **b** usted **c** ustedes

____ **3** los hijos de tu amigo

a tú **b** usted **c** ustedes

____ **4** una niña

a tú **b** usted **c** ustedes

____ **5** un nuevo cliente

a tú **b** usted **c** ustedes

____ **6** un paciente que también es amigo

a tú **b** usted **c** ustedes

____ **7** un paciente mayor

a tú **b** usted **c** ustedes

____ **8** Los Juárez

a tú **b** usted **c** ustedes

3B-PRIN-26

Read the sentences below and indicate which type of command is used. Then, explain why.

1 Laura, no te asustes, nos tienes a todos nosotros para apoyarte. Somos familia.

Tipo de mandato: ____________________

¿Por qué?: ____________________

____

2 Gracias por verme, doctora Estrada. Permítame presentarle a mi esposa.

Tipo de mandato: ____________________

¿Por qué?: ____________________

____

3 Alex, no me hables en inglés. Sabes que no lo manejo muy bien.

Tipo de mandato: ____________________

¿Por qué?: ____________________

____

4 Diviértanse esta noche y que lo pasen bien bailando salsa.

Tipo de mandato: ____________________

¿Por qué?: ____________________

____

5 Buenos días, doctor Cuenca. Por favor, ayúdeme a explicarle a mi madre que todo está bien.

Tipo de mandato: ____________________

¿Por qué?: ____________________

____

3B-PRIN-27

Create formal and informal commands by combining the elements found below. Don't forget to conjugate the verbs.

1 Víctor y Manuel / cubrir la boca antes de toser

____

____

____

2 Mamá / no darme aquel jarabe con sabor a cereza

____

____

____

3 Bueno mis queridos angelitos / no comportarse mal

____

____

____

4 Por favor doctor / repetir las instrucciones

____

____

____

5 Carmen / traernos las pastillas de la farmacia

____

____

____

6 Señor González / ponerse de pie

____

____

____

3B-PRIN-28

You are meeting with several different people today. Use the information provided below to help you create sentences that reflect the proper use of the formal and informal commands.

El Señor López Es mayor de edad. Es viudo. Sufre de cáncer.
Los señores Plata y García Vienen a revisar el presupuesto de la clínica.
Marta Tiene diecisiete años y le interesa aprender acerca de los distintos tipos de control de natalidad.
Los Sánchez Son los padres de William.
William Es un niño pequeño. Es VIH positivo. Nació prematuro.
La señora Perón Sufre de diabetes. Tiene treinta y cinco años. Es buena amiga de Duna.

1 ______________________________

____

2 ______________________________

____

3 ______________________________

____

4 ______________________________

____

5 ______________________________

____

6 ______________________________

____

7 ______________________________

____

8 ______________________________

____

3B-PRIN-29

One suggestion that Federico received to help him cope with the guilt of leaving his wife and children behind was to write them a letter containing everything he wishes he could say to them if he were there, regardless of whether he decides to send it. Help him to write his letter. Keep in mind the use of commands.

Querida familia:

Primero, perdónenme todos por no poder estar allí... ________________

SELF-REFLECTION

1. How does one determine which construction is the most appropriate?

Remember that the Spanish language often has several constructions available to express similar concepts. In the case of orders or requests, consider the type of order or request that you are making. Do you wish to express yourself indirectly or directly? Are you conversing with one person or more than one? Are you participating in the action? Consider the social setting in which the events are taking place. All of these factors will help you to select the most appropriate construction with which to convey your thoughts as precisely as possible.

2. What is the best way to learn the command forms?

Command forms actually are taken from other tenses or structures found in the Spanish language. Both the present indicative and the present subjunctive serve as the basis for all forms. If you learn these other tenses and structures well, you should have little or no difficulty managing the command forms. In addition, most of the spelling or stem-changes that occur in these forms also occur in other tenses or structures that you have studied; therefore, you should already be familiar with them. Still, memorization, practice, and time are your best tools for mastering these forms.

3. Is the position of the object pronoun important?

Yes, the placement of the object pronoun is extremely important. Not only does its position allow you to determine which pronoun is being used, but in the case of the affirmative command, it also serves to signal to the listener that a specific type of command was expressed. The placement of the object pronoun helps to guide the listener.

FOLLOW-UP TIPS

- Look to tenses and forms previously studied. More complicated and complex constructions usually build upon the basic ones. If you think you recognize a form, chances are that you have seen it before.
- Consider the social situation when trying to determine which is the most appropriate language structure. What are the relationships of the people involved? If there is more than one possibility, which is the most relevant for the present context?
- Keep in mind the importance of non-verbal cues. These cues often signal to the speaker that the idea being expressed is different from the previous one and that the content of the conversation is about to change. Furthermore, these cues can underscore the importance of the information that is about to be expressed, directing the listener to pay close attention.

DO YOU REMEMBER?

Answer the questions based on the explanations found in *Principios Unidad 3b* of the textbook. If you found any section particularly difficult, go back and try some of the exercises again. There are also links to Spanish language materials on the *Recursos* website.

1 What are the endings for the formal commands?

2 Give two examples of spelling changes that occur in the formal commands.

3 What are the formal command forms for the verb *dar*?

4 Which command type uses different forms depending on whether the command is affirmative or negative?

5 What are the irregular forms for the affirmative *tú* commands?

6 How do you form the affirmative *nosotros* command of a reflexive verb?

7 Where are object pronouns placed when the command is affirmative?

8 Which type of command would be used if a receptionist were speaking with a client?

9 You form the conditional by adding the appropriate endings to what?

10 How do you form the conditional for the verb *hablar*?

11 Which type of command would a child use when addressing an adult?

FOOD FOR THOUGHT

The following questions are intended to serve as a springboard for discussion. Think about them as you read the story.

- How can I develop trusting and respectful relationships with my patients and clients?
- How can I recognize and challenge my own assumptions?
- How can I learn to recognize my patients' and clients' strengths and to build on teachable moments?
- How can I become partners with colleagues who are bridges across culture, with other organizations in the community that have similar interests and with members of the community I hope to serve?

NOTES FROM THE FIELD

Ruth Efird is a nurse practitioner working in a public health department.

Six Hispanic ladies came to the Breast and Cervical Cancer Clinic accompanied by a church friend. Several had never had a pelvic or breast exam. They were dressed in church clothes and were very quiet. Our health educator and health clinician began by talking about breast cancer and doing a breast self-exam. The ladies were polite and very quiet until the breast models with lumps were passed around for them to feel. The mood changed; the women began to laugh as they passed the breast model from one to another. Then, they began to ask questions and share their personal concerns. Doing individual breast exams was much easier now that the women understood the objective and the exam.

Each woman left the exam room laughing and joking with the others. Everybody was more relaxed. The women were provided sack lunches, and they trooped off together for their first mammograms.

In this short interval, I learned the value of social support and group health education. The event became an annual social event with health prevention —a culturally appropriate moment for reaching so-called "hard-to-reach populations."

DISCUSSION QUESTIONS

Ruth describes a situation when she had to talk about a potentially very sensitive topic with middle-aged Hispanic women.

1 What can you learn from Ruth's comments that many of the women had never had a pelvic or breast exam before, that they came in their church clothes, that they were very quiet and polite?

2 What happened that changed the mood?

3 What do you think about Ruth's comment linking a "nice social event" with health prevention?

COMPROBACIÓN

DVD

Las preguntas de Comprobación *están diseñadas para evaluar tu habilidad de usar lo que has aprendido, en situaciones nuevas y diferentes. Aunque el contexto todavía es limitado y las respuestas están restringidas y guiadas, debes interpretar más.*

SECCIÓN A

¿Qué pasa en la Historia*? Escoge las palabras que completan mejor la oración. ¡Cuidado con la gramática!*

1 Carmina habla con Eliodoro, el joven paciente que temía haberse contagiado de SIDA y le dice: "Los mosquitos no son portadores del SIDA, (créame / créale / me crea)." Sin embargo, el joven todavía tiene miedo y le dice a ella: "Por favor, (hágame / me hace / me haga) un examen de sangre porque quiero estar muy seguro."

2 Después del examen, descubrimos que Eliodoro no tiene ningún problema y Ashleigh le dice: "No (preocúpese / preocuparse / se preocupe) más por este asunto.

3 A los jóvenes trabajadores les preocupa mucho el SIDA porque cada día hay más casos entre los inmigrantes. Si supiéramos por qué hay más casos ahora, (podíamos / podríamos / pudiéramos) evitar algunos de ellos. La (culpa / idea / razón) la tienen las condiciones de vida y la falta de información."

4 Por otro lado, Eliodoro está casado y su esposa espera un bebé. Carmina le aconseja: "Su esposa lo necesita, (cuídela / la cuida / la cuide) para que su bebé sea saludable. Tan pronto nazca el bebé, (regresa / regresan / regrese) a vernos y le haremos otro examen para estar seguros. No es necesario preocuparnos ahora, pero (no / quizás / sí) es importante que nos comunique cualquier cosa que cambie en su estado de salud."

SECCIÓN B

Estas oraciones describen por qué Rafa está investigando a Hugo Anderson y por qué Ángela está preocupada sobre esta situación. Escoge las palabras que mejor terminan cada oración.

abusa	errores
cabo	principio
comparten	quejas
consigues	regalos
defiende	regaños
equivocar	seria

Ángela le contó a Carmina que Rafa está investigando a Hugo Anderson porque piensa que él **(1)** ______________ de los inmigrantes. Ella teme que Rafa se pueda **(2)** ____________ y que se meta en líos muy serios con las autoridades. Sin embargo, Ángela piensa que es posible que Rafa tenga razón, al fin y al **(3)** _______________ los inmigrantes viven en malas condiciones y a veces varias familias **(4)** ____________________ una vivienda. La situación es **(5)** _____________ en muchos casos. Carmina dice que ha tratado de quejarse a las autoridades, pero hasta ahora sus **(6)** ____________________ no están dando resultado.

VIH/SIDA entre los hispanos o latinos

Datos de los CDC sobre el VIH/SIDA — Agosto de 2008

La epidemia del VIH/SIDA es una seria amenaza para la comunidad hispana o latina. En el 2005, el VIH/SIDA fue la cuarta causa principal de muertes entre hombres y mujeres de origen hispano o latino entre los 35 y 44 años [1].

LAS CIFRAS

El VIH/SIDA en el 2006

- Los hispanos o latinos representaron el 18% de los 35,314 nuevos diagnósticos de VIH/SIDA en los 33 estados que cuentan con sistemas prolongados de notificación nominal y confidencial del VIH [2].
- Los hispanos o latinos representaron el 17% de las 491,727 personas que viven con VIH/SIDA (entre las que se incluyen niños) en los 33 estados [2].
- En los hombres hispanos o latinos que viven con VIH/SIDA, las formas más comunes de transmisión del VIH fueron (en orden) el contacto sexual con otros hombres, el consumo de drogas inyectables y el contacto heterosexual de alto riesgo. En las mujeres hispanas o latinas que viven con VIH/SIDA, las formas más comunes de transmisión fueron el contacto heterosexual de alto riesgo y el consumo de drogas inyectables [2].

Raza o grupo étnico de las personas (incluidos los niños) a quienes se les diagnosticó el VIH/SIDA en el 2006

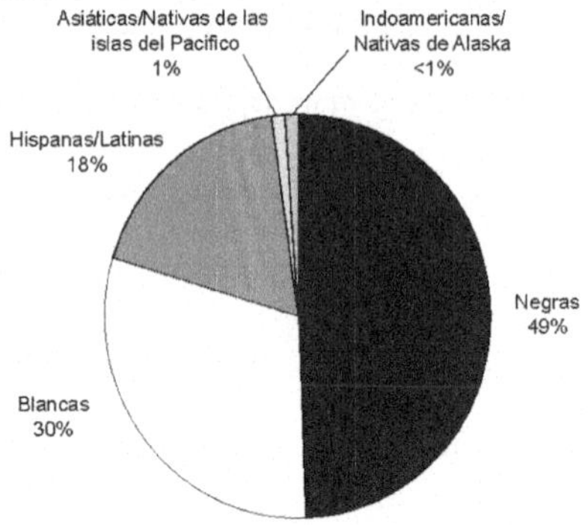

Núm. = 35,314

Datos basados en información de 33 estados que cuentan con sistemas prolongados de notificación nominal y confidencial del VIH.

El SIDA en el 2006

- Los hispanos o latinos representaron el 19% de los nuevos diagnósticos de SIDA y el 19% de todas las personas que viven con SIDA en los 50 estados y el Distrito de Columbia [2].
- La tasa de diagnósticos de SIDA en los hispanos o latinos fue la segunda más alta de todas las tasas de diagnósticos en adultos y adolescentes de todos los grupos raciales y étnicos [2].
- Aunque los hispanos o latinos comprenden solo el 13% de la población de los Estados Unidos, representan el 16% de los 982,498 casos de diagnósticos de SIDA en los 50 estados y el Distrito de Columbia desde el comienzo de la epidemia [2].
- Para finales del 2006, se calcula que habrían muerto 80,690 hispanos o latinos con SIDA en los 50 estados y el Distrito de Columbia [2].

RETOS PARA LOS ESFUERZOS DE PREVENCIÓN

Una variedad de factores culturales, socioeconómicos y relacionados con la salud contribuyen a propagar la epidemia del VIH y constituyen un reto para su prevención en la comunidad hispana o latina de los Estados Unidos.

- Los **factores de riesgo conductuales** relacionados con la infección por el VIH varían de acuerdo al país de origen. Por ejemplo, la información disponible parece indicar que los hispanos o latinos nacidos en Puerto Rico tienen más probabilidades que otros grupos de hispanos o latinos de contraer el VIH debido al consumo de drogas inyectables y el contacto heterosexual de alto riesgo. Por el contrario, el contacto sexual con otros hombres es la causa principal de infecciones por el VIH entre hombres hispanos o latinos nacidos en Centroamérica, Sudamérica, Cuba, México y los Estados Unidos [2].
- Las mujeres y hombres hispanos o latinos tienen más probabilidades de infectarse por el VIH por causa de tener **relaciones sexuales con hombres** [2]. Por lo tanto, el personal encargado de los programas de prevención necesita abordar los temas específicos para el grupo de hispanos o latinos al cual se dirige cada programa en particular: por ejemplo, el uso de condones (en hombres

1-800-CDC-INFO (232-4636)
En Inglés, en Español
24 horas/día
cdcinfo@cdc.gov
http://www.cdc.gov/hiv

CONTESTA LAS SIGUIENTES PREGUNTAS:

1 ¿Cuáles son las formas más comunes de transmisión del VIH entre los hombres hispanos? ¿Y entre las mujeres hispanas?

2 En 2006, los hispanos constituían el 13% de la población de los Estados Unidos, pero ¿qué porcentaje representaban en cuanto a los casos diagnosticados de SIDA?

3 Según la lectura, ¿cuáles son los retos para su prevención?

y mujeres) o el balance de poder en las relaciones (especialmente en las mujeres).

- El **consumo de drogas inyectables** continúa siendo un factor de riesgo entre los hispanos o latinos, especialmente los que viven en Puerto Rico [2]. Los usuarios ocasionales y crónicos de sustancias estupefacientes tienen más probabilidades de realizar conductas sexuales de alto riesgo, tales como las relaciones sexuales sin protección, cuando están bajo la influencia de las drogas o el alcohol.
- Las tasas de **enfermedades transmitidas sexualmente**, que pueden aumentar la posibilidad de contraer el VIH, son más altas en los hispanos o latinos. En el 2006, la tasa de infecciones por clamidia entre los hispanos o latinos fue cerca de 3 veces más alta que la tasa de los blancos (no hispanos o latinos), y las tasas de gonorrea y sífilis en los hispanos o latinos fue cerca del doble de la tasa de los blancos [3].
- Algunas **creencias culturales** pueden influir en el riesgo de infección por el VIH. Por ejemplo, entre los hombres, el machismo tiene implicaciones positivas para la prevención del VIH, como la fortaleza y la protección de la familia; sin embargo, el demostrar la masculinidad mediante el poder y la dominación puede llevar a los hombres hispanos o latinos, tanto heterosexuales como homosexuales, a realizar conductas sexuales riesgosas.
- Una mayor **aculturación en la cultura estadounidense** tiene efectos tanto negativos (adopción de conductas que aumentan el riesgo de adquirir la infección por el VIH) como positivos (comunicación con las parejas sobre las relaciones sexuales sin riesgo) en las conductas de los hispanos o latinos relacionadas con la salud.
- Más de 1 de cada 5 hispanos o latinos (21.9%) vive en la **pobreza** [4]. Los problemas asociados con la pobreza, entre los que se encuentran el desempleo, la falta de educación formal, el tener seguro de salud inadecuado y el acceso limitado a servicios de cuidados de salud de alta calidad, pueden incrementar el riesgo de adquirir el VIH.
- Los **patrones de migración**, la **estructura social**, las **barreras del idioma** y la **falta de acceso a la atención médica habitual** entre los inmigrantes hispanos o latinos transeúntes pueden afectar el conocimiento sobre los servicios de prevención y de atención médica para el VIH/SIDA y dificultar el acceso a los mismos.

QUÉ ESTÁN HACIENDO LOS CDC

Para reducir la incidencia de infecciones por el VIH, los CDC publicaron en el 2006 las recomendaciones: *Revised Recommendations for HIV Testing of Adults, Adolescents, and Pregnant Women in Health-Care Settings.* Estas nuevas recomendaciones aconsejan realizar las pruebas habituales del VIH en adultos, adolescentes y mujeres embarazadas en centros de atención médica en los Estados Unidos. Adicionalmente los CDC

- Realizan investigaciones epidemiológicas y conductuales centradas en los hispanos o latinos.
- Apoyan los esfuerzos para reducir las disparidades en la salud que se presentan en las comunidades de personas pertenecientes a minorías raciales o grupos étnicos expuestos a un alto riesgo de infección por el VIH.
- Ofrecen intervenciones con bases científicas y eficaces a las organizaciones que prestan servicios a la población de hispanos o latinos y están diseñando otras intervenciones conductuales eficaces para hispanos o latinos que tienen un riesgo alto de infectarse por el VIH.
- Fomentan la capacidad para establecer programas dirigidos a hispanos o latinos mediante las asociaciones con organizaciones nacionales, regionales y no gubernamentales.

En el 2006, los CDC otorgaron 56 subvenciones a organizaciones comunitarias en los Estados Unidos y Puerto Rico que se dirigen principalmente a los hispanos o latinos. Los CDC también proporcionan ayuda financiera a organizaciones que ofrecen servicios a esta población a través de los departamentos de salud estatales, territoriales y locales. Además, los CDC brindan capacitación para investigadores que pertenecen a minorías raciales o étnicas y en el 2002 lanzaron la Iniciativa para la Investigación del VIH/SIDA en las Minorías, (*Minority HIV/AIDS Research Initiative* o MARI) para fomentar asociaciones entre epidemiólogos e investigadores de los CDC que son miembros de razas o grupos étnicos minoritarios y que trabajan con comunidades de color. Los CDC invierten dos millones de dólares al año en este programa y desde 2003 han auspiciado el trabajo de 13 nuevos investigadores en 12 sitios en todo el país.

REFERENCIAS

1. CDC. WISQARS [Web-based Injury Statistics Query and Reporting System] leading causes of death reports, 2005. http://webapp.cdc.gov/sasweb/ncipc/leadcaus10.html.
2. CDC. HIV/AIDS Surveillance Report, 2006. Vol 18. US DHHS, CDC; 2008:1-55. http://www.cdc.gov/hiv/topics/surveillance/resources/reports.
3. CDC. Sexually Transmitted Disease Surveillance, 2006. Atlanta: US DHHS, CDC; 2007. http://www.cdc.gov/std/stats/toc2006.htm.
4. DeNavas-Walt C, et al. Income, Poverty, and Health Insurance Coverage in the United States: 2004. Washington, DC: US Government Printing Office; 2005. Current Population Reports P60-229. http://www.census.gov/prod/2005pubs/p60-229.pdf.

RECURSOS SOBRE EL VIH/SIDA

CDC VIH/SIDA
http://www.cdc.gov/hiv
Recursos de los CDC sobre el VIH/SIDA

CDC-INFO
1-800-232-4636
Información acerca de los riesgos personales y adónde ir para hacerse la prueba del VIH

Centro Nacional de Recursos para la Prueba del VIH de los CDC
http://www.hivtest.org
Lugares donde se hacen las pruebas del VIH

Centro Nacional de Prevención e Información de los CDC
1-800-458-5231
http://www.cdcnpin.org
Recursos, asistencia técnica y publicaciones de los CDC

AIDSinfo
1-800-448-0440
http://www.aidsinfo.nih.gov
Recursos sobre el tratamiento del VIH/SIDA y ensayos clínicos

Datos de los CDC sobre el VIH/SIDA — VIH/SIDA entre los hispanos

To read this article online, go to www.yalebooks.com/salud.

4 ¿Qué hacen los CDC para reducir la incidencia de infecciones por el VIH entre la población hispana?

Práctica con los mandatos:

Imagina que estás prestando servicio en una comunidad latina y tienes que preparar una lista para un grupo de adolescentes sobre la prevención del SIDA. Escribe diez mandatos, cada uno de ellos en forma tanto afirmativa como negativa (20 en total).

Modelo: No compartan jeringuillas nunca.

¡A CONVERSAR!

PERSONAJES

DVD *We meet Eliodoro in this segment. He introduces himself, and tells us a bit about himself: he tells us about his background, why he is in the U.S., and talks a little about his pregnant wife, Milagros.*

Eliodoro

Role-play a conversation between Eliodoro and one of his friends in which Eliodoro gives him the latest news, and then shares his plans for the future (use the future tense). Use the sentences below as a springboard for your conversation.

AMIGO: Ay, Eliodoro, ¿estás listo? Ser padre es...
ELIODORO: ¡Claro que sí! Seré el mejor padre...

¡A RESUMIR!

EPISODIO

Imagine that your instructor has asked you and your partner to give an oral presentation to the class about the episode. Discuss at least three of the following scenes from this episode with a classmate:

- The argument between Ángela and Rafa
- The conversation between Carmina and Laura
- The conversation between Jaime and Federico
- Eliodoro's health concerns and his conversation with Carmina
- Alex taking aspirin in the bathroom, and the conversation between Ángela and Jaime

APLICACIÓN

CONVERSAR

DVD

Watch this segment, and then discuss the following topics with a classmate:

Laura and Federico meet

a ¿Qué debe hacer una persona como Laura para conseguir un trabajo? ¿Qué tipo de trabajo puede hacer ella ahora, sin hablar muy bien el inglés? ¿Has trabajado tú con hispanohablantes? Si no, ¿conoces a alguien que sí haya trabajado con hispanohablantes?

b ¿Cómo aprendiste español? ¿Por qué estudias español? ¿Qué quieres hacer en el futuro?

ANALIZAR

DVD

Watch this segment and answer the following questions:

—¿Con quién habla?

—¿De qué habla?

Eliodoro has a telephone call

Role-play a conversation between Eliodoro and the person to whom he is speaking, basing your role-play on what Eliodoro says in this segment. You might begin by "filling in the blanks", providing dialogue for the other speaker. Expand on their conversation —add some original dialogue.

ELIODORO: Sí, estamos bien. Digo, ahí vamos.

AMIGO: ¿Y Mila? ¿Ya llegó de México?

ELIODORO: Sí, sí, eso está bien, ella llegó bien.

EN LA PRÁCTICA

How to give bad news

DVD

In this segment, Carmina gives Federico the bad news that he is HIV positive.

Carmina and Federico

Role-play a conversation between Carmina and Federico a few weeks or months in the future, after this scene. This time Federico will have several questions for Carmina. What will he want to know? What kind of advice should Carmina give him? Notice Carmina's use of formal commands in this conversation. Include formal commands in your dialogue, having Carmina tell Federico what he needs to do to improve his health.

FEDERICO: Doctora, hace tiempo usted me habló un poco del VIH. Ahora me gustaría hacerle algunas preguntas.

CARMINA: Claro, Federico. ¿Qué le gustaría saber?

LENGUA

DVD

In this segment, Rafa and Ángela discuss his concerns about the Latino community, and the possible abuses perpetrated on this community by Hugo Anderson.

¿Cuáles son los argumentos de Rafa contra Hugo Anderson? Escribe una lista de siete u ocho oraciones que Rafa puede usar para hablar con Hugo Anderson. Todas deben ser órdenes (mandatos). Menciona los siguientes puntos:

- el estado de las viviendas
- la responsabilidad social y económica
- las razones para mejorar la situación
- las condiciones que contribuyen al estado de casas

Después de escribir su lista, Rafa habla con Ángela. Ella le explica que sería mejor hablar con Hugo Anderson, y no darle órdenes. Rafa decide que Ángela tiene razón. Pero antes de hablar con Hugo Anderson, Rafa quiere ensayar *(practice)* una conversación con él. Representa una conversación entre Rafa y Ángela sobre las cosas de tu lista.

MÁS ALLÁ

Could you imagine writing a paper without capital letters, punctuation marks, and spaces? Even worse, could you imagine having to read that paper? Only the writer would be able to make sense of what was written. The reader would be lost in what would seem to be a never-ending stream of letters joined together without rhyme or reason. How would the reader know where one idea ended and another began? To eliminate this type of hit or miss approach you use visual cues, such as periods, commas, semicolons, etc., to let the reader know how to categorize and interpret the thoughts presented to him or her. Without these cues written communication would be very difficult.

Speech functions in a manner very similar to the written word. How do you let someone know that the conversation is about to change direction? Are you able to hold someone's attention in a conversation? What do you do to maintain the listener's interest? Gestures, facial expressions, pauses, and tone of voice are very common devices used to provide clues that help the listener follow your train of thought more easily. Without these cues it would be difficult to hold a conversation with anyone, let alone maintain his or her attention.

If you want to ensure that your message is understood, you need to make certain that your message is clear. Sometimes you rely on repetition and redundancy to make your point.

However, in face-to-face interaction, other, more effective tools are available. The tools enable you to separate and highlight the important aspect of the conversation; you point, you raise your hand, you raise your eyebrows, you pause, or you alter the tone of your voice. Whatever your method, your goal is to let the listener know that the next thought is different from the previous one. Engage your audience and make them active listeners.

ENTREVISTA

DVD

Read this summary in English of what both Carla Sánchez and Marilyn Brito say in their interviews before you watch them on the DVD. Remember that these interviews were conducted to include "authentic language" on the DVD. This means that the interviews are unscripted and at a natural conversational pace. Use the English summary to guide you.

Carla Sánchez (Carmina)

In fact my last project was a movie that became the third most successful Swiss project in Europe. And thanks to God, I had the chance to have a terrific role and to be part of a spectacular production that has changed my life.

[In the movie] I was a Cuban, [putting on accent] "Listen to me, kiddo, how are you?" She was a very —I loved that character because she wanted to leave Cuba and she did the impossible to do it. I'm not going to tell you how it comes out because that gives away the end of the movie, but everything was in preparation for that. During and after, the experience was marvelous in every way. A great experience for me as an actress because it was the first time that I had the chance to develop a really complete character. It also gave me a lot of experience in filmmaking and taught me a lot about helping the character and things that help me as an actress.

Lots of times people think that being an actress involves nothing more than learning the book and saying the lines but it turns out that it's a lot more, a lot more. That's why I take it so seriously and I like it so much because it's not just about giving me the book and learning the lines and, wow, that's it. It's a lot more than that. It's researching the character, finding out why she says what she says and why she does what she does, getting reactions, finding the sentimental part, the fragile part, the strong part so that people can connect with you, right? And so they say, "OK, that doesn't seem much like me, but that thing she did there, that's a lot like me." And, "Look, that seems a lot like that girl I met the other day," or, "Look, she's like that person," or, "She's just like me!" I like it a lot when people connect with me as a character.

I'm romantic, I'm very romantic. I think that as time goes by the romantic part —I am still a romantic but in a different way from before. Before I thought a lot about the prince that was going to come on his horse to rescue me from the tower... but not now. Now the prince has to have his feet a little more on the ground! Carmina is a romantic of the type who likes horses and blue-blooded princes, and she has this love for helping out her people, Hispanics, the Latino people. And in that she is a lot like me because I love to help people. I love to help people in general, but if those people are Latinos I like it even more. I feel like I've done my good deed for the day, you know? So in that regard she's a lot like me. And she has responsibilities in her life, with her cousin, and that seems to me to be very important. But at the same time she has a certain emptiness. You see, because someone trying to find someone is all well and good, but she has to be part of the culture. And it turns out that she's not married and she's going on 30 and in Latin culture, if you're not married by 30, you're finished! That's what I bring, what Carmina brings, from her mom, her family, and everything that her cousin tells her.

I love Venezuela. And I also like the United States. If I could work there, be there for a time working for X number of months but return here, that would be ideal. Unfortunately my country, well, it has a lot of insecurities and like other Latin American countries, we have our faults, you know? That's why I'm living here. But I love my people, I love Venezuelan *rumbas*. The beaches are spectacular with the fish right there. The sand, the sun —it's the ultimate. Ah, *arepas* with white cheese! That's another thing that slays me, for sure. And my favorite dish is fried plantains with white cheese. Divine! I love it.

Marilyn Brito (Laura)

I'm —I was born in Chicago but when I was very small I moved to Miami, so I consider myself a Miami native. I'm half Cuban, half Spanish, so I have a little bit of everything in me. In some respects I'm VERY Cuban, but in other respects I'm VERY Spanish. And in some other respects I'm very American. As I put it, "I'm a mutt." A little bit of everything.

I'm an actress. I consider that I work in everything but that I do it all full-time. I work as an actress doing theater, movies, lots of commercials, and all this is very fulfilling because I like to create stories. Or put another way, I love to live conning people. I also write because I like the creative part of creating stories and I like to write a lot. I write short stories, essays, short things because I don't have the patience to write something long. Some day, maybe. And I'm also a professor. I have a doctorate in social psychology from George Washington and I'm a part time professor, an "adjunct professor" as they say in English —I don't know how to say it in Spanish. So that I live by these three, combining the three things. It keeps me sharp, prepared, and energetic!

I'm not that different from Laura. I think not. There are some things in Laura that are very me. There are, perhaps, like I was when I was younger, like going out, going to parties. But in life there's a time for everything, right? And I went through that, but I still carry it in me. I'm a Gemini, so that I have two faces and in order to draw out Laura, I went a lot into my youth and into things that I wanted to do but perhaps didn't do. I'm actually a little shy. And I allowed myself, with the character of Laura, to get rid of that timidity and to put it all aside and be the person that I admire and be one of those people who's a little more adventuresome, a little more like, "Here I am!"

It's so difficult to work with someone so closely if you don't get along. It's happened to me [but Miguel René Moreno] was so nice to me, such a great person, so open to exploring that I instantly felt comfortable. And from the beginning we have spent a lot of time together, talking a lot, we got to know each other better and developed that intimacy so I felt very comfortable with him. Because that comes, that grows, it's not something that happens one day —with him I "clicked" and had instant chemistry and we could bring that to the scene. Yes, I like him. [He's a] great person.

I think that Alex's machismo is really socio-cultural, it's something learned, the boss, what a man has to be like. But inside he's profoundly not like that because he's a real person who loves Laura a lot, but the only way he's seen —the only way he's learned to express affection and to express being a man [is through machismo]. Well, I think that maybe he is like that that —bossy— but that he has the possibility of opening up because he begins to open up at the end just like I do.

Watch the interview with Carla and Marilyn once more, and discuss what they say regarding the following issues:

Carla Sánchez:

- su más reciente película
- cómo se preparó para hacer el papel de Carmina
- las diferencias entre su personalidad y la de Carmina
- Venezuela y su carrera profesional

Marilyn Brito:

- sus raíces
- su vida de creación
- lo que es parecido y lo que es diferente entre Laura y Marilyn
- cómo desarrolló el papel de Laura
- su relación con el actor que hace el papel de Alex
- el machismo de Alex y su relación con Laura en la película

Now do an Internet search on these actresses to discover what they are doing now.

UNIDAD 4a

NOTE TO THE STUDENT

As a language student, you come to rely a great deal on your dictionary. When you use the dictionary for writing or for speech, you are usually interested in a particular word with a particular meaning. Since most words have a number of different meanings, you scan all of them so that you have a general understanding of the range of words available. Finally, you focus on the meaning that is most closely related to the one you need. For the most part, this method works well for both the native language and the language you are studying because you are usually searching for isolated words and standard meanings. However, there are times when your reliance upon the dictionary can lead you astray. What happens when the word or words you are searching for do not reflect standard or conventional use? In other words, the process is not always so simple when it comes to slang or idiomatic expressions. Simply because a certain word choice is appropriate in English, does not mean that its Spanish equivalent is also the appropriate choice.

Imagine listening in on the following excerpts from a conversation between a doctor and the husband of one of his patients.

"What happened? She had a close call. Things like this don't just happen out of the blue... What would you do if you were in my shoes?... Let's not beat around the bush. We can operate first thing tomorrow morning... The doctors worked around the clock until the bleeding was stopped. So far, so good. Everything went smoothly, but we still have to keep a close eye on her. She should be up and around in a week or so. Can she go back to work? To be on the safe side, she should wait a bit. At this point, I don't want her to bite off more than she can chew."

Do you think that a literal, word for word translation into Spanish would convey the same ideas as in English? Slang and idioms rarely translate literally from one language to another. Slang and idiomatic expressions are commonly categorized as specialized vocabulary that lies outside of the conventional and standard usage, because their meanings are extended to new contexts. Sometimes the new meaning is so far removed from the original one that it is difficult to decipher the message, unless you have been repeatedly exposed to the expression. Since this type of communication is often based on shared cultural experiences and you do no share the same language experiences as native speakers of Spanish, it is unlikely that the two languages will share slang and idiomatic expressions.

DON'T PUT THE CART BEFORE THE HORSE

When speaking a language, you rely upon your own experiences for the meanings and general appropriateness of words and constructions. In fact, you have relied on these experiences to guide you since you first learned to talk. More often than not, you must rely upon your personal experiences to properly use and understand them. Your dictionary can aid and guide you in your word choices, but ultimately you must be aware of what is or is not appropriate for a specific context. In other words, you must learn to recognize your own language patterns and know when you are following convention or invention. Only you know what you are thinking.

MEASURE TWICE, CUT ONCE

When communicating in Spanish, you should consider the content of the message you wish to relay. Does it contain slang or fixed expressions that have been directly translated from English? Ask yourself this question: Are these concepts expressed similarly in Spanish? Does Spanish have its own way for expressing these notions? Is there a more conventional way to express this same idea? Take the time to examine the language you use. In time, you will learn which idioms and expressions are appropriate in Spanish. Just remember that practice makes perfect.

VOCABULARIO

Below are the vocabulary words highlighted in this unit. Remember that you can hear these words in action in the *Vocabulario* section of *Unidad 4a* on the *Recursos* webpage. After you've looked at them, write beside each one its English equivalent. If you have any doubt about the words' exact meanings, look them up in a good Spanish-English dictionary.

Review the words that you have written on the margins of *Vocabulario* so far. Look up the meanings of any words you don't know.

Remember to use this space to add new and useful words that you find in your study or work, but were not included in *Vocabulario*!

Verbos

acompañar

dar vergüenza

gritar

haber tiempo

hacer

hacerse cargo

insinuar

pedir disculpas

prescribir

renunciar

señalar

Adjetivos

agudo/a

cada ocho horas

frecuente

al día

recetada

nada

Sustantivos

la artritis reumatoide

las aspirinas

las cápsulas

las contracciones

las disculpas

la dosis

el grito

las mujercitas

el tiempo

el varón

¡A PRACTICAR!

4A-VOC-1

Choose the most appropriate word that completes the sentence.

1 Todos los días Alex sentía un dolor ___________ en las rodillas.

a agudo

b frecuente

c grito

2 Por el dolor, no podía pasar mucho ___________ sentado en la oficina.

a cápsulas

b tiempo

c varón

3 Cada ocho horas tomaba ___________ para sentirse mejor.

a aspirinas

b disculpas

c mujercitas

4 Le ___________ decirles a sus colegas que tenía una enfermedad.

a daba verguenza

b hacía cargo

c pedía disculpas

5 El comportamiento de Alex les ___________ que algo le pasaba.

a insinuaba

b renunciaba

c indicaba

6 De todos modos, Alex no hacía ___________ para mejorar su situación.

a dosis

b nada

c por día

4A-VOC-2

Fill in the correct word for each blank. Be careful with agreement between the new word and the rest of the sentence. If you need help, review Unidad 4a Vocabulario.

La señora López discute su visita al médico con su hija.

"Bueno, según la doctora, las pruebas muestran que sufro de **(1)** ___________ *(rheumatoid arthritis)*. Me dijo que es algo que se puede controlar, así que no tengo que **(2)** ___________ *(to quit)* al trabajo. Me **(3)** ___________ *(she prescribed)* una crema y unas pastillas para quitarme el dolor. ¿La crema? Me la pongo tres veces **(4)** ___________ *(a day)*. No, mi ángel, no me hace falta **(5)** ___________ *(nothing)* por ahora. Sí, tengo que volver en un mes. ¿Me puedes **(6)** ___________ *(accompany)*?"

4A-VOC-3

Complete the sentences below in a logical manner. If you need help, use the vocabulary from this section or previous sections studied.

En la clínica se escucha de todo. Termina las oraciones de abajo para saber lo que dice la gente.

1 Las contracciones señalan que ____________

____

____

2 La enfermera le pide disculpas al paciente por ______________________________

____

____

3 El paciente grita porque ____________

____

____

4 La mujer decidió renunciar a su trabajo por

____

____

____

5 Las medicinas prescritas sólo se obtienen después de ______________________

____

____

6 Recibió la dosis equivocada y por eso

____

____

____

4A-VOC-4

Take a look at the photo of Alex and Laura below. What do you think they are discussing? Use the vocabulary from Unidad 4a Vocabulario *to create a dialogue.*

____

____

____

____

____

____

____

____

____

____

____

____

____

____

____

USEFUL TERMS AND EXPRESSIONS

This section introduces new vocabulary and expressions related to themes found throughout *Historia 4a* of the DVD.

SUSTANTIVOS

El cuerpo

las caderas	hips
el cartílago	cartilage
las coyunturas	joints
la espalda	back
las rodillas	knees

La condición física

el bastón	cane
el estiramiento	stretching
el estreñimiento	constipation
la fatiga	fatigue
la gota	gout
la incontinencia	incontinence
los movimientos	movements
la propagación	spread
la radiación	radiation
la rigidez	stiffness
la silla de ruedas	wheelchair

La salud mental

el abandono	abandonment
las actitudes	attitudes
el ambiente	environment
la ansiedad	anxiety
la apatía	apathy
la conducta	conduct
el consuelo	comfort
la depresión	depression
los desafíos	challenges
el deambular	wandering
el desamparo	helplessness
la desesperación	desperation
la drogadiccíon	drug addiction
la duda	doubt
el enojo	anger
los episodios	episodes
el estado de ánimo	state of mind
las etapas	stages
el insomnio	insomnia
la ira	rage
las metas	goals
el odio	hate
el recipiente	recipient
los sedantes	sedatives
las preocupaciones	concerns
la psicoterapia	psychotherapy
la razón	reason

la soledad	loneliness
el suicidio	suicide
los trastornos	disorders
VERBOS	
acelerar	to accelerate
ahogar(se)	to drown
aliviar	to alleviate
aprobar	to approve
concentrar(se)	to concentrate
confiar	to trust
cuidar(se)	to take care of (oneself)
desempeñar	to carry out
detener	to stop
empeorar	to grow worse
ensayar	to try, test
entrevistar	to interview
gastar	to wear away
jalar	to pull
permanecer	to remain
raspar	to scrape
realizar	to fulfill
requerir	to require
sobrevivir	to survive
superar	to overcome
sustituir	to substitute
valorar	to value
variar	to vary
ADJETIVOS Y ADVERBIOS	
antidepresivo/a	anti-depressive
aterrorizado/a	terrified
capaz	capable
deprimido	depressed
detenido/a	detained
digestivo/a	digestive
disponible	available
eficaz	efficient
flexible	flexible
genérico/a	generic
leve	light
pesado/a	heavy
tenso/a	tense

Study the vocabulary before you begin *Principios* because it will be useful when practicing the grammar points of the unit. Remember that this section is not intended to be an exhaustive list of all relevant terms, but rather provides exposure to some of the basic vocabulary used in healthcare. The definitions given here are limited, because they are intended for the narrow use of the exercises found in *Principios*. Look the words up in a good Spanish-English dictionary if you want to know other meanings, how to pronounce them, the contexts in which the words can be found, sayings and common expressions using these words, and their derivatives (adjectives from nouns, nouns from verbs, etc.).

PRINCIPIOS

Imagine that you are a counselor speaking with a client who has recently escaped from a violent relationship. When you ask if her husband beat her recently, she responds, "I have been beaten by my husband." Similarly, when you ask her if her husband now knows where she is, she shamefacedly admits, "My husband has been contacted by me." As you speak with your client, you begin to realize that her language reflects her state of mind: she views herself as a passive agent being acted upon by her husband. The emotional assistance you give your client must change accordingly.

Perspective plays an important role both in how language is used, and in how care is given as well. This unit will further your understanding of the importance of perspective by examining constructions that provide you with a different frame of reference from which to view concepts studied in previous chapters. For example, actions can be expressed actively or passively, depending upon the focus of your sentence. Concepts expressed through the presence of nouns, adjectives, and adverbs can also be modified through the use of comparisons or superlatives. All of these elements serve to alter or reinforce the speaker's perspective. Being aware of such subtleties in language may help you to improve the understanding you have of your clients and patients.

PASSIVE VOICE

Up to this point we have studied tenses in the active voice. However, Spanish also makes use of a passive voice. The passive voice is used to show that someone or something is being acted upon by someone or something else. You might say that the subject receives the action, rather than performs the action. Compare the examples provided below.

PASSIVE	ACTIVE
He was killed by a drunk driver.	A drunk driver killed him.
She was committed by the psychiatrist.	A psychiatrist committed her.

Notice that there is an active counterpart for each passive construction. Both passive examples show that the subject is acted upon by some agent. The agent, or performer of the action, is indicated by a prepositional phrase. As for the active examples, the subject performs the action.

In Spanish, the formal passive voice is comprised of *ser* plus the past participle of the main verb. When joined with *ser,* the past participle functions as an adjective and agrees in gender and number with the subject. Go to *Unidad 2a* if you need a quick review of past participles.

SPANISH	ENGLISH
El daño a los órganos fue causad**o** por el alcohol.	The damage to the organs was caused by alcohol.
Los hombres fueron examinad**os** por el médico.	The men were examined by the doctor.
Las muestras fueron sacad**as** por la enfermera.	The samples were taken by the nurse.

Only verbs that can take objects can be used to form the past participle of the passive voice. Consequently, verbs of motion like *ir, venir*, and *salir* are never found in such constructions.

The passive voice can still be used even if the subject performing the action is unknown. The agent then becomes implied, signaling to the listener that the action was intentional, not accidental. In fact, this is one of the most appropriate times to use a passive construction, instead of an active one. Even though passive constructions may be used in these cases, however, it is more common to use the *se impersonal*. You will learn more about this later in the unit.

SPANISH	ENGLISH
La clínica fue cerrada.	The clinic was closed.
La propagación de la enfermedad fue detenida.	The spread of the disease was stopped.

In the examples given above, who or what acted upon the subject is not stated in the sentence, yet you can infer that the action was intentional in both cases.

Finally, the passive voice can occur in any tense.

INDICATIVE	SPANISH	ENGLISH
Present	El examen preliminar **es hecho** por la enfermera.	The preliminary exam **is done** by the nurse.
Preterit	Las células **fueron destruidas** por la radiación.	The cells **were killed** by the radiation.
Imperfect	La silla de ruedas **era usada** por el hombre.	The wheelchair **was used** by the man.
Future	Una cura **será encontrada** por los científicos.	A cure **will be found** by the scientists.
Conditional	Explicaron que la cuenta **sería pagada** por el seguro.	They explained that the bill **would be paid** by the insurance.

SUBJUNCTIVE	SPANISH	ENGLISH
Present	Es importante que los guantes **sean llevados** por ellos.	It is important that gloves **be (are) worn** by them.
Past	Fue necesario que la mujer **fuera llevada** al hospital.	It was necessary that the woman **was brough**t to the hospital.

Even though this construction exists in Spanish, native speakers usually consider the formal passive voice to be weak. Most prefer to use the active voice instead, especially in speech. Consequently, the formal passive has been slowly relegated to literary works and to instances in which the result is of more interest than the action that led to the result.

Take a look at the sentence below. Which type seems more direct and expressive to you?

PASSIVE	ACTIVE
Las drogas fueron vendidas por las pandillas.	Las pandillas vendieron las drogas.
The drugs were sold by the gangs.	Gangs sold the drugs.

How, then, can you avoid using the passive construction? Spanish has at least four tools available:

1 You can turn the passive construction around and create an active one.

PASSIVE	ACTIVE
Sufre de depresión porque **fue abusada por** su esposo.	Sufre de depresión porque su esposo **abusó** de ella.
She suffers from depression because she **was abused by** her husband.	She suffers from depression because her husband **abused** her.

2 If you are willing to leave the subject undertermined, you can make use of the *se impersonal* (also known as the passive with *se*).

PASSIVE	ACTIVE
Los mejores tratamientos **son recibidos** aquí.	Los mejores tratamientos **se reciben** aquí.
The best treatments **are received** here.	One (you) **receive(s)** the best treatment here.

3 You can use the third person plural.

PASSIVE	ACTIVE
La receta **es leída.**	**Leen** la receta.
The prescription **is read.**	They **read** the prescription.

4 You can use *uno* to express "one."

PASSIVE	ACTIVE
Los mejores tratamientos **se recibían** aquí.	**Uno recibía** los mejores tratamientos aquí.
The best treatments **were given** here.	One **received** the best treatments here.

¡A PRACTICAR!

4A-PRIN-1

Choose the most appropriate subject for the passive construction provided below.

1 son aceptadas

__ **a** el consejo __ **b** la responsabilidad

__ **c** las limitaciones __ **d** los problemas

2 fueron mantenidos

__ **a** la experiencia __ **b** las enfermedades

__ **c** las relaciones personales __ **d** los planes

3 fue sentida

__ **a** el ambiente __ **b** el dolor

__ **c** la tristeza __ **d** los problemas

4 son controladas

__ **a** el odio __ **b** la ira

__ **c** las emociones __ **d** los problemas

5 fueron superados

__ **a** el respeto __ **b** las actitudes

__ **c** los desafíos __ **d** los intereses

6 fue expresado

__ **a** el enojo __ **b** la duda

__ **c** la paciencia __ **d** los límites

4A-PRIN-2

Conjugate the infinitives below for the present, preterit and future passive.

1 el dolor / controlar

presente: ______________________

pretérito: ______________________

futuro: ______________________

2 las cuentas / pagar

presente: ______________________

pretérito: ______________________

futuro: ______________________

3 el trabajo / dar

presente: ______________________

pretérito: ______________________

futuro: ______________________

4 un artículo / escribir

presente: ______________________

pretérito: ______________________

futuro: ______________________

5 la clínica nueva / abrir

presente: ______________________

pretérito: ______________________

futuro: ______________________

6 los archivos / perder

presente: ______________________

pretérito: ______________________

futuro: ______________________

7 la enfermedad / prevenir

presente: ______________________

pretérito: ______________________

futuro: ______________________

8 la dosis / aumentar

presente: ______________________

pretérito: ______________________

futuro: ______________________

4A-PRIN-3

Alex can no longer stand the pain and decides to make an appointment with Carmina. Fill in the blanks with the correct form of the formal passive. Be careful with tense and agreement.

1 La Comunidad ______________________ *(conocer)* por todos en este barrio.

2 Esta mañana Alex visitó la clínica y ______________________ *(examinar)* por Carmina.

3 Durante la visita le ______________________ *(hacer)* un análisis de sangre.

4 Después de hacer el análisis ____________ ____________ *(descubrir)* algo por la médica: que Alex tenía artritis reumatoide.

5 Todos saben que la artritis ______________________ *(caracterizar)* por dolor, hinchazón y rigidez en las articulaciones.

6 Muchos de los problemas de la artritis ______________________ *(causar)* por la inflamación de las coyunturas.

7 Todos los tratamientos disponibles ______________________ *(discutir)* con Alex.

8 Mañana le ______________________ *(mostrar)* unos ejercicios de estiramiento por el terapeuta físico.

4A-PRIN-4

Ángela tells Rafa about some of the problems she encounters at the clinic. Rewrite the active sentences below as formal passive.

1 Compraron los medicamentos fuera de Estados Unidos.

____

____

2 El paciente no siguió las instrucciones indicadas en la etiqueta.

____

____

3 Las píldoras causan sueño y dolores de cabeza.

____

____

4 El médico le recetará pastillas para dormir.

____

____

5 El farmacéutico llena el recipiente con las píldoras.

____

____

6 El hombre tomó la medicina equivocada.

____

____

7 La enfermera especializada le escribió la información en español.

____

____

8 No aprueban la venta de algunos narcóticos en Estados Unidos.

____

____

4A-PRIN-5

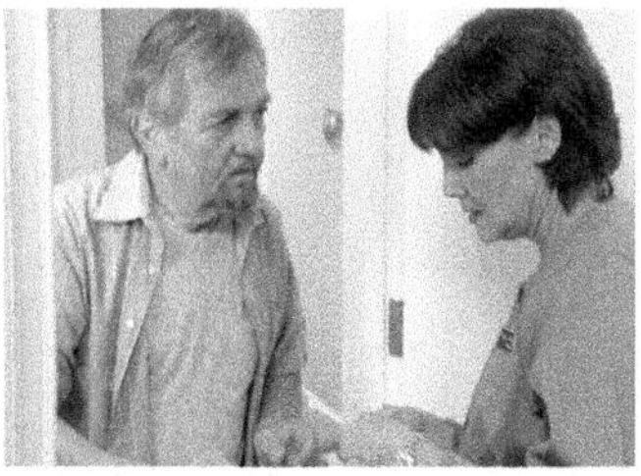

Study the photo below and describe what happened using the formal passive constructions. Write at least four sentences.

____

____

____

____

____

SE IMPERSONAL AND OTHER WAYS TO AVOID PASSIVE CONSTRUCTIONS

As previously stated, the formal passive voice in Spanish is slowly disappearing in speech. Native speakers use the *se impersonal* and the *se pasivo* instead to convey the same idea. In contrast to the formal passive, however, the subject of the action is expressed by *se*.

These *se* constructions are often used in healthcare settings since the agent performing the action is often unknown, indefinite, or irrelevant. In the sentence "They take more medicine than before," for example, "they" is undefined. "They" in this case could refer to a few patients at the clinic where you work, patients in every hospital in the country, or a specific group of people in a research study. What matters here is not "who" is performing the action but the information conveyed, because in most conversations the "who" is either understood through context or is not relevant (as in the example, "They say that many American children are overweight.")

	SPANISH	ENGLISH
Active	Toman más medicina que antes.	They take more medicine than before.
Passive *se*	**Se toma** más medicina que antes.	More medicine is taken now than before. (passive) People take more medicine now than before. (impersonal) They take more medicine now than before. (impersonal)
	Se entrevista al paciente.	The patient is interviewed. (passive)
third person plural	**Toman** más medicina que antes.	They take more medicine now than before.
Use of *uno*	**Uno toma** más medicina que antes.	One takes more medicine than before.

¡A PRACTICAR!

4A-PRIN-6

Read the paragraph below and circle all of the se impersonal *and the* pasiva refleja *constructions.*

Los trastornos depresivos pueden causar dolor y sufrimiento, pero todo esto se puede evitar con el tratamiento apropiado. Se sabe que hoy en día existen medicamientos y psicoterapias eficaces para los distintos tipos de depresión. Las psicoterapias se conocen por varios nombres y ayudan a aliviar el sufrimiento de la depresión más leve. Hay muchos factores que contribuyen al estado mental de una persona. Se puede heredar una predisposición biológica o el problema puede ser el resultado de alguna enfermedad física. Para encontrar el tratamiento adecuado, primero se entrevista al paciente y se hace un análisis de laboratorio. La mayoría de la gente recibe una combinación de tratamientos. Generalmente, no se ven resultados inmediatos y la dosis se debe ir aumentando hasta encontrar la dosis más efectiva.

4A-PRIN-7

Ángela addresses some concerns a patient has with respect to her medication. Use the cues provided to answer the following questions.

1 ¿Qué tipo de medicamentos se dan para la ansiedad? *(sedantes)* ____________________

____

____

2 ¿Se debe combinar los medicamentos sin consultar al médico? *(no)* ____________________

____

____

3 ¿Se crea hábito con el uso de los medicamentos antidepresivos? *(no)* ____________________

____

____

4 ¿Se experimentarán efectos adversos? *(boca seca y estreñimiento)* ____________________

____

____

5 ¿Se ofrecen tratamientos alternativos? *(la terapia naturista)* ____________________

____

____

6 ¿Con terapia se me quitará la depresión rápidamente? *(no)* ____________________

____

____

4A-PRIN-8

Almost everyone has experienced some type of grief in his or her life. Use the se impersonal *and the* pasiva se *to describe some ways in which people face it. Here are some suggestions to get you started.*

Palabras útiles

analizar	decisiones importantes
escribir	la situación completa
establecer	las prioridades
no tomar	un plan para el futuro
permitir	viejas amistades

1 ______________________________

2 ______________________________

3 ______________________________

4 ______________________________

5 ______________________________

4A-PRIN-9

At one time or another you have to explain a procedure or a process to a patient or a client. Select one of the most common procedures or processes and use the se impersonal *and the* pasiva se *to explain it below.*

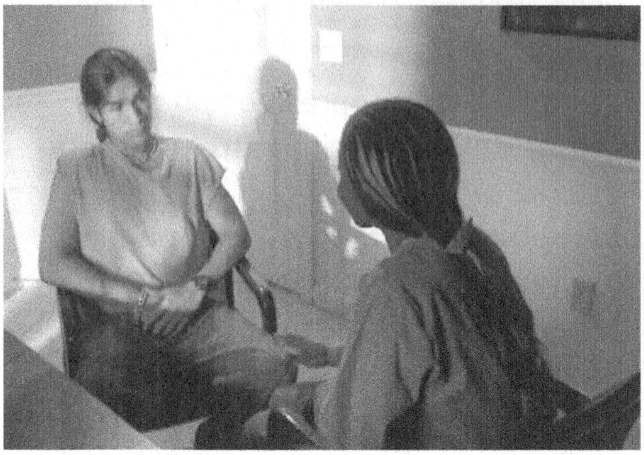

COMPARISONS

Imagine that you are a psychologist working with a depressed patient whom you feel is suicidal. You need to ask him/her if he/she feels more or less depressed than he/she did during his/her last depressive episode. In order to ask this question, you need to use the grammatical construction known as a comparison.

In English, making comparisons is easy: we simply add the suffix "-er than" to an adjective or say "more ... than" or "less ... than". Your patient might say, for example, "I feel more depressed than I did last year." To say that something is the same as it was before, a so-called comparison of equality, we say, "as ... as" or "as much as." Your patient might then add, "I am taking as much medicine as I did then." Fortunately for students of Spanish, saying this in Spanish is just as simple:

INEQUALITY	EQUALITY
...más ... que...	...tan ... como...
...menos ... que...	...tanto/a/s ... como...
...más que...	...tanto como...
...menos que...	

Choice of construction depends on what is being compared. Examine the sentences provided below:

■ Comparisons of Inequality:

SPANISH	ENGLISH
Laura tiene **más** problemas **que** Carmina.	Laura has **more** problems **than** Carmina.
Algunas viviendas están **más** sucias **que** otras.	Some housing units are dirt**ier** **than** others.
Ashleigh habla español **más** lentamente **que** los hispanoparlantes.	Ashleigh speaks Spanish slower **than** native speakers.
Aquella clínica ofrece **menos** servicios **que** ésta.	That clinic offers few**er** services **than** this one.
Algunos barrios son **menos** peligrosos **que** otros.	Some neighborhoods are **less** dangerous **than** others.
Las pastillas funcionan **menos** rápidamente **que** la inyección.	The pills work **less** quickly **than** the injection.
Este trabajo paga **más que** el que tenía.	This job pays **more than** the one I had.
Las gotas cuestan **menos que** las píldoras.	The drops cost **less than** the pills.

By examining the sentences above, you will notice that *...más ... que...* and *...menos ... que...* are used with nouns, adjectives and adverbs. If the expression of inequality only involves a verb, however, as in the sentence *Las gotas cuestan menos que las píldoras, ...más que ...* and *...menos que...* are kept together and are not separated by nouns, adjectives, or adverbs. Also, when using comparatives with numbers or ideas remember that *que* is replaced by *de*.

SPANISH	ENGLISH
Hay **más de** diez personas en la sala de espera.	There are **more than** ten people in the waiting room.
La situación es **más** grave **de** lo que pensaban.	The situation is **more** serious **than** they thought.

Of course, you will find some adjectives and adverbs that do not follow the regular methods of forming comparatives. Here are some of the most common irregular forms:

mejor que	*better than*	mayor que	*older than*
peor que	*worse than*	menor que	*younger than*

SPANISH	ENGLISH
Su estado de ánimo es **mejor que** el de ella.	His state of mind is **better than** hers.
Su estado mental está **peor que** antes.	His mental state is **worse than** before.
Rafa es **mayor que** Alex.	Rafa is **older than** Alex.

Nevertheless, constructions such as *...más bueno/a que..., ...menos bueno/a que..., ...más viejo/a que...,* and *más joven que...* are still very common in both spoken and written Spanish.

- **Comparisons of Equality:**

SPANISH	ENGLISH
Estos tratamientos son **tan** efectivos **como** aquellos.	These treatments are **as** effective **as** those.
Ángela cuenta los narcóticos **tan** cuidadosamente **como** le es posible.	Angela counts the drugs **as** carefully **as** possible.
Hay **tantas** mujeres **como** hombres que viven bajo estas condiciones.	There are **as** many women **as** men who live under these conditions.
Carmina trabaja **tanto como** Ángela.	Carmina works **as** much **as** Angela.

In expressions of equality, ...*tan* ... *como*... is found in combination with adjectives and adverbs. Once again, the word is placed in between the two comparative elements, and the adjectives will agree with the subject of the sentence. *Tanto/a/s* ... *como*... is the construction used to compare nouns; it agrees in gender and number with the first noun of the comparative expression, which is placed between the two comparative elements. Finally, the expression ... *tanto como*... serves to describe a verb. Like comparisons of inequality, this construction is never separated by the verb.

For the most part, comparatives are fairly straightforward. Still, you might encounter some problems. The most common difficulties occur with:

1 Word order

2 Verb agreement

3 Omitting comparative elements

4 Incorrectly combining comparative elements

5 Adjective agreement

Remember to pay special attention to these aspects of the comparisons.

¡A PRACTICAR!

4A-PRIN-10

Look at the chart and determine which comparisons reflect the information provided in the table.

Peso en libras	Tabletas masticables	Gotas	Jarabe
6-11	-	*.4 cc*	-
12-17	-	*.8 cc*	-
18-23	*1*	*1.2 cc*	*1 cucharadita*
24-35	*2*	*1.6 cc*	*1¼ cucharaditas*
36-47	*3*	-	*1¾ cucharaditas*
48-59	*4*	-	*2 cucharaditas*
más de 59	*Dosis para adultos*	-	-

1 Un niño de veinte libras puede tomar tantas tabletas como cucharaditas de jarabe.

Sí ______ ***No*** ______

2 Se toman menos gotas que jarabe si el niño pesa ocho libras.

Sí ______ ***No*** ______

3 Las gotas funcionan mejor para los niños chicos que para los niños más grandes.

Sí ______ ***No*** ______

4 Las tabletas son más efectivas que las gotas.

Sí ______ ***No*** ______

5 Se dan gotas en más ocasiones que tabletas.

Sí ______ ***No*** ______

6 Una niña de cincuenta libras necesita tomar más tabletas que cucharaditas de jarabe.

Sí ______ ***No*** ______

4A-PRIN-11

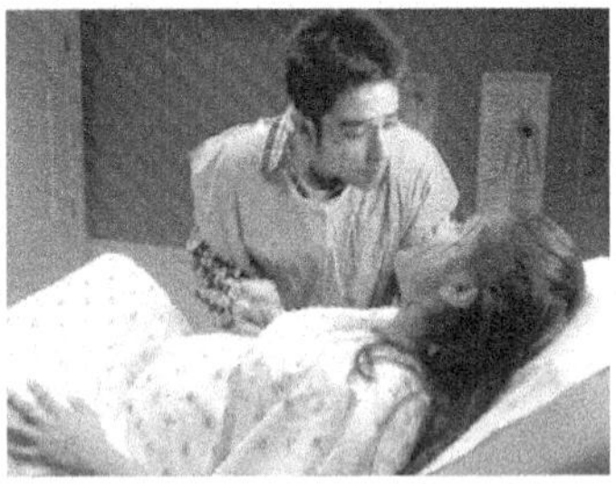

Mila is in labor. Use your knowledge of the Historia *to fill in the blanks with the missing component of the comparison.*

1 Mila siente ________ dolor que Eliodoro.

2 Las contracciones vienen más rápidamente ________ antes.

3 Las contracciones vienen en intervalos de menos ________ cinco minutos.

4 Mila tiene ________ miedo como su esposo.

5 Ángela no está ________ nerviosa como Eliodoro.

6 Ashleigh se preocupa ________ que Eliodoro.

7 Los padres nuevos son tan felices ________ los demás.

8 Eliodoro siente ________ emoción como Mila.

4A-PRIN-12

Manuel has been suffering from a lot of tension in his life. Help him describe how he feels by using the cues provided below to create comparisons of equality and inequality.

Modelo: La cabeza / el cuello / dolerle

Igualdad: La cabeza le duele tanto como el cuello.

Desigualdad: La cabeza le duele más que el cuello.

1 Los músculos de la espalda / los músculos del cuello / estar / tenso

Igualdad: ______________________________

____

Desigualdad: ______________________________

____

2 Un baño con agua tibia / un baño con agua fría / ayudar

Igualdad: ______________________________

____

Desigualdad: ______________________________

____

3 Dar un paseo / hacer ejercicio / ser / efectivo

Igualdad: ______________________________

____

Desigualdad: ______________________________

____

4 Problemas de dinero / problemas de trabajo / yo / tener

Igualdad: ______________________________

____

Desigualdad: ______________________________

____

5 Diversiones / preocupaciones / nosotros / tener

Igualdad: ______________________________

____

Desigualdad: ______________________________

____

4A-PRIN-13

Claudia maintains a weekly calendar of her feelings. Take a look at Claudia's chart for this week and use comparisons to describe how she feels. Use your imagination as well.

	apatía / apática	**abandono / abandonada**	**soledad / sola**	**desesperación / desesperada**	**desamparo / indefensa**
No presente	X				
Suave				X	
Moderado					X
Severo		X	X		

1 ______________________________

2 ______________________________

3 ______________________________

4 ______________________________

5 ______________________________

4A-PRIN-14

Examine the photograph below. What do the people at the clinic think of each other? Use comparisons and your knowledge of the people who work at the clinic to describe how they would characterize each other.

1 ______________________________

____

____

2 ______________________________

____

____

3 ______________________________

____

____

4 ______________________________

____

____

5 ______________________________

____

____

6 ______________________________

____

____

4A-PRIN-15

If a patient or client came to see you complaining about feeling tired, suffering from a loss of energy, and experiencing a lack of interest in activities that used to be enjoyable to her, what questions would you ask her to determine the cause or causes of her condition? What advice would you offer her? Use the comparisons below to help you create at least five sentences.

mayor que	...más... que...
mejor que	...menos... que...
menor que	...más que...
peor que	...menos que...
	...tanto/a/s... como
	...tan... como...
	...tanto como...

1 ______________________________

____

____

____

2 ______________________________

____

____

____

3 ______________________________

____

____

____

4 ______________________________

____

____

____

5 ______________________________

____

____

SUPERLATIVES

In order to describe a treatment as "the best", a medicine as "the newest", or a patient as "the least cooperative," you need to use a superlative. To form a superlative, use the correct definite article in combination with a comparison of inequality. Instead of using *que*, however, you will use *de*. You will be happy to know that Spanish does not have any irregular forms for the superlative.

SPANISH	ENGLISH
Ella es **la más** triste **de** todo el grupo.	She is the sadd**est of** the group.
Esta medicina es **la más** cara **de** todas.	This medicine is **the most** expensive **of** them all.
Laura es **la menos** responsable **del** grupo.	Laura is **the least** responsible **of** the group.
Jaime es **el mejor** obstetra **de** la clínica.	Jaime is **the best** obstetrician **at** the clinic.
No poder ayudar a la gente es **el peor** aspecto **de** mi trabajo.	Not being able to help people is **the worst** aspect **of** my job.
El señor Anderson es **el hombre más** poderoso **de** la comunidad.	Mr. Anderson is **the most** powerful man **in** the community.

Observe how both the definite article and the adjective agree with the subject of the sentence.

Sometimes concepts that can be expressed through superlative constructions in English do not have exact equivalents in Spanish. Therefore, the comparison is the most appropriate form to use. Such concepts usually involve only verbs; a concept such as "He works the hardest of them all" might be expressed as *Él trabaja más que los demás.*

¡A PRACTICAR!

4A-PRIN-16

Choose the construction that represents the correct way to form the superlative.

_______ **1 tratamiento / seguro**

a Es el tratamiento más segura de todos.
b Es el tratamiento más seguro de todas.
c Es el tratamiento más seguro de todos.
d Es la tratamiento más seguro de todas.

_______ **2 métodos**

a Son las mejoras métodos para aliviar el dolor.
b Son las mejores métodos para aliviar el dolor.
c Son los mejoras métodos para aliviar el dolor.
d Son los mejores métodos para aliviar el dolor.

_______ **3 medicinas / caro**

a La medicina es la menos caras en esta farmacia.
b La medicina es la menos caro en esta farmacia.
c Las medicinas son la menos cara en esta farmacia.
d Las medicinas son las menos caras en esta farmacia.

_______ **personas / importante**

a Mis hijos son la persona más importante demi vida.
b Mis hijos son las personas más importante de mi vida.
c Mis hijos son las personas más importantes de mi vida.
d Mis hijos son los personas más importantes de mi vida.

_______ **5 caso**

a Es el caso peor que he visto en La Comunidad.
b Es el peor caso que he visto en La Comunidad.
c Es la peor caso que he visto en La Comunidad.
d Son el peor caso que he visto en La Comunidad.

_______ **6 síntomas / severo**

a Son las síntomas menos severas de todas.
b Son los síntomas menos severas de todos.
c Son los síntomas menos severos de todas.
d Son los síntomas menos severos de todos.

4A-PRIN-17

Fill in the blanks with the most appropriate translation of the words.

1 Hay que elegir _______________ *(the most appropriate diet)* para su condición.

2 Los ejercicios que no ponen mucha tensión en las articulaciones son _______________ *(the best)*.

3 Los medicamentos no evaluados ni aprobados en los Estados Unidos _______________ *(are the least safe)*.

4 Busca _______________ *(the most effective treatment).*

5 Las cremas _______________ *(are the most useful medicines)* para mí.

4A-PRIN-18

Read the paragraph below. Based on what you read, create sentences using the superlative.

Gabriela y su familia acaban de mudarse a este país. Ella tiene tres niños: Jorge que tiene cinco años, Marco que tiene ocho años y Margarita que tiene once años. Todos viven en un apartamento de dos cuartos, pero no se quejan porque nunca han vivido en uno tan grande. Por suerte, Gabriela consiguió un trabajo en una fábrica que está a una cuadra del apartamento. No gana mucho dinero, pero no tiene que dejar a los niños solos por mucho tiempo. Había otros trabajos a una hora de distancia que pagaban más, pero los rechazó para poder estar cerca de los niños. No tiene mucho, pero Gabriela hace todo lo que puede por sus niños. Todos asisten a la escuela y por primera vez en la familia alguien se va a graduar del colegio.

1 ____________________________________

____

____

2 ____________________________________

____

____

3 ____________________________________

____

____

4 ____________________________________

____

____

5 ____________________________________

____

____

4A-PRIN-19

Duna is always so busy. Here is an excerpt from a pamphlet that she is translating into Spanish. Help her translate the paragraph below.

The best way to protect yourself is to ask questions. If you have any questions or concerns about your medication, the most important thing to do is to consult your doctor. Even the slightest doubt should not be ignored. Remember that some of the most dangerous situations can be avoided with the proper information.

4A-PRIN-20

How do you think these characters view their professions? Use superlative constructions to express what they might consider to be the most interesting, the most difficult, and the easiest aspect of their jobs.

Rafa

1 ____________________

2 ____________________

3 ____________________

Duna

1 ____________________

2 ____________________

3 ____________________

Federico

1 ____________________

2 ____________________

3 ____________________

Ángela

1 ____________________

2 ____________________

3 ____________________

CONCEPTO IMPORTANTE: USING NEGATIVE EXPRESSIONS

Being able to negate something is critical in healthcare settings. If a patient asks, "Should I take this medicine three times a day?," a pharmacist must be able to clarify, "No, do not take this medicine three times a day. Take the medicine once a day for three days." In the majority of cases, putting statements in the negative is not grammatically complicated in Spanish. Occasionally, however, English speakers learning Spanish end up affirming what they wish to deny and denying what they wish to affirm. Why and when this happens is the subject of the *Concepto importante* for this unit.

What We Know

Negative words can be pronouns, adjectives, adverbs, and prepositions. Each one has a positive counterpart.

NEGATIVE		POSITIVE	
no	*no*	sí	*yes*
nada	*nothing*	algo	*something*
nadie	*no one*	alguien	*someone*
nunca, jamás	*never*	siempre, a veces	*always, sometimes*
ninguno/a*	*none*	alguno/a/s*	*some*
tampoco	*neither, either*	también	*also*
ni ... ni	*neither ... nor*	o ... o	*either ... or*
sin	*without*	con	*with*

* *Note that as with other masculine adjectives,* alguno *and* ninguno *change to* algún *and* ningún *when placed in front of masculine singular nouns.* Ningún *is never plural since if there isn't even one object, there can't be more than one.*

In most cases, to make a sentence negative, simply place the word *no* or another negative word before the verb.

SPANISH	ENGLISH
Las mujeres embarazadas **no** deben fumar.	Pregnant women shouldn't smoke.
Las mujeres embarazadas **nunca** deben fumar.	Pregnant women should never smoke.

In some cases, however, you will want to reinforce or strengthen the negative idea in a sentence. You may do this by putting a negative word (or words) after the verb, but keep in mind that a negative word (or two) must then precede the verb as well.

SPANISH	ENGLISH
Nunca he estado tan deprimido.	I have never been so depressed.
No le he dicho nada sobre la enfermedad.	I have not told him anything about the illness.
Explicaron que nadie le ha dado nunca nada.	They explained that no one has ever given him anything.
El hombre se fue sin decirme nada.	The man left without telling me anything.

The Difficulty

The concept of the negative expression is not difficult to grasp; however, English speakers often make mistakes when trying to incorporate negative expressions into speech and writing. These errors primarily result from the fact that in English the use of the double negative is taboo. You might say that the double negative is a no-no in English. Let's reexamine a few of the sentences given above.

SPANISH	ENGLISH
No le he dicho nada sobre la enfermedad.	I have not told him anything about the illness.
Explicaron que nadie le ha dado nunca nada.	They explained that no one has ever given him anything.
El hombre se fue sin decirme nada.	The man left without telling me anything.

If you look at the English translations provided, you see that in each sentence only one negative word is present and the word accompanying the negative is positive. It is this positive word that creates so much difficulty for the language student. Unable to find its Spanish equivalent within the traditional list of negative and positive words, students will automatically try to translate "anything" by using the next best positive word available, which incorrectly results in *No le he dicho algo.* In many contexts, *algo* would be the appropriate choice. However, negative expressions in Spanish do not function in an identical manner to those of English. In fact, the two are quite opposite. Again, you see an example of why you must be careful not to use English as your crutch for learning the Spanish language. The two languages have different ways of expressing negative ideas. Other English terms of this type that do not have Spanish counterparts are "anyone," "ever," and "any."

Strategies

Try these simple strategies to help you better understand how to use negative expressions:

- Remember that negative words represent pronouns, adjectives, and adverbs. Consequently, these words reflect the characteristic of each category to which they belong. In other words, some forms will change for agreement and others will be invariable.

- Think about the placement of the negative words. Do you wish to reinforce or emphasize the negative aspect of your thought?
- Remember that the double negative is only taboo in English, not Spanish. In fact, the use of the double negative is quite prevalent in Spanish.
- Understand that not every word in English translates directly into Spanish. Some words may be unnecessary in Spanish, especially if the constructions are not parallel to one another.

¡A PRACTICAR!

4A-PRIN-21

Match the negative expression with its positive or negative counterpart.

1 No	______	**a** Nada
2 Algo	______	**b** Nadie
3 Alguien	______	**c** Ni... ni
4 Jamás	______	**d** Ninguno/a
5 Alguno/a/s	______	**e** Sí
6 También	______	**f** Siempre
7 O... o	______	**g** Sin
8 Con	______	**h** Tampoco

4A-PRIN-22

Read the paragraph below and circle all of the negative and positive expressions. There are 11 total.

No existe ninguna cura para la artritis. A veces las medicinas que se compran sin recetas pueden ayudar con el dolor. También un médico puede recetar alguna medicina. Desafortunadamente, algunas personas con esta enfermedad no pueden encontrar ningún tratamiento efectivo. Por esta razón, se encuentra una gran variedad de curas falsas en el mercado, pero estas curas tampoco funcionan.

4A-PRIN-23

Use either a negative or a positive expression to rewrite the sentences below so that they convey the opposite meaning.

1 Carlos siempre puede concentrarse.

____

____

2 A veces Pedro sufre de fatiga.

____

____

3 Nadie ha intentado suicidarse.

____

____

4 Cristina no toma drogas ni alcohol.

____

____

5 Carmen también sufre de insomnio.

____

____

6 Algo le molesta a Carlos.

____

____

7 Pedro no tiene ningún problema digestivo.

____

____

8 Uno no puede mejorar sin esperanza.

____

____

4A-PRIN-24

Create sentences using the cues provided below. Be careful with word order and be sure to make everything agree. In some cases, you may have to add a word or two.

1 (Yo) haber padecer de / alguno / problemas del estómago

____

____

2 Nunca / (él) haber sentir / ninguno / dolor en el pecho

____

____

3 Algunas veces / (ella) pensar / estar perdiendo la razón

____

____

4 (Yo) no tener / dificultades al respirar / ni… ni / sentir que ahogarse

____

____

5 También / (ellos) sufrir / temblores y escalofríos

____

____

6 Siempre / (ella) sentirse / aterrorizado / sin / razón / alguno

____

____

4A-PRIN-25

One of the women's support groups uses the clinic for its weekly meetings. Using either negative or positive words, write the questions that would bring about the answers given below.

1 ¿______________________________

______________________________?

Sí, he sufrido una depresión de posparto alguna vez.

2 ¿______________________________

______________________________?

Nadie me ayuda con el cuidado de los niños; soy madre soltera.

3 ¿______________________________

______________________________?

No, siento que no tengo ningún control ni sobre mi ambiente ni sobre mi vida.

4 ¿______________________________

______________________________?

Confío en mi familia y en la Iglesia.

5 ¿______________________________

______________________________?

No, no me hace falta nada en la vida. Bueno, dinero.

6 ¿______________________________

______________________________?

Sin el apoyo de mi familia no podría sobrevivir.

7 ¿______________________________

______________________________?

No, no tengo ni el tiempo ni el dinero para asistir a clases.

8 ¿______________________________

______________________________?

No, no me siento segura en mi casa, ni tampoco en mi barrio.

4A-PRIN-26

Laura is slowly realizing that in a few months she will be responsible for another person, and she is afraid. Complete the diary entry as if you were Laura. Discuss why you are afraid and what you will do to prepare yourself. Remember to include both positive and negative expressions.

Querido diario:
Soy yo otra vez. No tengo la menor idea de cómo ser madre. ____________________

4A-PRIN-27

Read the following lines written by Rafa. Before he goes to meet Mr. Anderson, Rafa thinks about the conversation they might have. Since he feels uncomfortable using English, he imagines the conversation in Spanish. What do they say to each other? Use both negative and positive expressions. Write at least five sentences.

"Hugo Anderson... Qué quiere... Bueno... 'To have a word,' dijo..."

1 ____________________

2 ____________________

3 ____________________

4 ____________________

5 ____________________

SELF-REFLECTION

1. What purpose does the passive voice serve?

Language is about expression. The passive voice provides you with one more tool with which to express yourself. Using the passive voice, you can present a different perspective to your listeners. Your focus can move from the action to the result of the action while still indicating intention. When you wish to emphasize who received the action over who performed the action, you can turn to the passive voice.

2. How do you know which se *is represented in a sentence?*

Look to the clues surrounding *se*. Is the verb in the singular or the plural? Are there object pronouns in the sentence? Which ones? Is the subject a person or a thing? Is there a prepositional phrase connected to *se*? You need to ask yourself these questions in order to determine what se expresses. After much practice, these questions will come to you automatically.

3. What is the best way to avoid confusing the different types of comparisons?

Once again, grouping like items together will help you to avoid misusing or confusing the various comparisons. Remember that some constructions can be combined with nouns, adjectives, and adverbs, but others are restricted to verbs. Also, think about the type of comparison you are making. What is the degree of the quality you wish to express? Are you comparing two elements or more than two?

FOLLOW-UP TIPS

- Learn to use these new constructions so that you are better able to express your meaning. Build your inventory and take the time to find the exact construction to express your thoughts. Of course, the greater your inventory, the easier it will be for you to find the most precise construction.
- Remember that most of the time we encounter several constructions in a single sentence. When the construction is unfamiliar or you are uncertain as to its function, look to the surrounding words, sentences, and paragraphs for clues to meaning.
- Some words can be used in several different contexts; as a result, these words take on new functions.

DO YOU REMEMBER?

Answer the questions based on the explanations found in *Principios Unidad 4a* of the textbook. If you found any section particularly difficult, go back and try some of the exercises again. There are also links to Spanish language materials on the *Recursos* website.

1 In formal passive constructions, what does the past participle agree with?

2 What is the purpose of the prepositional phrase in the formal passive construction?

3 In Spanish, what construction would you use to write "People say that he is very good"?

4 Which object pronouns can be used with the passive *se*?

5 Name the two types of comparatives. Give examples of each.

6 How many irregular comparatives are there?

7 How do you form the superlative?

8 What is the negative counterpart for *tampoco*?

9 Where in the sentence are negative expressions placed?

FOOD FOR THOUGHT

The following questions are intended to serve as a springboard for discussion. Think about them as you read the story.

- How can I develop trusting and respectful relationships with my patients and clients?
- How can I recognize and challenge my own assumptions?
- How can I learn to recognize my patients' and clients' strengths and to build on teachable moments?
- How can I become partners with colleagues who are bridges across culture, with other organizations in the community that have similar interests and with members of the community I hope to serve?

NOTES FROM THE FIELD

Karen Current is a social worker. At the time of this story, she was pursuing her master's degree.

When I started my first social work internship working with Mexican clients, my Spanish language experience had been mostly with Central and South Americans. One Mexican high school student talked about how she was having a hard time studying with all the noise in her house and the chamaquitos running around. The way she talked, I thought chamacos were rodents or cockroaches. Fortunately I asked and found out that she meant too many little children!

It took me longer to decipher a lo mejor," another Spanish expression. I could tell it had to do with the chance that something would happen. For example, one might hear it in response to Would you like to come to a support group? A lo mejor word for word translated means to the best. I figured it meant probably, and was glad that so many kids wanted to participate in our programs. Later I learned it means maybe, which is as close as some of our clients, not wanting to sound impolite, will ever get to telling you "no way!"

DISCUSSION QUESTIONS

Look at how Karen breaks down the meaning of a lo mejor as she tries to understand the underlying message that the expression implies. How we say "Yes" or "No" is very often defined by cultural expectations.

1 What kind of words do you sometimes substitute for "yes", "no" or "maybe" responses?

2 What kinds of situations might arise in a provider/patient interaction if the provider is not aware of cultural variation in describing possibility or giving consent?

SALUD

KIMMEL, bajo el bisturí

A JIMMY KIMMEL, el divertidísimo presentador de *Jimmy Kimmel Live*, de la cadena ABC, acaban de extirparle el apéndice... y ya se está riendo de eso.

RD: ¿Cómo fue el diagnóstico?
Kimmel: Aunque sentí dolor de estómago justo antes del programa, como tengo muchos problemas gastrointestinales, no le di importancia. Pero el dolor empeoró y al día siguiente falté al trabajo, cosa que nunca antes había hecho. Sólo por curiosidad, busqué "apendicitis" en Internet. Como describía exactamente mis síntomas, llamé a mi médico y le dije: "Creo que tengo apendicitis". Se rió de mí y dijo que podían ser otras 20 cosas, pero cuando me vio, dijo: "Posiblemente seas la primera persona que se diagnostica correctamente por Internet". Me hicieron una tomografía y di a luz un hermoso apéndice de nueve libras.

RD: Es una broma, ¿verdad?
Kimmel: Claro, el apéndice es pequeño, como un dedo meñique.

RD: ¿Cómo fue la cirugía?
Kimmel: Fue laparoscopia. Hicieron tres incisiones y me inflaron el estómago con CO_2 para poder sacar el órgano. Me veía como si estuviera listo para flotar en el Desfile de Acción de Gracias.

RD: ¿Te quedaron cicatrices?
Kimmel: Tres pequeñas, y han arruinado mi cuerpo, que antes era perfecto. Pero en una semana van a estar cubiertas de pelo.

RD: Dicen que los hombres actúan como niños cuando están enfermos. ¿Qué tipo de paciente eres tú?
Kimmel: Lo opuesto. Regresé a trabajar al día siguiente de la operación y les arruiné los planes a todos, porque pensaban que iban a tener la semana libre.

RD: "Apéndice" es una palabra graciosa. ¿Hay alguna parte del cuerpo que lo sea más?
Kimmel: Es una buena palabra; significa "inútil". La úvula es una parte del cuerpo graciosa. Pero creo que la mejor es el bazo.

RD: ¿Recibiste buenos regalos por tu convalecencia?
Kimmel: Barbara Walters, Eminem y Larry King me mandaron algo. Howie Mandel me envió una plantita. Ni siquiera es una planta: es una maceta con tierra y un palito, y 75 páginas de instrucciones sobre cómo cuidarla. Me dieron muchas cosas. Fue mejor que cumplir años. Quisiera tener otro apéndice, porque me regalaron de todo.

RD: Todavía te queda el bazo, ¿verdad?
Kimmel: Creo que sí, pero me parece que puedes morirte sin eso.

RD: Yo creo que es otro órgano "extra".
Kimmel: Ah, pues entonces es el próximo que me voy a quitar.

JODY L. ROHLENA

CONTESTA LAS SIGUIENTES PREGUNTAS:

1 ¿Has visto alguna vez el programa de Jimmy Kimmel? ¿Te gustan los programas de humor y/o las películas cómicas?

2 Kimmel indica que él mismo se diagnosticó tras buscar la palabra "apendicitis" en Internet. ¿Cómo reaccionó su médico ante ese diagnóstico?

La cura del humor

AHORA QUE YA TE HAS REÍDO con la entrevista a Jimmy Kimmel sobre sus experiencias bajo el bisturí, estás más sano que antes. La risa, una habilidad innata, reduce el estrés, mejora la memoria y es beneficiosa para el corazón. Y nuevos estudios revelan que reír no sólo es bueno para nosotros, sino que, además, es contagioso. Si los programas cómicos de televisión son más graciosos cuando estamos en grupo, es porque cuando otra persona se ríe, nuestro cerebro parece activar "neuronas reflejo" que provocan ataques de risa.

Un poco de alegría puede generar una actitud más positiva en situaciones cotidianas, dice la doctora Kelly McGonigal, psicóloga de la Universidad de Stanford. McGonigal enseña risa guiada, una técnica grupal con la que se acondiciona el cuerpo para el trabajo físico de reír a fin de aprovechar los beneficios: alegría e interacción social. "En lugar de preocuparnos por reducir el estrés, deberíamos concentrarnos en reír", señala.

LA TERAPIA DEL HUMOR ALGÚN DÍA PODRÍA SER PARTE DEL CUIDADO PREVENTIVO. UNA BUENA CARCAJADA NOS AYUDA A:

Quemar calorías Reír de 10 a 15 minutos aumenta el ritmo cardiaco entre 10 y 20 por ciento, quemando de 10 a 40 calorías adicionales al día. En un año, la pérdida de peso podría ascender a cuatro libras.

Aliviar el dolor Un estudio de la UCLA financiado por Rx Laughter (grupo que promueve la investigación sobre la conexión entre el humor y la salud) reveló que los niños toleraban mejor el dolor si veían un programa o un video gracioso.

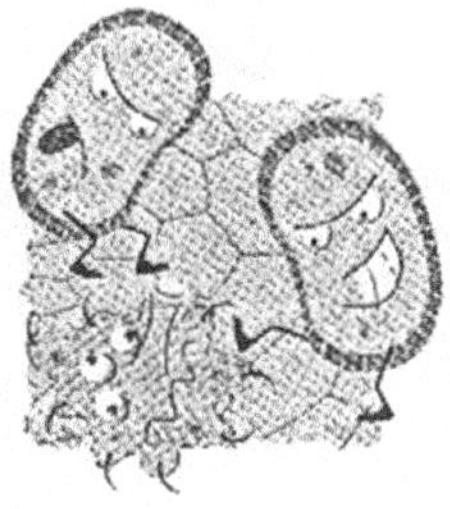

Mantenernos sanos El humor aumenta la producción y la efectividad de células inmunitarias que aniquilan a los microbios. Su número se eleva durante por lo menos 12 horas después de ver sólo una hora del monólogo de George López sobre el Ratón Mickey, por ejemplo.

KATHRYN M. TYRANSKI

To read this article online, go to www.yalebooks.com/salud.

3 ¿Qué opina Kimmel de la operación que le hicieron? ¿Crees que tiene buen sentido del humor, o que está loco? ¿Tienes buen sentido del humor?

4 ¿Crees que el humor puede curar? Explica tu respuesta.

COMPROBACIÓN

DVD *Las preguntas de* Comprobación *están diseñadas para evaluar tu habilidad de usar lo que has aprendido, en situaciones nuevas y diferentes. Aunque el contexto todavía es limitado y las respuestas están restringidas y guiadas, debes interpretar más.*

SECCIÓN A

¿Qué pasa en la Historia*? Escoge las palabras que completan mejor la oración. ¡Cuidado con la gramática!*

1 Hoy fue uno de los días más agitados en la clínica. Todo el mundo trabajó (más / mucho / muy).

2 Primero, Mila tuvo a su hija en la clínica (asistida / asistidos / asistiendo) por Jaime, Carmina y Ashleigh.

3 Eliodoro también estuvo en la sala, aunque al principio él (nadie / no / nunca) quería entrar.

4 Como oía los (agudas / gritos / mujercitas) de Mila en la sala, Eliodoro quería quedarse afuera.

5 Ángela lo ayudó a decidirse y eso fue lo (mayor / mejor / menor) porque Mila se sintió (mejor / mucho / muy) feliz de estar acompañada (a / para / por) su marido en una situación (más / menos / tan) importante y complicada. Al final del día, todos estaban muy contentos y aliviados.

SECCIÓN B

Estas oraciones describen este día tan agitado en la clínica. Escoge las palabras que completan mejor cada oración.

agudo	nada
cargo	nadie
contracciones	ningún
corregir	prescrita
dosis	vergüenza
insinuar	

Primero ocurrió que Ashleigh se equivocó al explicarle la **(1)** __________ de una receta a un paciente. Como consecuencia, Ángela tuvo que **(2)** __________ lo que Ashleigh le había explicado, y no pasó **(3)** __________. Entonces llegó Mila con **(4)** __________ y hubo que ayudarla a dar a luz allí mismo. Como si no fuera suficiente, llegó Laura con Alex que tenía un dolor **(5)** __________. Inmediatamente Carmina se hizo **(6)** __________ de él y al final todo quedó resuelto. Pero, ¡qué día!

¡A CONVERSAR!

PERSONAJES

DVD

In this segment we meet Ricardito, Jaime's nephew. What does he say about himself? About his parents? What does he say about living in the U.S., and about leaving his friends behind in Puerto Rico? In your opinion, are the high school years difficult? What about for a teenager whose parents have recently separated? Do you think these years are more difficult for immigrants? In what way? Discuss these questions with a friend, using the sentences below as a way to get started.

Ricardito

ESTUDIANTE 1: Creo que Ricardito tiene problemas porque...
ESTUDIANTE 2: Bueno, la situación de Ricardito no es tan difícil como la situación de otros inmigrantes porque por lo menos tiene el apoyo de su tío Jaime...

¡A RESUMIR!

EPISODIO

A local radio station has a program dedicated to Latino health issues. The host has heard of La Comunidad *and is encouraging his listeners to see it. With your partner, call the program and summarize the* Episodio *for this unit, being sure to mention the following issues:*

- Alex and his chronic pain
- The phone conversation between Jaime and his "*hermanita*"
- The conversation between Alex and Laura
- Milagros and Eliodoro
- What Rafa has to say about Hugo Anderson
- The conversation between Ángela and Carmina
- The phone call that Jaime receives at the end of the episode

APLICACIÓN

ESCUCHAR

DVD

View the conversation between Jaime and Ricardito, and then discuss the following issues with a classmate:

1. ¿De qué hablan?
2. ¿Por qué Jaime está preocupado?
3. ¿Cómo reacciona Ricardito?
4. A Ricardito no le gusta que Jaime diga que es un "niño." ¿Tiene razón de estar molesto Ricardito?

Jaime and Ricardito

Imagine another conversation between them: alter their attitudes and give them a new dialogue. Practice this new scene with a classmate. How does the scene end?

JAIME: Bueno, Ricardito, comprendo exactamente cómo te sientes.
RICARDITO: Gracias, tío. Aprecio mucho tu ayuda, especialmente tus recomendaciones de que ...

ANALIZAR

DVD

In this scene a patient picks up his prescription from Ángela, and she reviews the instructions with him. Why is he confused?

Role-play a more extended conversation between Ángela and the patient. Practice giving prescription instructions. To make sure that the "patient" understands, have him/ her repeat the instructions back to you. Use the sentences below as a conversation starter.

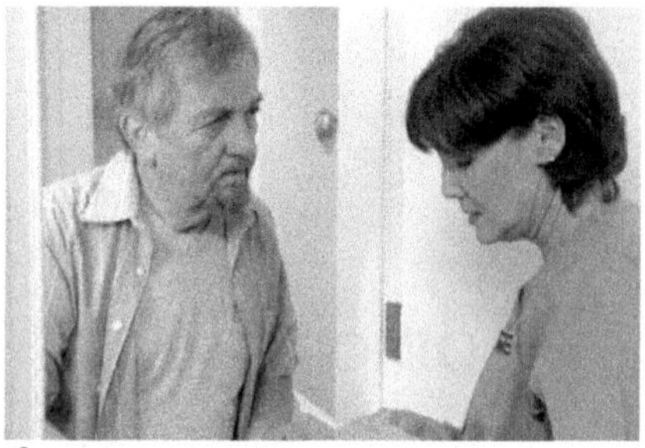

Ángela and a patient

ÁNGELA: Señor, es importante no tomar más de...

PACIENTE: Gracias. ¿Puedo manejar cuando tomo este medicamento?

Now role-play a conversation between Ángela and Ashleigh. You may wish to use the sentence that follows as a way to start your dialogue.

ÁNGELA: Ashleigh, gracias por ayudarme con el paciente, pero es importante...

EN LA PRÁCTICA

DVD

Ricardito reacts as a typical teenager when Duna asks him about his experiences in high school. What does he say? Keep in mind that children in immigrant families may have more difficulties with feelings of isolation and maladjustment. Do you think this is the case with Ricardito? What kind of advice can Duna give him?

Duna speaks with Ricardito

Role-play a conversation between Duna and Ricardito in which she gives him more specific advice on adjusting to life in the U.S. How does he react to her advice in your scene? Use the following sentence as a way to start this difficult conversation.

DUNA: Ricardito, la vida en la secundaria es difícil a veces. Pero tomar alcohol...

LENGUA

DVD

Después de escuchar el regaño de su madre, las preguntas de Duna y los consejos de Jaime, Ricardito le escribe un mensaje electrónico a un amigo en Puerto Rico contándole todo el asunto desde el principio, desde su punto de vista.

Escribe el mensaje de Ricardito a su amigo. Puedes incluir los siguientes puntos:

- estábamos bebiendo
- nos descubrieron
- mi madre me regañó, Duna me habló, Jaime me aconsejó
- mi opinión del asunto
- qué voy a hacer ahora

b Representa una conversación entre Ricardito y su amigo, en la que Ricardito cuenta lo que pasó y el amigo le hace preguntas y le da consejos.

RICARDITO: Mira, el otro día pasó algo terrible...
AMIGO: Ay, sí, es horrible. Los padres no entienden nada...

MÁS ALLÁ

Even though questions containing negative expressions are formed differently in Spanish than they are in English, you respond to them in a similar fashion. Students, however, tend to experience problems when it comes to this aspect of the Spanish language. How do you respond to negative questions that require a yes or no answer?

First, you need to understand that typically there are two parts to the answer: the yes/no and the main content. You should respond with "no" and a negative statement if you are in agreement with the negative question. If you are in disagreement, then your response should begin with *sí* and end with an affirmative statement.

SPANISH	ENGLISH
¿Alex no toma nada para el dolor?	Alex doesn't take anything for the pain?
—No, no toma nada para el dolor.	—No, he doesn't take anything for the pain.
¿Alex no toma nada para el dolor?	Alex doesn't take anything for the pain?
—Sí, toma algo para el dolor.	—Yes, he takes something for the pain.

Notice how the majority of the content from the original question is incorporated into the response. This use of repetition helps to clarify the meaning intended by the speaker, as well as to avoid any possible misunderstandings.

Speakers of English sometimes employ another method of responding to negative questions. In some instances, you choose to confirm and then supplement with additional unsolicited information. In other words, you agree with the negative question but are offering information not previously mentioned or sought after. The context allows you to add rather than contradict, especially because these constructions are perceived to be assumptions, not questions. Consequently, you opt to avoid the yes/no portion of the question and respond with two separate and complete thoughts: the first indicates the correctness or incorrectness of the question, whereas the second presents the new information. Look at the following examples:

SPANISH	ENGLISH
¿No muestra ningún síntoma de depresión?	He doesn't show any signs of depression?
—Tiene razón. Muestra síntomas de fatiga.	—You're right. He shows signs of fatigue.

The above method of responding to negative questions is very common in the English language; however, it simply does not work in Spanish. As a result, you might encounter difficulty when learning this aspect of the Spanish language. In Spanish, if you wish to affirm a question that contains a negative, you must also respond in the negative. You can then add extra information.

SPANISH	ENGLISH
¿No muestra ningún síntoma de depresión?	He doesn't show any signs of depression?
—No, no muestra ninguno. Pero muestra síntomas de fatiga.	—No, he doesn't show any. But he does show signs of fatigue.

Practice incorporating these elements into your speech so that you grow accustomed to how they function. Rather than trust direct translations from English, consider how Spanish handles these expressions. More specifically, consider your response to a question containing a negative expression. Do you agree or disagree? Have you made your opinion clear?

ENTREVISTA

DVD

Read this summary in English of what Miguel René Moreno says in his interview before you watch it on the DVD. Remember that these interviews were conducted to include "authentic language" on the DVD. This means that the interviews are unscripted and at a natural conversational pace. Use the English summary to guide you.

Miguel René Moreno

I like the character a lot. He's a very deep character. He has a lot inside. He gives you a lot to grab onto. He's not a lightweight person in terms that he doesn't do something and then is done with it. No. He's a complicated person in that he has a lot of changes of attitude, and he's got a lot of passion inside him. I love that because in that way he's somewhat like me. Yes, well, I'm also a little explosive and also apprehensive with the people I love. But I don't go to such extremes. But Alex is good. He means well, he wants to be someone important. He knows that he's helping the community and is happy about it. He knows that he's doing something for his people, for the part of him that is Mexican-American, the part that is Mexican and Latino. He knows his people, what they are suffering, what they have suffered, and is very involved in the community.

As far as the script is written, he doesn't hit her, but it could be... There are some women that yes, he hits. Well, the character of Alex that I created had a girlfriend and he hit her once. She kept going out with him and didn't leave him because of it, but he felt bad about what he had done... That's my way of creating a back-story for the character. But with Laura he doesn't dare, because in spite of the fact that she is a bit of —I don't know if I can say this word— a bastard (laughs), she's somewhat of a bastard, but he loves her. She's a good girl and is very fragile.

I have a girlfriend, to the pain of some and the delight of others. We've been going out for eight years. The way I talk about it you'd think it was twenty, right? It's a big thing, but I don't want to get married yet, no, no, no. It's not for me. Marriage is not for me. I think I'm doing just fine. What are they laughing about back there?! (laughs)

In the beginning it didn't seem like it had to go that way. But the scene was very emotional, wasn't it? It was a little bit over the top, but Alex's passion and courage rose up in me and the truth is that all of a sudden, when I saw their faces looking at me, it seemed like something real and I began to give back this energy and that surprised me even more. Because there came a moment when I wanted to hit one of them and fight them because they were saying things to me... and I think that someone came out from inside of me who was hidden because I'm very calm, Miguel René is very calm, I don't get into disputes. I can learn a lot from these things because really I'm very calm on a physical level.

Up in the North the *machismo* thing is very common. It's like, "You, woman over there! Go cook, hurry! Make me some eggs for dinner!" and the man is watching the TV or something. If there are get togethers, the woman is with the women and the man with the men. Everything is very separated... Please, be quiet back there! (laughs)

Actually, getting the part of Alex was a surprise because my casting was for Rafa. I was afraid because Rafa is a bigger character than I am but Rocío [the assistant director] and everyone told me, "You're going to be Alex." I hadn't known Alex until that day but as I looked into it I felt more affinity for him and felt more like myself.

[Marilyn Brito, who plays Laura] is marvelous. She's a pretty girl, very sweet, more than you can believe. She gives a lot of affection. I love to hug her —it's just a joke! (laughs) I love hugging her and besides, she's got good relationships with all of the actors. She's great, pretty, sweet. When she's in front of me, I push aside many things from inside myself for the scene. She brings me a lot even in real life and these days that we've spent together have been great because she's helped me with my job. She's also from another country, and that's important because our work involves different ways of thinking, attitudes, ways of life, relationships, and quality of life. Everything is different and that influences me, but I also think that we've developed a nice friendship and "hot damn!" Excuse me! That was the word but... I'm Mexican and I'm from the north, excuse me.

Watch the interview with Miguel René Moreno (Alex) once more, and discuss the following items with a classmate:

- el personaje de Alex
- el parecido entre Alex y Miguel
- la violencia entre Alex y Laura
- cómo Miguel construyó el personaje de Alex
- Laura y su relación con Alex
- la relación que Miguel tiene con su novia en la vida real
- la pelea en La Pueblita
- el machismo en el norte de México
- cómo Miguel consiguió el papel de Alex
- la actriz que hace el papel de Laura y la relación entre ellos

Discuss this interview with a classmate. Make comparisons between "Alex", the character, and Miguel, the actor, for example: Miguel es más tranquilo que Alex.

Watch the interview with Rocío Quiñones once more, and answer the following questions:

- ¿Cómo se interesó en la odontología?
- ¿Cómo es un día típico en su vida profesional?
- ¿Cómo llegó a los Estados Unidos?

UNIDAD 4b

NOTE TO THE STUDENT

Knowing vocabulary does not automatically make you fluent in any language, but you are certainly off to a strong start. However, your ability to express yourself depends upon your entire language inventory, which includes knowing how to combine the vocabulary to express meaningful thoughts and ideas. True, there is no simple way to acquire all of the skills necessary to communicate effectively in the Spanish language, but through dedication, practice, and experimentation fluency is certainly an attainable goal.

DON'T JUST SETTLE

Limit the use of those comfortable and overworked words that have no precise meaning because they have been extended to so many different contexts that their meaning has become diluted. Such words and expressions as "good," "bad," "interesting," and "I like it" are examples of these overused elements. While these types of words and expressions might be the first to come to mind, you will most likely discover a better and more precise term or construction if you take the time to explore your language inventory. Most important, if you use the same few words to describe different people, actions, and situations, you are not taking advantage of the variety that the Spanish language has to offer.

EXPLORE YOUR OPTIONS

Remember that there are many ways to convey the same basic idea. Using a variety of constructions can add color to your language and improve your ability to express yourself. Consider how many different ways there are in Spanish to express the idea "good job."

- *¡Vaya esfuerzo!*
- *Ahora ya lo sabes.*
- *Así es cómo se hace.*
- *Bien hecho.*
- *Buen trabajo.*
- *¡Cuánto mejor!*
- *Estupendo.*
- *Excelente.*
- *Felicitaciones.*
- *Lo ha logrado.*
- *Lo hizo usted bien.*
- *Muy bien.*
- *No podría sobrevivir sin usted.*
- *Perfecto.*
- *Qué rápido aprende usted.*
- *Usted es el mejor.*

The list could go on and on, but we'll stop here. Notice how the basic message remains the same, although, some expressions might be more appropriate than others. Regardless, you always have more than one option available.

FINAL OBSERVATIONS

Although speaking English seems perfectly natural to you now, there was a time when it was not. Starting at an early age you probably struggled with learning the language. Eventually, you learned how to express yourself in your own way. Your experience with the Spanish language will be that much richer if you learn to examine critically your own language abilities. Be observant when interacting with others and consider the whole picture. Train yourself to be both an active listener and an active speaker.

VOCABULARIO

Below are the vocabulary words highlighted in this unit. Remember that you can hear these words in action in the *Vocabulario* section of *Unidad 4b* on the *Recursos* webpage. After you've looked at them, write beside each one its English equivalent. If you have any doubt about the words' exact meaning, look them up in a good Spanish-English dictionary.

Review the words that you have written on the margins of *Vocabulario* so far. Look up the meanings of any words you don't know.

Remember to use this space to add new and useful words that you find in your study or work, but were not included in *Vocabulario*!

Verbos

admitir

agradecer

arreglar

cepillar

cobrar

complacer

corregir

desaparecer

optar

otorgar

patrocinar

ponerse mejor

prometer

resolver

tener

tocarle a él

Adjetivos

adecuado

alocada

desaparecidos

insoportable

otorgado

resuelto

Sustantivos

el abogado

el anuncio

los dientes

la esperanza

el incremento

el infierno

el tratamiento

¡A PRACTICAR!

4B-VOC-1

Match the picture with the sentence that most accurately describes the scene.

1 ____ Agradece a toda la gente por su apoyo y trabajo duro.

2 ____ Los niños aprenden a cepillarse los dientes.

3 ____ Admite que tiene un problema y quiere recibir el tratamiento apropiado.

4 ____ Patrocinan una feria de salud.

5 ____ Promete arreglar su vida alocada.

a

b

c

d

e

4B-VOC-2

Fill in each blank with the correct word. Be careful with agreement between the new word and the rest of the sentence. If you need help, review Unidad 4b Vocabulario, *or go back to the first exercise in this section.*

Duna le da consejos a un paciente de la clínica que sufre de drogadicción.

Lo primero que usted **(1)** ____________ *(have)* que hacer es **(2)** ____________ *(admit)* que hay un problema. Después de reconocer esto, sugiero que vaya al Departamento de Salud y haga una cita con el doctor Rodríguez. No se preocupe si no tiene seguro porque no **(3)** ____________ *(they charge)* mucho dinero, y además aceptan Medicaid. Allí lo pueden ayudar a encontrar **(4)** ____________ *(the appropriate treatment)* para que **(5)** ____________ *(you get better)*. **(6)** ____________ *(Promise me)* que hará la cita cuanto antes.

4B-VOC-3

Look at the photos below. Use the vocabulary provided to write one or two sentences that describe each scene. You can choose to follow the story line or to use your imagination. Be sure to incorporate grammar that you have studied up to this point.

1 un infierno
agradecer
tener

2 anunciar
patrocinar
otorgado

3 abogado
arreglar
la esperanza

4 complacer
prometer
insoportable

1 ______________________________

2 ______________________________

3 ______________________________

4 ______________________________

4B-VOC-4

We have now come to the final chapter of our story. What do you think will happen next? How will the story end? Were all of the issues resolved? Using the vocabulary found in Unidad 4b, create your own ending for one or more of the following characters: Carmina, Laura, Ángela, Rafa, Alex, Jaime, Duna, Ashleigh, Federico, Ricardito, Eliodoro, and/or Milagros.

USEFUL TERMS AND EXPRESSIONS

This section introduces new vocabulary and expressions related to themes found throughout *Historia 4b* on the DVD.

SUSTANTIVOS

La gente

el/la casero/a	homeowner
el/la ciudadano/a	citizen
el/la cuñado/a law	brother/sister-in-
el/la juez/a	judge
el/la nieto/a	grandchild
el/la obrero/a	worker
el/la sobrino/a	niece/nephew

Las condiciones físicas

la convalescencia	convalescence
el entumecimiento	numbness
la intervención	intervention
los signos vitales	vital signs

Las condiciones físicas

la aprobación previa	prior approval
los beneficios	benefits
la cobertura	coverage
la confidencialidad	confidentiality
el costo íntegro	entire cost
el empleo	employment
las estampillas de comida	food stamps
el estatus	status
los fondos	funds
la guardería	daycare
el hogar	home
el ingreso	income
la junta	board, committee
la ley	law
el maltrato	mistreatment
el manejo	management
el pago	pay
el papeleo	paperwork
el poder	power
la póliza de seguro	insurance policy
el préstamo	loan
las prioridades	priorities
la privacidad	privacy
la raza	race
las represalias	retaliation
los requisitos	requirements
el Seguro Social	Social Security
la solicitud	application
el sueldo	salary
el talón	heel; check (money)
el vecindario	neighborhood

VERBOS	
acudir	to go to
advertir	to warn
aflojar(se)	to loosen
alquilar	to rent
atraer	to attract
atrasar(se)	to delay
autorizar	to authorize
calificar	to qualify
consentir	to allow
cumplir	to fulfill
desalojar	to evict
descansar	to rest
engañar	to deceive
fallecer	to pass away, die
fomentar	to foster
localizar	to locate
perjudicar(se)	to harm
promover	to promote
rechazar	to reject
reclamar	to demand
rentar	to rent
restar	to deduct
rogar	to beg
sacar de quicio	to drive crazy
solicitar	to apply
someter(se)	to undergo
torcer(se)	to twist
valer	to be worth
ADJETIVOS Y ADVERBIOS	
a largo plazo	long-term
adjunto/a	enclosed
encargado/a	in charge
financiero/a	financial
preventivo/a	preventative
sobrepeso	overweight
tiempo completo	full-time
tiempo parcial	part-time

Study the vocabulary before you begin *Principios* because it will be useful when practicing the grammar points of the unit. Remember that this section is not intended to be an exhaustive list of all relevant terms, but rather to give you exposure to some of the basic vocabulary used in healthcare. The definitions given here are limited, because they are intended for the narrow use of the exercises found in *Principios*. Look the words up in a good Spanish-English dictionary if you want to know other meanings, how to pronounce them, the contexts in which the words can be found, sayings and common expressions using these words, and their derivatives (adjectives from nouns, nouns from verbs, etc.).

PRINCIPIOS

So far, with the exception of the commands, you have focused primarily on tenses that belong to the indicative mood. In this final chapter, you will study the three most common tenses of the subjunctive mood: present, present perfect, and past. In English, we tend to ignore or forget this mood since it is used so infrequently, but the Spanish language employs the subjunctive mood in a wide variety of contexts; therefore, it is an important tool for accurately communicating in this language.

MOOD

First, what is meant by the term "mood"? Usually, you think of someone's particular state of mind when you hear this word. This explanation is pretty close to how mood is defined in terms of language, so you're half way there. Mood lets you know the speaker's attitude toward the information that is conveyed. For example, the mood tells the listener if the information is representative of fact, of possibility, of a feeling or emotion, or of an opinion. In other words, you learn the state of mind of the speaker through the use of moods.

What, then, is the difference between the indicative and the subjunctive moods? Whenever the sentence represents something believed to be true —an objective fact or a truth— or you want to assert that something is fact, you should use one of the indicative tenses: present, preterit, imperfect, present perfect, pluperfect, future, or conditional.

SPANISH	ENGLISH
Viven juntos porque **es** la mejor manera de ahorrar dinero.	They **live** together because it **is** the best way to save money.
Me **recomendaron** un abogado muy bueno.	They **recommended** a very good lawyer to me.
El grupo **se reunirá** mañana por la noche.	The group **will meet** tomorrow night.

Each of the sentences above expresses a fact or a concept that the speaker believes to be true.

So when should you use the subjunctive? You should use the subjunctive if you want to express a possibility or a subjective opinion or feeling.

SPANISH	ENGLISH
Es importante que **tengan** un programa de servicio de alimentos de verano.	It's important **to have** a Summer Food Service Program.
Recomiendo que los niños **asistan** a este programa.	I recommend that the children **attend** this program.

In the above sentences where the subjunctive is used, the speaker is expressing an opinion or an idea that is subjective and not necessarily representative of fact.

SUBJUNCTIVE SIGNALS

Before we begin our discussion of the subjunctive forms, a brief review of when to use the subjunctive is in order. The subjunctive is usually dependent on a particular expression or clause, one that reflects an attitude or opinion of some type. In fact, it is this expression or clause that triggers the use of the subjunctive. Let's call these expressions subjunctive signals. *Que* is the element that most often connects the verb in the subjunctive with the expression or signal. Typically, the signals used to introduce the subjunctive are categorized in the following manner:

Wishes and Desires:

Aconsejar que...	Pedir que...
Decir que...	Permitir que...
Desear que...	Preferir que...
Insistir en que...	Prohibir que...
Mandar que...	Querer que...
Necesitar que...	Recomendar que...
Ojalá que...	Sugerir que...

Emotions:

Alegrarse de que...	Molestar que...
Enojarse de que...	Sentir que...
Esperar que...	Sorprender que...
Estar contento/a de que...	Temer que...
Gustar que...	Tener miedo de que...
Lamentar que...	

Impersonal Expressions:

Es una lástima que...	Es indispensable que...
Es bueno que...	Es malo que...
Es difícil que...	Es mejor que...
Es dudoso que...	Es necesario que...
Es extraño que...	Es posible que...
Es fácil que...	Es preciso que...
Es importante que...	Es probable que...
Es imposible que...	Es urgente que...
Es increíble que...	

These expressions receive their name from the fact that they do not have a specific subject. In fact, the English concept "it" is contained within the verb.

Doubt and Denial:

Dudar que...	Presumir que...
Negar que...	Quizás...
No creer que...	Tal vez...
No pensar que...	

Indefinite:

There are no fixed expressions for this group of signals. Basically, the subjunctive is required whenever the signal refers to something unknown or unidentified. English concepts such as *any*, *anything*, or anyone are often associated with this category. It might help to think of this category as also falling under "doubt and denial" since the existence of something is called into question.

SPANISH	ENGLISH
¿**Existe alguna ley que** establezca el pago mínimo?	**Does any law exist that** establishes minimum pay?

Negative:

Similar to the indefinite category, this group doesn't have any fixed expressions. Here the subjunctive is required whenever the signal refers to something nonexistent or negative.

SPANISH	ENGLISH
No encuentro ningún trabajo de tiempo parcial que me ofrezca seguro médico.	**I can't find any part-time job that** provides me medical insurance.

Guesses:

Once again, there are no fixed expressions for this group of signals. A signal of this type refers to something hypothetical or conjecture. Most conjunctions and the conditional + *sí* clauses fit into this category.

SPANISH	ENGLISH
Usted tiene derecho a recibir los beneficios **mientras cumpla** con los requisitos.	You have the right to receive benefits **as long** as you fulfill the requirements.
Usted puede recibir Medicaid **con tal de que** sus ingresos no sean demasiado altos.	You can receive Medicaid **provided that** your income **is** not too high.
Lo contrataría **si pudiera.**	I would hire you **if I could.**

Notice how all of the signals provided here express subjective value judgments. A popular convention used to remember which type of expressions require the subjunctive is the acronym **WEDDING**.

W:	Wishes, Wants
E:	Emotions
D:	Desires
D:	Doubts
I:	Impersonal, Indefinite
N:	Negative
G:	Guesses

This acronym is quite apropos, especially since the English concept of a wedding embodies all of the categories described above (although hopefully "impersonal" and "negative" are not words you would use to describe too many weddings!).

PRESENT SUBJUNCTIVE

You have already seen glimpses of the present subjunctive when you studied the commands. If you recall, both affirmative and negative formal, negative informal, and *nosotros* commands actually use the present subjunctive as their base. Here is the complete distribution of present subjunctive endings for each verb type:

SUBJECT	-AR	-ER	-IR
yo	-e	-a	-a
tú	-es	-as	-as
usted, él, ella	-e	-a	-a
nosotros	-emos	-amos	-amos
ustedes, ellos, ellas	-en	-an	-an

Observe that the first person singular (*yo*) ending and the third person singular (*usted*, *él*, *ella*) ending are identical. Also, note that once again the *-er* and *-ir* verb conjugations follow the same pattern.

Do you recall how to form the subjunctive? For most verbs, take the stem of the *yo* form of the verb in the present indicative (the first present tense you studied) and add the appropriate subjunctive endings for the infinitive type.

INFINITIVE	PRESENT INDICATIVE - YO FORM	PRESENT SUBJUNCTIVE
hablar	habl(o)	habl(emos) *nosotros*
fomentar	foment(o)	foment(e) *la clínica*
venir	veng(o)	veng(an) *los niños*
vivir	viv(o)	viv(a) *el paciente*

Another way to look at how to form the subjunctive is to take the *yo* form of the verb in the present indicative and simply switch or reverse the distribution of the present indicative endings. In other words, *-ar* verbs now take the *-er* verb endings and *-er* / *-ir* verbs take the *-ar* verb endings (except for the first person singular, the *yo* conjugations.)

	FOMENTAR	PROMETER	AÑADIR
Indicativo:	fomento	prometo	añado
	fomentas	prometes	añades
	fomenta	promete	añade
	fomentamos	prometemos	añadimos
	fomentan	prometen	añaden
Subjuntivo:	fomente	prometa	añada
	fomentes	prometas	añadas
	fomente	prometa	añada
	fomentemos	prometamos	añadamos
	fomenten	prometan	añadan

Use whichever method works best for you. Review *Unidad 1b* if you feel you need a review of the present tense verb forms.

SPANISH	ENGLISH
Es difícil que **hablemos** con él hoy.	It's unlikely that we **talk** with him today.
Es importante que **fomente** una buena relación con la comunidad.	It's important that the clinic **foster** a good relationship with the community.
Me alegro de que los niños **vengan** a verme.	I am glad that the children **come** to see me.
Es dudoso que **viva** el paciente.	It's doubtful that the patient **will live**.

Understand that the patterns described above only apply to those verbs that do not exhibit stem changes in the first person form (*yo*) or require spelling changes in every form. Both stem changing verbs and spelling changes will be discussed in the sections that follow.

¡A PRACTICAR!

4B-PRIN-1

Read the paragraph below and circle the verbs in the present subjunctive. There are six verbs.

Es ilegal que su patrón le quite dinero de su sueldo por cosas o artículos que usted no le ha comprado. Si usted alquila un trailer o apartamento, la ley requiere que el patrón tenga una orden del juez por escrito para desalojarlo. Además es necesario que el patrón provea de agua caliente y fría, calefacción en el invierno y un lugar limpio y seguro. Si usted sufre de maltrato en el trabajo, es importante que reclame sus derechos. Desgraciadamente, muchos trabajadores temen que el patrón los corra del trabajo por reclamar sus derechos. Por eso, es importante entender que la ley prohíbe que su empleador tome represalias.

4B-PRIN-2

Conjugate the infinitives below in the present subjunctive. Then, write down their meaning in a phrase in English.

1 cumplir (yo)

Forma: ______________________

Significado: ______________________

2 establecer (tú)

Forma: ______________________

Significado: ______________________

3 consumir (ellas)

Forma: ______________________

Significado: ______________________

4 preguntar (nosotros)

Forma: ______________________

Significado: ______________________

5 preparar (ella)

Forma: ______________________

Significado: ______________________

6 servir (la escuela)

Forma: ______________________

Significado: ______________________

7 presionar (ellos)

Forma: ______________________

Significado: ______________________

8 recibir (tú)

Forma: ______________________

Significado: ______________________

9 reconocer (nosotros)

Forma: ______________________

Significado: ______________________

10 necesitar (yo)

Forma: ______________________

Significado: ______________________

11 proveer (la comida)

Forma: ______________________

Significado: ______________________

12 poner (tú)

Forma: ______________________

Significado: ______________________

4B-PRIN-3

Carmina, Ángela, Duna, and Ashleigh prepare for the upcoming health fair. Combine the cues below to create logical sentences using the present subjunctive.

1 Quiero que / preparar (ustedes) / una lista de nuestras prioridades

____

____

2 Es importante que / escribir (Rafa) / un artículo para *La Voz*

____

____

3 Espero que / recibir (la clínica) / los fondos necesarios

____

____

4 Pido que / compartir (nosotras) / la información con otras organizaciones

____

____

5 Tengo miedo de que / olvidarse (nosotros) / de algo importante

____

____

6 Es posible que / no atraer (la feria) / a toda la comunidad

____

____

7 Es necesario que / cubrir (nosotras) / todos los asuntos más importantes

____

____

8 Sugiero que / distribuir (nosotras) / información sobre los programas de intervención

____

____

4B-PRIN-4

Giving bad news is never pleasant; however, the language you use can help to soften the severity of the news. Read the sentences below. Then use the present subjunctive to present the information in a more comforting manner.

1 "Señor García usted tiene SIDA."

____

____

2 "Su cáncer es terminal."

____

____

3 "Ponga usted todos sus asuntos en orden porque le doy unos dos meses."

____

____

4 "Su esposo fallecerá pronto."

____

____

5 "Vamos a amputar la pierna."

____

____

6 "El bebé padece de muchos problemas muy graves porque es prematuro."

____

____

7 "Sufres de problemas cardíacos porque estás pasado de peso."

____

____

8 "No funciona el tratamiento."

____

____

9 "No vale la pena hacerle la operación."

____

____

4B-PRIN-5

Sometimes what is said does not reflect what was meant; therefore, the listener must learn to interpret what was said to avoid misunderstandings and to find the underlying message. Below are lines from throughout the Historia. *Read the sentences. Then combine the expressions provided or others that you might think of with the present subjunctive to give your interpretation of the message.*

Palabras útiles

Dudar que...	Lamentar que...
Es bueno que...	Necesitar que...
Es difícil que...	Querer que...
Es importante que...	Sugerir que..
Es preciso que...	Tal vez...
Esperar que...	Temer que...

MODELO:

Tú nunca me ayudas con nada.

Necesito que me ayudes por favor.

1 La clínica no está igual que antes de yo irme a México.

____

____

2 Ya ven, nada funciona bien en esta casa.

____

____

3 Ya tengo bastante con lo que me pasó y encima tú vienes a someterme a un interrogatorio.

____

____

4 Claro que le caes mal, siempre vienes a hacerme escenas.

____

____

5 Pues, a tu edad cualquiera se preocupa.

____

____

6 Tan "perfecto", que es insoportable...

____

____

7 Es su actitud, tan machista. Me saca de quicio.

____

____

8 No actúes impulsivamente contra gente con poder.

____

____

9 ¡Y seguro que son ellos quienes arruinan las viviendas porque son "brutos"!

____

____

10 ¡Lo que pasa es que tú eres como todos los americanos!

____

____

11 Bueno, mucho gusto, doctor... Verá, lo que ocurre es algo... delicado...

____

____

12 Lo siento, Abe... Pero Lois Lane ama a Superman y ¡no a Clark Kent!

____

____

VERBS WITH STEM CHANGES IN THE PRESENT SUBJUNCTIVE

You must pay close attention to whether a verb stem changes in the *yo* form, especially the type of stem change that occurs. In the present subjunctive, some stem changing verbs will undergo a transformation in the *nosotros* form, yet others will follow the regular pattern and not stem change at all. All of the verbs that undergo this additional stem change belong to the *-ir* conjugation. Here are the two types of stem changes that occur in the present subjunctive:

- *-ir* verbs that stem change from *-e-* to *-ie-* and *-e-* to *-i-* will stem change to *-i-* in the *nosotros* form.

	DIVERTIR (E > IE)	MENTIR (E > IE)	DECIR (E > I)
yo	divierta	mienta	diga
tú	diviertas	mientas	digas
usted, él, ella	divierta	mienta	diga
nosotros	**divirtamos**	**mintamos**	**digamos**
ustedes, ellos, ellas	diviertan	mientan	digan

- *-ir* verbs that stem change from *-o-* to *-ue-* will stem change from *-o-* to *-u-* in the *nosotros* command.

	DORMIR (E > IE)	MORIR (E > IE)
yo	duerma	muera
tú	duermas	mueras
usted, él, ella	duerma	muera
nosotros	**durmamos**	**muramos**
ustedes, ellos, ellas	duerman	mueran

Verbs that belong to the *-ar* and *-er* conjugations will not show signs of any stem change in the *nosotros* form.

INFINITIVE	PRESENT INDICATIVE	PRESENT SUBJUNCTIVE
PENSAR	pienso	piense
	piensas	pienses
	piensa	piense
	pensamos	**pensemos**
	piensan	piensen
PODER	puedo	pueda
	puedes	puedas
	puede	pueda
	podemos	**podamos**
	pueden	puedan

¡A PRACTICAR!

4B-PRIN-6

For each infinitive, mark the forms that will undergo a stem change in the present subjunctive.

1 **perder:** yo _____ tú _____ él, ella, usted _____ nosotros _____ ellos, ellas, ustedes _____

2 **convertir(se):** yo _____ tú _____ él, ella, usted _____ nosotros _____ ellos, ellas, ustedes _____

3 **comenzar:** yo _____ tú _____ él, ella, usted _____ nosotros _____ ellos, ellas, ustedes _____

4 **consentir:** yo _____ tú _____ él, ella, usted _____ nosotros _____ ellos, ellas, ustedes _____

5 **pensar:** yo _____ tú _____ él, ella, usted _____ nosotros _____ ellos, ellas, ustedes _____

6 **entender:** yo _____ tú _____ él, ella, usted _____ nosotros _____ ellos, ellas, ustedes _____

7 **pedir:** yo _____ tú _____ él, ella, usted _____ nosotros _____ ellos, ellas, ustedes _____

8 **querer:** yo _____ tú _____ él, ella, usted _____ nosotros _____ ellos, ellas, ustedes _____

9 **recordar:** yo _____ tú _____ él, ella, usted _____ nosotros _____ ellos, ellas, ustedes _____

10 **divertir(se):** yo _____ tú _____ él, ella, usted _____ nosotros _____ ellos, ellas, ustedes _____

11 **dormir:** yo _____ tú _____ él, ella, usted _____ nosotros _____ ellos, ellas, ustedes _____

12 **decir:** yo _____ tú _____ él, ella, usted _____ nosotros _____ ellos, ellas, ustedes _____

4B-PRIN-7

Provide the subject/s and the infinitive for each verb listed below.

1 muera **Sujeto:** ______________
Infinitivo: ______________

2 te acuerdes **Sujeto:** ______________
Infinitivo: ______________

3 sigamos **Sujeto:** ______________
Infinitivo: ______________

4 sirvan **Sujeto:** ______________
Infinitivo: ______________

5 pruebe **Sujeto:** ______________
Infinitivo: ______________

6 elijamos **Sujeto:** ______________
Infinitivo: ______________

7 cierres **Sujeto:** ______________
Infinitivo: ______________

8 midamos **Sujeto:** ______________
Infinitivo: ______________

9 repitan **Sujeto:** ______________
Infinitivo: ______________

10 durmamos **Sujeto:** ______________
Infinitivo: ______________

11 demuestre **Sujeto:** ______________
Infinitivo: ______________

12 aprieten **Sujeto:** ______________
Infinitivo: ______________

4B-PRIN-8

Duna is working with some clients who need to apply for Medicaid. Help her out by combining words from each of the three columns to create logical sentences in the present subjunctive. More than one answer is possible for each sentence!

Palabras útiles

Aconsejo que...	conseguir	...copias de su póliza de seguro de salud o de vida
El departamento de servicios sociales quiere que...	buscar	...copias de todos los talones de su sueldo
Ellos requieren que...	escribir	...documentos de estados financieros
Es bueno que...	llevar	...el acta de nacimiento
Es importante que...	mostrar	...prueba de su embarazo
Es mejor que...	proveer	...prueba de su estatus migratorio
Pido que...	tener	...su tarjeta de Seguro Social
Sugiero que...	pedir	...una lista de los vehículos que usted posee

1 ______________________________

____

2 ______________________________

____

3 ______________________________

____

4 ______________________________

____

5 ______________________________

____

6 ______________________________

____

7 ______________________________

____

8 ______________________________

____

4B-PRIN-9

Read the following lines by Laura. Based on what she says, what advice would you offer her?

Soy un desastre, Carmina... Desde que me diagnosticaron la diabetes, mi vida ha sido un infierno... No quise aceptarlo... Opté por llevar una vida alocada, como si nada importara... No he hecho nada que valga la pena, ni he estudiado... Y ahora, de pronto, la responsabilidad de ser madre... Con todos los riesgos... Tú sabes...

1 ______________________________

____

2 ______________________________

____

3 ______________________________

____

4 ______________________________

____

5 ______________________________

____

6 ______________________________

____

4B-PRIN-10

Imagine that the man in the photo is trying to find out about the health services offered at the clinic. Use what you have learned to create a dialogue of at least eight sentences. Remember to use the present subjunctive.

1 ______________________________

____

2 ______________________________

____

3 ______________________________

____

4 ______________________________

____

5 ______________________________

____

6 ______________________________

____

7 ______________________________

____

8 ______________________________

____

VERBS WITH SPELLING CHANGES IN THE PRESENT SUBJUNCTIVE

Some verbs will undergo spelling changes to the stem before adding the subjunctive endings. You already practiced these spelling changes when you studied the preterit in *Unidad 2b* and the commands in *Unidad 3b*. Here are the three most common spelling changes that occur:

- Examples of *-car* changing to *-qu* before *-e*:

	SACAR	SECAR	MARCAR
yo	saque	seque	marque
tú	saques	seques	marques
usted, él, ella	saque	seque	marque
nosotros	saquemos	sequemos	marquemos
ustedes, ellos, ellas	saquen	sequen	marquen

- Examples of *-gar* changing to *-gu* before *-e*:

	TRAGAR	LLEGAR	PAGAR
yo	trague	llegue	pague
tú	tragues	llegues	pagues
usted, él, ella	trague	llegue	pague
nosotros	traguemos	lleguemos	paguemos
ustedes, ellos, ellas	traguen	lleguen	paguen

- Examples of *-zar* changing to *-c* before *-e*:

	REZAR	CRUZAR	ALCANZAR
yo	rece	cruce	alcance
tú	reces	cruces	alcances
usted, él, ella	rece	cruce	alcances
nosotros	recemos	crucemos	alcancemos
ustedes, ellos, ellas	recen	crucen	alcancen

¡A PRACTICAR!

4B-PRIN-11

Conjugate the verbs listed below in the present subjunctive.

1 rogar:
yo ____________
tú ____________
él, ella, usted ____________
nosotros ____________
ellos, ellas, ustedes ____________

2 forzar:
yo ____________
tú ____________
él, ella, usted ____________
nosotros ____________
ellos, ellas, ustedes ____________

3 buscar:
yo ____________
tú ____________
él, ella, usted ____________
nosotros ____________
ellos, ellas, ustedes ____________

4 colgar:
yo ____________
tú ____________
él, ella, usted ____________
nosotros ____________
ellos, ellas, ustedes ____________

5 explicar:
yo ____________
tú ____________
él, ella, usted ____________
nosotros ____________
ellos, ellas, ustedes ____________

4B-PRIN-12

One of the clinic's patients tries to convince her husband to follow the doctor's orders. Fill in the blanks with the correct form of the verb in the present subjunctive.

arriesgar	gozar
empezar	perjudicarse
equivocarse	realizar

Dudo que el médico **(1)** ____________. Es importante que tú no **(2)** ____________ la salud. Según él, es probable que **(3)** ____________ si no cambias tus hábitos alimenticios. Insisto en que **(4)** ____________ mañana con el programa de ejercicios. Quiero que tú **(5)** ____________ de una vida larga y saludable. Espero que nosotros **(6)** ____________ nuestros sueños juntos.

4B-PRIN-13

Duna discusses Medicaid with one of her clients. Provide the questions that would bring about the answers given. Use the present subjunctive.

Modelo:

¿Es necesario que llegue a tiempo?

Sí, tiene que llegar a tiempo.

1 ¿ ____?

Sí, usted puede calificar para Medicaid.

2 ¿ ____?

Sí, el médico tiene que certificar que usted permanece en casa.

3 ¿ ____?

Sí, usted tiene que pagar el costo íntegro si no recibe aprobación previa.

4 ¿ ____?

No, usted no tiene que buscar un plan de salud.

5 ¿ ____?

No, un médico de cabecera no tiene que autorizar todos los servicios.

6 ¿ ____?

Sí, le pueden negar la cobertura.

IRREGULAR PRESENT SUBJUNCTIVE

Like every other tense you have studied, the present subjunctive has irregular verbs. Can you guess which verbs are irregular? Verbs like *ser*, *ir*, *saber*, and *haber* change their form entirely. Others such as *estar* and *dar* add an accent. (These accents help distinguish them from other words such as the preposition *de*.) Here are the present subjunctive forms for the irregular verbs:

	SER	**IR**	**SABER**	**HABER**
yo	sea	vaya	sepa	haya
tú	seas	vayas	sepas	hayas
usted, él, ella	sea	vaya	sepa	haya
nosotros	seamos	vayamos	sepamos	hayamos
ustedes, ellos, ellas	sean	sequen	sepan	hayan

	ESTAR	**DAR**
yo	esté	dé
tú	estés	des
usted, él, ella	esté	dé
nosotros	estemos	demos
ustedes, ellos, ellas	estén	den

¡A PRACTICAR!

4B-PRIN-14

Read the paragraph below and circle all forms of the irregular present subjunctive. There are five in all.

Es importante que sea el mismo farmacéutico todo el mes. Al terminar el mes, usted puede cambiar de farmacia si quiere. También es necesario que sepa que no le dan más de seis recetas al mes a menos que tenga una enfermedad que ponga en riesgo su vida. Si usted pierde la tarjeta, es posible que le den otra sin el talón de farmacia adjunto. Si usted tiene alguna pregunta, recomiendo que vaya a hablar con su trabajadora social. Espero que ella la haya ayudado.

4B-PRIN-15

Fill in the blanks with the correct form of the present subjunctive.

No hay nada que **(1)** ______________ *(ser)* más importante que la comunidad en que vivo. Por eso, busco un barrio en que **(2)** ______________ *(haber)* una gran variedad de gente y de culturas. También, prefiero que nosotros **(3)** ______________ *(estar)* cerca de las escuelas y tiendas porque sólo tenemos un auto. Por ahora, vivimos en casa de mi hermano con mi cuñada y mis sobrinos porque tenemos que ahorrar dinero. Cuando tenga dinero suficiente, compraré una casa nueva con tal de que el banco me **(4)** ______________ *(dar)* un préstamo. Mi sueño es que mis hijos **(5)** ______________ *(estar)* contentos porque los quiero tanto. Ojalá que ellos lo **(6)** ______________ *(saber)*.

4B-PRIN-16

Ashleigh pays a visit to Mila to check on how she and the baby are doing. Respond to the questions below using the present subjunctive.

1 ¿Hay alguien que lo ayuda con el cuidado de la niña mientras Eliodoro trabaja?

No, ______________________________

____

____

____

2 ¿Buscan ustedes un apartamento que sea más grande?

No, ______________________________

____

____

____

3 ¿Quieren ustedes que la niña vaya a una guardería?

No, ______________________________

____

____

____

4 ¿Le molesta que sus padres no estén para ver a la niña?

Si, ______________________________

____

____

____

4B-PRIN-17

We all have expectations of people we work with. What do you expect of or require from someone who works for or with you? Use the irregular present subjunctive to give five examples.

Exijo que…

1 ______________________________

____

____

____

____

2 ______________________________

____

____

____

____

3 ______________________________

____

____

____

____

4 ______________________________

____

____

____

____

5 ______________________________

____

____

____

____

PRESENT PERFECT SUBJUNCTIVE

To form the present perfect subjunctive, join the present subjunctive of *haber* —*haya*, *hayas*, *haya*, *hayamos*, *hayan*— with the past participle of the main verb. Go to *Unidad 2a* if you need a quick refresher on past participles. Don't forget that nothing can be placed between *haber* and the past participle and that the past participles do not change for gender or number.

	OPTAR	AGRADECER	ADMITIR
yo	haya optado	haya agradecido	haya admitido
tú	hayas optado	hayas agradecido	hayas admitido
usted, él, ella	haya optado	haya agradecido	haya admitido
nosotros	hayamos optado	hayamos agradecido	hayamos admitido
ustedes, ellos, ellas	hayan optado	hayan agradecido	hayan admitido

The only difference between the use of the present perfect subjunctive and the present perfect indicative is that the present perfect subjunctive constructions are restricted to contexts that are introduced by subjunctive signals. In these contexts, the present perfect subjunctive can be interpreted as meaning that an action has or may have taken place.

SPANISH	ENGLISH
Tal vez la tarjeta **haya llegado**.	Maybe the card **has arrived**.
Ojalá que nos **hayan otorgado** la beca.	I hope that they **have awarded** us the grant.

¡A PRACTICAR!

4B-PRIN-18

Write the correct form of the present perfect subjunctive for the verbs listed below.

1 que mi familia y yo / volver

____

2 que las organizaciones / patrocinar

____

3 que la junta / ser

____

4 que yo / recibir

____

5 que usted / prevenir

____

6 que tú / perder

____

7 que la clínica / desarrollar

____

8 que la feria / traer

____

9 que los programas de intervención / ayudar

____

10 que nosotros / poner

____

4B-PRIN-19

Duna meets with one of her clients to discuss the WIC program. Use the present perfect subjunctive with the cues provided to form complete sentences.

1 Tal vez / sus niños / estar en riesgo

____

____

2 Me alegro de que / usted / poder participar en el programa de nutrición WIC para mujeres, infantes y niños

____

____

3 Me gusta que / establecerse / un sistema de prioridades

____

____

4 Espero que / nosotros / discutir todos los alimentos recomendados

____

____

5 Es bueno que / usted / decidir darle el pecho

____

____

6 No pienso que / ellos / mandarle el cheque todavía

____

____

4B-PRIN-20

Duna meets with a woman who describes some of the obstacles she has faced while trying to find a home for her family. What do you think about what has happened to her? Use the cues below to respond to the following sentences in the present perfect subjunctive.

Modelo: Un casero no me vendió la casa por ser una mujer soltera con niños.
Siento que no le haya vendido la casa.

Expresiones útiles:

Dudo que...	No creo que...
Es imposible que...	No me gusta que...
Es mejor que...	Ojalá que...
Es una lástima que...	Qué bueno que...
Me molesta que...	Siento que...

1 Un casero se negó a alquilarme el apartamento.

____

____

2 Un agente me mintió acerca de la disponibilidad de la casa.

____

____

3 Algunos agentes intentaron persuadirme para no comprar en cierto vecindario.

____

____

4 Una vez un casero me desalojó de la vivienda.

____

____

5 Algunos caseros querían cobrarme un depósito muy alto.

____

____

4B-PRIN-21

Before Mr. Anderson met with Rafa, he consulted with his lawyer. What do you think the two discussed on the phone? Write a brief conversation of at least five sentences. Use ojalá *and the present perfect subjunctive.*

1 ______________________________

____

____

____

2 ______________________________

____

____

____

3 ______________________________

____

____

____

4 ______________________________

____

____

____

5 ______________________________

____

____

____

PAST SUBJUNCTIVE

The past subjunctive (often called the "imperfect subjunctive") again shows why it is so important to learn your verb forms well, because you must use the preterit as your base. Go back to *Unidad 2b* if you need a quick review of the preterit. Here is the distribution of endings for the past subjunctive:

	-AR	**-ER**	**-IR**
yo	-ra	-ra	-ra
tú	-ras	-ras	-ras
usted, él, ella	-ra	-ra	-ra
nosotros	-ramos	-ramos	-ramos
ustedes, ellos, ellas	-ran	-ran	-ran

As you will notice, the endings for the past subjunctive are the same for each infinitive type. In addition, both the first person (*yo*) and the third person (*él*, *ella*, *usted*) singular make use of the same endings.

To form the past subjunctive, you drop the *-ron* ending of the the third person plural form (*ellos*, *ellas*, *ustedes*) of the preterit and add the endings listed above:

	-AR	**-ER**	**-IR**
yo	apoyara	perdiera	asistiera
tú	apoyaras	perdieras	asistieras
usted, él, ella	apoyara	perdiera	asistiera
nosotros	apoyáramos	perdiéramos	asistiéramos
ustedes, ellos, ellas	apoyaran	perdieran	asistieran

Observe that the *nosotros* form adds an accent mark. Although we will concentrate on the endings shown above, there are alternate endings for the past subjunctive: *-se, -ses, -se, -semos, -sen*. This second group, however, is restricted to formal writing. Still, you should learn to recognize them.

When do you use the past subjunctive? Like the present, the past subjunctive is used to express attitudes, opinions, feelings, and hypothetical situations; however, the action or state is conveyed in the past. In addition, the past subjunctive can be extended to *si* clauses when the concept being expressed is hypothetical. Along these same lines, the past subjunctive can be used in certain contexts that permit the conditional. For example, because of the uncertain nature of whether an act will be carried out, the past subjunctive can be used with verbs such as *querer* and *poder* to make polite requests.

SPANISH	ENGLISH
Para expresar el pasado:	**To express the past:**
Ella no quería que **cancelaran** la feria.	She didn't want them **to cancel** the fair.
Lamento que el programa **rechazara** su solicitud.	I regret that the program **rejected** your application.
En claúsulas de *si*:	**In *si* clauses:**
Aprovecharía los programas disponibles si **supiera** algo de ellos.	I would take advantage of the programs if I **knew** something about them.
Laura se comporta como si no **estuviera** enferma.	Laura behaves as if she **were** not ill.
En lugar del condicional:	**In place of the conditional:**
Quisiera obtener información sobre los servicios ofrecidos por la clínica.	I **would like** to obtain information about the services offered by the clinic.
Ustedes debieran hablar con el médico.	**You should** really speak with the doctor.

¡A PRACTICAR!

4B-PRIN-22

Write the correct form of the present perfect subjunctive for the verbs listed below.

1 ser (yo) **Forma:** ____________
Significado: ____________

2 llegar (tú): **Forma:** ____________
Significado: ____________

3 morir (ellas) **Forma:** ____________
Significado: ____________

4 traer (nosotros) **Forma:** ____________
Significado: ____________

5 llamar (ella) **Forma:** ____________
Significado: ____________

6 comprar (el hombre) **Forma:** ____________
Significado: ____________

7 recontar (ellos) **Forma:** ____________
Significado: ____________

8 beber (tú) **Forma:** ____________
Significado: ____________

9 cubrir (nosotros) **Forma:** ____________
Significado: ____________

10 poner (yo) **Forma:** ____________
Significado: ____________

11 querer (la mujer) **Forma:** ____________
Significado: ____________

12 poder (tú) **Forma:** ____________
Significado: ____________

4B-PRIN-23

Fill in the blanks with the correct forms of the verbs in the past subjunctive.

Me dijeron que **(1)** ____________ *(ir)* nosotros a su oficina para pedir una solicitud. Querían que yo **(2)** ____________ *(traer)* dos copias de todos los documentos requeridos para que no **(3)** ____________ *(atrasarse)* el proceso. Fue necesario que nosotros **(4)** ____________ *(pedir)* un intérprete porque no hablamos inglés. No creo que **(5)** ____________ *(poder)* haber llenado los formularios sin que él nos **(6)** ____________ *(ayudar)*. Pero, por fin, ya está hecho todo y sólo podemos esperar. Si después de dos semanas no recibo nada por correo, me recomendaron que **(7)** ____________ *(llamar)* la oficina para avisarles de la situación. Quizás ellos **(8)** ____________ *(tener)* mejor control si **(9)** ____________ *(aceptar)* los papeles en persona y no por correo. Bueno, si **(10)** ____________ *(haber)* problemas con este sistema, ya nos lo habrían indicado.

4B-PRIN-24

One of Duna's clients, Claudia, is speaking with her neighbor. Claudia compares the health programs in which she participates now with those she participated in as a young woman. Rewrite the sentences in the past, remembering to use the past subjunctive when necessary.

1 Es posible que una persona vea al médico cuando se siente enferma.

____

____

2 Les importa que los clientes esperen privacidad y confidencialidad.

____

____

3 No se prohíbe que tú cambies tu médico de cabecera.

____

____

4 Nos dejan que seleccionemos un médico de cabecera de una lista de participantes.

____

____

5 Está bien que un cliente presente quejas o recomendaciones para hacer cambios.

____

____

6 No se permite que un paciente sea maltratado.

____

____

7 Es posible que los clientes participen en la toma de decisiones con respecto a su salud.

____

____

4B-PRIN-25

Sometimes things are not always as they seem. Respond to the sentences using como si *combined with the past subjunctive.*

Modelo:

Rafa acaba de conocer al señor Anderson, pero habla como si lo conociera de toda la vida.

1 Laura es diabética y está embarazada.

Pero ______________________________

____

____

2 Alex sufre de artritis reumatoide.

Pero ______________________________

____

____

3 Carmina sueña con otro hombre.

Pero ______________________________

____

____

4 Federico extraña a su familia.

Pero ______________________________

____

____

5 Ashleigh sabe español bastante bien.

Pero ______________________________

____

____

6 Ricardito bebe alcohol con sus amigos aunque es un menor.

Pero ______________________________

____

____

INDIRECT COMMANDS

Once you have mastered how to form the subjunctive, indirect command constructions will not present much of a challenge to you. To form indirect commands you need only place *que* in front of the verb in the subjunctive. In Spanish, these constructions express concepts equivalent to English "let" and "have."

SPANISH	ENGLISH
Que me llamen mañana para hacer una cita.	Have them call me tomorrow to make an appointment.
Que me explique él lo que pasó con los narcóticos.	Let him explain to me what happened to the narcotics.

Indirect commands are not considered alternatives to the informal and formal command forms because as their name implies, indirect commands are not used to convey the request or order directly to the person who will carry out the action. Instead, the request is communicated to a third party who in turn relays the message.

¡A PRACTICAR!

4B-PRIN-26

It's a hot day for the fair. People who work outside are more likely to suffer from heat exhaustion. To find out what to do when this occurs match the sentences in Spanish with the appropriate translation in English.

1 Que descanse un poco.

2 Que se afloje la ropa.

3 Que se ponga un pañuelo mojado en la frente.

4 Que se siente en la sombra.

5 Que se tome un vaso de agua.

a Have him drink a glass of water.

b Have him loosen his clothing.

c Have him sit in the shade.

d Have him rest a bit.

e Have him put a wet handkerchief on his forehead.

4B-PRIN-27

Carmina has met the man of her dreams. Now she has to let Abe know. What should she do? Use indirect commands to tell Laura what to tell Carmina.

1 (escribirle una carta)

____

____

2 (dejar de llamarlo)

____

____

3 (decirle la verdad)

____

____

4 (presentarle a otra mujer)

____

____

5 (no aceptar sus llamadas)

____

____

6 (explicarle que hay otras mujeres para él)

____

____

4B-PRIN-28

Translate the following sentences into Spanish using indirect commands.

1 Have your grandchild join a program for those who abuse alcohol and drugs.

____

____

____

2 Let your cousin move in with you.

____

____

____

3 Have your friends speak to a social worker.

____

____

____

4 Have your cousin demand his rights.

____

____

____

5 Let your children become active members in the community.

____

____

____

6 Have your aunt meet with a lawyer.

____

____

____

4B-PRIN-29

Imagine that you are on the phone with a woman whose husband was just stung by a bee. He is allergic to bee stings. What instructions would you give to her? Use indirect commands.

1 ______________________________________

____

____

____

____

____

2 ______________________________________

____

____

____

____

____

3 ______________________________________

____

____

____

____

____

4 ______________________________________

____

____

____

____

____

CONCEPTO IMPORTANTE: USING THE SUBJUNCTIVE

Think of a sentence that uses the subjunctive in English. If you're a typical English speaker, you are having trouble doing this. Most speakers of English are barely aware of the existence of the subjunctive mood in their own language and misuse it when they do need to use it. Think of all the times you have heard someone say, "If it was me..." or "If I was king for a day" (instead of "If it were" and "If I were"). Did you even realize that the subjunctive was needed? Grasping this somewhat unfamiliar concept in a foreign language can seem overwhelming at first. However, to communicate effectively in Spanish, you need to gain reasonable control over the subjunctive constructions.

What We Know

Sentences containing verbs in the subjunctive usually consist of two clauses connected by a conjunction —in other words, two sets of words, each with its own verb and subject. With the exception of a select group of verbs, the subjects do not refer to the same person or group of people. Generally, the verb in the first clause is in the indicative mood and the verb in the second clause is in the subjunctive.

SPANISH	ENGLISH
Es probable que lo **hagan**.	**It's** probable that **they will do** it.
Estoy contento de que **usted se mejore**.	**I am** happy that **you are getting** better.
No **había** nada que **pudiera** hacer.	**There was** nothing that **I could** do.
No **es** posible que **ellos vengan** hoy.	**It's** not possible for **them to come** today.

The subjunctive mood is required whenever you wish to do one of the following:

1 Indicate something potentially (but not necessarily) true

2 Express thoughts distorted by emotion

3 Express your opinion or attitude toward something

4 Indicate something potentially not true

5 Express subjective thoughts

Usually, the four basic contexts described above are indicated through the use of subjunctive signals.

SPANISH	ENGLISH
Es probable que...	It's probable that...
Estoy contento de que...	I am happy that...
No hay nada que...	There is nothing that...
No es posible que...	It's not possible that...

For the most part, if you do not employ a subjunctive signal, you should use one of the tenses belonging to the indicative mood. The subjunctive is not required when there is only one subject, even though there are two verbs. Instead, the second verb appears as an infinitive.

SUBJUNTIVO	INFINITIVO
(Yo) Necesito que (tú) hables con el señor Anderson.	**(Yo) Necesito hablar** con el señor Anderson.

Knowing that the subjunctive usually consists of two clauses joined by *que* and set off by certain triggers such as uncertainty or emotion makes it relatively easy to recognize, but deciding when to use the subjunctive in a conversation with a native Spanish speaker is not as easy. Why?

The Difficulty

To put it simply, we are not used to paying attention to the hypothetical or emotional on a linguistic level in English. The distinction between whether or not something is definitely going to happen or might possibly happen certainly matters in terms of content: we care about the distinction between whether or not we will need (or might possibly need) surgery. On a linguistic level, however, it matters not at all. Spanish, on the other hand, highlights the content of what is being said on the level of the language itself.

Imagine a photo of a family picnic taken two months ago. The colors are bright, the edges of the figures crisp. To describe this photograph, you might say, "Mom was so happy that day," or in Spanish, *Mamá estuvo tan contenta ese día*. Now imagine that the photo was taken 100 years ago and that everything is cast in sepia tones. You might describe the picture by saying, "It's possible that Grandma was happy in those days," or *Es posible que Abuelita estuviera contenta en aquellos días* since you can't be sure from looking at the photo. The subjunctive mood casts everything in a hypothetical or emotional light. Using the subjunctive is like overlaying your language with a more doubtful or emotional tinge.

Understanding the difference between the two moods is not so complicated. Now you have to overcome the automatic response of translating directly from English.

The English language, with the exception of the verb "to be" (be, were) and the forms used to represent the third person singular (take, have, come, etc.), makes no distinction between the indicative and the subjunctive moods, but the Spanish language does. Spanish uses two sets of forms to represent the two moods. Take a look at the examples provided here:

	PRESENT INDICATIVE	PRESENT SUBJUNCTIVE
Spanish	Es verdad que ellos **tienen** SIDA.	Es triste que ellos **tengan** SIDA.
English	It's true that they **have** AIDS.	It's sad that they **have** AIDS.

Since English, in most instances, employs a single set of forms regardless of the mood, you tend to mistakenly associate these contexts with the indicative forms that you first encountered in your studies, overlooking the fact that Spanish has two separate sets of forms.

To complicate matters further, English employs alternative expressions that make use of infinitives or prepositional phrases where Spanish would employ the subjunctive. Once again, direct translation and incorrect association can lead to the use of incorrect forms.

SPANISH	ENGLISH
Le aconsejé que **fuera** a la clínica.	I advised her **to go** to the clinic.
Querían que **viniera** él.	They wanted him **to come**.
Es importante que **siga** con el tratamiento.	It's important **for him to continue** with the treatment.

In addition, you now have to train yourself to ask questions that you never had to ask before. How do you feel about the message you are conveying? What is your attitude? In the beginning of this unit, you reviewed expressions that reflect attitudes and feelings. Certain words and expressions, however, are not so clear-cut because they can introduce either the indicative or the subjunctive mood. Therefore, you must know which mood is associated with the particular word or expression you wish to use. Is the word or expression a subjunctive signal or not?

In this first group, whether to choose the subjunctive or the indicative mood depends on whether the expression is affirmative or negative.

SUBJUNTIVO	INDICATIVO
no pensar que...	pensar que...
no creer que del ...	creer que...
dudar que...	no dudar que...
negar que...	no negar que...
no ser verdad que...	ser verdad que...
no ser seguro que...	ser seguro que...
no ser cierto que...	ser cierto que...
no estar seguro de que...	estar seguro de que...

The subjunctive is used only those expressions that represent uncertainty, emotion, opinion, or negatives.

Unlike the first group, here the choice between subjunctive and indicative is determined by whether the information is factual or uncertain. The verb *decir* falls in this group.

SPANISH	ENGLISH
Le dije que **descansara**.	I told him **to rest**.
Le dije que **descansaba**.	I told him that **he was resting**.

The use of *que* is quite straightforward because it is separate from the signal itself. You know that the conjunction que can serve to connect the signal with the verb in the subjunctive.

SPANISH	ENGLISH
Es necesario que tenga una receta para recibir algunos tipos de medicamentos.	**It is necessary that you have** a prescription in order to receive some types of medicines.
Está prohibido que ustedes usen información de otras personas.	**It is prohibited for you to use** someone else's information.

Still, students will often omit this word because English does. You need to remember that in Spanish the conjunction is not optional; it must be used to separate two verbs with different subjects.

SPANISH	ENGLISH
Espero **que** sepan cómo hacerlo.	I hope they know how to do it.
Quieren **que** vayas al mercado.	They want you to go to the store.

Some conjunctions and adverbial expressions, however, serve as both the signal and the connection between the two clauses. Here are the most common ones:

To indicate condition:	a condición de que (s)	as long as
	a fin de que (s)	so that
	a menos que (s)	unless
	a no ser que (s)	unless
	como	if
	con tal de que (s)	provided that
	de manera que	so that
	de modo que	so that
	donde	wherever
	en caso de que (s)	so that
	para que (s)	so that
	salvo que (s)	unless
	según	according to
	sin que (s)	without
To indicate time:	antes de que (s)	before
	apenas	as soon as
	cuando	when
	después de que	after
	en cuanto	as soon as
	hasta que	until
	mientras	as long as
	tan pronto como	as soon as
To indicate a contrast:	aunque	even though
	no obstante	in spite of
	a pesar de que	in spite of

Those forms followed by (s) are used exclusively with the subjunctive, while the others only require the subjunctive when the intended meaning is hypothetical or conjecture. Do some of these conjunctions seem familiar to you? You studied many of them in *Unidad 2b*. If, however, you compare the meanings found here with those meanings found in *Unidad 2b*, you will note that they are not always identical. Once again, the determining factor is one of certainty versus uncertainty.

SPANISH	ENGLISH
Indicativo:	**Translation of Indicative:**
Como no sigues las recomendaciones del médico, no mejorarás.	**Since you don't follow** the doctor's recommendations, you will not get better.
Tendremos la feria **aunque llueve**.	We will have the fair **even though it is raining**.
Subjuntivo:	**Translation of Subjunctive:**
Como no sigas las recomendaciones del médico, no mejorarás.	**If you don't follow** the doctor's recommendations, you will not get better.
Tendremos la feria **aunque llueva**.	We will have the fair **even though it might rain**.

Strategies

Try these simple strategies to help you better understand how to use the subjunctive:

- Consider your message. How do you want others to interpret your message? Is it fact or opinion?
- When in doubt, remember that the subjunctive is used whenever you wish to express the uncertainty of a statement or you wish to express your subjunctive feelings.
- Keep in mind that the subjunctive is usually employed in a subordinate or dependent clause. In other words, a preceding element or group of elements will signal you to use or listen for the subjunctive.
- Remember that you usually have two verbs with two different subjects and that you must place *que* between the signal and the verb in the subjunctive.

¡A PRACTICAR!

4B-PRIN-30

In English, explain in your own words the difference between the subjunctive and indicative moods.

____

____

____

____

____

____

____

____

____

____

4B-PRIN-31

Indicate whether the words in bold would be expressed by the subjunctive, indicative, or infinitive in Spanish.

1 I always take my card whenever **I go** to the doctor.

______ ***Subjuntivo***

______ ***Indicativo***

______ ***Infinitivo***

2 I wouldn't do it, unless **you feel** it's necessary.

______ ***Subjuntivo***

______ ***Indicativo***

______ ***Infinitivo***

3 Is there anyone here **who speaks** Spanish?

______ ***Subjuntivo***

______ ***Indicativo***

______ ***Infinitivo***

4 We hope that this treatment **works**.

______ ***Subjuntivo***

______ ***Indicativo***

______ ***Infinitivo***

5 It's important **to bring** a list of your medications.

______ ***Subjuntivo***

______ ***Indicativo***

______ ***Infinitivo***

6 He told me **to take** two tablets a day.

______ ***Subjuntivo***

______ ***Indicativo***

______ ***Infinitivo***

7 I have **to visit** with clients at their homes.

______ ***Subjuntivo***

______ ***Indicativo***

______ ***Infinitivo***

8 I need you **to tell** me where it hurts.

______ ***Subjuntivo***

______ ***Indicativo***

______ ***Infinitivo***

9 I think that this **will work** better.

______ ***Subjuntivo***

______ ***Indicativo***

______ ***Infinitivo***

10 You need to rest so that your body **will heal**.

______ ***Subjuntivo***

______ ***Indicativo***

______ ***Infinitivo***

4B-PRIN-32

Ashleigh is preparing for her next home visit with a woman who needs some information about Medicaid. In English, explain why the subjunctive is or is not used in Spanish. Then translate the sentence.

Modelo:

Está bien que nos reunamos ahora.

Razón: The subjunctive is used because there are two verbs, two subjects, and the impersonal signal *está bien.*

Traducción: It's fine that we meet now.

1 Es mejor que **vaya** usted a la sala de emergencia sólo cuando **se trate** de una emergencia.

Razón: ____________________

Traducción: ____________________

2 **Estaba** segura de que estos servicios no **requerían** la aprobación previa de un médico de cabecera puesto que **eran** servicios dentales.

Razón: ____________________

Traducción: ____________________

3 Es importante **acudir** a los servicios de cuidado preventivo.

Razón: ____________________

Traducción: ____________________

4 Antes de que **visite** a un especialista, necesita **hablar** con su médico de cabecera.

Razón: ____________________

Traducción: ____________________

5 Primero, sugiero que **escoja** su médico de cabecera ya que él **tiene** que **coordinar** su cuidado.

Razón: ____________________

Traducción: ____________________

6 Sentí que no **pudiéramos** verla el otro día.

Razón: ____________________

Traducción: ____________________

4B-PRIN-33

Here is an excerpt from a pamphlet describing one of the summer meal programs available for children of immigrants. Translate the paragraph into Spanish.

It is important to have a summer food program because the children don't attend school during this time. Through this program, the children of low-income migrant families receive free food so that the families can save money and buy other things necessary for the maintenance of all of the family members. These children can receive up to three meals a day and all migrant children are eligible unless they are more than eighteen years of age. Since the hours are flexible, they can eat whenever they want. In addition, it's not necessary that the families fill out an application.

____

____

____

____

____

____

____

____

____

____

____

____

____

____

4B-PRIN-34

Read the diagnosis provided below. Use your powers of persuasion to convince this patient that your particular line of treatment is the best way to go. Discuss both the pros and cons. Write at least five sentences.

El Señor Ruíz es obrero. Tiene 45 años. Sufre de presión alta. Las pruebas muestran una alta concentración de glucosa en la sangre. También se queja de palpitaciones, dolores en los riñones y entumecimiento de los pies. Además se ha notado que sus encías han comenzado a deteriorarse.

1 ____

____

____

____

2 ____

____

____

____

3 ____

____

____

____

4 ____

____

____

____

5 ____

____

____

4B-PRIN-35

David wants to know how to go about organizing a health fair for the health center where he works. What aspects of your profession or future profession would you advise him to include?

1

2

3

4

5

6

SELF-REFLECTION

1. What is the purpose of the subjunctive signal?

Obviously, these signals introduce the subjunctive; however, they do have an even greater purpose. Subjunctive signals enable you to let the listener know exactly how you feel about the message you are conveying. Through the use of subjunctive signals, you enable the listener to step into your shoes so that he or she can better understand your personal perspective.

2. How do I avoid using indicative forms when I should be using subjunctive ones?

The best way to remember to use the subjunctive is to commit to memory the signals that introduce it. Another option is to take time to think about your message. Is there more than one way to express your idea? If there is more than one, are both viable options in Spanish? For example, in English you can say "It's important for them to communicate with each other"or "It's important that they communicate with each other;" however, only the second sentence is acceptable in Spanish.

3. What do I need to remember when using indirect commands?

First, you only need *que* and a verb in the subjunctive to form them. Second, indirect commands are considered third person or third party commands. In other words, you are never speaking directly with the person who is told to perform the action.

FOLLOW-UP TIPS

- Keep in mind the more complex your message, the more likely it is that you will have to employ complex constructions. But this isn't meant as license to use only short cryptic sentences.
- Remember that certain words and expressions require the use of specific constructions.
- Try not to avoid constructions simply because they are new or challenging to you. All of them are essential parts of the Spanish language that enable you to truly personalize the manner in which you communicate with others.

DO YOU REMEMBER?

Answer the questions based on the explanations found in *Principios Unidad 4b* of the textbook. If you found any section particularly difficult, go back and try some of the exercises again. There are also links to Spanish language materials on the *Recursos* website.

1 Name the 8 basic categories used to organize the subjunctive signals.

2 In which clause is the verb in the subjunctive usually found?

3 Which is the most common conjunction used to introduce the subjunctive?

4 How do you form the present subjunctive?

5 Which types of verbs stem-changes in the *nosotros* form of the present subjunctive?

6 How do you conjugate the verb *dormir* in the present subjunctive?

7 Name the three types of spelling changes that occur in the present subjunctive.

8 How many irregular verb forms does the present subjunctive have? List them.

9 How do you form the present perfect subjunctive?

10 How do you form the past subjunctive?

11 What type of construction is *Que traigan a la niña a mi oficina*?

FOOD FOR THOUGHT

The following questions are intended to serve as a springboard for discussion. Think about them as you read the story.

- How can I develop trusting and respectful relationships with my patients and clients?
- How can I recognize and challenge my own assumptions?
- How can I learn to recognize my patients' and clients' strengths and to build on teachable moments?
- How can I become partners with colleagues who are bridges across culture, with other organizations in the community that have similar interests and with members of the community I hope to serve?

NOTES FROM THE FIELD

Theresa Costello is a physical therapist working on an advanced degree.

As I began to conduct interviews for my research on musculoskeletal discomfort and related relief seeking behaviors, I found myself a bit apprehensive. I had never interacted with male Latinos and I remembered some negative stereotypes from my childhood about Latino men. The farm workers who gathered to be interviewed had just come from church and were neatly dressed and impeccably groomed. I remember being surprised that someone who had spent the whole week working in the fields showed up so well dressed! I marveled at their composure and grace. Scientific literature tells us that "Latinos" and others at the low end of the socioeconomic scale have a sense of fatalism and limited personal control. The men before me, however, appeared proud yet respectful of themselves and others.

Initially I did not see any signs of pain or discomfort. "These folks don't need my help," I thought to myself. Once we started interviewing, however, and a level of trust developed, the men lined up to ask questions. Some shared tips and techniques used to reduce their aches and pains. I learned more than can ever be reflected in scientific publications. The experience made me realize that research is never "value-free" or totally objective. We always bring our perceptions and viewpoints to the field with us which affects how we "see" and what we choose to "hear." It is important to "step out of the way" and accurately perceive the true sentiments and concerns of the people we are hoping to help.

I still visit these workers when I can to offer physical therapy; I like being part of the community and feel honored to have been included in their world.

DISCUSSION QUESTIONS

During a dental encounter with a father and his young daughter, Randy makes several observations.

1 What do you think about her comments?

- Research is never "value-free."
- Our own perceptions and viewpoints affect how we "see" and what we choose to "hear."
- It is important to recognize and acknowledge our own agendas so that we can "step out of the way."

2 Can you give examples from your own experience that support what Theresa says?

3 Think about what all the storytellers featured in *Principios Salud* have said and reflect upon your own work. Where will your new insights and skills take you?

COMPROBACIÓN

DVD *Las preguntas de* Comprobación *están diseñadas para evaluar tu habilidad de usar lo que has aprendido, en situaciones nuevas y diferentes. Aunque el contexto todavía es limitado y las respuestas están restringidas y guiadas, debes interpretar más.*

SECCIÓN A

¿Qué pasa en la Historia*? Escoge las palabras que completan mejor la oración. ¡Cuidado con la gramática!*

1 Laura y Alex se reconcilian y Alex puede seguir trabajando en la clínica con tal de que (sigue / siga / siguiera) un tratamiento para su enfermedad.

2 Rafa convence a Hugo Anderson para que le (da / dé / diera) fondos a la clínica y la feria que Carmina organizó se (lleva / llevara / lleve) a cabo.

3 Mientras tanto, un extranjero llega a la clínica y sorprende a Carmina como si (es / estuviera / fuera) Superman.

4 Cuando Abe llega, ya es muy tarde; Carmina no (es / está / fue). Sin embargo, todos piensan que la feria (es / está / sea) un éxito.

5 Con los nuevos fondos, la clínica (pueda / puede / pudo) seguir funcionando por muchos años más.

6 ¡Hasta es posible que Jaime (resolver / resuelva / resuelve) su problema con las llamadas telefónicas! Pues, ¿quién sabe?

SECCIÓN B

Estas oraciones describen la Feria de Salud, organizada por Carmina. Escoge las palabras que completan mejor cada oración.

admite	mejore
agradecer	optan
cepillarse	organicen
cobrar	paguemos
lleguen	patrocinan
mantener	va a poner

¡Es un día precioso! Niños y adultos vienen a la feria donde se **(1)** ____________ a todos sin costo. Hugo Anderson y Asociados **(2)** ____________ el evento y La Comunidad no tiene que **(3)** ____________ la entrada a la feria. En la salita los niños aprenden a **(4)** ____________ los dientes para **(5)** ____________ una buena salud dental. Afuera, los adultos **(6)** ____________ por estudiar los panfletos y hablar con los representantes de los grupos que traen información a la comunidad. Hay bebidas, palomitas de maíz, globos y mucha alegría.

Preguntas y Respuestas sobre: VIVIENDA JUSTA

El propósito de las leyes de vivienda justa es proteger el derecho a ser dueño, comprar, vender o alquilar la vivienda que se escoja sin temor a ser víctima de discriminación ilegal. Las leyes de vivienda justa tienen por objeto permitir que todas las personas tengan igual acceso a la vivienda. Las leyes federales y estatales de vivienda justa prohiben la discriminación en el mercado de la vivienda por razones de **raza, color de la piel, sexo, religión, país de origen, discapacidad o condición (estado) familiar**. Es ilegal discriminar contra una persona por pertenecer a alguna de estas categorías protegidas.

Este folleto se refiere principalmente a las leyes de vivienda justa del estado de Carolina del Norte.

P: ¿Se aplican las leyes de vivienda justa a todas las transacciones relativas a la vivienda?

R: Sí, excepto en las siguientes excepciones limitadas:

- Alquilar una unidad en una vivienda multifamiliar de menos de cuatro unidades cuando el dueño, o uno de sus familiares, vive en una de las unidades
- Alquilar una habitación o habitaciones en una casa particular en que el dueño o uno de sus familiares vive en la casa
- Pensión de propiedad u operada por clubes privados que dan preferencia a sus miembros
- Instituciones religiosas, caritativas o educacionales u organizaciones que son operadas, supervisadas o controladas por organizaciones o instituciones religiosas que le dan preferencia a las transacciones inmobiliarias de sus miembros, a condición de que la organización no excluya a personas de categorías protegidas
- Dormitorios sólo para hombres o sólo para mujeres

Prácticas discriminatorias

P: ¿Cuáles son algunos de los actos ilegales más comunes de discriminación?

R: Negarse a vender, alquilar (rentar) o negociar. Es ilegal tomar cualquiera de las siguientes medidas en razón de que una de las personas pertenezca a una de las categorías protegidas:

- Negarse a participar en una transacción inmobiliaria
- Negarse a alquilar o vender una vivienda
- Discriminar en cuanto a términos, condiciones o privilegios por la venta o alquiler de una vivienda
- Negarse a recibir, o no transmitir, una oferta válida para celebrar una transacción inmobiliaria
- Decir que la vivienda no está disponible cuando de hecho lo está
- Discriminar proporcionando diferentes instalaciones o servicios
- Negarse a negociar por la vivienda

Direccionamiento. Desanimar a una persona en su búsqueda de vivienda en una comunidad, un vecindario o una urbanización en particular porque la persona pertenece o no pertenece a una categoría protegida. Por ejemplo un agente de bienes raíces le muestra una vivienda a una persona negra en vecindarios predominantemente negros o a una persona blanca en vecindarios predominantemente blancos.

Interferencia, coacción o intimidación. Intentar limitar los beneficios de alquilar o vender una vivienda en un área determinada porque la persona pertenece a una categoría protegida. Esto incluye tratar de coaccionar, amenazar, intimidar, tomar represalias o interferir de cualquier manera con el uso y disfrute de la vivienda.

Publicidad discriminatoria. Hacer publicidad o declaraciones que indiquen directa o indirectamente una intención de limitar, especificar o discriminar a personas que pertenecen a categorías protegidas.

Ahuyentar (también conocido como tráfico de pánico). Intentar, de manera directa o sutil, de atemorizar a una persona para que se vaya de un vecindario diciendo que una persona de una de las categorías protegidas está considerando mudarse o de hecho se ha mudado al vecindario. Por ejemplo, es ilegal decir que el vecindario declinaría o que la proporción de delitos aumentaría si los integrantes de una categoría protegida se mudan al vecindario.

Marcación. Negar o aplicar condiciones más estrictas a las solicitudes de préstamo para una propiedad en un área en particular debido a la composición racial del área. Esto se refiere a préstamos para comprar, construir, mejorar, reparar o mantener las viviendas.

CONTESTA LAS PREGUNTAS SIGUIENTES:

1 ¿Cuáles son las categorías de vivienda protegidas contra la discriminación en el mercado? ¿Cuál de ellas tendría más importancia para Rafa en su investigación sobre Hugo Anderson?

2 ¿Cuáles son los actos ilegales discriminatorios más comunes?

3 ¿Qué dice el folleto sober la discriminación de familias con niños?

P: **¿Puede una persona que no sea el vendedor o el dueño de la propiedad ser culpable de infracciones a las leyes de vivienda justa?**
R: Sí. Toda persona que participe en una transacción inmobiliaria que discrimine en función de una categoría protegida ha cometido una infracción contra las leyes de vivienda justa. Por ejemplo, es ilegal que un banquero local informe a un agente de bienes raíces que si permite a personas con niños mudarse al vecindario, el banco no tratará más con él o con sus clientes.

P: **¿Tiene el dueño de una propiedad la obligación de alquilar o vender a una persona solamente porque la persona pertenece a una categoría protegida?**
R: No. Los dueños pueden alquilar o vender a quienquiera que sea con tal de que sus decisiones no se basen en que el posible inquilino o comprador pertenezca a una categoría protegida. Si una persona perteneciente a una categoría protegida se convierte en inquilino, el dueño debe aplicar al inquilino los mismos estándares de comportamiento y desempeño que aplica a los demás.

P: **¿Pueden los dueños de propiedades protegerse a sí mismos contra quejas de discriminación cuando rechazan a una persona perteneciente a una categoría protegida?**
R: Sí. Los dueños de propiedades deben tener estándares detallados para decidir quién es aceptable como inquilino y quién no. Sin embargo, estos estándares no pueden basarse en que un posible inquilino o comprador pertenezca a una categoría protegida. Si una persona perteneciente a una categoría protegida pasa a ser inquilino, el dueño debe aplicar al inquilino los mismos estándares de comportamiento y desempeño que aplica a los demás. Tales estándares son especialmente importantes cuando se rechaza la solicitud de un inquilino por razones de crédito inadecuado y cuando se pone a los posibles inquilinos en «lista de espera». El dueño de la propiedad debe aplicar estos estándares por igual a todos los inquilinos solicitantes. Si usa una lista de espera, el dueño de la propiedad debe de hecho poner en la lista los nombres de todos los solicitantes a quienes ha indicado que lo hará y, en el momento correspondiente, debe notificar a cada solicitante de la lista que su turno ha llegado.

Condición (estado) familiar

P: **¿Puede negárseles la vivienda a las personas con niños porque tienen niños?**
R: No. Las leyes de vivienda justa protegen a las personas que (1) tienen un niño menor de 18 años, (2) tienen la custodia legal de un niño, (3) son nombradas por el padre o la madre para cuidar a un niño (a condición de que la persona nombrada tenga permiso escrito del padre o de la madre) (4) están embarazadas y (5) están en el proceso de obtener la custodia legal de un niño. Sin embargo, las leyes de vivienda justa no protegen a las personas a quienes se les niega vivienda porque son solteros, casados o viven con alguien.

P: **¿Se permiten las comunidades «sólo para adultos»?**
R: No. A menos que queden bajo una de las dos exenciones que permiten sólo adultos en las viviendas para personas de edad. [Aviso: Hay muchos requisitos que cumplir para tener derecho a estas exenciones. Comuníquese con la Comisión de Relaciones Humanas de Carolina del Norte (North Carolina Human Relations Commission, NCHRC) para obtener más detalles]. Si una comunidad habitacional tiene derecho a exención de discriminación por edad, tal comunidad puede discriminar únicamente en función de la condición o estado familiar. No puede discriminar en función de ninguna de las otras categorías protegidas.

P: **¿Puede el dueño de la propiedad o agente segregar a las familias con niños de las de otros inquilinos?**
R: No. Los integrantes de las categorías protegidas no pueden ser asignados a una sección específica de una comunidad, vecindario o urbanización o a un piso de un edificio específico por ser integrantes de una categoría en particular.

P: **¿Puede un dueño de propiedad o agente limitar el número de niños que se permite en una habitación, o prohibir que niños de sexo opuesto compartan las habitaciones?**
R: No. Aunque el dueño de la propiedad puede establecer «estándares de ocupación» en cuanto a la cantidad total de personas que se permite vivir en una unidad, los estándares no deben basarse en la edad o el sexo de las personas.

To read this article online, go to www.yalebooks.com/salud.

Práctica con el subjuntivo:

Escribe diez oraciones utilizando los "Subjunctive Signals" que aparecen en la Unidad 4b.

Modelo: Es una lástima que dueños de apartamentos como Hugo Anderson se aprovechen de los inmigrantes.

Práctica con las "cláusulas de si":

Repasa las explicaciones de las "cláusulas de si" en las unidades 3b y 4b. Después, escribe por lo menos cinco oraciones utilizando esta estructura.

Modelo: Si yo fuera Rafa, hablaría directamente con Hugo Anderson sobre las condiciones insalubres de las viviendas.

¡A CONVERSAR!

PERSONAJES

Jaime speaks about the clinic, *La Comunidad*

DVD

What does Jaime say about the clinic?
What is your opinion?

¡A RESUMIR!

EPISODIO

Imagine that you and your partner are preparing for a test on the content of the Historia. In order to study better, you orally summarize the episodes together. Discuss the final episode, including at least three of the following scenes:

- Laura and her former attitude towards her diagnosis of diabetes
- Jaime and his concerns about Alex
- The contribution that Hugo Anderson makes to the clinic
- The health fair
- David Mora –Does he look familiar?

Be sure to incorporate the subjunctive mood into your conversation:

- Es bueno que Hugo Anderson quiera patrocinar la clínica de la comunidad.
- Es necesario que Laura haga frente a su enfermedad.

APLICACIÓN

CONVERSAR

Ashleigh and Carmina

DVD *In this segment Ashleigh asks Carmina for advice on how to improve her Spanish. Watch it, and then discuss the following with a classmate:*

1 ¿Qué haces para practicar el español?

2 ¿A veces te da miedo hablar español? ¿Qué haces cuando te da miedo?

3 ¿Qué más le puedes recomendar a Laura?

ANALIZAR

Carmina and David Mora

DVD *Watch this segment, and discuss the following questions with a classmate:*

1 ¿Qué relación inicial hay entre Carmina y David Mora?

2 ¿Puedes imaginar una pregunta que Carmina debe hacerle a David Mora?

3 Imagínate que es Abe con quien Carmina está hablando. ¿Cómo cambia la conversación?

EN LA PRÁCTICA

DVD

Watch this segment, and discuss the following issues with a classmate:

- ¿Cómo se demuestran Ashleigh y Mila su confianza y su aprecio?
- ¿Sería difícil ajustarte a una cultura y un idioma diferente? ¿Crees que sea difícil criar a un hijo en un país extranjero? ¿Por qué?

Ashleigh and Milagros

LENGUA

DVD

El sueño de Carmina

Ha pasado un año desde que Carmina se encontró perseguida por un sueño particular. ¿Con quién soñaba ella? ¿Qué ocurrió después? ¿Encontró Carmina la solución al sueño? Escribe tu versión de La Comunidad II *y explica por qué piensas que tu historia es la mejor solución. Comenta tus ideas con un/a compañero/a de clase.*

ESTUDIANTE 1: Carmina conoció al hombre de sus sueños cuando conoció a David Mora...

ESTUDIANTE 2: No estoy de acuerdo. Abe es un hombre simpático, y es perfecto para ella...

MÁS ALLÁ

Since the distinction between formal and informal interactions is an integral part of the many Hispanic cultures, the Spanish language offers many alternatives for demonstrating this difference. In Spanish, formality and informality can be witnessed through both the use of the language and the conduct of the people. For example, you are already aware of the fact that Spanish uses of the pronouns *tú*, *usted*, and *ustedes* to define the social context and to demonstrate the varying levels of respect. In addition, verb forms are used to reflect these same notions. Still, there are other devices used to help underscore this formal and informal distinction, most of which normally accompany the use of pronouns and verb forms.

Like English, Spanish defines a relationship through the use of terms of endearment, first names, last names, or titles that refer to one's professional or social standing. As a result, you come across terms like *amor, cielo, querido/a, angelito/a, señor/a, doctor/a, licenciado/a*, etc. Which terms are chosen depends on the level of intimacy the speaker wishes to create. Greetings and farewells also serve to distinguish between formal and informal situations because you have an opportunity to show respect at the beginning and at the end of a conversation. For example, *Hola* is considered to be much more informal than *Buenos días* or *Buenas tardes*. Consequently, *Hola* would be more appropriate for informal or intimate situations. Finally, a handshake, kisses, nods, and waves are also used to indicate whether a situation is informal or formal. Which action would be more appropriate for first encounters? for professional relationships? between friends? In other words, the way in which you acknowledge a person lets them know how you perceive this relationship.

Nevertheless, there may be times when you are uncertain as to how to address a particular individual or group of individuals. When you find yourself in such a situation, take cues from those around you. You can always play it safe and start out using formal manners of address; if you recall, this is how David Mora handled his first encounter with Carmina. Another possible solution is to let your audience know how to address you; this type of approach can help to alleviate some of the awkwardness of the situation. In fact, this is the method employed by Carmina in the *Analizar* section of this unit when she says to David, *Podemos tratarnos de tú, ¿verdad?* She this creates an informal situation. Again, remember that the methods you use, as well as how you choose to combine these methods, will establish the type of relationship between others and yourself.

ENTREVISTA

DVD *Read this summary in English of what Debora David says in her interview before you watch it on the DVD. Remember that these interviews were conducted to include "authentic language" on the DVD. This means that the interviews are unscripted and at a natural conversational pace. Use the English summary to guide you.*

Debora David

Celia Cruz is a very, very famous singer in the Latin world and well, she chose me to be in her video and I'm very happy about that. There was a lot of acting [in the video], a lot of handling the camera, flirting a lot with the camera and this is what I did.

I'm from Livingston. In Guatemala there are black people as well. Where I'm from, well, we're a minority: 0000.0000001% of the Guatemalan population. And I'm also Garifuna. I'm from the Garifuna culture. My dialect is a mixture of English, French and Spanish. Everything is like, [speaks in Garifuna]. This is, "Hi. How are you? Are you well? OK. I'm also doing well." That's what that means.

In 1994 I was Miss America, Guatemala. And in 1997 I was Miss Guatemala, which caused a lot of controversy because I did not represent the country very well, because of what I look like. And later I had to get out of there because I wanted to see new things and I told myself, "No, no, what they did to you wasn't right."

I'm single and yes, I have a boyfriend. He lives in Mexico; he's Mexican... Well, right now we're in a stage where he's trying to understand my work, my career. Now I'm traveling more outside of Mexico. So we're entering into a new phase right now.

I think that a lot of it has to do with my culture. It's a culture that, since it doesn't have a lot of resources, leads to us having to share and help each other a lot. We have to help each other out a lot and to support each other because there just aren't a lot of resources. We have to be very hospitable. For example, in the morning the neighbor might get up as say, "Neighbor! What's going on?" "Neighbor, did you eat yet?" "No, neighbor, there's no food." "Well I got up early and made food. Would you like to share it with me?" It's a culture in which you have to share because there isn't much else to rely on, at times resources are scarce, so you have to be like that. I think that that's where I got some of the inspiration for taking on the role of Duna, because we have to share, sometimes there just wasn't a lot to live on, and we had to give to each other. I think that's somewhat where Duna comes from. And the word "duna," in my language, means "water." And water is, well, I think it's clarity; water hydrates, water gives energy. And so I can understand Duna as *duna*, as water. And I can associate her with that and that's what gives me the energy to be Duna.

Mira la entrevista con Debora David otra vez, y presta atención a lo que ella dice con relación a las siguientes cosas:

- Celia Cruz y su nuevo video
- su cultura y sus raíces étnicas
- sus experiencias en los concursos de belleza
- el efecto de su vida profesional en su vida privada
- cómo su cultura le ayuda a darle energía al personaje de Duna
- el significado de "Duna" en su idioma

GLOSARIO ESPAÑOL - INGLÉS

a (prep.)	*at, to*
a condición de que (conj.)	*as long as*
a fin de que (conj.)	*so that*
a menos que (conj.)	*unless*
a menudo (adv.)	*often*
a no ser que (conj.)	*unless*
a pesar de que (conj.)	*in spite of*
a veces (adv.)	*sometimes*
abajo (prep.)	*below*
abandonar (v.)	*to abandon*
abandono (n., m.)	*abandonment*
abdominal (adj.)	*abdominal*
abierto, -a (adj.)	*open*
abogado, -a (n.)	*lawyer*
aborto (n., m.)	*abortion*
abrigo (n., m.)	*coat*
abrir (v.)	*to open*
abuelo, -a (n.)	*grandfather, grandmother, grandparents (pl.)*
aburrido, -a (adj.)	*boring, bored*
aburrir(se) (v.)	*to bore, to get bored*
abusar (v.)	*to abuse*
abuso (n., m.)	*abuse*
acá (adv.)	*here*
acabar de (v.)	*to have just*
acaso (adv.)	*perhaps*
accidente (n., m.)	*accident*
acelerar (v.)	*to accelerate*
aceptar (v.)	*to accept*
acerca de (adv.)	*about, concerning*
acercar(se) (v.)	*to approach*
ácido (n., m.)	*acid*
ácido fólico (n., m.)	*folic acid*
acompañar (v.)	*to accompany*
aconsejar (v.)	*to advise*
acordarse (v.)	*to agree*
acosador, -a (n.)	*assaulter, abuser*
acoso (n., m.)	*assault; harassment*
acostarse (v.)	*to go to bed*
acostumbrar (v.)	*to use to, to be accustomed to*
acta de nacimiento (n., f.)	*birth certificate*
actitud (n., f.)	*attitude*
actividad (n., f.)	*activity*
activo, -a (adj.)	*active*
actual (adj.)	*current*
actuar (v.)	*to act, to behave*
acuático, -a (adj.)	*aquatic*
acudir (v.)	*to go to*
acuerdo (n., m.)	*agreement*
acusar (v.)	*to accuse*
adecuar (v.)	*to adapt, to make suitable*
adelgazar (v.)	*to slim down, to get thin*
además (adv.)	*besides*
adicional (adj.)	*additional*
adicto, -a (adj.)	*addicted*
adicto, -a (n.)	*addict*
adjunto, -a (adj.)	*enclosed*
administración (n., f.)	*administration*
administrar (v.)	*to administrate*
admitir (v.)	*to admit*
adolescente (adj.)	*adolescent, teenager*
adulto, -a (adj.)	*adult*
adverso, -a (adj.)	*adverse*
advertir (v.)	*to warn*
afectar (v.)	*to affect*
aflojar (v.)	*to loosen*
afortunadamente (adv.)	*fortunately*
africano, -a (adj., n.)	*African*
afuera (adv.)	*outside*
agarrar (v.)	*to hold on to*
agencia (n., f.)	*agency*
agente (n., m. or f.)	*agent*
agobiado, -a (adj.)	*overwhelmed*
agradecer (v.)	*to thank for*
agrandar (v.)	*to grow larger, to get bigger*
agresivo, -a (adj.)	*aggressive*
agrícola (adj.)	*agricultural*
agua (n., f.)	*water*
aguantar (v.)	*to tolerate*
agudo, -a (adj.)	*sharp*
aguja (n., f.)	*needle*
agujero (n., m.)	*hole*
ahogarse (v.)	*to drown*
ahora (adv.)	*now*
ahora que (conj.)	*since*
ahorrar (v.)	*to save, to economize*
aire acondicionado (n., m.)	*air conditioning*
aislar (v.)	*to isolate, to insulate*
aislarse (v.)	*to isolate oneself*
alcanzar (v.)	*to reach*
alcohol (n., m.)	*alcohol*
alegrarse (v.)	*to be happy*
alegre (adj.)	*happy*
alejar(se) (v.)	*to move away*
alergia (n., f.)	*allergy*
alérgico, -a (adj.)	*allergic*
algo (pron.)	*something*
algodón (n., m.)	*cotton*
alguien (pron.)	*someone*
algún (adj.)	*some*
alguna, alguno (adj, indet. pron.)	*someone, somebody*
aliento (n., m.)	*breath*
alimentación (n., f.)	*feeding, nourishment*
alimenticio, -a (adj.)	*nutritious*
alimento (n., m.)	*nourishment, food*
aliviar (v.)	*to alleviate*
allá (adv.)	*there (over there)*
allí (adv.)	*there (less exact place than "allá")*
almohada (n., f.)	*pillow*
almorzar (v.)	*to eat lunch*
almuerzo (n., m.)	*lunch*
alocado, -a (adj.)	*wild, reckless*
alquilar (v.)	*to rent*
alternativa (n., f.)	*alternative*
alto, -a (adj.)	*tall, high*
amable (adj.)	*friendly*
amamantar (v.)	*to breastfeed*
amar (v.)	*to love*
amarillo, -a (adj.)	*yellow*
ambiente (n., m.)	*environment*
ambos, -as (adj., pron.)	*both*
ambulancia (n., f.)	*ambulance*
amenazar (v.)	*to threaten*
americano, -a (adj, n.)	*American, from the Americas*
amigo, -a (n.)	*friend*
amistad (n., f.)	*friendship*
amor (n., m.)	*love*
ampolla (n., f.)	*blister*
amputar (v.)	*to amputate*
añadir (v.)	*to add*
análisis (n., m.)	*analysis*
analizado, -a (adj.)	*analyzed*
analizar (v.)	*to analyze*
andar (v.)	*to walk, to move*
andar en bicicleta (v.)	*to ride a bike*
ángel (n., m.)	*angel*
angustiado, -a (adj.)	*anguished, distressed*
animal (n., m.)	*animal*
animar (v.)	*to encourage*
ánimo (n., m.)	*state of mind, mood, spirit*
año (n., m.)	*year*
anoche (adv.)	*last night*
anormal (adj.)	*abnormal*
anotar (v.)	*to write down*
ansiedad (n., f.)	*anxiety*
ansioso, -a (adj.)	*anxious*
anteayer (adv.)	*the day before yesterday*
antepasado (n., m.)	*ancestor*
antes (adv.)	*before*
antes de (prep.)	*before*
antibiótico (n., m.)	*antibiotic (also an adjective)*
anticonceptivo, -a (adj.)	*contraceptive*
antidepresivo, -a (adj.)	*antidepressant*
antiguo, -a (adj.)	*old, ancient*
anunciar (v.)	*to announce*
anuncio (n., m.)	*announcement*
apariencia (n., f.)	*appearance*
apartamento (n., m.)	*apartment*
apatía (n., f.)	*apathy*
apático, -a (adj.)	*apathetic*
apenas (conj.)	*as soon as*
apetito (n., m.)	*appetite*
apostema (n., f.)	*pus*
apoyar (v.)	*to support*
apoyo (n., m.)	*support*
aprender (v.)	*to learn*
apresurar(se) (v.)	*to hurry up*
apretar (v.)	*to squeeze*
aprisa (adj.)	*in a hurry*
aprobación (n., f.)	*approval*
aprobar (v.)	*to approve*
apropiado, -a (adj.)	*appropriate, proper*
aprovecharse de (v.)	*to take advantage*
apuntar (v.)	*to write down*
aquel (adj.)	*that*
aquello, -a (adj.)	*that (for abstract, ideas)*
aquí (adv.)	*here*
archivo (n., m.)	*file*
ardor (n., m.)	*ardor, burning sensation*

área (n., f.)	*area*
argentino, -a (adj., n.)	*Argentinian, from Argentina*
arma (n., f.)	*weapon*
arreglar (v.)	*to arrange, to fix, to tidy*
arreglarse (v.)	*to reach an agreement, to manage (colloq.)*
arriba (prep.)	*up*
arriesgar (v.)	*to risk*
arruinado, -a (adj.)	*ruined*
arruinar (v.)	*to ruin*
arterial (adj.)	*arterial*
articulación (n., f.)	*joint*
artículo (n., m.)	*article*
artritis (n., f.)	*arthritis*
artritis reumatoide (n., f.)	*rheumatoid arthritis*
asar (v.)	*to roast*
ascensor (n., m.)	*elevator*
asegurar (v.)	*to secure, to make sure*
asegurarse (v.)	*to make sure*
así (adv.)	*thus, so*
asiento (n., m.)	*seat*
asistencia (n., f.)	*assistance*
asistir (v.)	*to attend (a function or event)*
aspecto (n., m.)	*aspect*
aspirina (n., f.)	*aspirin*
asunto (n., m.)	*issue, matter, question*
asustar (v.)	*to frighten*
asustarse (v.)	*to be frightened*
atacar (v.)	*to attack*
ataque (n., m.)	*attack*
atención (n., f.)	*attention*
atender (v.)	*to attend to, to take care of*
aterrorizado, -a (adj.)	*frightened, terrified*
atraer (v.)	*to attract*
atrasar(se) (v.)	*to set back, to be late*
audiólogo, -a (n.)	*audiologist*
aumentar (v.)	*to increase*
aumento (n., m.)	*increase*
aun (adv.)	*even*
aún (adv.)	*still, yet*
aunque (conj.)	*although, even though*
autoestima (n., f.)	*self-esteem*
auto (n., m.)	*car*
automóvil (n., m.)	*automobile*
autorizar (v.)	*to authorize*
avaricia (n., f.)	*greed*
avergonzado, -a (adj.)	*ashamed*
averiguar (v.)	*to verify*
avisar (v.)	*to warn*
ayer (adv.)	*yesterday*
ayuda (n., f.)	*help*
ayudante (n., m. or f.)	*helper, assistant*
ayudar (v.)	*to help*
azúcar (n., m.)	*sugar*
azucarado, -a (adj.)	*sugary, sweetened*
bachillerato (n., m.)	*high school*
bacteria (n., f.)	*bacteria*
bailar (v.)	*to dance*
bajar (v.)	*to lower*
bajo (adv.)	*below*
bajo, -a (adj.)	*short, low*
bala (n., f.)	*bullet*
balanceado, -a (adj.)	*balanced*
bañar (v.)	*to bathe (someone else)*
bañar(se) (v.)	*to bathe (oneself)*
bañera (n., f.)	*bathtub*
banco (n., m.)	*bank*
baño (n., m.)	*bathroom, bath*
bar (n., m.)	*bar (establishment)*
barra (n., f.)	*bar, rail*
barrio (n., m.)	*neighborhood*
básico, -a (adj.)	*basic*
bastante (adv.)	*enough*
bastón (n., m.)	*cane*
basurero (n., m.)	*garbage can*
bebé (n., m. or f.)	*baby*
beber (v.)	*to drink*
beca (n., f.)	*grant, scholarship*
béisbol (n., m.)	*baseball*
beneficio (n., m.)	*benefit*
besar (v.)	*to kiss*
biberón (n., m.)	*baby bottle*
bicicleta (n., f.)	*bicycle*
bien (adv.)	*well*
bienestar (n., m.)	*well-being*
bilirrubina (n., f.)	*bilirubin*
billetera (n., f.)	*wallet*
biológico, -a (adj.)	*biological*
bloque (n., m.)	*building block*
boca (n., f.)	*mouth*
boca abajo (prep.)	*face down*
boca arriba (prep.)	*face up*
bofetada (n., f.)	*slap*
bola (n., f.)	*ball*
boletín (n., m.)	*bulletin*
boliviano, -a (adj., n.)	*Bolivian, from Bolivia*
bolsa (n., f.)	*bag*
bolso (n., m.)	*handbag*
bonito, -a (adj.)	*pretty*
botar (v.)	*to throw away, to expel*
botella (n., f.)	*bottle*
brasileño, -a (adj., n.)	*Brazilian, from Brazil*
brazo (n., m.)	*arm*
bruto, -a (adj.)	*ignorant*
bucal (adj.)	*oral, mouth*
buen (adj.)	*good, kind*
bueno, -a (adj.)	*good, kind*
buscar (v.)	*to look for*
cabecera, médico, -a de (n.)	*family doctor, Primary Care Physician (PCP)*
caber (v.)	*to fit*
cabeza (n., f.)	*head*
cabo (n., m.)	*end*
cada (adj.)	*each, every*
cadera (n., f.)	*hip*
caer (v.)	*to fall*
caerse (v.)	*to fall down*
cajero, -a (n.)	*cashier*
calcio (n., m.)	*calcium*
calefacción (n., f.)	*heating*
calentador (n., m.)	*heater*
calentamiento (n., m.)	*warm-up*
calentar (v.)	*to warm-up, to heat*
calidad (n., f.)	*quality*
caliente (adj.)	*hot*
calificar (v.)	*to grade, to qualify*
callar(se) (v.)	*to quiet, to become quiet*
calle (n., f.)	*street*
calmar(se) (v.)	*to calm down*
calor (n., m.)	*heat, warmth*
caloría (n., f.)	*calorie*
cama (n., f.)	*bed*
cambiar (v.)	*to change*
cambio (n., m.)	*change*
camilla (n., f.)	*stretcher*
caminar (v.)	*to walk*
camino (n., m.)	*road, path, way*
camisa (n., f.)	*shirt*
campesino, -a (n.)	*farmer, peasant*
campo (n., m.)	*field*
cancelar (v.)	*to cancel*
cáncer (n., m.)	*cancer*
cansancio (n., m.)	*tiredness, weariness*
cansado, -a (adj.)	*exhausted, tired*
cansar (v.)	*to tire*
cansarse (v.)	*to get tired*
cantar (v.)	*to sing*
cantidad (n., f.)	*quantity*
capaz (adj.)	*capable*
capellán (n., m.)	*chaplain*
cápsula (n., f.)	*capsule*
caracterizar (v.)	*to characterize*
carbohidrato (n., m.)	*carbohydrate*
cárcel (n., f.)	*jail, prison*
cardíaco, -a (adj.)	*cardiac, heart*
cargos (n., m.)	*financial charges*
caries (n., f., sing. or pl.)	*cavity, cavities*
carne (n., f.)	*meat*
caro, -a (adj.)	*expensive*
carro (n., m.)	*car*
carta (n., f.)	*letter*
carta de incapacidad (n., f.)	*work excuse*
cartel (n., m.)	*poster*
cartílago (n., m.)	*cartilage*
casa (n., f.)	*house*
casa rodante (n., f.)	*trailer*
casarse (v.)	*to marry*
casero, -a (adj.)	*home-made*
casero, -a (n.)	*landlord*
casi (adv.)	*almost*
caso (n., m.)	*case*
castigar (v.)	*to punish*
casualidad (n., f.)	*coincidence*
cataplasma (n., f.)	*poultice*
catarata (n., f.)	*cataract*
causa (n., f.)	*cause*
causar (v.)	*to cause*
ceguera (n., f.)	*blindness*
celebrar (v.)	*to celebrate*
celos (n., m.)	*jealousy*
célula (n., f.)	*cell*
cena (n., f.)	*dinner*
cenar (v.)	*to dine, to eat dinner*
centroamericano, -a (adj., n.)	*Central American*

cepillar(se) (v.)	*to brush*
cepillo (n., m.)	*brush*
cerca (prep.)	*close, near*
cercano, -a (adj.)	*close, nearby*
cereal (n., m.)	*cereal*
cerebral (adj.)	*cerebral, brain*
cerebro (n., m.)	*brain*
cereza (n., f.)	*cherry*
cerrado, -a (adj.)	*closed*
cerradura (n., f.)	*lock, lockset (keyhole, knob, handle, lock)*
cerrar (v.)	*to close*
certeza (n., f.)	*certainty*
certificado (n., m.)	*certificate*
certificado, -a (adj.)	*certified*
certificar (v.)	*to certify*
cerveza (n., f.)	*beer*
cesárea (n., f.)	*cesarean*
cheque (n., m.)	*check*
chico, -a (adj.)	*small*
chico, -a (n.)	*child*
chichón (n., m.)	*booboo, raised bump*
chileno, -a (adj., n.)	*Chilean, from Chile*
chocar (v.)	*to crash*
chupar (v.)	*to suck*
chupete (n., m.)	*pacifier*
ciclo (n., m.)	*cycle*
cielo (n., m.)	*sky, dear (term of endearment)*
cien (adj.)	*(one) hundred*
científico, -a (n.)	*scientist*
cierto, -a (adj.)	*certain, sure*
cifra (n., f.)	*figure, number*
cinco (adj.)	*five*
cincuenta (adj.)	*fifty*
circulatorio, -a (adj.)	*circulatory*
circunstancia (n., f.)	*circumstance*
cirujano, -a (n.)	*surgeon*
cita (n., f.)	*appointment, date*
ciudad (n., f.)	*city*
ciudadano, -a (n.)	*citizen*
claramente (adv.)	*clearly*
clarificar (v.)	*to clarify*
claro, -a (adj.)	*clear*
clase (n., f.)	*class*
cliente (n., m. or f.)	*client*
clientela (n., f.)	*clientele*
clima (n., m.)	*climate, weather*
clínica (n., f.)	*clinic*
club (n., m.)	*club*
cobertura (n., f.)	*coverage (i.e. medical, insurance)*
cobrar (v.)	*to collect (money), to charge*
cocinar (v.)	*to cook*
coger (v.)	*to grab*
coincidencia (n., f.)	*coincidence*
colar (v.)	*to strain, to filter*
colega (n., m. or f.)	*colleague*
colegio (n., m.)	*school*
colesterol (n., m.)	*cholesterol*
colgar (v.)	*to hang (up)*
cólico (n., m.)	*colic*
collar (n., m.)	*necklace*
colocar (v.)	*to place*
colombiano, -a (adj., n.)	*Colombian, from Colombia*
color (n., m.)	*color*
columna (n., f.)	*column*
combatir (v.)	*to combat, to fight*
combinación (n., f.)	*combination*
combinar (v.)	*to combine*
comenzar (v.)	*to begin, to start*
comer (v.)	*to eat, to have a meal*
comezón (n., f.)	*itching*
comida (n., f.)	*food, meal*
como (adv.)	*as, since*
cómo (interr.)	*how*
cómodo, -a (adj.)	*comfortable*
compañero, -a (n.)	*companion, friend*
compañía (n., f.)	*company*
compartir (v.)	*to share*
competente (adj.)	*competent*
complacer (v.)	*to please*
complejo, -a (adj.)	*complex*
completo, -a (adj.)	*complete*
complicación (n., f.)	*complication*
complicado, -a (adj.)	*complicated*
componer (v.)	*to fix, to compose (music)*
comportamiento (n., m.)	*behavior, conduct*
comportarse (v.)	*to behave, to act*
comprar (v.)	*to buy*
comprender (v.)	*to understand*
comprobar (v.)	*to verify, to check*
compuesto, -a (adj.)	*composed*
común, -a (adj.)	*common*
comunicarse (v.)	*to communicate*
comunidad (n., f.)	*community*
con (prep.)	*with*
con respecto a (adv.)	*with respect to, with regard to*
con tal de que (conj.)	*provided that*
concentración (n., f.)	*concentration*
concentrarse (v.)	*to concentrate*
condado (n., m.)	*county*
condición (n., f.)	*condition*
condón (n., m.)	*condom*
conducta (n., f.)	*conduct*
confianza (n., f.)	*trust, confidence*
confiar (v.)	*to have trust in, to confide, to entrust*
confidencialidad (n., f.)	*confidentiality*
confusión (n., f.)	*confusion, mistake*
congelar(se) (v.)	*to freeze*
conmigo (pron.)	*with me*
conmoción (n., f.)	*commotion*
conocer (v.)	*to know a person, to be familiar with, to meet*
conocimiento (n., m.)	*knowledge*
consecuencia (n., f.)	*consequence*
conseguir (v.)	*to obtain*
consejero, -a (n.)	*counselor*
consejo (n., m.)	*advice*
consentir (v.)	*to allow, to consent*
considerar (v.)	*to consider*
constantemente (adv.)	*constantly*
constante (adj.)	*constant*
construcción (n., f.)	*construction*
construir (v.)	*to construct*
consuelo (n., m.)	*comfort*
consultar (v.)	*to consult*
consumir (v.)	*to consume*
contactar (v.)	*to contact*
contacto (n., m.)	*contact*
contador, -a (n.)	*accountant*
contagiar (v.)	*to transmit, to infect*
contagiarse (v.)	*to get infected*
contagio (n., m.)	*contagion, infection*
contar (v.)	*to tell, to count*
contener (v.)	*to contain*
contenido (n., m.)	*content*
contento, -a (adj.)	*happy*
contigo (prep.)	*with you*
continuación (n., f.)	*continuation*
continuar (v.)	*to continue*
continuo, -a (adj.)	*continuous*
contra (prep.)	*against*
contracción (n., f.)	*contraction*
contraer (v.)	*to contract, to catch an illness*
contratar (v.)	*to hire*
contribuir (v.)	*to contribute*
control (n., m.)	*control*
control de natalidad (n., m.)	*birth control*
controlar (v.)	*to control*
convalecencia (n., f.)	*convalescence*
convencer (v.)	*to convince*
convertir (v.)	*to convert*
convertirse (v.)	*to become*
coordinar (v.)	*to coordinate*
copia (n., f.)	*copy*
copiar (v.)	*to copy*
coraje (n., m.)	*courage, anger*
corazón (n., m.)	*heart*
cordón umbilical (n., m.)	*umbilical chord*
corporal (adj.)	*corporal, body*
correctamente (adv.)	*correctly*
correcto, -a (adj.)	*correct*
corregir (v.)	*to correct*
correo (n., m.)	*mail*
correo electrónico (n., m.)	*email*
correr (v.)	*to run*
cortadura (n., f.)	*cut*
cortar (v.)	*to cut*
corto, -a (adj.)	*short*
cosa (n., f.)	*thing*
costar (v.)	*to cost*
costarricense (adj., n., m. or f.)	*Costa Rican, from Costa Rica*
costo (n., m.)	*cost*
costoso, -a (adj)	*costly*
costumbre (n., f.)	*custom, habit*
coyuntura (n., f.)	*joint*
crear (v.)	*to create*
creer (v.)	*to think, to believe*
crema (n., f.)	*cream*
criticar (v.)	*to criticize*
cruzar (v.)	*to cross*
cuadra (n., f.)	*city block*
cuál (interr.)	*who, which*

cual (pron.) *which*
cualquier, -a (adj.) *any*
cuando (adv.) *when*
cuándo (interr.) *when*
cuánto (interr.) *how much (unmeasurable amount)*
cuánto, -s (interr.) *how many (measurable quantity)*
cuanto, -a (adj.) *as much as*
cuarto (n., m.) *room*
cuarto, -a (adj.) *fourth*
cuatro (adj.) *four*
cubierto, -a (adj.) *covered*
cubano, -a (adj., n.) *Cuban, from Cuba*
cubrir (v.) *to cover*
cucharadita (n., f.) *teaspoon*
cuello (n., m.) *neck*
cuenta (n., f.) *bill*
cuerpo (n., m.) *body*
cuestión (n., f.) *issue, matter, question*
cuidado (n., m.) *care, carefulness*
cuidar (v.) *to care for*
cuidarse (v.) *to take care of oneself*
culpa (n., f.) *fault, blame*
culpable (adj.) *guilty*
culpar (v.) *to blame*
cultura (n., f.) *culture*
cumplir (v.) *to accomplish, to carry out, to fulfill*
cuna (n., f.) *crib*
cuñado, -a (n.) *brother-in-law, sister-in-law*
cupón (n., m.) *coupon, vale*
cura (n., m.) *priest*
cura (n., f.) *cure*
curandero, -a (n.) *healer*
curar (v.) *to cure*
curarse (v.) *to be cured*
curita (n., f.) *band aid*
cuyo, -a (pron.) *whose*
dañado, -a (adj.) *damaged*
dañar (v.) *to damage, to harm*
dañarse (v.) *to get hurt*
daño (n., m.) *damage, harm*
dar (v.) *to give*
dar a luz (v.) *to give birth*
dar el pecho (v.) *to breastfeed*
dar la bienvenida (v.) *to welcome*
dar miedo (v.) *to scare*
dar un paseo (v.) *to take a walk*
darse cuenta (v.) *to realize*
dar vuelta (v.) *to turn around, to turn over*
darse vuelta (v.) *to turn around (oneself)*
darse prisa (v.) *to hurry up*
dato (n., m.) *fact, data*
de (prep.) *from, of*
de manera que (conj.) *so that*
de modo que (conj.) *so that*
de repente (adv.) *suddenly*
de vez en cuando (adv.) *sometimes*
deber (v.) *to have to, must*
débil (adj.) *weak*
debilitarse (v.) *to become weak*
decaer (v.) *to fall out*
decaído, -a (adj.) *weak, depressed, fallen*
decidir (v.) *to decide*
decir (v.) *to say*
decisión (n., f.) *decision*
declaración (n., f.) *statement*
dedicado, -a (adj.) *dedicated*
dedicar(se) (v.) *to dedicate, to devote*
dedo (n., m.) *finger, toe*
defecto (n., m.) *defect*
defender(se) (v.) *to defend, to assert oneself*
defensa (n., f.) *defense*
dejar (v.) *to leave something behind, to allow*
dejar de (v.) *to stop, to quit*
delicado, -a (adj.) *delicate*
demandar (v.) *to demand*
demás (adj.) *other, rest*
demasiado (adv.) *too much*
demasiado, -a (adj.) *too much*
demostrar (v.) *to demonstrate*
dentadura postiza (n., f.) *dentures, false teeth*
dental (adj.) *dental*
dentista (n., m. or f.) *dentist*
departamento (n., m.) *apartment, department*
depender (v.) *to depend*
deporte (n., m.) *sport*
depósito (n., m.) *deposit*
depresión (n., f.) *depression*
deprimido, -a (adj.) *depressed*
derecha (adj.) *right side*
derecho (adv.) *direct, straight ahead*
derecho (n., m.) *right*
derrame (n., m.) *spill*
derrame cerebral (n., m.) *brain hemorrhage, stroke*
desafío (n., m.) *challenge*
desafortunadamente (adv.) *unfortunately*
desalojar (v.) *to evict*
desambular (v.) *to wander*
desamparo (n., m.) *helplessness*
desaparecer (v.) *to disappear*
desarrollar(se) (v.) *to develop*
desarrollo (n., m.) *development*
desastre (n., m.) *disaster*
desayunar (v.) *to have breakfast*
desayuno (n., m.) *breakfast*
descansar (v.) *to rest, to take a break*
descanso (n., m.) *rest, break*
desconocido, -a (adj.) *unknown, unfamiliar*
describir (v.) *to describe*
descubierto, -a (adj.) *discovered, uncovered*
descubrir (v.) *to discover*
desde (prep.) *from, since*
desear (v.) *to desire*
desempeñar (v.) *to carry out*
desesperado, -a (adj.) *desperate*
desesperanza (n., f.) *despair, desperation*
desesperarse (v.) *to despair*
designado, -a (adj.) *designated*
designar (v.) *to designate*
desigualdad (n., f.) *inequality*
despedir (v.) *to fire, to lay off*
despertar (v.) *to wake up*
despertarse (v.) *to wake up, to awaken*
despierto, -a (adj.) *awake*
desprenderse (v.) *to detach, to become loose*
después (adv.) *afterwards, later*
después de (prep.) *after*
destruir (v.) *to destroy*
detalle (n., m.) *detail*
detectar (v.) *to detect*
detener (v.) *to stop, to retain*
deterioro (n., m.) *deterioration*
deteriorarse (v.) *to deteriorate*
determinar (v.) *to determine*
devolver (v.) *to return something*
día (n., m.) *day*
diabetes (n., f.) *diabetes*
diabético, -a (adj.) *diabetic*
diagnóstico (n., f.) *diagnosis*
diagnosticar (v.) *to diagnose*
diálisis (n., f.) *dialysis*
diariamente (adv.) *daily*
diario, -a (adj.) *daily*
diario (n., m.) *diary, journal*
dibujo (n., m.) *drawing*
dicho, -a (adj.) *mentioned*
diecisiete (adj.) *seventeen*
diente (n., m.) *tooth*
dieta (n., f.) *diet*
dietista (n., m. or f.) *dietician*
diez (adj.) *ten*
diferencia (n., f.) *difference*
diferente (adj.) *different*
difícil (adj.) *difficult*
dificultad (n., f.) *difficulty*
difteria (n., f.) *diphtheria*
digerir (v.) *to digest*
digestivo, -a (adj.) *digestive*
dilatación (n., f.) *dilatation*
dinero (n., m.) *money*
Dios (n., m.) *God*
dirección (n., f.) *address, direction*
directo, -a (adj.) *direct*
director, -a (n.) *director*
dirigir (v.) *to direct*
disculpa (n., f.) *apology*
disculpar (v.) *to forgive*
disculparse (v.) *to apologize*
discutir (v.) *to discuss, to argue*
disgustar (v.) *to dislike*
disminuir (v.) *to reduce, to decrease*
disparo (n., m.) *shot*
disponibilidad (n., f.) *availability*
disponible (adj.) *available*
distinguir (v.) *to distinguish*
distinto, -a (adj.) *distinct*
distribuir (v.) *to distribute*
diversión (n., f.) *amusement, diversion*
diverso, -a (adj.) *diverse*

divertir (v.) *to amuse*
divertirse (v.) *to have a good time*
doctor, -a (n.) *doctor*
documento (n., m.) *document*
dólar (n., m.) *dollar*
doler (v.) *to ache, to hurt*
dolor (n., m.) *ache, pain*
doloroso, -a (adj.) *painful*
doméstico, -a (adj.) *domestic*
dominicano, -a (adj., n.) *Dominican, from Dominican Republic*
donar (v.) *to donate*
donde (adv.) *where*
dónde (interr.) *where*
dormir (v.) *to sleep*
dormirse (v.) *to fall asleep*
dos (adj.) *two*
dosificación (n., f.) *dosage*
dosis (n., f.) *dose, dosage*
drama (n., m.) *drama*
droga (n., f.) *drug*
drogadicción (n., f.) *drug addiction*
ducha (n., f.) *shower*
duda (n., f.) *doubt*
dudar (v.) *to doubt*
dudoso, -a (adj.) *doubtful*
dulce (adj.) *sweet*
dulce (n., m.) *candy, sweet*
durante (adv.) *during*
durar (v.) *to last*
duro, -a (adj.) *hard, tough*
e (conj.) *and (used instead of "y" when the next word begins with "i" or "h")*
echar (v.) *to throw*
ecografía (n., f.) *echogram*
ecuatoriano, -a (adj., n,) *Ecuadorian, from Ecuador*
edad (n., f.) *age*
edificio (n., m.) *building*
editorialista (n., m. or f.) *editorialist*
educación (n., f.) *education*
efectivo, -a (adj.) *effective*
efecto (n., m.) *effect*
eficaz (adj.) *efficient*
ejemplo (n., m.) *example*
ejercicio (n., m.) *exercise*
el (art.) *the*
él (pron.) *he*
electo, -a (adj.) *elect*
electricidad (n., f.) *electricity*
electrónico, -a (adj.) *electronic*
elegir (v.) *to choose, to elect*
elegible (adj.) *eligible*
eliminar (v.) *to eliminate*
ella (pron.) *she*
ellas (pron.) *they*
ellos (pron.) *they*
embarazar (v.) *to make pregnant*
embarazarse (v.) *to become pregnant*
embarazo (n., m.) *pregnancy*
emergencia (n., f.) *emergency*
emoción (n., f.) *emotion*
emotivo (adj.) *emotional*
empanada (n., f.) *stuffed pastry, turnover*
empeño (n., m.) *determination*
empeorar (v.) *to make worse*
empezar (v.) *to begin, to start*
empleado, -a (n.) *employee*
empleo (n., m.) *employment, job*
empujar (v.) *to push (something)*
en (prep.) *in, on, at*
en vez de (adv.) *instead of*
enamorado, -a (adj.) *in love*
enamorarse (v.) *to fall in love*
encantado, -a (adj.) *delighted, pleased*
encantador, -a (adj.) *charming, delightful*
encantar (v.) *to love, to delight*
encargado, -a (adj.) *in charge*
enchufe (n., m.) *electrical socket, plug*
encías (n., f.) *gums*
encima de (prep.) *on top of*
encontrar (v.) *to find*
encontrarse (v.) *to meet each other, to find oneself*
enfadarse (v.) *to get angry*
enfermarse (v.) *to get sick*
enfermedad (n., f.) *illness*
enfermero, -a (n.) *nurse*
enfermo, -a (adj.) *sick*
enfrentar (v.) *to face, to confront*
enfriamiento (n., m.) *cool down, chill*
enfriar (v.) *to cool, to chill*
enfriarse (v.) *to get cold, to catch a cold*
engañar (v.) *to deceive*
engordar (v.) *to fatten, to gain weight*
grasoso, -a (adj.) *greasy, fatty*
enjuague bucal (n., m.) *mouthwash*
enlatado, -a (adj.) *canned*
enojarse (v.) *to get angry*
enojo (n., m.) *anger*
enrojecimiento (n., m.) *redness*
ensayar (v.) *to test, to try*
enseguida (adv.) *at once*
enseñar (v.) *to teach, to show*
entender (v.) *to understand*
enterarse (v.) *to become aware*
entero, -a (adj.) *entire, whole*
entonces (adv.) *then*
entrar en (v.) *to enter*
entre (prep.) *between*
entrenamiento (n., m.) *training*
entrevistar (v.) *to interview*
entumecimiento (n., m.) *numbness*
envase (n., m.) *container*
envenenamiento (n., m.) *poisoning*
envenenar (v.) *to poison*
enviar (v.) *to send*
envolver (v.) *to wrap up*
epidemia (n., f.) *epidemic*
episodio (n., m.) *episode*
equipo (n., m.) *equipment, team*
equivocar (v.) *to mistake*
equivocarse (v.) *to be mistaken*
erupción (n., f.) *rash*
escalera (n., f.) *stair, staircase, ladder*
escalofríos (n., m.) *chills*
escapar (v.) *to escape*
escena (n., f.) *scene*
esclavo, -a (n.) *slave*
escoger (v.) *to choose*
escolar (adj.) *school, scholastic*
esconder(se) (v.) *to hide*
escribir (v.) *to write*
escrito, -a (adj.) *written*
escuchar (v.) *to listen*
escuela (n., f.) *school*
escupir (v.) *to spit*
ese, -a (adj.) *that (pl. those)*
esfuerzo (n., m.) *effort*
eso (pron.) *that (for ideas)*
espacio (n., m.) *space*
espalda (n., f.) *back*
español, -a (adj., n.) *Spanish, Spaniard*
espantoso, -a (adj.) *scary, frightening*
espasmo (n., m.) *spasm*
especial (adj.) *special*
especialista (n., m. or f.) *specialist*
especializado, -a (adj.) *specialized*
específico, -a (adj.) *specific*
espejo (n., m.) *mirror*
esperanza (n., f.) *hope*
esperar (v.) *to wait, to hope, to expect*
espeso, -a (adj.) *thick, dense*
espiritista (n., m. or f.) *spiritualist*
esposo, -a (n.) *spouse, husband, wife*
esputo (n., m.) *spit*
estable (adj.) *stable*
establecer (v.) *to establish*
estación (n., f.) *station, season*
estado (n., m.) *state*
estado de ánimo (n., m.) *state of mind*
Estados Unidos (n., m., pl.) *United States*
estadounidense (adj., n., m. or f.) *American, from the U.S.*
estampilla (n., f.) *stamp*
estar (v.) *to be*
este, -a (adj.) *this (pl. those)*
esterilidad (n., f.) *sterility*
estimular (v.) *to stimulate*
estiramiento (n., m.) *stretching*
estirarse (v.) *to stretch*
esto (pron.) *this (for ideas)*
estómago (n., m.) *stomach*
estornudar (v.) *to sneeze*
estrategia (n., f.) *strategy*
estreñimiento (n., m.) *constipation*
estrés (n., m.) *stress*
estricto, -a (adj.) *strict*
estudiante (n., m. or f.) *student*
estudiar (v.) *to study*
estupendamente (adv.) *stupendously*
estupendo, -a (adj.) *stupendous*
etapa (n., f.) *stage*

etiqueta (n., f.)	*label*
evento (n., m.)	*event*
evidencia (n., f.)	*evidence*
evitar (v.)	*to avoid*
exacto, -a (adj.)	*exact*
examen (n., m.)	*exam*
examinar (v.)	*to examine*
examinarse (v.)	*to have an examination*
excelente (adj.)	*excellent*
excesivamente (adv.)	*excessively*
excesivo, -a (adj.)	*excessive*
excremento (n., m.)	*stool*
exhibir (v.)	*to exhibit, to show*
exigir (v.)	*to demand*
existir (v.)	*to exist*
éxito (n., m.)	*success*
experiencia (n., f.)	*experience*
experimentar (v.)	*to experience, to experiment*
experto, -a (adj.)	*expert*
explicación (n., f.)	*explanation*
explicar (v.)	*to explain*
explotar (v.)	*to explode*
exponer (v.)	*to expose*
exposición (n., f.)	*exposure*
expresar(se) (v.)	*to express*
expuesto, -a (adj.)	*exposed*
extenderse (v.)	*to extend*
extrañar (v.)	*to miss (to long for something)*
extranjero (n., m.)	*abroad, foreigner*
extranjero, -a (adj.)	*foreign*
extraño, -a (adj.)	*foreign, strange*
fábrica (n., f.)	*factory*
fabuloso, -a (adj.)	*fabulous*
fácil (adj.)	*easy*
facilidad (n., f.)	*ease*
fácilmente (adv.)	*easily*
factor (n., m.)	*factor*
fallar (v.)	*to fail*
fallecer (v.)	*to pass away*
falso, -a (adj.)	*false*
faltar (v.)	*to miss (as in the sense of to be lacking something)*
familia (n., f.)	*family*
familiar (adj.)	*familiar*
farmacéutico, -a (n.)	*pharmacist*
farmacia (n., f.)	*pharmacy*
fatiga (n., f.)	*fatigue*
fatigar(se) (v.)	*to wear out, to tire*
favor (n., m.)	*favor*
favorito, -a (adj.)	*favorite*
felicidad (n., f.)	*happiness*
felicitaciones (n., f.)	*congratulations*
feliz (adj.)	*happy*
feria (n., f.)	*fair*
fibra (n., f.)	*fiber*
fibroma (n., m.)	*fibroid*
fiebre (n., f.)	*fever*
fiesta (n., f.)	*party*
fin (n., m.)	*end*
financiero, -a (adj.)	*financial*
finanzas (n., f.)	*finances*
físicamente (adv.)	*physically*
físico, -a (adj.)	*physical*
flaco, -a (adj.)	*thin, skinny*
flexible (adj.)	*flexible*
flojo, -a (adj.)	*loose, lazy*
fluido (n., m.)	*fluid*
flujo (n., m.)	*discharge*
flúor (n., m.)	*fluoride*
folleto (n., m.)	*pamphlet*
fomentar (v.)	*to foster*
fondos (n., m.)	*funds*
foniatra (n., m. or f.)	*speech pathologist*
forma (n., f.)	*form, shape, way*
formal (adj.)	*formal*
formar (v.)	*to form*
fórmula (n., f.)	*formula*
formulario (n., m.)	*form (paper)*
fortalecer (v.)	*to strengthen*
forzar (v.)	*to force*
foto (n., f.)	*photo*
fotografía (n., f.)	*photograph*
frasco (n., m.)	*bottle, flask*
frase (n., f.)	*phrase*
frecuente (adj.)	*frequent, common*
frecuentemente (adv.)	*frequently*
fregar (v.)	*to scrub, to wash*
freír (v.)	*to fry*
frente (n., f.)	*forehead*
frío (n., m.)	*cold (temperature)*
frío, -a (adj.)	*cold*
frito, -a (adj.)	*fried*
fruta (n., f.)	*fruit*
fuente (n., f.)	*source*
fuera (adv.)	*outside*
fuerte (adj.)	*strong*
fuertemente (adv.)	*strongly*
fumar (v.)	*to smoke*
funcionar (v.)	*to function*
furioso, -a (adj.)	*furious*
futuro (n., m.)	*future*
futuro, -a (adj.)	*future*
gafas (n., f.)	*eyeglasses*
ganar (v.)	*to win*
ganas (n., f.)	*desire, wish*
ganglio (n., m.)	*glanglion*
ganglios linfáticos (n., m.)	*lymph glands*
garganta (n., f.)	*throat*
garífuna (adj., n.)	*Garifuna (Guatemalan indigenous group)*
gastar (v.)	*to spend*
gastarse (v.)	*to wear away*
gel (n., m.)	*gel*
gemelo, -a (n.)	*twin*
general (adj.)	*general*
generalmente (adv.)	*generally*
genérico, -a (adj.)	*generic*
genético, -a (adj.)	*genetic*
genital (adj.)	*genital*
gente (n., f.)	*people*
germen (n., m.)	*germ*
gimnasio (n., m.)	*gymnasium*
glaucoma (n., m.)	*glaucoma*
glucosa (n., f.)	*glucose*
gobernar (v.)	*to govern, to control*
gobierno (n., m.)	*government*
golpe (n., m.)	*blow*
golpear (v.)	*to hit*
gonorrea (n., f.)	*gonorrhea*
gordo, -a (adj.)	*fat, stout*
gota (n., f.)	*drop, gout*
gozar (v.)	*to enjoy*
gracias (n., f.)	*thanks*
graduarse (v.)	*to graduate*
grande (adj.)	*big, large*
grasa (n., f.)	*fat (food), grease*
gratis (adj.)	*free*
grave (adj.)	*serious*
gravedad (n., f.)	*seriousness, gravity*
gripe (n., f.)	*flu*
gritar (v.)	*to shout, to yell*
grito (n., m.)	*shout, yell*
grupo (n., m.)	*group*
guante (n., m.)	*glove*
guapo, -a (adj.)	*good-looking, handsome*
guardar (v.)	*to keep, to put away*
guardería (n., m.)	*daycare*
guardia, estar de (v.)	*to be on duty, on call*
guatemalteco, -a (adj., n.)	*Guatemalan, from Guatemala*
guerra (n., f.)	*war*
gustar (v.)	*to like*
gusto (n., m.)	*pleasure*
haber (aux. v.)	*to have*
habilidad (n., f.)	*ability*
habitación (n., f.)	*room*
hábito (n., m.)	*habit*
habla (n., f.)	*speech*
hablar (v.)	*to speak, to talk*
hace (adv.)	*ago*
hacer (v.)	*to make, to do*
hacer preguntas (v.)	*to ask questions*
hacerse (v.)	*to become*
hacerse cargo de (v.)	*to be in charge*
hacia (prep.)	*toward*
hambre (n., f.)	*hunger*
hasta (prep.)	*until*
heces (n., f.)	*feces*
hecho, -a (adj.)	*done*
hemorragia (n., f.)	*hemorrhage, bleeding*
hepatitis (n., f.)	*hepatitis*
heredar (v.)	*to inherit*
herencia (n., f.)	*heredity, inheritance*
herida (n., f.)	*wound, injury*
herido, -a (adj.)	*wounded, injured*
herir (v.)	*to wound, to injure*
hermano, -a (n.)	*sibling, brother, sister*
hervir (v.)	*to boil*
Hib (n.)	*Haemophilus Influenza B*
hielo (n., m.)	*ice*
hígado (n., m.)	*liver*
hijo, -a (n.)	*child, son, daughter*
hilo (n., m.)	*thread*
hilo dental (n., m.)	*dental floss*
hinchar (v.)	*to swell up*
hincharse (v.)	*to become swollen*
hinchazón (n., f.)	*swelling*
hipertensión (n., f.)	*hypertension*
hipoglucemia (n., f.)	*hypoglycemia*

hispano, -a (adj.)	*Hispanic*
histérico, -a (adj.)	*hysterical*
historia (n., f.)	*history, record*
historial (n, m.)	*record*
hogar (n., m.)	*home*
hola (interj.)	*hello*
hombre (n., m.)	*man*
hondureño, -a (adj., n,)	*Honduran, from Honduras*
honesto, -a (adj.)	*honest*
hora (n., f.)	*hour*
horario (n., m.)	*schedule*
hormona (n., f.)	*hormone*
hornear (v.)	*to bake*
hospital (n., m.)	*hospital*
hoy (adv.)	*today*
hueso (n., m.)	*bone*
huir (v.)	*to flee, to escape*
humano, -a (adj.)	*human*
humillado, -a (adj.)	*humiliated*
humor (n., m.)	*humor*
idea (n., f.)	*idea*
identidad (n., f.)	*identity*
identificar (v.)	*to identify*
idioma (n., m.)	*language*
idiota (adj.)	*idiotic, stupid*
iglesia (n., f.)	*church*
ignorar (v.)	*to ignore*
igual (adj.)	*equal*
igualdad (n., f.)	*equality*
ilegal (adj.)	*illegal*
imaginar (v.)	*to imagine*
imitar (v.)	*to imitate*
impacto (n., m.)	*impact*
implantar (v.)	*to implant*
importante (adj.)	*important*
importar (v.)	*to matter, to import*
imposible (adj.)	*impossible*
impulsivamente (adv.)	*impulsively*
inactivo, -a (adj.)	*inactive*
incapacidad (n., f.)	*incapacity, disability*
incidente (n., m.)	*incident*
incluir (v.)	*to include*
incluso (adv.)	*even*
incómodo, -a (adj.)	*uncomfortable*
incontinencia (n., f.)	*incontinence*
increíble (adj.)	*incredible*
incremento (n., m.)	*increment*
indefenso, -a (adj.)	*defenseless*
independientemente (adv.)	*independently*
indispensable (adj.)	*indispensable, essential*
indicado, -a (adj.)	*indicated*
indicar (v.)	*to indicate*
indicio (n., m.)	*indication, sign*
indio, -a (adj., n.)	*Indian*
individuo, -a (n.)	*individual*
industrioso, -a (adj.)	*industrious*
infantil (adj.)	*infantile, childish*
infección (n., f.)	*infection*
infectado, -a (adj.)	*infected*
infierno (n., m.)	*hell*
inflamación (n., f.)	*inflammation*
información (n., f.)	*information*

informar (v.)	*to inform*
informativo, -a (adj.)	*informative*
inglés, inglesa (adj., n.)	*English, British*
ingresar (v.)	*to join a corporation, club; to be admitted into a hospital, clinic*
ingresos (n., m.)	*income*
inhalar (v.)	*to inhale*
iniciar (v.)	*to initiate*
injusticia (n., f.)	*injustice*
inmaduro, -a (adj.)	*immature*
inmediatamente (adv.)	*immediately*
inmediato, -a (adj.)	*immediate*
inmigrante (n., m. or f.)	*immigrant*
inocente (adj.)	*innocent*
inquieto, -a (adj.)	*restless*
insalubre (adj.)	*unhealthy*
inseguro, -a (adj.)	*insecure*
insinuar (v.)	*to insinuate*
insistir (v.)	*to insist*
insomnio (n., m.)	*insomnia*
insoportable (adj.)	*intolerable, insufferable*
instalar (v.)	*to install*
instituto (n., m.)	*institute*
instrucción (n., f.)	*instruction*
insulina (n., f.)	*insulin*
íntegro, -a (adj.)	*entire*
inteligente (adj.)	*intelligent*
intensivo, -a (adj.)	*intensive*
intentar (v.)	*to try, to attempt*
interés (n., m.)	*interest*
interesante (adj.)	*interesting*
interesar (v.)	*to interest*
intérprete (n., m. or f.)	*interpreter*
interrogatorio (n., m.)	*interrogation*
intervalo (n., m.)	*interval*
intervención (n., f.)	*intervention*
íntimo, -a (adj.)	*close, intimate*
introducir (v.)	*to introduce (something into something)*
inventario (n., m.)	*inventory*
investigación (n., f.)	*investigation*
invierno (n., m.)	*winter*
invisible (adj.)	*invisible*
invitar (v.)	*to invite*
inyección (n., f.)	*injection*
inyectar (v.)	*to inject*
ir (v.)	*to go (to a specific destination)*
ir de compras (v.)	*to shop*
ira (n., f.)	*rage*
irresponsable (adj.)	*irresponsible*
irritabilidad (n., f.)	*irritability*
irritación (n., f.)	*irritation*
irse (v.)	*to go, to leave (with no specific destination)*
izquierdo, -a (adj.)	*left*
jalar (v.)	*to pull*
jalea (n., f.)	*jelly*
jamás (adv.)	*never, ever*
jamón (n., m.)	*ham*
jarabe para la tos (n., m.)	*cough syrup*

jefe, -a (n.)	*boss, employer*
jeringa (n., f.)	*syringe*
joven (adj.)	*young*
juez, -a (n.)	*judge*
jugar (v.)	*to play*
jugo (n., m.)	*juice*
junta (n., f.)	*meeting*
junto, -a (adj.)	*together*
laboratorio (n., m.)	*laboratory*
lado (n., m.)	*side*
lamentar (v.)	*to regret*
largo, -a (adj.)	*long*
lástima (n., f.)	*shame*
lastimar (v.)	*to hurt*
látex (n., m.)	*latex*
latido (n., m.)	*beat*
latido del corazón (n., m.)	*heartbeat*
latino, -a (adj.)	*Latin*
latinoamericano, -a (adj., n.)	*Latin American*
lavar (v.)	*to wash*
leche (n., f.)	*milk*
leer (v.)	*to read*
legislador, -a (n.)	*legislator*
lejos (prep.)	*far*
lengua (n., f.)	*tongue*
lentamente (adv.)	*slowly*
lentes (n., m.)	*eyeglasses*
lento, -a (adj.)	*slow*
leucemia (n., f.)	*leukemia*
levantar(se) (v.)	*to lift (oneself), to get up*
leve (adj.)	*light*
ley (n., f.)	*law*
libra (n., f.)	*pound*
libre (adj.)	*free*
libro (n., m.)	*book*
limitación (n., f.)	*limitation*
limitar (v.)	*to limit*
límite (n., m.)	*limit*
limpiar (v.)	*to clean*
limpieza (n., f.)	*cleanliness*
limpio, -a (adj.)	*clean*
linfático, -a (adj.)	*lymph*
líquido, -a (adj.)	*liquid*
líquido (n., m.)	*liquid*
lista (n., f.)	*list*
listo, -a (adj.)	*ready, smart*
llaga (n., f.)	*sore*
llamada telefónica (n., f.)	*phone call*
llamado, -a (adj.)	*called, named*
llamar (v.)	*to call*
llamarse (v.)	*to be called*
llegar (v.)	*to arrive*
llenar (v.)	*to fill*
lleno, -a (adj.)	*full*
llevar (v.)	*to take, to wear, to carry*
llevarse (v.)	*to get along*
llorar (v.)	*to cry*
llover (v.)	*to rain*
local (adj.)	*local*
localizar (v.)	*to locate*
loco, -a (adj.)	*crazy*
lograr (v.)	*to achieve, to attain*

lugar (n., m.)	*place*
lunar (n., m.)	*mole, birthmark*
luz (n., f.)	*light*
machista (adj.)	*chauvinistic*
madera (n., f.)	*wood*
madre (n., f.)	*mother*
maduro, -a (adj.)	*mature, ripe*
maestro, -a (n.)	*teacher*
magulladura (n., f.)	*bruise, contusion*
mal (adv.)	*badly, wrong*
malestar (n., m.)	*discomfort*
maltratar (v.)	*to mistreat*
maltrato (n., m.)	*mistreatment*
mamá (n., f.)	*mom*
mamadera (n., f.)	*baby bottle*
mamografía (n., f.)	*mammogram*
mañana (adv.)	*tomorrow*
mañana (n., f.)	*morning*
mancha (n., f.)	*spot, stain*
mandar (v.)	*to send*
mandato (n., m.)	*mandate, command*
manejar (v.)	*to drive, to handle*
manejo (n., m.)	*management*
manera (n., f.)	*way (as in the way to do something)*
mano (n., f.)	*hand*
mantener (v.)	*to maintain, to support financially*
mantenimiento (n., m.)	*maintenance*
mantequilla (n., f.)	*butter*
manzana (n., f.)	*apple*
mapa (n., m.)	*map*
máquina (n., f.)	*machine*
marca (n., f.)	*brand name, mark*
marcar (v.)	*to mark, to dial*
mareado, -a (adj.)	*dizzy*
marearse (v.)	*to get dizzy*
mareos (n., m.)	*dizziness*
marido (n., m.)	*husband*
más (adv.)	*more*
masa (n., f.)	*mass*
máscara (n., f.)	*mask*
masticable (adj.)	*chewable*
masticar (v.)	*to chew*
matar (v.)	*to kill*
materno, -a (adj.)	*maternal*
matrimonio (n., m.)	*marriage*
mayor (adj.)	*older, greater*
mayoría (n., f.)	*majority*
medicamento (n., m.)	*medication*
medicina (n., f.)	*medicine*
médico, -a (adj.)	*medical*
médico, -a (n.)	*medical doctor*
medio ambiente (n., m.)	*environment*
medio, -a (adj.)	*half*
mediodía (n., m.)	*noon*
medir (v.)	*to measure*
mejor (adj.)	*better*
mejora (n., f.)	*improvement*
mejorar (v.)	*to better, to improve*
memoria (n., f.)	*memory*
mencionar (v.)	*to mention*
menor (adj.)	*younger, smaller, minor*
menos (adv.)	*less, fewer*
mensualmente (adv.)	*monthly*
mental (adj.)	*mental*
mente (n., f.)	*mind*
mentir (v.)	*to lie*
mentira (n., f.)	*lie*
mercado (n., m.)	*market*
merecer (v.)	*to deserve*
merendar (v.)	*to snack*
merienda (n., f.)	*snack*
mes (n., m.)	*month*
mesa (n., f.)	*table*
meta (n., f.)	*goal*
meterse (v.)	*to get involved*
método (n., m.)	*method*
mexicano, -a (adj., n.)	*Mexican, from Mexico*
mezcla (n., f.)	*mixture*
mi (adj.)	*my*
miedo (n., m.)	*fear*
miel (n., f.)	*honey*
miembro (n., m.)	*member, limb*
mientras (adv.)	*while*
migratorio, -a (adj.)	*migratory*
mínimo (n., m.)	*minimum*
mínimo, -a (adj.)	*minimal, lowest*
minuto (n., m.)	*minute*
mío, -a (adj.)	*my, mine*
mirar (v.)	*to look at*
mismo, -a (adj.)	*same*
moco (n., m.)	*mucus*
modelo (n., m. or f.)	*model*
moderado, -a (adj.)	*moderate, controlled, restrained*
modo (n., m.)	*way, manner*
mojado, -a (adj.)	*wet*
molestar (v.)	*to bother, to annoy*
molestia (n., f.)	*bother, pain*
momento (n., m.)	*moment*
moretón (n., m.)	*bruise*
morir (v.)	*to die*
mostrar (v.)	*to show*
mover (v.)	*to move*
movimiento (n., m.)	*movement*
mucho, -a (adj.)	*a lot, much*
mudarse (v.)	*to change residence, to move out*
mudo, -a (adj.)	*mute*
muerto, -a (adj)	*dead*
muestra (n., f.)	*sample*
mujer (n., f.)	*woman*
muletas (n., f.)	*crutches*
mundo (n., m.)	*world*
muñeca (n., f.)	*wrist, doll*
músculo (n., m.)	*muscle*
muslo (n., m.)	*thigh*
muy (adv.)	*very*
nacer (v.)	*to be born*
nacimiento (n., m.)	*birth*
nada (pron.)	*nothing*
nadie (pron.)	*nobody*
naranja (n., f.)	*orange*
narcótico (n., m.)	*narcotic*
nariz (n., f.)	*nose*
natalidad, tasa de (n., f.)	*birth-rate*
nativo, -a (adj.)	*native*
naturalmente (adv.)	*naturally*
naturista (adj.)	*naturist*
náusea (n., f.)	*nausea*
necesario, -a (adj.)	*necessary*
necesidad (n., f.)	*necessity*
necesitar (v.)	*to need*
negar (v.)	*to deny*
negativo, -a (adj.)	*negative*
negocio (n., m.)	*business*
negro, -a (adj.)	*black*
neonatólogo, -a (n.)	*neonatologist*
nervio (n., m.)	*nerve*
nervioso, -a (adj.)	*nervous*
neumonía (n., f.)	*pneumonia*
ni (conj.)	*neither, nor*
ni siquiera (adv.)	*not even*
nieto, -a (n.)	*grandchild, grandson, granddaughter*
niñez (n., f.)	*childhood*
ningún (adj.)	*not any*
ninguno, -a (adj.)	*not any*
ninguno, -a (pron.)	*nobody*
niño, -a (n.)	*child, boy, girl*
nivel (n., m.)	*level*
no obstante (conj.)	*however, notwithstanding*
noche (n., f.)	*night*
nocturno, -a (adj.)	*nocturnal*
nombre (n., m.)	*name*
normal (adj.)	*normal*
normalmente (adv.)	*normally*
norteamericano, -a (adj., n.)	*North American*
nosotros (pron.)	*we*
notar (v.)	*to notice*
noticia (n., f., sing.)	*news*
noticias (n., f., pl.)	*news*
novio, -a (n.)	*boyfriend, girlfriend*
nuestro, -a (adj.)	*our*
nueve (adj.)	*nine*
nuevo, -a (adj.)	*new*
número (n., m.)	*number*
nunca (adv.)	*never*
nutrición (n., f.)	*nutrition*
nutricionista (n., m. or f.)	*nutritionist*
o (conj.)	*or*
obedecer (v.)	*to obey*
obesidad (n., f.)	*obesity*
objeto (n., m.)	*object*
obligar (v.)	*to obligate, to force*
obrero, -a (n.)	*worker (blue collar)*
obstetra (n., m. or f.)	*obstetrician*
obtener (v.)	*to obtain*
ocasión (n., f.)	*occasion*
ocho (adj.)	*eight*
octavo, -a (adj.)	*eighth*
oculista (n., m. or f.)	*oculist, ophtalmologist*
ocupacional (adj.)	*occupational*
ocupado, -a (adj.)	*busy, occupied*
ocurrir (v.)	*to occur, to happen*
odio (n., m.)	*hate*
oficina (n., f.)	*office*
ofrecer (v.)	*to offer*
ofrecerse (v.)	*to volunteer*

oftamólogo, -a (n.)	*ophthamologist*
oído (n., m.)	*inner ear*
oír (v.)	*to hear*
ojalá (interj.)	*hopefully*
ojo (n., m.)	*eye*
oler (v.)	*to smell*
olvidar (v.)	*to forget*
olvidarse (v.)	*to forget*
omóplato (n., m.)	*shoulder blade*
once (adj.)	*eleven*
opción (n., f.)	*option*
operación (n., f.)	*operation*
opinar (v.)	*to opine, to be of the opinion*
oportunidad (n., f.)	*opportunity*
oprimir (v.)	*to oppress*
optar (v.)	*to opt, to choose*
optometrista (n., m. or f.)	*optometrist*
orden (n., m.)	*order*
orden (n., f.)	*mandate*
oración (n., f.)	*sentence*
oreja (n., f.)	*outer ear*
organización (n., f.)	*organization*
organizar (v.)	*to organize*
órgano (n., m.)	*organ*
orgullo (n., m.)	*pride*
orgulloso, -a (adj.)	*proud*
orina (n., f.)	*urine*
orinar (v.)	*to urinate*
oscuro, -a (adj.)	*obscure, dark*
osteoporosis (n., f.)	*osteoporosis*
otorgar (v.)	*to award, to grant*
otro, -a (adj.)	*other, another*
paciencia (n., f.)	*patience*
paciente (adj.)	*patient*
paciente (n., m. or f.)	*patient*
padecer (v.)	*to suffer*
padre (n., m.)	*father, parents (pl.), priest*
pagar (v.)	*to pay*
pago (n., m.)	*payment*
país (n., m.)	*country*
palabra (n., f.)	*word*
paladar (n., m.)	*palate*
pálido, -a (adj.)	*pale*
palpitación (n., f.)	*palpitation*
pan (n., m.)	*bread*
panameño, -a (adj., n.)	*Panamanian, from Panama*
pañal (n., m.)	*diaper*
páncreas (n., m.)	*pancreas*
pandilla (n., f.)	*gang*
pandillero, -a (n.)	*gang member*
pañuelo (n., m.)	*handkerchief*
pañuelo desechable (n., m.)	*disposable tissue*
papel (n., m.)	*paper, role*
papeleo (n., m.)	*paperwork*
paperas (n., f.)	*mumps*
para (prep.)	*for, to, by*
paraguayo, -a (adj., n.)	*Paraguayan, from Paraguay*
para que (conj.)	*so that*
parar (v.)	*to stop*
parcial (adj.)	*partial*
parecer (v.)	*to seem*
parecerse (v.)	*to resemble*
pared (n., f.)	*wall*
pareja (n., f.)	*pair, couple*
pariente, -ta (n.)	*relative*
parque (n., m.)	*park*
parte (n., f.)	*part*
partera (n., f.)	*midwife*
participante (n., m. or f.)	*participant*
participar (v.)	*to participate*
particular (adj.)	*particular*
parto (n., m.)	*delivery, childbirth*
pasado (n., m.)	*past*
pasado, -a (adj.)	*past, last*
pasar (v.)	*to pass, to happen, to spend time*
paseo (n., m.)	*walk, stroll*
paso (n., m.)	*step*
pasta (n., f.)	*paste*
pasta dental (n., f.)	*toothpaste*
pastel (n., m.)	*cake*
pastilla (n., f.)	*pill*
patria (n., f.)	*homeland*
patrocinar (v.)	*to sponsor*
patrón, -a (n.)	*boss*
pecho (n., m.)	*chest*
pedazo (n., m.)	*piece*
pediatra (n., m. or f.)	*pediatrician*
pedir (v.)	*to ask for*
pedir disculpas (v.)	*to ask forgiveness, to apologize*
pedir prestado (v.)	*to borrow*
pegajoso, -a (adj.)	*sticky*
pegar (v.)	*to hit*
pegarse (v.)	*to stick to, to hit oneself*
pelear (v.)	*to fight*
peligro (n., m.)	*danger*
peligroso, -a (adj.)	*dangerous*
pena (n., f.)	*grief, sorrow*
pene (n., m.)	*penis*
pensar (v.)	*to think*
peor (adj.)	*worse*
pequeño, -a (adj.)	*little, small*
perder (v.)	*to lose*
pérdida (n., f.)	*loss*
perdonar (v.)	*to pardon, to forgive*
perezoso, -a (adj.)	*lazy*
perfecto, -a (adj.)	*perfect*
periódico, -a (adj.)	*periodical*
periódico (n., m.)	*newspaper*
periodista (n., m. or f.)	*journalist*
período (n., m.)	*period (of time), menstrual cycle*
periodontitis (n., f.)	*periodontitis*
perjudicar (v.)	*to harm, to jeopardize*
perjudicial (adj.)	*harmful*
permanecer (v.)	*to remain*
permanente (adj.)	*permanent*
permitir (v.)	*to permit, to allow*
pero (conj.)	*but*
persistente (adj.)	*persistent*
persona (n., f.)	*person*
personaje (n., m.)	*character (in a story)*
personal (adj.)	*personal*
personal (n., m.)	*personnel, staff*
personalidad (n., f.)	*personality*
persuadir (v.)	*to persuade*
pertenecer (v.)	*to belong*
peruano, -a (adj., n.)	*Peruvian, from Peru*
pesadilla (n., f.)	*nightmare*
pesado, -a (adj.)	*heavy, tiresome*
pesar (v.)	*to weigh*
peso (n., m.)	*money, weight*
pesticidas (n., f.)	*pesticides*
picadura (n., f.)	*insect bite*
picar (v.)	*to prick, to bite*
picazón (n., f.)	*itching*
picotear (v.)	*to snack*
pie (n., m.)	*foot*
piel (n., f.)	*skin*
pierna (n., f.)	*leg*
pijama (n., f.)	*pajamas*
píldora (n., f.)	*pill*
pinta (n., f.)	*pint*
pintar (v.)	*to paint*
pintura (n., f.)	*paint*
pipí (n.)	*pee pee*
placa de rayos X (n.)	*x-ray*
placer (n., m.)	*pleasure*
plan (n., m.)	*plan*
plan de salud	*Health Maintenance Organization (HMO)*
planta (n., f.)	*plant*
plasma (n., m.)	*plasma*
plazo (n., m.)	*term, installment*
plomo (n., m.)	*lead*
población (n., f.)	*population*
pobre (adj.)	*poor*
pobreza (n., f.)	*poverty*
poco (adv.)	*little, few*
poco, -a (adj.)	*little*
poder (n., m.)	*power*
poder (v.)	*to be able to*
poderoso, -a (adj.)	*powerful*
policía (n., m. or f.)	*police, policeman/policewoman*
polio (n., m.)	*polio*
póliza (n., f.)	*insurance policy*
polvo (n., m.)	*dust*
poner (v.)	*to place, to put*
poner(se) (v.)	*to put on, to become*
ponerse de pie (v.)	*to stand up*
por (prep.)	*for, because of, by, through*
porción (n., f.)	*portion*
porque (conj.)	*because*
por qué (interr.)	*why*
portador (n., m.)	*carrier*
portarse (v.)	*to behave*
posibilidad (n., f.)	*possibility*
posible (adj.)	*possible*
positivo, -a (adj.)	*positive*
posparto (n., m.)	*postpartum*
postema (n., f.)	*pus*
postizo, -a (adj.)	*false*
practicar (v.)	*to practice*
precioso, -a (adj.)	*precious*
precisión (n., f.)	*precision*

preciso, -a (adj.)	precise, accurate, necessary
predisposición (n., f.)	predisposition
preferible (adj.)	preferable
preferido, -a (adj.)	preferred
preferir (v.)	to prefer
pregunta (n., f.)	question
preguntar (v.)	to question, to ask
prejuicio (n., m.)	prejudice
preliminar (adj.)	preliminary
prematuro, -a (adj.)	premature
prenatal (adj.)	prenatal
preocupación (n., f.)	concern
preocupar(se) (v.)	to worry
preparación (n., f.)	preparation
preparar (v.)	to prepare
prescribir (v.)	to prescribe
prescrito, -a (adj.)	prescribed
presencia (n., f.)	presence
presentar (v.)	to present
presentar cargos (v.)	to present charges
presión (n., f.)	pressure
presión arterial (n., f.)	blood pressure
presionar (v.)	to pressure
préstamo (n., m.)	loan
prestar (v.)	to lend
presumir (v.)	to presume
presupuesto (n., m.)	budget
pretender (v.)	to pretend
prevenir (v.)	to prevent
preventivo, -a (adj.)	preventive
previo, -a (adj.)	previous, prior
primario, -a (adj.)	primary
primer (adj.)	first
primero, -a (adj.)	first
primo, -a (n.)	cousin
principal (adj.)	main, principle
principio (n., m.)	beginning
prioridad (n., f.)	priority
prisa (n., f.)	hurry
privacidad (n., f.)	privacy
privado, -a (adj.)	private
privar (v.)	to deprive
probable (adj.)	probable
probablemente (adv.)	probably
probar (v.)	to test, to try
problema (n., m.)	problem
procedimiento (n., m.)	procedure
proceso (n., m.)	process
producción (n., f.)	production
producido, -a (adj.)	produced
producir (v.)	to produce
producto (n., m.)	product
profesional (adj.)	professional
profesional (n., m. or f.)	professional
profundo, -a (adj.)	deep
programa (n., m.)	program
programa de nutrición WIC para mujeres, infantes y niños	WIC program
progresar (v.)	to progress
prohibir (v.)	to prohibit
prometer (v.)	to promise
promover (v.)	to promote
pronto (adv.)	soon
propagación (n., f.)	spread
propiedad (n., f.)	property
propietario, -a (n.)	owner
propio, -a (adj.)	own, proper
proponer (v.)	to propose
propósito (n., m.)	purpose
próstata (n., f.)	prostate
protección (n., f.)	protection
protector, -a (n.)	protector
protector bucal (n., m.)	mouthpiece
proteger (v.)	to protect
proteína (n., f.)	protein
protestar (v.)	to protest
proveer (v.)	to provide
provinciano, -a (adj.)	from a rural area
provocar (v.)	to provoke
próximo, -a (adj.)	next
proyecto (n., m.)	project
prueba (n., f.)	test, proof
prueba de Papanicolaou (n., f.)	pap smear
psicológico, -a (adj.)	psychological
psicoterapia (n., f.)	psychotherapy
público, -a (adj.)	public
pueblo (n., m.)	town
pueblerino, -a (adj.)	from a rural area
puertorriqueño, -a (adj., n.)	Puerto Rican, from Puerto Rico
pues (conj.)	since, as
puesto, -a (adj.)	dressed, placed
puesto (n., m.)	position, place
puesto que (conj.)	since
pujar (v.)	to push (during delivery)
pulgar (n., m.)	thumb
pulmón (n., m.)	lung
puntual (adj.)	punctual
pupila (n., f.)	eye pupil
pupú (n., m.)	poop
puro, -a (adj.)	pure
pus (n., m.)	pus
qué (interr.)	what
que (pron.)	who, that, which
quedar (v.)	to remain, to be leftover
quedarse (v.)	to stay behind, to remain or to be left doing something
quehacer (n., m.)	chore
queja (n., f.)	complaint
quejarse (v.)	to complain
querer (v.)	to want, to love
querido, -a (adj.)	dear, loved
quién (interr.)	who
quien (pron.)	who, whom
quijada (n., f.)	jaw
químico, -a (adj.)	chemical
quiste (n., m.)	cyst
quitar (v.)	to remove, to take off, to take away
quizás (adv.)	maybe
rabia (n., f.)	rage, fury
radiación (n., f.)	radiation
radiar (v.)	to radiate
radiografía (n., f.)	x-ray
ranchero, -a (n.)	ranchman, cattle farmer, cowboy/cowgirl
rápidamente (adv.)	quickly
raro, -a (adj.)	rare, scarce, odd
raspar (v.)	to scrape
rato (n., m.)	while, moment
raza (n., f.)	race
razón (n., f.)	reason
reacción (n., f.)	reaction
reaccionar (v.)	to react
realidad (n., f.)	reality
realizar (v.)	to fulfill, to achieve, to carry out
recepción (n., f.)	reception
recepcionista (n., m. or f.)	receptionist
receta (n., f.)	prescription
recetado, -a (adj.)	prescribed
recetar (v.)	to prescribe
rechazar (v.)	to reject
recibir (v.)	to receive
recién, recientemente (adv.)	recently
reciente (adj.)	recent
recipiente (n., m.)	recipient
reclamar (v.)	to complain
recoger (v.)	to collect, to gather, to pick up
recomendación (n., f.)	recommendation
recomendar (v.)	to recommend
reconocer (v.)	to recognize
recontar (v.)	to recount, to retell
récord (n., m.)	record, best result in an activity, deed
recordar (v.)	to remind
recuerdo (n., m.)	souvenir, memory
recuperación (n., f.)	recovery
recuperar (v.)	to recover
recurso (n., m.)	resource
reducido, -a (adj.)	reduced
reducir (v.)	to reduce
refrigerador (n., m.)	refrigerator
regalo (n., m.)	gift
regañar (v.)	to scold
regla (n., f.)	rule, menstrual cycle
regresar (v.)	to return
regularmente (adv.)	regularly
reina (n., f.)	queen
reír (v.)	to laugh
reírse de (v.)	to laugh about something
relación (n., f.)	relation, link
relacionado, -a (adj.)	related
relajamiento (n., m.)	relaxation
relajar (v.)	to relax
religioso, -a (adj.)	religious
rellenar (v.)	to refill, to fill something in
remedio (n., m.)	remedy
remojado, -a (adj.)	soaked
remojar (v.)	to soak
renal (adj.)	renal
rentar (v.)	to rent

renunciar (v.)	*to quit, to give up*
repetitivo, -a (adj.)	*repetitive*
repetir (v.)	*to repeat, to have seconds*
reportado, -a (adj.)	*reported*
reportar (v.)	*to report*
represalias (n., f.)	*retaliation*
representante (n., m. or f.)	*representative*
reprimenda (n., f.)	*reprimand*
requerir (v.)	*to require*
requisito (n., m.)	*requirement*
resfriado (n., m.)	*cold (illness)*
resolver (v.)	*to resolve*
respetar (v.)	*to respect*
respeto (n., m.)	*respect*
respiración (n., f.)	*breathing*
respirar (v.)	*to breathe*
respiratorio, -a (adj.)	*respiratory*
responder (v.)	*to respond*
responsabilidad (n., f.)	*responsibility*
responsable (adj.)	*responsible*
respuesta (n., f.)	*answer*
restar (v.)	*to deduct, to subtract*
restaurante (n., m.)	*restaurant*
resto (n., m.)	*rest*
resultado (n., m.)	*result*
resultar (v.)	*to result*
retar (v.)	*to challenge*
retener (v.)	*to retain*
retenido, -a (adj.)	*retained*
retina (n., f.)	*retina*
reto (n., m.)	*challenge*
retraso (n., m.)	*delay*
reunión (n., f.)	*meeting*
reunirse (v.)	*to get together*
revisar (v.)	*to revise, to check, to review*
rey (n., m.)	*king*
rezar (v.)	*to pray*
rico, -a (adj.)	*rich, delicious, wealthy*
riesgo (n., m.)	*risk*
rigidez (n., f.)	*rigidity*
riñón (n., m.)	*kidney*
robar (v.)	*to rob, to steal*
rodilla (n., f.)	*knee*
rogar (v.)	*to beg*
rojo, -a (adj.)	*red*
romper (v.)	*to break*
ropa (n., f.)	*clothing*
roto, -a (adj.)	*broken*
rubéola (n., f.)	*rubella*
ruido (n., m.)	*noise*
rutina (n., f.)	*routine*
saber (v.)	*to know*
sabor (n., m.)	*flavor, taste*
sacar (v.)	*to take out*
sacar de quicio (v.)	*to drive crazy*
sal (n., f.)	*salt*
sala (n., f.)	*room*
salado, -a (adj.)	*salty*
salir (v.)	*to leave*
salón (n., m.)	*lounge, room*
salsa (n., f.)	*salsa (dance and music), sauce (food)*
salud (n., f.)	*health*
saludable (adj.)	*healthy*
salvadoreño, -a (adj.)	*Salvadoran, from El Salvador*
salvo que (conj.)	*unless*
sándwich (n., m.)	*sandwich*
sangrar (v.)	*to bleed*
sangre (n., f.)	*blood*
sanguíneo, -a (adj.)	*sanguine, blood related*
sanitario, -a (adj.)	*sanitary*
santo, -a (n.)	*saint*
sarampión (n., m.)	*measles*
sarro (n., m.)	*plaque, tartar*
satisfacer (v.)	*to satisfy*
secar (v.)	*to dry*
sección (n., f.)	*section*
seco, -a (adj.)	*dry*
secreción (n.)	*discharge*
secundario, -a (adj.)	*secondary*
sed (n., f.)	*thirst*
seda (n., f.)	*silk*
sedante (n., m.)	*sedative*
seguir (v.)	*to follow, to continue*
según (conj.)	*according to*
segundo (n., m.)	*second (as in time)*
seguro (n., m.)	*insurance*
seguro, -a (adj.)	*safe, sure*
Seguro Social (n.)	*Social Security*
seis (adj.)	*six*
seleccionar (v.)	*to select*
selladores dentales (n., m.)	*sealants*
semana (n., f.)	*week*
semanalmente (adv.)	*weekly*
semejante (adj.)	*similar*
semen (n., m.)	*semen*
señal (n., f.)	*signal, sign*
señalar (v.)	*to signal*
seno (n., m.)	*breast*
señor, -a (n.)	*sir, Mr., man, madam, Mrs., lady*
sensación (n., f.)	*sensation*
sensibilidad (n., f.)	*sensitivity*
sensible (adj.)	*sensitive*
sentado, -a (adj.)	*seated*
sentar(se) (v.)	*to sit*
sentimiento (n., m.)	*feeling*
sentir (v.)	*to feel*
separar (v.)	*to separate*
septiembre (n., m.)	*September*
ser (v.)	*to be*
sereno, -a (adj.)	*calm, peaceful*
serie (n., f.)	*series*
serio, -a (adj.)	*serious*
servicio (n., m.)	*service*
servir (v.)	*to serve*
severamente (adv.)	*severely*
severo, -a (adj.)	*severe*
sexo (n., m.)	*sex*
sexual (adj.)	*sexual*
sí (adv.)	*yes*
si (conj.)	*if*
SIDA (n., m.)	*AIDS*
siempre (adv.)	*always*
siesta (n., f.)	*nap*
significado (n., m.)	*meaning*
significar (v.)	*to mean, to signify*
signo (n., m.)	*sign*
signos vitales (n., m.)	*vital signs*
siguiente (adj.)	*following, next*
silencio (n., m.)	*silence*
silla (n., f.)	*chair*
silla de ruedas (n., f.)	*wheelchair*
simpático, -a (adj.)	*nice*
simple (adj.)	*simple*
sin (prep.)	*without*
sin embargo (adv.)	*nevertheless*
sin (conj.)	*without*
sino (conj.)	*but*
síntoma (n., m.)	*symptom*
siquiera (conj.)	*even*
sistema (n., m.)	*system*
situación (n., f.)	*situation*
sobre (prep.)	*about, over*
sobrepeso (n., m.)	*overweight*
sobrevivir (v.)	*to survive*
sobrino, -a (n.)	*nephew, niece*
social (adj.)	*social*
sodio (n., m.)	*sodium*
sol (n., m.)	*sun*
solamente (adv.)	*only*
soledad (n., f.)	*loneliness, solitude*
soler (v.)	*to use to*
solicitar (v.)	*to apply for, to request*
solicitud (n., f.)	*application, request*
solo, -a (adj.)	*alone, only*
soltero, -a (adj.)	*single, unmarried*
sombra (n., f.)	*shade*
someterse (v.)	*to subject to, to surrender to*
somnoliento, -a (adj.)	*sleepy*
soñar (v.)	*to dream*
soñar con (v.)	*to dream about*
sonido (n., m.)	*sound*
sonreír (v.)	*to smile*
soportar (v.)	*to support, to bear*
sordo, -a (adj.)	*deaf*
sorprender (v.)	*to surprise*
sorprenderse (v.)	*to be surprised*
sospecha (n., f.)	*suspicion*
sospechar (v.)	*to suspect*
sospechoso, -a (adj.)	*suspicious*
sostener (v.)	*to sustain, to support, to maintain*
su (adj.)	*his, her, your, its, their (pl.), your (pl.)*
suave (adj.)	*soft*
suavizar (v.)	*to soften*
subir (v.)	*to climb, to go up*
suceder (v.)	*to happen*
sucio, -a (adj.)	*dirty*
sudor (n., m.)	*perspiration*
sueldo (n., m.)	*salary*
suelo (n., m.)	*floor*
sueño (n., m.)	*dream*
suerte (n., f.)	*luck*
suficiente (adj.)	*sufficient*
sufrimiento (n., m.)	*suffering*

sufrir (v.)	*to suffer*
sugerido, -a (adj.)	*suggested*
sugerir (v.)	*to suggest*
suicidarse (v.)	*to commit suicide*
suicidio (n., m.)	*suicide*
sumamente (adv.)	*extremely*
superar (v.)	*to overcome*
superficie (n., f.)	*surface*
supervisión (n., f.)	*supervision*
supervisor, -a (n.)	*supervisor*
suplemento (n., m.)	*supplement*
suponer (v.)	*to suppose, to assume*
suramericano, -a (adj., n.)	*South American*
surtir (v.)	*to supply, to provide*
sustantivo (n., m.)	*noun*
sustituir (v.)	*substitute*
suyo, -a (adj.)	*his, her, your, its, their (pl.), your (pl.)*
tableta (n., f.)	*tablet*
tablilla (n., f.)	*splint*
tal (adj.)	*such*
tal vez (adv.)	*perhaps, maybe*
talón (n., m.)	*check stub, heel*
también (adv.)	*also, too*
tampoco (adv.)	*neither*
tan (adv.)	*so, such*
tanto, -a (adj.)	*so much, so many*
tapar (v.)	*to cover*
taparse (v.)	*to be clogged*
tardar (v.)	*to be late*
tarde (adv.)	*late*
tarde (n., f.)	*afternoon*
tarea (n., f.)	*task, job, homework, chore*
tarjeta (n., f.)	*card*
té (n., m.)	*tea*
técnico (n., m.)	*technician*
tejido (n., m.)	*tissue, fabric, textile*
telefónico, -a (adj.)	*telephone*
teléfono (n., m.)	*telephone*
tema (n., m.)	*theme*
temblor (n., m.)	*shake, tremor*
temer (v.)	*to fear*
temor (n., m.)	*fear*
temperatura (n., f.)	*temperature*
temprano (adv.)	*early*
tender a (v.)	*to have the tendency to*
tener (v.)	*to have*
tener en cuenta (v.)	*to keep in mind, to consider*
tenis (n., m.)	*tennis*
tensión (n., f.)	*tension*
tenso, -a (adj.)	*tense*
terapeuta (n., m. or f.)	*therapist*
terapia (n., f.)	*therapy*
tercer (adj.)	*third*
tercero, -a (adj.)	*third*
terminal (adj.)	*terminal*
terminar (v.)	*to finish*
terrible (adj.)	*terrible*
territorio (n., m.)	*territory*
tétanos (n., m.)	*tetanus*
texto (n., m.)	*text*
tibio, -a (adj.)	*lukewarm, tepid*
tiempo (n., m.)	*time, weather*
tiempo completo (adj.)	*full-time*
tiempo parcial (adj.)	*part-time*
tienda (n., f.)	*store*
tímido, -a (adj.)	*timid, shy*
tina (n., f.)	*bathtub*
tío, -a (n.)	*uncle, aunt*
tipo (n., m.)	*type*
tirado, -a (adj.)	*thrown, spread out*
tirita (n., f.)	*band aid*
tiritar (v.)	*to shiver*
tiro (n., m.)	*shot*
tirón (n., m.)	*tug, tic*
toalla (n., f.)	*towel*
tobillo (n., m.)	*ankle*
tocar (v.)	*to touch*
tocar(le) (v.)	*to be (one's) turn*
todavía (adv.)	*still*
todo (pron.)	*every, all*
todo, -a (adj.)	*everything*
tomar (v.)	*to take, to drink*
tórax (n., m.)	*thorax*
torcer (v.)	*to twist, to sprain*
torcido, -a (adj.)	*twisted, sprained*
toro (n., m.)	*bull*
tos (n., f.)	*cough*
tos ferina (n., f.)	*pertussis*
toser (v.)	*to cough*
tostado, -a (adj.)	*toasted*
trabajador, -a (adj.)	*hard-working*
trabajador, -a (n.)	*worker*
trabajar (v.)	*to work*
trabajo (n., m.)	*work, job*
traducción (n., f.)	*translation*
traer (v.)	*to bring*
tragar (v.)	*to swallow*
tráiler (n., m.)	*trailer, mobile home*
tranquilamente (adv.)	*calmly*
tranquilizarse (v.)	*to calm down*
tranquilo, -a (adj.)	*calm, tranquil*
transmisión (n., f.)	*transmission*
transmitir (v.)	*to transmit*
transplante (n., m.)	*transplantation*
tras (prep.)	*after*
trastorno (n., m.)	*disorder*
tratamiento (n., m.)	*treatment*
tratar (v.)	*to treat, to try to*
tratarse de (v.)	*to be about*
traumático, -a (adj.)	*traumatic*
treinta (adj.)	*thirty*
tres (adj.)	*three*
triste (adj.)	*sad*
tristeza (n., f.)	*sadness*
tu (adj.)	*your*
tú (pron.)	*you*
tuberculino, -a (adj.)	*tuberculin*
tuberculosis (n., f.)	*tuberculosis*
tuyo, -a (adj.)	*yours*
u (conj.)	*or (used instead of "o" when the following word begins with "o" or "ho")*
últimamente (adv.)	*lately*
último, -a (adj.)	*last*
uña (n., f.)	*fingernail, toenail*
único, -a (adj.)	*only, unique*
unido, -a (adj.)	*united, close*
uno, -a (adj.)	*one*
urgente (adj.)	*urgent*
urinario, -a (adj.)	*urinary*
uruguayo, -a (adj., n.)	*Uruguayan, from Uruguay*
usar (v.)	*to use*
uso (n., m.)	*use*
usted (pron.)	*you*
útero (n., m.)	*uterus*
útil (adj.)	*useful*
utilizar (v.)	*to use*
vaca (n., f.)	*cow*
vacaciones (n., f.)	*vacation*
vacuna (n., f.)	*vaccine*
vacunar (v.)	*to vaccinate*
vagina (n., f.)	*vagina*
valer (v.)	*to be worth*
valorar (v.)	*to value*
variado, -a (adj.)	*varied, mixed*
variar (v.)	*to vary*
varicela (n., f.)	*chickenpox*
variedad (n., f.)	*variety*
vario, -a (adj.)	*various, different*
varón (n., m.)	*male*
vaso (n., m.)	*glass, vessel*
vaso sanguíneo (n., m.)	*blood vessel*
vecindario (n., m.)	*neighborhood*
vecino, -a (n.)	*neighbor*
vegetal (n., m.)	*vegetable*
vehículo (n., m.)	*vehicle*
veinte (adj.)	*twenty*
vejez (n., f.)	*old age*
vejiga (n., f.)	*bladder*
vender (v.)	*to sell*
vendido, -a (adj.)	*sold*
veneno (n., m.)	*poison*
venezolano, -a) (adj., n.)	*Venezuelan, from Venezuela*
venir (v.)	*to come*
venta (n., f.)	*sale*
ventana (n., f.)	*window*
ventilar (v.)	*to ventilate*
ver (v.)	*to see*
verano (n., m.)	*summer*
verdad (n., f.)	*truth*
verdadero, -a (adj.)	*true, real*
verde (adj.)	*green*
vergüenza (n., f.)	*shame*
verificar (v.)	*to verify, to confirm*
vestir(se) (v.)	*to dress, to wear*
vez (n., f.)	*time, occasion*
vía (n., f.)	*line, pathway, tract, way*
vía arterial (n., f.)	*arterial line*
vía respiratoria (n., f.)	*airway*
vía urinaria (n., f.)	*urinary tract*
viajar (v.)	*to travel*
viaje (n., m.)	*trip*
víctima (n., f.)	*victim*
vida (n., f.)	*life*
viejo, -a (adj.)	*old*

viento (n., m.)	*wind*
vigilar (v.)	*to watch over, to observe, to guard*
VIH (n., m.)	*HIV*
violar (v.)	*to violate, to rape*
violencia (n., f.)	*violence*
violento, -a (adj.)	*violent*
virus (n., m.)	*virus*
visión (n., f.)	*vision*
visita (n., f.)	*visit*
visitar (v.)	*to visit*
vista (n., f.)	*vision, sight*
visto, -a (adj.)	*seen*
vital (adj.)	*vital*
vitamina (n., f.)	*vitamin*
viudo, -a (n.)	*widower, widow*
vivienda (n., f.)	*dwelling*
vivir (v.)	*to live*
vivo, -a (adj.)	*alive*
vocabulario (n., m.)	*vocabulary*
voluntario, -a (n.)	*volunteer*
volver (v.)	*to go back*
vomitar (v.)	*to vomit*
vómito (n., m.)	*vomit*
vos	*you (fam., sing.)*
vosotros (pron.)	*you*
voz (n., f.)	*voice*
vuelta (n., f.)	*turn*
vuestro, -a (adj.)	*your*
y (conj.)	*and*
ya (adv.)	*already*
yerbabuena, té de (n., f.)	*peppermint tea*
yerbero, -a (n.)	*herbalist*
yeso (n., m.)	*cast*
yo (pron.)	*I*
yogur (n., m.)	*yogurt*

ENGLISH - SPANISH GLOSSARY

a	*un, -a (art.)*
a lot	*mucho, -a (adj.)*
abandon	*abandonar (v.)*
abandonment	*abandono (n., m.)*
abdominal	*abdominal (adj.)*
ability	*habilidad (n., f.)*
abnormal	*anormal (adj.)*
abortion	*aborto (n., m.)*
about	*acerca de (prep.); sobre (prep.)*
abroad	*extranjero (n., m.)*
abuse	*abusar (v.); abuso (n., m.)*
accelerate	*acelerar (v.)*
accept	*aceptar (v.)*
accident	*accidente (n., m.)*
accompany	*acompañar (v.)*
according to	*según (conj.)*
accountant	*contador, -a (n.)*
accurate	*preciso, -a (adj.)*
accuse	*acusar (v.)*
accustomed to	*acostumbrar (v.); soler (v.)*
ache	*doler (v.); dolor (n., m.)*
achieve	*lograr (v.); realizar (v.)*
acid	*ácido (n., m.)*
act	*comportarse (v.); actuar (v.); acto (n., m.)*
active	*activo, -a (adj.)*
activity	*actividad (n., f.)*
adapt	*adecuar (v.)*
add	*añadir (v.)*
addict	*adicto, -a (n.)*
additional	*adicional (adj.)*
address	*dirección (n., f.)*
adequate	*adecuado, -a (adj.)*
adequately	*adecuadamente (adv.)*
administrate	*administrar (v.)*
administration	*administración (n., f.)*
admit	*admitir (v.)*
adolescent	*adolescente (adj.)*
adult	*adulto, -a (n.)*
adverse	*adverso, -a (adj.)*
advice	*consejo (n., m.)*
advise	*aconsejar (v.)*
affect	*afectar (v.)*
affected	*afectado, -a (adj.)*
African	*africano, -a (adj.)*
after	*después de (prep.); tras (prep.)*
afternoon	*tarde (n., f.)*
afterwards	*después (adv.)*
against	*contra (prep.)*
age	*edad (n., f.)*
agency	*agencia (n., f.)*
agent	*agente (n., m. or f.)*
aggressive	*agresivo, -a (adj.)*
ago	*hace (adv.)*
agree	*acordar (v.)*
agreement	*acuerdo (n., m.)*
agricultural	*agrícola (adj.)*
AIDS	*SIDA (n., m.)*
air conditioning	*aire acondicionado (n., m.)*
airway	*vía respiratoria (n., f.)*
alcohol	*alcohol (n., m.)*
alive	*vivo, -a (adj.)*
all	*todo (pron.)*
allergic	*alérgico, -a (adj.)*
allergy	*alergia (n., f.)*
alleviate	*aliviar (v.)*
allow	*consentir (v.); dejar (v.); permitir (v.)*
almost	*casi (adv.)*
alone	*solo, -a (adj.)*
already	*ya (adv.)*
also	*también (adv.)*
alternative	*alternativa (n., f.)*
although	*aunque (conj.); siquiera (conj.)*
always	*siempre (adv.)*
ambulance	*ambulancia (n., f.)*
American	*americano, -a (adj., n.), estadounidense (adj., n., m. or f.)*
amputate	*amputar (v.)*
an	*un, -a (art.)*
analysis	*análisis (n., m.)*
analyze	*analizar (v.)*
ancestor	*antepasado (n., m.)*
ancient	*antiguo, -a (adj.)*
and	*y (conj.); e (conj.)*
angel	*ángel (n., m.)*
anger	*coraje (n., m.); enojo (n.)*
animal	*animal (n., m. or f.)*
ankle	*tobillo (n., m.)*
announce	*anunciar (v.)*
announcement	*anuncio (n., m.)*
annoy	*molestar (v.)*
another	*otro, -a (adj.)*
answer	*respuesta (n.); responder (v.); contestar (v.)*
antibiotic	*antibiótico (n., m.)*
antidepressant	*antidepresivo, -a (adj.)*
anxiety	*ansiedad (n., f.)*
anxious	*ansioso, -a (adj.)*
any	*cualquier, -a (adj.)*
apartment	*apartamento (n., m.), departamento (n., m.)*
apathetic	*apático, -a (adj.)*
apathy	*apatía (n., f.)*
apologize	*disculparse (v.)*
apology	*disculpa (n., f.)*
appearance	*apariencia (n., f.); aspecto (n., m.); aparición (the act of appearing) (n., f.)*
appetite	*apetito (n., m.)*
apple	*manzana (n., f.)*
application	*solicitud (n., f.)*
apply for	*solicitar (v.)*
appointment	*cita (n., f.)*
approach	*acercarse (v.)*
appropriate	*apropiado, -a (adj.)*
approval	*aprobación (n., f.)*
approve	*aprobar (v.)*
aquatic	*acuático, -a (adj.)*
area	*área (n., f.)*
Argentinian	*argentino, -a (adj., n.)*
argue	*discutir (v.)*
arm	*brazo (n., m.)*
arrive	*llegar (v.)*
arterial	*arterial (adj.)*
arterial line	*vía arterial (n., f.)*
arthritis	*artritis (n., f.)*
article	*artículo (n., m.)*
as	*como (adv.); pues (conj.)*
as long as	*a condición de que (conj.)*
as much as	*cuanto, -a (adj.); tanto como (adv.)*
as soon as	*apenas (conj.)*
ashamed	*avergonzado, -a (adj.)*
ask	*preguntar (v.)*
ask for	*pedir (v.)*
ask forgiveness	*pedir disculpas (v.)*
ask questions	*hacer preguntas (v.)*
aspect	*aspecto (n., m.)*
aspirin	*aspirina (n., f.)*

assault	*asaltar (v.); asalto (n., m.); acosar (v.); acoso (n., m.)*
assaulter	*acosador, -a (n.); asaltante (n., m. or f.)*
assert	*afirmar (v.)*
assistance	*asistencia (n., f.)*
assistant	*ayudante (n., m. or f.)*
assume	*suponer (v.)*
at	*en (prep.); a (prep.)*
at once	*en seguida (adv.)*
attack	*ataque (n.); atacar (v.)*
attain	*lograr (v.)*
attend to	*atender (v.)*
attend	*asistir – to a function or event (v.)*
attention	*atención (n., f.)*
attitude	*actitud (n., f.)*
attract	*atraer (v.)*
audiologist	*audiólogo, -a (n.)*
aunt	*tía (n., f.)*
authorize	*autorizar (v.)*
automobile	*automóvil (n., m.)*
availability	*disponibilidad (n., f.)*
available	*disponible (adj.)*
avoid	*evitar (v.)*
awake	*despierto, -a (adj.)*
awaken	*despertarse (v.)*
award	*otorgar (v.); premio (n., m.)*
baby	*bebé (n., m. or f.)*
baby bottle	*biberón (n., m.); mama dera (n., f.)*
back	*espalda (n., f.)*
bacteria	*bacteria (n., f.)*
bad	*mal (adv.)*
badly	*mal (adv.)*
bag	*bolsa (n., f.)*
bake	*hornear (v.)*
balanced	*equilibrado, -a (adj.)*
ball	*bola, pelota (n., f.)*
band aid	*curita (n., f.); tirita (n., f.)*
bank	*banco (n., m.)*
bar	*barra - for exercise (n., f.); bar - establishment (n., f.)*
baseball	*béisbol (n., m.)*
basic	*básico, -a (adj.)*
bath	*baño (n., m.)*
bathe	*bañar (v.); bañarse (v.)*
bathroom	*baño (n., m.)*
bathtub	*tina, bañera (n., f.)*
be	*estar (v.); ser (v.)*
be able	*poder (v.)*
be about	*tratarse de (v.)*
be born	*nacer (v.)*
be familiar with	*conocer (v.)*
be frightened	*asustarse (v.)*
be happy	*alegrarse (v.)*
be hurt	*lastimarse (v.)*
be in charge	*hacerse cargo (v.)*
be mistaken	*equivocarse (v.)*
be of the opinion	*opinar (v.)*
be (one's) turn	*tocarle (a uno/a) (v.)*
be surprised	*sorprenderse (v.)*
be worth	*valer (v.)*
bear	*soportar (v.)*
beat	*latido (n., m.); latir (v.)*
because	*porque (conj.)*
because of	*por, a causa de (prep.)*
become a member	*ingresar a (v.)*
become loose	*desprenderse (v.)*
become pregnant	*embarazarse (v.)*
become swollen	*hincharse (v.)*
become	*convertirse (v.); hacerse (v.)*
bed	*cama (n., f.)*
beer	*cerveza (n., f.)*
before	*antes (adv.); antes de (prep.)*
beg	*rogar (v.)*
begin	*comenzar (v.); empezar (v.)*
beginning	*principio (n., m.)*
behave	*comportarse (v.); portarse (v.); actuar (v.)*
behavior	*comportamiento (n., m.)*
believe	*creer (v.)*
belong	*pertenecer (v.)*
below	*abajo (prep.); bajo (adv.)*
benefit	*beneficio (n., m.)*
besides	*además (adv.)*
better	*mejor (adj.); mejorar (v.)*
between	*entre (prep.)*
bicycle	*bicicleta (n., f.)*
big	*grande (adj.)*
bilirubin	*bilirrubina (n., f.)*
bill	*cuenta (n., f.)*
biological	*biológico, -a (adj.)*
birth	*nacimiento (n., m.)*
birth certificate	*acta de nacimiento (n., f.)*
birth control	*control de natalidad (n., m.)*
birth-rate	*tasa de natalidad (n., f.)*
bite	*picar - animal (v.); morder - human (v.)*
black	*negro, -a (adj.)*
bladder	*vejiga (n., f.)*
blame	*culpar (v.); culpa (n., f.)*
bleed	*sangrar (v.)*
bleeding	*hemorragia (n., f.)*
blind	*ciego, -a (adj.)*
blindness	*ceguera (n., f.)*
blister	*ampolla (n., f.)*
block	*bloque - building block (n., m.); cuadra - city block (n., f.)*
blood	*sangre (n., f.); sanguíneo, -a (adj.)*
blood pressure	*presión arterial (n., f.)*
blood vessel	*vaso sanguíneo (n., m.)*
blow	*golpe (n., m.); soplar (v.); soplo (n., m.)*
board	*junta (n., f.)*
body	*cuerpo (n., m.); corporal (adj.)*
boil	*hervir (v.)*
Bolivian	*boliviano, -a (adj., n.)*
bone	*hueso (n., m.)*
booboo	*chichón (n., m.)*
book	*libro (n., m.)*
boring	*aburrido, -a (adj.)*
born	*nacido, -a (adj.)*
borrow	*pedir prestado (v.)*
boss	*patrón, -a (n.); jefe, -a (n.)*
both	*ambos, -as (adj., pron.)*
bother	*molestar (v.); molestia (n., f.)*
bottle	*botella (n., f.); frasco (n., m.)*
boy	*niño (n., m.); chico (n., m.)*
boyfriend	*novio (fiancee) (n., m.); amigo (n., m.)*
brain	*cerebral (adj.); cerebro (n., m.)*
brain hemorrhage	*derrame cerebral (n., m.)*
brand name	*marca (n., f.)*
Brazilian	*brasileño, -a (adj., n.)*
bread	*pan (n., m.)*
break	*descanso (n., m.); romper (v.); romperse (v.)*
breakfast	*desayuno (n., m.)*
breast	*seno (n., m.); busto (n., m.)*
breastfeed	*amamantar (v.); dar el pecho (v.)*
breath	*aliento (n., m.)*
breathe	*respirar (v.)*
breathing	*respiración (n., f.)*
bring	*traer, llevar (v.)*
broken	*roto, -a (adj.)*
brother	*hermano (n., m.)*
brother-in-law	*cuñado (n., m.)*
bruise	*moretón (n., m.); magulladora (n., f.)*
brush	*cepillar (v.); cepillarse (v.); cepillo (n., m.)*
budget	*presupuesto (n., m.)*
building	*edificio (n., m.)*
bull	*toro (n., m.)*
bullet	*bala (n., f.)*
bulletin	*boletín (n., m.)*
bump	*chichón (n., m.); protuberancia (n., f.)*
burning	*ardor (n., m.)*
business	*negocio (n., m.)*
busy	*ocupado, -a (adj.)*
but	*pero (conj.)*
butter	*mantequilla (n., f.)*
buy	*comprar (v.)*
by	*por (prep.); para (prep.)*
cake	*pastel (n., m.)*
calcium	*calcio (n., m.)*
call	*llamar (v.); llamada (n.)*
called, to be	*llamarse (v.)*
calm down	*calmar(se) (v.); tranquilizar(se) (v.)*
calm	*sereno, -a (adj.); tranquilo, -a (adj.)*
calmly	*tranquilamente (adv.)*
calorie	*caloría (n., f.)*
cancel	*cancelar (v.)*
cancer	*cáncer (n., m.)*
cane	*bastón (n., m.)*
canned	*enlatado, -a (adj.)*
capable	*capaz (adj.)*
capsule	*cápsula (n.)*
car	*carro (n., m.); auto (n., m.)*
carbohydrate	*carbohidrato (n., m.)*
card	*tarjeta (n., f.)*
cardiac	*cardíaco, -a (adj.)*
care for	*cuidar (v.); cuidarse (v.)*
care	*cuidado (n., m.)*
carefully	*cuidadosamente (adv.)*

carefulness	*cuidado (n., m.)*
carrier	*portador (n., m.)*
carry	*llevar (v.)*
carry out	*desempeñar (v.); cumplir (v.)*
cartilage	*cartílago (n., m.)*
case	*caso (n., m.)*
cashier	*cajero, -a (n., m.)*
cast	*yeso (n., m.)*
cataract	*catarata (n., f.)*
catch a cold	*resfriarse (v.)*
catch an illness	*contraer (v.)*
cause	*causa (n.); causar (v.)*
cavity	*caries (n., f., sing.)*
cavities	*caries (n., f., pl.)*
celebrate	*celebrar (v.)*
cell	*célula (n., f.)*
Central American	*centroamericano, -a (adj., n.)*
cereal	*cereal (n., m.)*
cerebral	*cerebral, brain (adj.)*
certain	*cierto, -a (adj.)*
certainty	*certeza (n., f.)*
certificate	*certificado (n., m.)*
certify	*certificar (v.)*
cesarean	*cesárea (n., f.)*
chair	*silla (n., f.)*
challenge	*desafío (n., m.); retar (v.); reto (n., m.)*
change	*cambiar (v.); cambio (n., m.)*
chaplain	*capellán (n., m.)*
character m.)	*personaje - in a story (n.,*
characterize	*caracterizar (v.)*
charge	*cobrar - money (v.); cargo (n., m.)*
charming	*encantador, -a (adj.)*
chauvinistic	*machista (adj.)*
check	*cheque (n., m.); comprobar (v.); revisar (v.)*
check stub	*talón de cheque (n., m.)*
chemical	*químico (adj.)*
cherry	*cereza (n., f.)*
chest	*pecho (n., m.)*
chew	*masticar (v.)*
chewable	*masticable (adj.)*
chickenpox	*varicela (n., f.)*
child	*hijo, -a (n.); niño, -a (n.); chico, -a (n.)*
childbirth	*parto (n., m.)*
childhood	*niñez (n., f.)*
Chilean	*chileno, -a (adj., n.)*
chills	*escalofríos (n., m.)*
cholesterol	*colesterol (n., m.)*
choose	*escoger (v.); optar (v.); elegir (v.)*
chore	*quehacer (n., m.); tarea (n., f.)*
church	*iglesia (n., f.)*
circulatory	*circulatorio (adj.)*
circumstance	*circunstancia (n., f.)*
citizen	*ciudadano, -a (n.)*
city	*ciudad (n., f.)*
clarify	*clarificar (v.)*
class	*clase (n., f.)*
clean	*limpiar (v.); limpio, -a (adj.)*
cleanliness	*limpieza (n., f.)*
clear	*claro, -a (adj.)*
clearly	*claramente (adv.)*
client	*cliente (n., m. or f.)*
clientele	*clientela (n., f.)*
climate	*clima (n., m.)*
climb	*subir (v.)*
clinic	*clínica (n., f.)*
clog	*tapar (v.)*
close	*cerca (prep.); cercano, -a (adj.); íntimo, -a (adj.); unido, -a (adj.); cerrar (v.)*
clothing	*ropa (n., f.)*
club	*club (n., m.)*
coat	*abrigo (n., m.)*
coincidence	*casualidad (n., f.); coincidencia (n., f.)*
cold	*resfriado - illness (n., m.); frío - temperature (n., m.); frío, -a (adj.)*
colic	*cólico (n., m.)*
collar	*collar (n., m.)*
colleague	*colega (n., m. or f.)*
collect	*cobrar - money (v.); recoger (v.)*
college	*universidad (n., f.)*
Colombian	*colombiano, -a (adj., n.)*
color	*color (n., m.)*
column	*columna (n., f.)*
combat	*combatir (v.)*
combination	*combinación (n., f.)*
combine	*combinar (v.)*
come	*venir (v.)*
comfort	*consuelo (n., m.)*
comfortable	*cómodo, -a (adj.)*
command	*orden (n., f.); mandato (n., m.)*
commit suicide	*suicidarse (v.)*
committee	*comité (n., m.)*
common	*común (adj.); frecuente (adj.)*
commotion	*conmoción (n., f.)*
communicate	*comunicar (v.)*
community	*comunidad (n., f.)*
companion	*compañero, -a (n.)*
company	*compañía (n., f.)*
competent	*competente (adj.)*
complain	*quejarse (v.)*
complaint	*queja (n., f.)*
complete	*completo, -a (adj.)*
complex	*complejo, -a (adj.)*
complication	*complicación (n., f.)*
composed	*compuesto, -a (adj.)*
concentrate	*concentrarse (v.)*
concentration	*concentración (n., f.)*
concern	*preocupación (n., f.); concernir (v.); preocupar (v.)*
concerning	*acerca de (prep.)*
condition	*condición (n., f.)*
condom	*condón (n., m.)*
conduct	*conducta (n., f.); comportamiento (n., m.)*
confide in	*confiar en (v.)*
confidence	*confianza (n., f.)*
confidentiality	*confidencialidad (n., f.)*
confirm	*verificar (v.)*
confront	*enfrentar (v.)*
confusion	*confusión (n., f.)*
congratulations	*felicitaciones (n., f.)*
consent	*consentir (v.)*
consequence	*consecuencia (n., f.)*
consider	*considerar (v.)*
consist	*componer(se) (v.); consistir (v.)*
constant	*constante (adj.)*
constantly	*constantamente (adv.)*
constipation	*estreñimiento (n., m.)*
construct	*construir (v.)*
construction	*construcción (n., f.)*
consult	*consultar (v.)*
consume	*consumir (v.)*
contact	*ponerse en contacto con (v.); contacto (n., m.); enchufe - connection (n., m.)*
contagion	*contagio (n., m.)*
contagious	*contagioso, -a (adj.)*
contain	*contener (v.)*
container	*envase (n., m.)*
content	*contenido (n., m.)*
continuation	*continuación (n., f.)*
continue	*continuar (v.); seguir (v.)*
continuous	*continuo, -a (adj.)*
contraceptive	*anticonceptivo, -a (adj.)*
contract	*contraer - an illness (v.); contrato - legal paper (n., m.)*
contraction	*contracción (n., f.)*
contribute	*contribuir (v.)*
control	*control (n., m.); controlar (v.); gobernar (v.)*
controlled	*moderado, -a (adj.)*
convalescence	*convalecencia (n., f.)*
convert	*convertir (v.)*
convince	*convencer (v.)*
cook	*cocinar (v.)*
cool down	*enfriamiento (n., m.)*
coordinate	*coordinar (v.)*
copy	*copia (n., f.); copiar (v.)*
corporal	*corporal (adj.)*
correct	*corregir (v.); correcto, -a (adj.)*
correctly	*correctamente (adv.)*
cost	*costar (v.); costo (n., m.)*
Costa Rican	*costarricense (adj., n., m. or f.)*
costly	*costoso, -a (adj)*
cotton	*algodón (n., m.)*
cough	*tos (n., f.); toser (v.)*
cough syrup	*jarabe para la tos (n., m.)*
counselor	*consejero, -a (n.)*
count	*contar (v.)*
country	*país (n., m.)*
county	*condado (n., m.)*
couple	*pareja (n., f.)*
coupon	*vale (n., m.); cupón (n., m.)*
cousin	*primo, -a (n.)*
cover	*cubrir (v.); tapar (v.)*
coverage	*cobertura (n., f.)*
covered	*cubierto, -a (adj.)*
cow	*vaca (n., f.)*
crash	*chocar (v.)*

crazy	*loco, -a (adj.)*
cream	*crema (n., f.)*
create	*crear (v.)*
crib	*cuna (n., f.)*
criticize	*criticar (v.)*
cross	*cruzar (v.); cruz (n., f.)*
crutches	*muletas (n., f.)*
cry	*llorar (v.); grito (n., m.)*
Cuban	*cubano, -a (adj., n.)*
culture	*cultura (n., f.)*
cure	*cura (n., f.); curar (v.)*
current	*actual (adj.)*
custom	*costumbre (n., f.)*
cut	*cortada, cortadura (n., f.); cortar (v.)*
cycle	*ciclo (n., m.)*
cyst	*quiste (n., m.)*
daily	*al día (adv.); diariamente (adv.); diario, -a (adj.)*
damage	*dañar (v.); dañarse (v.); daño (n., m.)*
damaged	*dañado, -a (adj.)*
dance	*bailar (v.)*
danger	*peligro (n., m.)*
dangerous	*peligroso, -a (adj.)*
dark	*oscuro, -a (adj.)*
date	*cita (n., f.); fecha (n., f.)*
daughter	*hija (n., f.)*
day	*día (n., m.)*
daycare	*guardería (n., f.)*
dead	*muerto, -a (adj)*
deaf	*sordo, -a (adj.)*
dear	*cielo -term of endearment (n.); querido, -a (adj.)*
deceive	*engañar (v.)*
decide	*decidir (v.)*
decision	*decisión (n., f.)*
decrease	*disminuir (v.)*
dedicate	*dedicar (v.)*
deduct	*restar (v.); deducir (v.)*
deep	*profundo, -a (adj.)*
defect	*defecto (n., m.)*
defend	*defender(se) (v.)*
defense	*defensa (n., f.)*
defenseless	*indefenso, -a (adj.)*
delay	*atrasarse (v.); retraso (n., m.)*
delicate	*delicado, -a (adj.)*
delight	*encantar (v.)*
delightful	*encantador, -a (adj.)*
delivery	*parto - childbirth (n., m.)*
demand	*demandar (v.); exigir (v.); reclamar (v.)*
demonstrate	*demostrar (v.)*
dense	*espeso, -a (adj.)*
dental	*dental (adj.)*
dental floss	*hilo dental (n.)*
dentist	*dentista (n., m. or f.)*
dentures	*dentadura postiza (n., f.)*
deny	*negar (v.)*
department	*apartamento (n., m.); departamento (n., m.)*
depend	*depender (v.)*
deposit	*depósito (n., m.)*
depressed	*decaído, -a (adj.); deprimido, -a (adj.)*
depression	*depresión (n., f.)*
depressive	*deprimente (adj.); depresivo -a (adj.)*
depressant	*depresivo, -a (adj.)*
deprive	*privar (v.)*
describe	*describir (v.)*
deserve	*merecer (v.)*
designate	*designar (v.)*
designated	*designado, -a (adj.)*
desire	*desear (v.); ganas (n., f.); deseo (n., m.)*
despair	*desesperación (n., f.); desesperar (v.)*
desperate	*desesperado, -a (adj.)*
desperation	*desesperanza (n., f.)*
destroy	*destruir (v.)*
detach	*desprender (v.)*
detail	*detalle (n., m.)*
detect	*detectar (v.)*
deteriorate	*deteriorarse (v.)*
deterioration	*deterioro (n.); deterioración (n., f.)*
determination	*empeño (n., m.); determinación (n., f.)*
determine	*determinar (v.)*
develop	*desarrollar (v.); desarrollarse (v.)*
development	*desarrollo (n., m.)*
devote	*dedicarse (v.)*
diabetes	*diabetes (n., f.)*
diagnose	*diagnosticar (v.)*
diagnosed	*diagnosticado, -a (adj.)*
diagnosis	*diagnóstico (n., m.)*
dial	*marcar (v.)*
dialysis	*diálisis (n., f.)*
diaper	*pañal (n., m.)*
diary	*diario, -a (adj.); diario (n., m.)*
die	*morir (v.); morirse (v.)*
diet	*dieta (n., f.)*
dietician	*dietista (n., m. or f.)*
difference	*diferencia (n., f.)*
different	*diferente, -s (adj.); varios, -as (adj., pl.)*
difficult	*difícil (adj.)*
difficulty	*dificultad (n., f.)*
digest	*digerir (v.)*
digestive	*digestivo, -a (adj.)*
dilatation	*dilatación (n., f.)*
dine	*cenar (v.)*
dinner	*cena (n., f.)*
diphtheria	*difteria (n., f.)*
direct	*directo, -a (adj.); dirigir (v.)*
direction	*dirección (n., f.)*
director	*director, -a (n.)*
dirty	*sucio, -a (adj.)*
disability	*incapacidad (n., f.)*
disappear	*desaparecer (v.)*
disaster	*desastre (n., m.)*
discharge	*flujo (n., m.); secreción (n., f.)*
discomfort	*malestar (n., m.)*
discover	*descubrir (v.)*
discovered	*descubierto, -a (adj.)*
discuss	*discutir (v.)*
dislike	*disgustar (v.)*
disorder	*desorden (n., m.); trastorno (n., m.)*
distinct	*distinto, -a (adj.)*
distinguish	*distinguir (v.)*
distressed	*angustiado, -a (adj.)*
distribute	*distribuir (v.)*
distributed	*distribuido, -a (adj.)*
diverse	*diverso, -a (adj.)*
dizziness	*mareo (n., m.)*
dizzy	*mareado, -a (adj.)*
do	*hacer (v.)*
doctor	*doctor, -a (n.); médico, -a (n.)*
document	*documento (n., m.)*
dollar	*dólar (n., m.)*
domestic	*doméstico, -a (adj.)*
domicile	*domicilio (n., m.)*
Dominican	*dominicano, -a (adj., n.)*
donate	*donar (v.)*
done	*hecho, -a (adj.)*
dosage	*dosificación (n., f.); dosis (n., f.)*
dose	*dosis (n., f.)*
doubt	*duda (n., f.); dudar (v.)*
doubtful	*dudoso, -a (adj.)*
drama	*drama (n., m.)*
drawing	*dibujo (n., m.)*
dream	*soñar (v.); sueño (n., m.)*
dream about	*soñar con (v.)*
dress	*vestir (v.); vestirse (v.)*
drink	*tomar (v.); beber (v.); trago - glass of alcoholic drink (n., m.)*
drive	*manejar (v.)*
drive crazy	*sacar de quicio (v.); volver loco, -a (v.)*
drop	*gota (n., f.); dejar caer -let fall (v.)*
drown	*ahogar(se) (v.)*
drug	*droga (n., f.)*
drug addiction	*drogadicción (n., f.)*
dry	*secar (v.); seco, -a (adj.)*
due	*debido, -a (adj.)*
during	*durante (adv.)*
dust	*polvo (n., m.)*
duty	*obligación (n., m.)*
dwelling	*vivienda (n., f.)*
each	*cada (adj.)*
ear	*oído -inner ear (n., m.); oreja -outer ear (n., f.)*
early	*temprano (adv.)*
easily	*fácilmente (adv.)*
easy	*fácil (adj.)*
eat	*comer (v.)*
eat dinner	*cenar (v.)*
eat lunch	*almorzar (v.)*
echogram	*ecografía (n., f.)*
Ecuadorian	*ecuatoriano, -a (adj., n.)*
editorialist	*editorialista (n., m. or f.)*
education	*educación (n., f.)*
effect	*efecto (n., m.)*
effective	*efectivo, -a (adj.)*
efficient	*eficaz (adj.); eficiente (adj.)*
effort	*esfuerzo (n., m.)*
eight	*ocho (adj.)*
eighth	*octavo, -a (adj.)*
elect	*elegir (v.); electo, -a (adj.)*
electricity	*electricidad (n., f.)*

electronic	*electrónico, -a (adj.)*
elevator	*ascensor (n., m.); elevador (n., m.)*
eleven	*once (adj.)*
eligible	*elegible (adj.)*
eliminate	*eliminar (v.)*
email	*correo electrónico (n., m.)*
emergency	*emergencia (n., f.)*
emotion	*emoción (n., f.)*
emotional	*emocional (adj.); emotivo (adj.)*
employee	*empleado, -a (n.)*
employer	*jefe, -a (n.); patrón (n., m.)*
employment	*empleo (n., m.)*
enclosed	*adjunto, -a (adj.)*
encourage	*animar (v.)*
end	*fin (n., m.)*
English	*inglés, inglesa (adj., n.)*
enjoy	*gozar (v.)*
enough	*bastante (adv.)*
enter	*entrar (v.)*
entire	*entero, -a (adj.); íntegro, -a (adj.)*
environment	*ambiente (n., m.); medio ambiente (n., m.)*
epidemic	*epidemia (n., f.)*
episode	*episodio (n., m.)*
equal	*igual (adj.)*
equality	*igualdad (n., f.)*
equipment	*equipo (n., m.)*
escape	*escapar(se) (v.); huir (v.)*
essential	*indispensable (adj.); esencial (adj.)*
establish	*establecer (v.)*
even	*aun (adv.); incluso (adv.); par (n., m.); siquiera (adv.)*
even though	*aunque (conj.)*
event	*evento (n., m.)*
ever	*jamás (adv.)*
every	*cada (adj.); todo (pron.)*
everything	*todo, -a (adj.)*
evict	*desalojar (v.)*
evidence	*evidencia (n., f.)*
exact	*exacto, -a (adj.)*
exam	*examen (n., m.)*
examine	*chequear (v.); examinar (v.)*
example	*ejemplo (n., m.)*
excellent	*excelente (adj.)*
except	*sino (conj.); excepto (adv.)*
excessive	*excesivo, -a (adj.)*
excessively	*excesivamente (adv.)*
exercise	*ejercicio (n., m.)*
exhausted	*agotado, -a (adj.); cansado, -a (adj.)*
exhibit	*exhibir (v.); exhibición (n., f.)*
exist	*existir (v.)*
expect	*esperar (v.)*
expel	*botar (v.); expulsar (v.)*
expensive	*caro, -a (adj.)*
experience	*experiencia (n., f.); experimentar (v.)*
expert	*experto, -a (adj.)*
explain	*explicar (v.)*
explanation	*explicación (n., f.)*
explode	*explotar (v.)*
expose	*exponer (v.)*
exposed	*expuesto, -a (adj.)*
exposure	*exposición (n., f.)*
express	*expresar (v.); expresarse (v.)*
extend	*extender(se) (v.)*
extremely	*sumamente (adv.)*
eye	*ojo (n., m.)*
eye pupil	*pupila (del ojo) (n., f.)*
eyeglasses	*anteojos (n., m.); lentes (n., m.); gafas (n., f.)*
fabric	*tela - material (n., f.); tejido - woven material (n., m.)*
fabulous	*fabuloso, -a (adj.)*
face	*enfrentar (v.); cara (n., f.)*
face down	*boca abajo (prep.)*
face up	*boca arriba (prep.)*
facility	*edificio -building (n., m.); instalaciones -buildings (n., f.); facilidad -ability (n., f.)*
fact	*dato (n., m.); hecho (n., m.)*
factor	*factor (n., m.)*
factory	*fábrica (n., f.)*
fail	*fallar (v.)*
fair	*feria (n., f.); justo, -a (adj.)*
fall	*caer (v.)*
fall asleep	*dormirse (v.)*
fall down	*caerse (v.)*
fall in love	*enamorarse (v.)*
fallen	*decaído, -a (adj.)*
false teeth	*dentadura postiza (n., f.)*
false	*falso, -a (adj.); postizo, -a (adj.)*
familiar	*conocido, -a (adj.); familiar (adj.); familiar -relative (n., m. or f.)*
family	*familia (n., f.)*
far	*lejos (prep.)*
farmer	*granjero, -a (n.); campesino, -a (n.); ranchero, -a - cattle farmer (n.)*
fat	*grasa - food (n., f.); gordo, -a (adj.)*
fatty	*grasoso, -a (adj.)*
father	*padre (n., m.); priest (n., m.)*
fatigue	*fatiga (n., f.)*
fatten	*engordar (v.)*
fault	*culpa (n., f.)*
favor	*favor (n., m.)*
favorite	*favorito, -a (adj.)*
fear	*miedo (n., m.); temer (v.); temor (n., m.)*
feces	*heces (n., f.)*
feeding	*alimentación (n., f.)*
feel	*sentir (v.); sentirse (v.)*
feeling	*sentimiento (n., m.)*
festival	*festival (n., m.)*
fever	*fiebre (n., f.)*
few	*poco, -s (adv.)*
fewer	*menos (adv.)*
fiber	*fibra (n., f.)*
fibroid	*fibroma (n., m.)*
field	*campo (n., m.)*
fifty	*cincuenta (adj.)*
fight	*combatir (v.); pelea (n., f.); pelear (v.); pelearse (v.)*
figure	*cifra - number (n., f.)*
file	*archivo (n., m.)*
fill	*llenar (v.)*
fill in	*rellenar (v.)*
filter	*filtro (n., m.); colar (v.)*
finances	*finanzas (n., f.)*
financial	*financiero, -a (adj.)*
find out	*enterarse (v.)*
find	*encontrar (v.)*
finger	*dedo de la mano (n., m.)*
fingernail	*uña (n., f.)*
finish	*acabar (v.); terminar (v.)*
finished	*acabado, -a (adj.); terminado, -a (adj.)*
fire	*despedir (v.); fuego (n., m.)*
first	*primer (adj.); primero, -a (adj.)*
fit	*caber (v.)*
five	*cinco (adj.)*
fix up	*arreglar (v.)*
flask	*frasco (n., m.)*
flavor	*sabor (n., m.)*
flee	*huir (v.)*
flexible	*flexible (adj.)*
floor	*suelo (n., m.)*
flu	*gripe (n., f.)*
fluid	*fluido (n., m.)*
fluoride	*flúor (n., m.)*
folic acid	*ácido fólico (n., m.)*
follow	*seguir (v.)*
following	*siguiente (adj.)*
food	*alimento (n., m.); comida (n., f.)*
foot	*pie (n., m.)*
for	*por (prep.); para (prep.)*
force	*obligar (v.); forzar (v.)*
forehead	*frente (n., f.)*
foreign	*extranjero, -a (adj.); extraño, -a (adj.)*
forget	*olvidar (v.); olvidarse (v.)*
forgive	*perdonar (v.)*
form	*forma - shape (n., f.); formar (v.); formulario - paper (n., m.)*
formal	*formal (adj.)*
formula	*fórmula (n., f.)*
fortunately	*afortunadamente (adv.)*
foster	*fomentar (v.)*
four	*cuatro (adj.)*
fourth	*cuarto, -a (adj.)*
free	*gratis (adj.); libre (adj.)*
freeze	*congelar (v.)*
frequent	*frecuente (adj.)*
frequently	*frecuentemente (adv.)*
fried	*frito, -a (adj.)*
friend	*amigo, -a (n.); compañero, -a (n.)*
friendship	*amistad (n., f.)*
frighten	*asustar (v.)*
frightened	*aterrorizado, -a (adj.)*
frightening	*espantoso, -a (adj.)*
from	*de (prep.); desde - since (prep.)*
fruit	*fruta (n., f.)*
fry	*freír (v.)*
fulfill	*cumplir (v.); realizar (v.)*

full	*lleno, -a (adj.)*
full-time	*tiempo completo (adj.)*
fun	*diversión (n., f.); divertido, -a (adj.)*
function	*funcionar (v.)*
funds	*fondos (n., m., pl.)*
furious	*furioso, -a (adj.)*
fury	*rabia (n., f.)*
future	*futuro (n., m.); futuro, -a (adj.)*
gain weight	*engordar (v.)*
gang member	*pandillero, -a (n.)*
gang	*pandilla (n., f.)*
garbage can	*basurero (n., m.)*
Garifuna	*garífuna (adj., n.)*
gather	*reunir (v.); recoger (v.)*
gel	*gel (n., m.)*
general	*general (adj.)*
generally	*generalmente (adv.)*
generic	*genérico, -a (adj.)*
genetic	*genético, -a (adj.)*
genital	*genital (adj.)*
germ	*germen (n., m.)*
get along	*llevarse - with another person (v.)*
get angry	*enfadarse (v.); enojarse (v.)*
get better	*mejorar (v.)*
get bored	*aburrirse (v.)*
get cold	*enfriarse (v.)*
get hurt	*lastimarse (v.)*
get infected	*contagiarse (v.)*
get involved	*involucrarse (v.)*
get poisoned	*envenenarse (v.)*
get sick	*enfermarse (v.)*
get thin	*adelgazar (v.)*
get tired	*cansarse (v.)*
get up	*levantarse (v.)*
get worse	*empeorar (v.)*
gift	*regalo (n., m.)*
girl	*niña (n., f.); chica (n., f.)*
girlfriend	*novia (n., f.); amiga (n., f.)*
give	*dar (v.)*
give birth	*dar a luz (v.)*
gland	*glándula (n., f.)*
glass	*vaso (n., m.)*
glaucoma	*glaucoma (n., m.)*
glove	*guante (n., m.)*
glucose	*glucosa (n., f.)*
go	*ir (v.); irse (v.)*
go down	*bajar (v.)*
go to bed	*acostarse (v.)*
go up	*subir (v.)*
goal	*meta (n., f.)*
God	*Dios (n.)*
gonorrhea	*gonorrea (n., f.)*
good	*buen (adj.); bueno, -a (adj.)*
good-looking	*guapo, -a (adj.)*
gout	*gota (n., f.)*
govern	*gobernar (v.)*
government	*gobierno (n., m.)*
graduate	*graduarse (v.); egresado, -a (n.); graduado, -a (adj., n.)*
grandchild	*nieto, -a (n.)*
grandfather	*abuelo (n., m.)*
grandmother	*abuela (n., f.)*
grandparents	*abuelos (n.)*
grant	*beca (n., f.); otorgar (v.)*
gravity	*gravedad (n., f.)*
grease	*grasa (n., f.)*
greasy	*grasoso, -a (adj.)*
greater	*mayor (adj.)*
greed	*avaricia (n., f.)*
green	*verde (adj.)*
grief	*pena (n., f.)*
group	*grupo (n., m.)*
grow larger	*agrandar (v.)*
guard	*proteger (v.)*
Guatemalan	*guatemalteco, -a (adj., n.)*
guilty	*culpable (adj.)*
gums	*encías (n., f.)*
gymnasium	*gimnasio (n., m.)*
habit	*costumbre (n., f.); hábito (n., m.)*
Haemophilus Influenza B	*Hib (n., f.)*
half	*medio, -a (adj.); mitad (n., f.)*
ham	*jamón (n., m.)*
hand	*mano (n., f.)*
handbag	*bolso (n., m.)*
handkerchief	*pañuelo (n., m.)*
handle	*manejar (v.)*
handsome	*guapo, -a (adj.)*
hang up	*colgar (v.)*
happen	*pasar (v.); suceder (v.)*
happiness	*felicidad (n., f.)*
happy	*alegre (adj.); contento, -a (adj.); feliz (adj.)*
harass	*acosar (v.)*
harassment	*acoso (n., m.)*
hard	*duro, -a (adj.)*
hard-working	*trabajador, -a (adj.)*
harm	*dañar (v.); daño (n., .m.); perjudicar (v.)*
harmful	*dañino (adj.); perjudicial (adj.)*
hate	*odio (n., m.)*
have	*haber (aux. v.); tener (v.)*
get dizzy	*marearse (v.)*
have a good time	*divertirse (v.)*
have a snack	*merendar (v.)*
have an examination	*examinarse (v.)*
have breakfast	*desayunar (v.)*
have just (+ verb in the inf.)	*acabar de + (verbo en inf.) (v.)*
have seconds	*repetir (v.)*
have sex	*tener relaciones sexuales (v.)*
have the tendency to	*tender a (v.)*
have to	*tener que (v.)*
he	*él (pron.)*
head	*cabeza (n., f.)*
healer	*curandero, -a (n.)*
health	*salud (n., f.)*
healthy	*saludable (adj.)*
hear	*oír (v.)*
hearing	*oído (n., m.); audición (n., f.)*
heart	*corazón (n., m.); cardíaco, -a (adj.)*
heartbeat	*latido del corazón (n., m.)*
heat up	*calentar (v.)*
heat	*calor (n., m.)*
heater	*calentador (n., m.)*
heating	*calefacción (n., f.)*
heavy	*pesado, -a (adj.)*
heel	*talón (n., m.)*
hell	*infierno (n., m.)*
hello	*hola (interj.)*
help	*ayuda (n., f.); ayudar (v.)*
helper	*ayudante (n., m. or f.)*
helplessness	*desamparo (n., m.)*
hepatitis	*hepatitis (n., f.)*
herbalist	*yerbero, -a (n.)*
here	*acá (adv.); aquí (adv.)*
heredity	*herencia (n., f.)*
hide	*esconder (v.); esconderse (v.)*
high	*alto, -a (adj.)*
high school	*bachillerato (n., m.); preparatoria (n., f.)*
hip	*cadera (n., f.)*
hire	*contratar (v.)*
Hispanic	*hispano, -a (adj.)*
history	*historia (n., f.); historial (n., m.)*
hit	*golpear (v.); pegar (v.)*
HIV	*VIH (n., m.)*
HMO (Health Maintenance Organization)	*plan de salud (n, m.)*
hold on to	*agarrarse a (v.); aferrarse a (v.)*
hole	*agujero (n., m.)*
home	*hogar (n., m.)*
homeland	*patria (n., f.)*
home-made	*casero, -a (adj.)*
homeowner	*dueño, -a de la casa (n.); casero, -a - landlord (n.)*
Honduran	*hondureño, -a (adj., n.)*
honest	*honesto, -a (adj.)*
honey	*miel (n., f.)*
hope	*esperanza (n., f.); esperar (v.)*
hopefully	*ojalá (interj.)*
hormone	*hormona (n., f.)*
hospital	*hospital (n., m.)*
hot	*caliente (adj.)*
hour	*hora (n., f.)*
house	*casa (n., f.)*
how	*cómo (interr.)*
however	*sin embargo (conj.); no obstante (conj.)*
how many	*cuánto, -s (interr.)*
how much	*cuánto (interr.)*
human	*humano, -a (adj.)*
humiliated	*humillado, -a (adj.)*
humor	*humor (n., m.)*
hundred (one)	*cien (adj.); ciento (adj.)*
hunger	*hambre (n., f.)*
hurry	*prisa (n., f.)*
hurry up	*apresurar(se) (v.); darse prisa (v.)*
hurt	*lastimar(se) (v.); doler (v.)*
husband	*esposo (n., m.); marido (n., m.)*
hypertension	*hipertensión (n., f.)*
hypoglycemia	*hipoglucemia (n., f.)*

hysterical	*histérico, -a (adj.)*
ice	*hielo (n., m.)*
idea	*idea (n., f.)*
identify	*identificar (v.); identificarse (v.)*
identity	*identidad (n., f.)*
idiotic	*idiota (adj.)*
if	*si (conj.)*
ignorant	*ignorante (adj.)*
ignore	*ignorar (v.)*
illegal	*ilegal (adj.)*
illness	*enfermedad (n., f.)*
imagine	*imaginar(se) (v.)*
imitate	*imitar (v.)*
immature	*inmaduro, -a (adj.)*
immediate	*inmediato, -a (adj.)*
immediately	*inmediatamente (adv.)*
immigrant	*inmigrante (n., m. or f.)*
impact	*impacto (n., m.)*
implant	*implantar (v.); implante (n., m.)*
importance	*importancia (n., f.)*
important	*importante (adj.)*
impossible	*imposible (adj.)*
improve	*mejorar (v.)*
improvement	*mejora (n., f.); mejoría - health (n., f.); mejoramiento (n., m.)*
impulsively	*impulsivamente (adv.)*
in	*en (prep.)*
in charge, person	*encargado, -a (adj.)*
in love	*enamorado, -a (adj.)*
in spite of	*a pesar de (que, conj.)*
inactive	*inactivo, -a (adj.)*
incapacity	*incapacidad (n., f.)*
incident	*incidente (n., m.)*
include	*incluir (v.)*
income	*ingreso, -s (n., m.)*
incontinence	*incontinencia (n., f.)*
increase	*aumentar (v.); aumento (n., m.)*
incredible	*increíble (adj.)*
increment	*incremento (n., m.)*
independently	*independientemente (adv.)*
Indian	*indio, -a (adj., n.)*
indicate	*indicar (v.)*
indicated	*indicado, -a (adj.)*
indication	*indicación (n., f.); indicio (n., m.)*
indispensable	*indispensable (adj.)*
individual	*individuo, -a (n.); individual (adj.)*
industrious	*diligente (adj.); trabajador, -a (adj.)*
inequality	*desigualdad (n., f.)*
infantile	*infantil (adj.)*
infect	*contagiar (v.); infectar (v.)*
infected	*infectado, -a (adj.)*
infection	*infección (n., f.)*
inflammation	*inflamación (n., f.)*
inflate	*hinchar (v.)*
inform	*informar (v.)*
information	*información (n., f.)*
informative	*informativo, -a (adj.)*
inhale	*inhalar (v.)*
inherit	*heredar (v.)*
initiate	*iniciar (v.)*
inject	*inyectar (v.); inyectarse (v.)*
injection	*inyección (n., f.)*
injure	*herir (v.)*
injured	*herido, -a (adj.)*
injury	*herida (n., f.)*
injustice	*injusticia (n., f.)*
inner ear	*oído (n., m.)*
innocent	*inocente (adj.)*
insect bite	*picadura (n., f.)*
insecure	*inseguro, -a (adj.)*
insinuate	*insinuar (v.)*
insist	*insistir (v.)*
insomnia	*insomnio (n., m.)*
install	*instalar (v.)*
installment	*plazo (n., m.)*
instead of	*en vez de (adv.)*
institute	*instituto (n, m..)*
instruction	*instrucción (n., f.)*
insufferable	*insoportable (adj.)*
insulate	*aislar (v.)*
insulin	*insulina (n., f.)*
insurance	*seguro (n., m.)*
intelligent	*inteligente (adj.)*
intensive	*intensivo, -a (adj.)*
interest	*interés (n., m.); interesar (v.)*
interesting	*interesante (adj.)*
interpreter	*intérprete (n., m. or f.)*
interrogation	*interrogatorio (n., m.)*
interval	*intervalo (n., m.)*
intervention	*intervención (n., f.)*
interview	*entrevistar (v.); entrevista (n., f.)*
intimate	*íntimo, -a (adj.)*
intolerable	*insoportable (adj.); intolerable (adj.)*
introduce	*introducir - into something (v.)*
inventory	*inventario (n., m.)*
investigation	*investigación (n., f.)*
invisible	*invisible (adj.)*
invite	*invitar (v.)*
involve	*involucrar(se) (v.)*
involved	*involucrado, -a (adj.)*
irresponsible	*irresponsable (adj.)*
irritability	*irritabilidad (n., f.)*
irritation	*irritación (n., f.)*
isolate	*aislar (v.); aislarse (v.)*
itching	*comezón (n., f.); picazón (n., f.)*
jail	*cárcel (n., f.)*
jaw	*quijada (n., f.)*
jealousy	*celos (n., m.)*
jelly	*jalea (n., f.)*
job	*trabajo (n., m.); empleo (n., m.); tarea (n., f.)*
joint	*articulación (n., f.); coyuntura (n., f.)*
journalist	*periodista (n., m. or f.)*
judge	*juez, -a (n.)*
juice	*jugo (n., m.)*
keep	*mantener (v.); guardar - to keep away (v.)*
keep in mind	*tener en cuenta (v.)*
kidney	*riñón (n., m.)*
kill	*matar (v.)*
kind	*buen (adj.); bueno, -a (adj.); tipo (n., m.)*
king	*rey (n., m.)*
kiss	*besar (v.); beso (n., m.)*
knee	*rodilla (n., f.)*
know	*conocer - someone (v.); saber - something (v.)*
knowledge	*conocimiento (n., m.)*
known	*conocido, -a (adj.)*
label	*etiqueta (n., f.)*
laboratory	*laboratorio (n., m.)*
lack	*falta (n., f.); faltar (v.)*
lady	*dama (n., f.); señora (n., f.); señorita (n., f.)*
language	*idioma (n., m.)*
large	*grande (adj.)*
last	*durar (v.); último, -a (adj.)*
last night	*anoche (adv.)*
late	*tarde (adv.)*
lately	*últimamente (adv.)*
later	*después (adv.)*
latex	*látex (n., m.)*
Latin	*latino, -a (adj.)*
Latin American	*latinoamericano, -a (adj., -n.)*
laugh	*reír (v.); reírse (v.)*
law	*ley (n., f.)*
lawyer	*abogado, -a (n.)*
lazy	*perezoso, -a (adj.); flojo, -a (adj.)*
lead	*plomo (n., m.); guiar (v.)*
learn	*aprender (v.)*
leave	*dejar - something behind (v.); irse (v.); salir (v.)*
left	*izquierdo, -a (adj.)*
leg	*pierna (n., f.)*
legislator	*legislador, -a (n.)*
lend	*prestar (v.)*
less	*menos (adv.)*
letter	*carta (n., f.)*
leukemia	*leucemia (n., f.)*
level	*nivel (n., m.)*
liberated	*libre (adj.)*
lie	*mentira (n., f.); mentir (v.)*
life	*vida (n., f.)*
light	*luz (n., f.); leve (adj.); ligero - weight (adj.)*
like	*gustar (v.); como (adv.); similar, parecido, -a (adj.)*
limb	*miembro - extremity (n., m.)*
limit	*límite (n., m.); limitar (v.)*
limitation	*limitación (n., f.)*
line	*línea (n., f.); vía (n., f.)*
link	*relación (n., f.); enlace - Web (n., m.)*
liquid	*líquido (n., m.)*
list	*lista (n., f.)*
listen	*escuchar (v.)*
little	*pequeño, -a - size (adj.); poco (adv.); poco, -a - amount (adj.)*
live	*vivir (v.)*
liver	*hígado (n., m.)*
loan	*préstamo (n., m.); prestar (v.)*
local	*local (adj.)*
locate	*localizar (v.); ubicar (v.)*

lock	*cerradura (n., m.); candado (n., m.)*
loneliness	*soledad (n., f.)*
long	*largo, -a (adj.)*
look at	*mirar (v.)*
look for	*buscar (v.)*
loose	*flojo, -a (adj.)*
loosen	*aflojar(se) (v.)*
lose	*perder (v.)*
loss	*pérdida (n., f.)*
lounge	*salón (n., m.)*
love	*amor (n., m.); querer (v.); amar (v.); encantar (v.)*
loved	*querido, -a (adj.)*
low	*bajo, -a (adj.)*
lower	*bajar (v.); bajarse (v.)*
lowest	*mínimo, -a (adj.)*
luck	*suerte (n., f.)*
lunch	*almuerzo (n., m.)*
lung	*pulmón (n., m.)*
lymph gland	*ganglio linfático (n., m.)*
lymph	*linfático, -a (adj.)*
machine	*máquina (n., f.)*
madam	*señora (n., f.)*
mail	*correo (n., m.)*
main	*principal (adj.)*
maintain	*mantener (v.); mantenerse (v.)*
maintenance	*mantenimiento (n., m.)*
majority	*mayoría (n., f.)*
make	*hacer (v.)*
make bigger	*agrandar (v.)*
make pregnant	*embarazar (v.)*
make suitable	*adecuar (v.)*
make sure	*asegurarse de (v.)*
make worse	*empeorar (v.)*
male	*masculine (adj.); hombre (n., m.); varón - people (n., m.); macho - animal (n., m.)*
mammogram	*mamografía (n., f.)*
man	*hombre (n., m.); señor (n., m.)*
manage	*dirigir - lead (v.); administrar (v.); arreglar - solve (v.)*
management	*dirección (n., f.); administración (n., f.)*
manner	*manera (n., f.); modo (n., m.)*
many	*mucho, -a (adj.)*
map	*mapa (n., m.)*
mark	*marcar (v.); marca (n., f.)*
market	*mercado (n., m.)*
marriage	*matrimonio (n., m.)*
married	*casado, -a (adj.)*
marry	*casar(se) (v.)*
mask	*máscara (n., f.)*
mass	*masa (n., f.); misa - church service (n., f.)*
maternal	*materno, -a (adj.)*
matter	*asunto (n., m.); importar (v.)*
mature	*maduro, -a (adj.)*
maybe	*quizás (adv.); tal vez (adv.)*
meal	*comida (n., f.)*
mean	*significar (v.)*
meaning	*significado (n., m.)*
measles	*sarampión (n., m.)*
measure	*medir (v.)*
meat	*carne (n., f.)*
medical	*médico, -a (adj.)*
medication	*medicamento (n., m.)*
medicine	*medicina (n., f.)*
meet	*conocer (v.); reunirse (v.); encontrarse (v.)*
meeting	*reunión (n., f.); junta (n., f.)*
member	*miembro (n., m.)*
memory	*memoria (n., f.); recuerdo (n., m.)*
menstrual cycle	*menstruación (n., f.); período (n., m.); regla (n., f.)*
mental	*mental (adj.)*
mention	*mencionar (v.)*
mentioned	*dicho, -a (adj.)*
method	*método (n., m.)*
Mexican	*mexicano, -a (adj., n.)*
midwife	*partera (n., f.)*
migratory	*migratorio, -a (adj.)*
milk	*leche (n., f.)*
mind	*mente (n., f.)*
mine	*mío, -a (adj.)*
minimal	*mínimo, -a (adj.)*
minimum	*mínimo (n., m.)*
mint tea	*té de yerbabuena (n., m.)*
minute	*minuto (n., m.)*
mirror	*espejo (n., m.)*
miss	*extrañar (v.); señorita (n., f.)*
missing	*desaparecido, -a (adj.)*
mistake	*error (n., m.); equivocar(se) (v.)*
mistaken	*equivocado, -a (adj.)*
mistreat	*maltratar (v.)*
mistreatment	*maltrato (n., m.); maltratamiento (n., m.)*
mixed	*variado, -a (adj.)*
mixture	*mezcla (n., f.)*
model	*modelo (n., m.)*
mole	*lunar (n., m.)*
mom	*mamá (n., f.)*
moment	*momento (n., m.); rato (n., m.)*
money	*dinero (n., sing.); peso, -s (n. Spain)*
month	*mes (n., m.)*
monthly	*mensualmente (adv.)*
more	*más (adv.)*
morning	*mañana (n., f.)*
mother	*madre (n., f.)*
mouth	*boca (n., f.); bucal (adj.)*
mouthpiece	*protector bucal (n., m.)*
mouthwash	*enjuague bucal (n., m.)*
move	*mover (v.); moverse (v.); mudarse - from a place (v.)*
move away	*alejarse (v.)*
movement	*movimiento (n., m.)*
move out	*mudarse (v.)*
Mr.	*señor (n., m.)*
Mrs.	*señora (n., f.)*
mucus	*moco (n., m.)*
mumps	*paperas (n., f., pl.)*
muscle	*músculo (n., m.)*
must	*deber (v.)*
mute	*mudo, -a (adj.)*
name	*nombre (n., m.)*
named	*llamado, -a (adj.)*
nap	*siesta (n., f.)*
narcotic	*narcótico (n., m.)*
native	*nativo, -a (adj.); oriundo de - born (adj.); ser de (v.)*
naturally	*naturalmente (adv.)*
naturist	*naturista (adj.)*
nausea	*náusea (n., f.)*
near	*cerca (prep.)*
nearby	*cercano, -a (adj.)*
necessary	*necesario, -a (adj.); preciso, -a (adj.)*
necessity	*necesidad (n., f.)*
neck	*cuello (n., m.)*
neck brace	*collar (n., m.)*
need	*necesitar (v.); necesidad (n., f.)*
needle	*aguja (n., f.)*
negative	*negativo, -a (adj.)*
neighbor	*vecino, -a (n.)*
neighborhood	*barrio (n., m.); vecindario (n., m.)*
neither	*tampoco (adv.); ni (conj.)*
neonatologist	*neonatólogo, -a (n.)*
nephew	*sobrino (n., m.)*
nerve	*nervio (n., m.)*
nervous	*nervioso, -a (adj.)*
never	*nunca (adv.); jamás (adv.)*
nevertheless	*sin embargo (adv.)*
new	*nuevo, -a (adj.)*
news	*noticia, -s (n., f., sing.or pl.)*
newspaper	*periódico (n., m.)*
next	*próximo, -a (adj.); siguiente (adj.)*
nice	*simpático, -a (adj.)*
niece	*sobrina (n., f.)*
night	*noche (n., f.); nocturno, -a (adj.)*
nightmare	*pesadilla (n., f.)*
nine	*nueve (adj.)*
no	*no (adv.)*
nobody	*nadie (pron.); ninguno, -a (pron.)*
nocturnal	*nocturno, -a (adj.)*
noise	*ruido (n., m.)*
noon	*mediodía (n., m.)*
nor	*ni (conj.)*
normal	*normal (adj.)*
normally	*normalmente (adv.)*
North American	*norteamericano, -a (adj., n.)*
nose	*nariz (n., f.)*
not	*no (adv.)*
not any	*ningún (adj.); ninguno, -a (adj.)*
not even	*ni siquiera (adv.)*
nothing	*nada (pron.)*
notice	*notar (v.); aviso (n., m.)*
noun	*sustantivo (n., m.)*
now	*ahora (adv.)*
number	*número (n., m.)*
numbness	*entumecimiento (n., m.)*
nurse	*enfermero, -a (n.)*

nutrient	*nutriente (n., m.)*
nutrition	*nutrición (n., f.)*
nutritionist	*nutricionista (n., m. or f.)*
nutritious	*alimenticio, -a (adj.); nutritivo, -a (adj.)*
obesity	*obesidad (n., f.)*
obey	*obedecer (v.)*
object	*objeto (n., m.); objetar (v.)*
obligate	*obligar (v.)*
obstetrician	*obstetra (n., m. or f.)*
obtain	*obtener (v.); conseguir (v.);*
occasion	*ocasión (n., f.); vez (n., f.)*
occupational	*ocupacional (adj.)*
occupied	*ocupado, -a (adj.)*
occur	*ocurrir (v.)*
odd	*raro, -a (adj.)*
of	*de (prep.)*
offer	*ofrecer (v.)*
offered	*ofrecido, -a (adj.)*
office	*oficina (n., f.)*
often	*a menudo (adv.)*
old	*antiguo, -a (adj.); viejo, -a (adj.)*
old age	*vejez (n., f.)*
older	*mayor (adj.)*
on	*en (prep.); encima (prep.); sobre (prep.)*
once	*una vez (adv.)*
on top of	*encima de (prep.)*
one	*uno, -a (adj.)*
only	*solamente (adv.); único, -a (adj.)*
open	*abrir (v.); abierto, -a (adj.)*
operation	*operación (n., f.)*
ophthalmologist	*oculista (n., m. or f.); oftalmólogo, -a (n.)*
opportunity	*oportunidad (n., f.)*
oppress	*oprimir (v.)*
opt	*optar (v.)*
option	*opción (n., f.)*
optometrist	*optometrista (n., m. or f.)*
or	*o (conj.); u (used instead of "o" when the following word begins with "o" or "ho") (conj.)*
oral	*bucal (adj.); oral (adj.)*
orange	*naranja (n., f.)*
order	*orden - mandate (n., f.); - order of things (n., m.)*
organ	*órgano (n., m.)*
organization	*organización (n., f.)*
organize	*organizar (v.)*
osteoporosis	*osteoporosis (n., f.)*
other	*otro, -a (adj.)*
our	*nuestro, -a (adj.)*
outside	*afuera (adv.); fuera (adv.)*
over	*sobre (prep.)*
overcome	*superar (v.)*
overweight	*sobrepeso, -a (adj.)*
overwhelmed	*agobiado, -a (adj.)*
owe	*deber (v.)*
own	*propio, -a (adj.); tener (v.)*
owner	*propietario, -a (n.); dueño, -a (n.)*
pacifier	*chupete (n., m.)*
package	*paquete (n., m.)*
pain	*dolor (n., m.)*
painful	*doloroso, -a (adj.)*
paint	*pintar (v.); pintura (n., f.)*
painted	*pintado, -a (adj.)*
pair	*pareja (n.); par - set (n., m.)*
pajamas	*pijama (n., f.)*
palate	*paladar (n., m.)*
pale	*pálido, -a (adj.)*
palpitation	*palpitación (n., f.)*
pamphlet	*folleto (n., m.)*
Panamanian	*panameño, -a (adj., n.)*
pancreas	*páncreas (n., m.)*
pap smear	*prueba de Papanicolaou (n., f.)*
paper	*papel - material (n., m.); trabajo - written work (n., m.)*
paperwork	*papeleo (n., m.)*
Paraguayan	*paraguayo, -a (adj., n.)*
pardon	*perdonar (v.); perdón (n., m.)*
parents	*padres (n., m.)*
park	*parque (n., m.); estacionar(se) (v.)*
parking lot	*estacionamiento (n., m.); playa de estacionamiento (n., f.); parqueo (n., f. Spain)*
part	*parte (n., f.)*
partial	*parcial (adj.)*
participant	*participante (n., m. or f.)*
participate	*participar (v.)*
particular	*particular (adj.)*
part-time	*medio tiempo (adj.); tiempo parcial (adj.)*
party	*fiesta (n., f.)*
pass	*pasar (v.)*
pass away	*fallecer (v.)*
past	*pasado (n., m.); pasado, -a (adj.)*
paste	*pasta (n., f.)*
path	*camino (n., m.); sendero (n., m.)*
pathway	*camino (n., m.); vía (n., f.)*
patience	*paciencia (n., f.)*
patient	*paciente (n., m. or f.); paciente (adj.)*
pay	*pagar (v.); pago (n., m.)*
peaceful	*sereno, -a (adj.)*
pediatrician	*pediatra (n., m. or f.)*
pee pee	*pipí (n., m.)*
penis	*pene (n., m.)*
people	*gente (n., f.)*
perfect	*perfecto, -a (adj.)*
perhaps, maybe	*acaso (adv.); a lo mejor (adv.); quizá o quizás (adv.); tal vez (adv.)*
period	*punto (n., m.); período (n., m.); ciclo (n., m.); menstruación (n., f.); regla - menstruation (n., f.)*
periodontitis	*periodontitis (n., f.)*
permanent	*permanente (adj.)*
permit	*dejar (v.); permitir (v.)*
persistent	*persistente (adj.)*
person	*persona (n., f.)*
person from a rural area	*pueblerino, -a (adj.); provinciano, -a (adj.)*
personal	*personal (adj.)*
personality	*personalidad (n., f.)*
personnel	*personal - staff (n., m.)*
perspiration	*sudor (n., m.)*
persuade	*persuadir (v.)*
pertussis	*tos ferina (n., f.)*
Peruvian	*peruano, -a (adj., n.)*
pesticides	*pesticidas (n., m.)*
petrolatum	*petrolato (n., m.)*
pharmacist	*farmacéutico, -a (n.)*
pharmacy	*farmacia (n., f.)*
phone call	*llamada telefónica (n., f.)*
photo	*foto (n., f.)*
photograph	*fotografía (n., f.)*
phrase	*frase (n., f.)*
physical	*examen físico / médico (n., m.)*
physically	*físicamente (adv.)*
piece	*pedazo (n., m.)*
pill	*pastilla (n., f.); píldora (n., f.)*
pillow	*almohada (n., f.)*
pint	*pinta - measure (n., f.)*
place	*colocar (v.); lugar (n., m.); puesto (n., m.); poner (v.)*
plan	*plan (n., m.)*
plant	*planta (n., f.)*
plaque	*placa - plate, sheet, sign (n., f.); sarro - teeth (n., m.)*
plasma	*plasma (n., m.)*
play	*jugar (v.)*
please	*complacer (v.)*
pleased	*encantado, -a (adj.)*
pleasure	*gusto (n.); placer (n., m.)*
plug	*enchufe (n., m.)*
pneumonia	*neumonía (n., f.)*
poison	*envenenar (v.); veneno (n., m.)*
poisoning	*envenenamiento (n., m.)*
police	*policía (n., m. or f.)*
policy	*póliza (n., f.)*
polio	*polio (n., f.)*
poo poo	*pupú (n., m.)*
poor	*pobre (adj.)*
population	*población (n., f.)*
portion	*porción (n., f.)*
position	*posición (n., f.); puesto - job (n., m.)*
positive	*positivo, -a (adj.)*
possibility	*posibilidad (n., f.)*
possible	*posible (adj.)*
poster	*cartel (n., m.)*
postpartum	*posparto (n., m.)*
poultice	*cataplasma (n., f.)*
pound	*libra (n., f.)*
poverty	*pobreza (n., f.)*
power	*poder (n., m.)*
powerful	*poderoso, -a (adj.)*
practice	*practicar (v.)*
pray	*rezar (v.)*
precious	*precioso, -a (adj.)*
precise	*preciso, -a (adj.)*
precision	*precisión (n., f.)*
predisposition	*predisposición (n., f.)*
prefer	*preferir (v.)*
preferable	*preferible (adj.)*
preferred	*preferido, -a (adj.)*

pregnancy — *embarazo (n., m.)*
pregnant — *embarazada (adj.)*
prejudice — *prejuicio (n., m.)*
preliminary — *preliminar (adj.)*
premature — *prematuro, -a (adj.)*
prenatal — *prenatal (adj.)*
preparation — *preparación (n., f.)*
prepare — *preparar (v.)*
prescribe — *prescribir (v.); recetar (v.)*
prescribed — *prescrito, -a (adj.); recetado, -a (adj.)*
prescription — *receta (n., f.)*
presence — *presencia (n., f.)*
present — *presentar (v.)*
pressure — *presión (n., f.); presionar (v.)*
presume — *presumir (v.)*
pretty — *bonito, -a (adj.)*
prevent — *prevenir (v.)*
preventive — *preventivo, -a (adj.)*
previous — *previo, -a (adj.)*
prick — *picar (v.); pinchazo (n., m.); picazón (n., f.)*
pride — *orgullo (n., m.)*
priest — *cura (n., m.)*
primary — *primario, -a (adj.)*
PCP (Primary Care Physician) — *médico, -a de cabecera (n.), médico, -a familiar (n.)*
principle — *principal (adj.); principio (n., m.)*
prior — *previo, -a (adj.)*
priority — *prioridad (n., f.)*
prison — *prisión (n., f.); cárcel (n., f.)*
privacy — *privacidad (n., f.)*
private — *privado, -a (adj.)*
probable — *probable (adj.)*
probably — *probablemente (adv.)*
problem — *problema (n., m.)*
procedure — *procedimiento (n., m.)*
process — *proceso (n., m.)*
produce — *producir (v.); vegetales (n., m.)*
produced — *producido, -a (adj.)*
product — *producto (n., m.)*
production — *producción (n., f.)*
professional — *profesional (adj.); profesional (n., m. or f.)*
program — *programa (n., m.)*
progress — *progresar (v.)*
prohibit — *prohibir (v.)*
project — *proyectar (v); proyecto (n., m.)*
promise — *promesa (n., f.); prometer (v.)*
promote — *promover (v.)*
proof — *prueba (n., f.)*
proper — *adecuado, -a (adj.); apropiado, -a (adj.)*
properly — *adecuadamente (adv.); apropiadamente (adv.)*
property — *propiedad (n., f.)*
propose — *proponer (v.)*
prostate — *próstata (n., f.)*
protect — *proteger (v.)*
protected — *protegido, -a (adj.)*
protection — *protección (n., f.)*
protector — *protector, -a (adj., n.)*
protein — *proteína (n., f.)*
protest — *protestar (v.)*
proud — *orgulloso, -a (adj.)*
provide — *proveer (v.); dar (v.); ofrecer (v.), brindar (v.)*
provided that — *con tal de que (conj.)*
provoke — *provocar (v.)*
psychiatrist — *psiquiatra (n., m. or f.)*
psychologist — *psicológo, -a (n.)*
psychotherapy — *psicoterapia (n., f.)*
public — *público, -a (adj.)*
Puerto Rican — *puertorriqueño, -a (adj., n.)*
pull — *jalar (v.)*
punctual — *puntual (adj.)*
punish — *castigar (v.)*
pure — *puro, -a (adj.)*
purpose — *propósito (n., m.)*
pus — *postema (n., f.); pus (n., m.)*
push — *empujar - something (v.); pujar - during delivery (v.)*
put — *poner (v.); puesto, -a (adj.)*
put on — *ponerse (v.)*
put to trial — *probar (v.)*
qualify — *calificar (v.); llenar los requisitos (v.)*
quality — *calidad (n., f.)*
quantity — *cantidad (n., f.)*
queen — *reina (n., f.)*
question — *asunto (n., m.); pregunta (n., f.); preguntar (v.)*
quickly — *rápidamente (adv.)*
quiet — *quieto (adj.); callar(se) (v.)*
quit — *dejar de (v.); renunciar (v.)*
race — *raza (n., f.)*
radiate — *radiar (v.); extender(se) (v.); difundir (v.)*
radiation — *radiación (n., f.)*
rage — *ira (n., f.); rabia (n., f.)*
rail — *barra (n., f.)*
rain — *llover (v.); lluvia (n., f.)*
rape — *violar (v.); violación (n., f.)*
rare — *raro, -a (adj.)*
rash — *erupción (n., f.)*
reach — *alcanzar (v.)*
react — *reaccionar (v.)*
reaction — *reacción (n., f.)*
read — *leer (v.)*
ready — *listo, -a (adj.)*
real — *verdadero, -a (adj.)*
reality — *realidad (n., f.)*
realize — *darse cuenta de (v.)*
reason — *razón (n., f.)*
receive — *recibir (v.)*
recent — *reciente (adj.)*
recently — *recién (adv.); recientemente (adv.)*
reception — *recepción (n., f.)*
receptionist — *recepcionista (n., m. or f.)*
recipient — *recipiente (n., m. or f.); envase - container (n., m.)*
reckless — *imprudente (adj.); alocado, -a (adj.)*
recognize — *reconocer (v.)*
recommend — *recomendar (v.)*
recommendation — *recomendación (n., f.)*
recommended — *recomendado, -a (adj.)*
record — *historia - medical history (n., f.); historial - personal history (n., m.); expediente (n., m.); datos - data, information (used always in pl.) (n., m.); récord - sports (n., m.); anotar (v.); apuntar (v.)*
recount — *relatar - to tell (v.); contar - to tell (v.); recontar - to count something again (v.)*
recover — *recuperar (v.); recuperarse (v.)*
recovery — *recuperación (n., f.)*
red — *rojo, -a (adj.)*
redness — *enrojecimiento (n., m.)*
reduce — *reducir (v.); disminuir (v.)*
reduced — *reducido, -a (adj.)*
refill — *rellenar (v.); surtir - a prescription (v.)*
refrigerator — *refrigerador (n., m.)*
regret — *arrepentirse (v.); lamentar (v.)*
regularly — *regularmente (adv.)*
reject — *rechazar (v.)*
related — *relacionado, -a (adj.)*
relation — *relación (n., f.)*
relative — *pariente, -a (n.); relativo, -a (adj.)*
relax — *relajarse (v.)*
relaxation — *relajamiento (n., m.)*
religious — *religioso, -a (adj.)*
relocate — *mudarse (v.); reubicarse (v.)*
remain — *permanecer (v.); quedarse (v.)*
remedy — *remedio (n., m.)*
remember — *recordar (v.); acordarse de (v.)*
remind — *recordar (v.)*
remove — *quitar (v.); quitarse (v.)*
renal — *renal (adj.)*
rent — *alquilar (v.); alquiler (n., m.); renta - yield (n., f.)*
repeat — *repetir (v.)*
repetitive — *repetitivo, -a (adj.)*
report — *reportar (v.)*
reported — *reportado, -a (adj.)*
representative — *representante (n., m. or f.)*
reprimand — *reprimenda (n., f.)*
request — *solicitud (n., f.); solicitar (v.)*
require — *requerir (v.)*
required — *requerido, -a (adj.)*
requirement — *requisito (n., m.)*
resemble — *parecerse (v.)*
resolve — *resolver (v.); solucionar (v.)*
resource — *recurso (n., m.)*
respect — *respetar (v.); respeto (n., m.)*
respiratory — *respiratorio, -a (adj.)*
respond — *responder (v.)*
responsibility — *responsabilidad (n., f.)*
responsible — *responsable (adj.)*
rest — *resto (n., m.); demás (adj.); descansar (v.);*

	descanso (n., m.)
restaurant	restaurante (n., m.)
restless	inquieto, -a (adj.)
result	resultado (n., m.); resultar (v.)
retain	detener (v.); retener (v.)
retained	retenido, -a (adj.)
retaliation	represalias (n., f.)
retell	contar de nuevo (v.)
retina	retina (n., f.)
return	devolver - something (v.); regresar (v.); volver (v.)
review	revisar (v.)
revise	revisar (v.)
rheumatoid arthritis	artritis reumatoide (n., f.)
rich	rico, -a (adj.)
ride a bike	andar en bicicleta (v.)
right	derecha - right side (adj.); derecho - direct, straight ahead (adv.); human right (n., m.)
rigidity	rigidez (n., f.)
ripe	maduro, -a (adj.)
risk	arriesgar (v.); riesgo (n., m.)
road	camino (n., m.)
roast	asar (v.)
rob	robar (v.)
room	cuarto (n., m.); habitación (n., f.); sala (n., f.)
routine	rutina (n., f.)
rubella	rubéola (n., f.)
ruin	arruinar (v.); echar a perder (v.)
run	correr (v.)
running	manejo (n., m.)
sad	triste (adj.)
sadness	tristeza (n., f.)
safe	seguro, -a (adj.)
saint	santo, -a (n.)
salary	sueldo (n., m.)
sale	venta (n., f.)
salsa	salsa (n., f.)
salt	sal (n., f.)
salty	salado, -a (adj.)
Salvadoran	salvadoreño, -a (adj., n.)
same	mismo, -a (adj.)
sample	muestra (n., f.)
sandwich	sándwich (n., m.); emparedado (n., m.)
sanguine	sanguíneo, -a (adj.)
sanitary	sanitario, -a (adj.)
satisfy	satisfacer (v.)
save	ahorrar - money (v.); salvar - people (v).
say	decir (v.)
scarce	escaso, -a; insuficiente - not abundant (adj.); raro, -a - uncommon (adj.)
scare	dar miedo (v.); susto (n., m.)
scary	espantoso, -a (adj.)
scene	escena (n., f.)
schedule	horario (n., m.)
scholastic	escolar (adj.)
school	colegio (n., m.); escuela (n., f.)
scientist	científico, -a (n.)
scold	regañar (v.)
scrape	raspar (v.); rasparse (v.)
scrub	fregar (v.)
sealants	selladores dentales (n., m.)
season	estación (n., f.)
seat	asiento (n., m.)
seated	sentado, -a (adj.)
second	segundo, -a (adj.)
secondary	secundario, -a (adj.)
section	sección (n., f.)
secure	asegurar (v.); seguro, -a (adj.)
sedative	sedante (n., m.)
see	ver (v.)
seem	parecer (v.)
seen	visto, -a (adj.)
select	seleccionar (v.)
self-esteem	autoestima (n., f.)
sell	vender (v.)
semen	semen (n., m.)
send	enviar (v.); mandar (v.)
sensation	sensación (n., f.)
sensitive	sensible (adj.)
sensitivity	sensibilidad (n., f.)
sentence	oración (n., f.)
separate	separado, -a (adj.)
separate	separar(se) (v.)
series	serie, -s (n., f.)
serious	grave (adj.); serio, -a (adj.)
seriousness	gravedad (n., f.); seriedad (n., f.)
serve	servir (v.)
service	servicio (n., m.)
seventeen	diecisiete (adj.)
severe	severo, -a (adj.); grave (adj.)
severely	severamente (adv.)
sex	sexo (n., m.)
sexual	sexual (adj.)
shade	sombra (n., f.)
shake	temblor (n., m.)
shame	lástima (n., f.); vergüenza (n., f.)
shape	forma (n., f.)
share	compartir (v.)
sharp	agudo, -a - pain (adj.); filoso, -a - able to cut (adj.)
shirt	camisa (n., f.)
shop	ir de compras (v.); tienda (n., f.)
short	corto, -a (adj.); bajo, -a (adj.)
shot	disparo; tiro - gun (n., m.); inyección (n., f.)
shoulder blade	omóplato (n., m.)
shout	gritar (v.); grito (n., m.)
show	enseñar (v.); exhibición (n., f.); exhibir (v.); mostrar (v.); muestra (n., f.)
shower	ducha (n., f.); ducharse (v.)
shy	tímido, -a (adj.)
sibling	hermano, -a (n.)
sick	enfermo, -a (adj.)
side	lado (n., m.)
sight	vista (n., f.); visión (n., f.)
sign	señal (n., m.); signo (n., m.)
signal	señalar (v.); señal (n., m.)
signify	significar (v.)
silence	silencio (n., m.)
similar	semejante (adj.)
simple	simple (adj.)
since	desde (prep.); ahora que (conj.); como (adv.); pues (conj.); puesto que (conj.)
sing	cantar (v.)
single	solo, -a (adj.); soltero, -a (adj.)
sir	señor (n., m.)
sister	hermana (n., f.)
sister-in-law	cuñada (n., f.)
sit	sentar(se) (v.)
situation	situación (n., f.)
six	seis (adj.)
skin	piel (n., f.)
skinny	flaco, -a (adj.)
sky	cielo (n., m.)
slap	bofetada (n., f.)
slave	esclavo, -a (n.)
sleep	dormir (v.)
sleepy	somnoliento, -a (adj.)
slim down	adelgazar (v.)
slow	lento, -a (adj.)
slowly	lentamente (adv.)
small	chico, -a (adj.); pequeño, -a (adj.)
smaller	menor (adj.)
smart	listo, -a (adj.)
smell	oler (v.); olor (n., m.)
smile	sonreír (v.)
smoke	fumar (v.); humo (n., m.)
snack	merendar (v.); merienda (n., f.); picotear (v.)
sneeze	estornudar (v.)
so	así (adv.); tan (adv.)
so many	tanto, -a - measurable quantity (adj.)
so much	tanto, -a - not measurable amount (adj.)
so that	a fin de que (conj.); de manera que (conj.); de modo que (conj.); para que (conj.)
soak	remojar (v.)
soaked	remojado, -a (adj.)
Social Security	Seguro Social (n.)
social	social (adj.)
sodium	sodio (n., m.)
soft	suave (adj.)
soften	suavizarse (v.)
sold	vendido, -a (adj.)
solitude	soledad (n., f.)
some	algún (adj.); alguno, -a (adj.); unos, -as (art.);
somebody	alguien, (pron.); alguno (pron.)
someone	alguien (pron.); alguno (pron.)
something	algo (pron.)
sometimes	a veces (adv.); de vez en cuando (adv.)
son	hijo (n., m.)
soon	pronto (adv.)
sore	llaga (n., f.)
sorrow	pena (n., f.); tristeza (n., f.)

sort out *clasificar (v.); arreglar (v.)*
sound *sonido (n., m.)*
source *fuente (n., f.)*
South American *suramericano, -a (adj., n.)*
souvenir *recuerdo (n., m.)*
space *espacio (n., m.)*
Spanish *español, -a (adj., n.)*
Spaniard *español, -a (n.)*
spasm *espasmo (n., m.)*
speak *hablar (v.)*
special *especial (adj.)*
specialist *especialista (n., m. or f.)*
specialized *especializado, -a (adj.)*
specific *específico, -a (adj.)*
speech pathologist *foniatra (n., m. or f.)*
speech *habla (n., m.)*
spend time *pasar tiempo (v.)*
spill *derrame (n., m.); derramar (v.)*
spirit *espíritu (n., m.); ánimo - mood (n., m.)*
spiritualist *espiritista (n., m. or f.)*
spit *escupir (v.); esputo (n., m.)*
splint *tablilla (n., f.)*
split *dividir (v.)*
sponsor *patrocinar (v.); patrocinador, -a (n.)*
sport *deporte (n., m.)*
spot *mancha (n., f.)*
spouse *esposo, -a (n.)*
sprain *torcer (v.)*
sprained *torcido, -a (adj.)*
spread *extender(se); tender(se) - unfold (v.); untar - smear (v.); esparcir - scatter (v.)*
spread out *tendido, -a (adj.)*
squeeze *apretar (v.)*
stable *estable (adj.)*
stage *etapa (n., f.)*
staircase *escalera (n., f.)*
stamp *estampilla (n., f.)*
stand *ponerse de pie (v.)*
start *comenzar (v.); empezar (v.)*
state *estado (n., m.)*
state of mind *estado de ánimo (n., m.)*
statement *declaración (n., f.)*
station *estación (n., f.)*
stay *quedarse (v.)*
steal *robar (v.)*
step *paso - foot movement (n., m.); escalón - stair, rung (n., m.)*
sterility *esterilidad (n., f.)*
stick out *sobresalir (v.)*
stick to *pegar(se) (v.); adherir(se) (v.)*
sticky *pegajoso, -a (adj.)*
still *todavía (adv.); aún (adv.)*
stimulate *estimular (v.)*
stomach *estómago (n., m.)*
stool *excremento (n., m.)*
stop *dejar de (v.); parar de - doing something (v.); detener - movement (v.)*
store *tienda (n., f.)*
strain *colar (v.)*
strange *extraño, -a (adj.)*
strategy *estrategia (n., f.)*
street *calle (n., f.)*
strengthen *fortalecer (v.)*
stress *tensión (n., f.); esfuerzo (n., m.); estrés (n., m.)*
stretch *estirar(se) (v.)*
stretcher *camilla (n., f.)*
stretching *estiramiento (n., m.)*
strict *estricto, -a (adj.)*
strong *fuerte (adj.)*
strongly *fuertemente (adv.)*
student *estudiante (n., m. or f.)*
study *estudiar (v.)*
stuffed pastry *empanada (n., f.)*
stupendous *estupendo, -a (adj.)*
stupendously *estupendamente (adv.)*
stupid *idiota (adj.); estúpido, -a (adj.)*
subject to *someterse (v.)*
substitute *sustituir (v.)*
success *éxito (n., m.)*
such *tal (adj.); tan (adv.)*
suck *chupar (v.)*
suddenly *de repente (adv.)*
suffer *sufrir (v.)*
suffer *padecer (v.); sufrir (v.)*
suffering *sufrimiento (n., m.)*
sufficient *suficiente (adj.)*
sugar *azúcar (n., m.)*
suggest *sugerir (v.)*
suggested *sugerido, -a (adj.)*
suicide *suicidio (n., m.)*
summer *verano (n., m.)*
sun *sol (n., m.)*
supervision *supervisión (n., f.)*
supervisor *supervisor, -a (n.)*
supplement *suplemento (n., m.)*
supply *proveer (v.); surtir (v.)*
support *apoyar (v.); apoyo (n., m.); mantener - financial support (v.); sostener (v.); soportar (v.)*
suppose *suponer (v.)*
sure *seguro, -a (adj.); cierto, -a (adj.)*
surface *superficie (n., f.)*
surgeon *cirujano, -a (n.)*
surprise *sorprender (v.)*
surrender to *rendirse (v.); someterse (v.)*
survive *sobrevivir (v.)*
suspect *sospechar (v.)*
suspicion *sospecha (n., f.)*
suspicious *sospechoso, -a (adj.)*
sustain *sostener (v.)*
swallow *tragar (v.)*
sweet *dulce (n., m.); dulce (adj.)*
sweetened *azucarado, -a (adj.)*
swell up *hinchar (v.)*
swelling *hinchazón (n., f.)*
symptom *síntoma (n., m.)*
syringe *jeringa (n., f.)*
system *sistema (n., m.)*
table *mesa (n., f.)*
tablet *tableta (n., f.)*
take *tomar (v.); tomarse (v.)*
take a break *descansar (v.)*
take a walk *dar un paseo (v.)*
take advantage *aprovecharse de (v.)*
take away *quitar (v.)*
take care of *atender (v.); cuidar (v.)*
take off *quitar (v.); quitarse (v.)*
take out *sacar (v.)*
take time *tardar (v.)*
tall *alto, -a (adj.)*
tartar *placa dental (n., f.); sarro (n., f.)*
task *tarea (n., f.)*
taste *probar (v.)*
tea *té (n., m.)*
teach *enseñar (v.)*
teacher *maestro, -a (n.)*
team *equipo (n., m.)*
teaspoon *cucharilla - spoon (n., f.); cucharadita - the amount (n., f.)*
technician *técnico, -a (n.)*
telephone *teléfono (n., m.); telefónico, -a (adj.)*
tell *decir (v.); contar (v.)*
temperature *temperatura (n., f.)*
ten *diez (adj.)*
tennis *tenis (n., m.)*
tense *tenso, -a (adj.)*
tension *tensión (n., f.)*
term *plazo (n., m.)*
terminal *terminal (adj.)*
terrible *terrible (adj.)*
terrified *aterrorizado, -a (adj.)*
territory *territorio (n., m.)*
test *ensayar (v.); probar (v.); prueba (n., f.)*
tetanus *tétanos (n., m.)*
text *texto (n., m.)*
textile *tejido (n., m.)*
thank for *agradecer (v.); dar gracias (v.)*
thanks *gracias (n., f.)*
the day before yesterday *anteayer (adv.)*
theme *tema (n., m.)*
then *entonces (adv.)*
therapist *terapeuta (n., m. or f.)*
therapy *terapia (n., f.)*
there *allá (adv.); allí (adv.)*
these *estos, -as (pron.)*
thick *espeso, -a (adj.)*
thigh *muslo (n., m.)*
thin *flaco, -a (adj.)*
thing *cosa (n., f.)*
think *pensar (v.); creer (v.)*
third *tercer (adj.); tercero, -a (adj.)*
thirst *sed (n., f.)*
thirty *treinta (adj.)*
this *este, -a (adj.); esto (pron.)*
thorax *tórax (n., m.)*
those *esos, esas, aquellos, aquellas (pron.)*
thread *hilo (n., m.)*
threaten *amenazar (v.)*
three *tres (adj.)*
throat *garganta (n., f.)*

through	*por (prep.); a través de (prep.)*
throw	*echar (v.)*
throw away	*botar (v.); tirar (v.)*
thrown	*tirado, -a (adj.)*
thumb	*pulgar (n., m.)*
thus	*así (adv.); de manera que (adv.)*
time	*hora (n., f.); tiempo (n., m.); vez (n., f.)*
timid	*tímido, -a (adj.)*
tire	*cansar(se) (v.); fatigar(se) (v.)*
tired	*cansado, -a (adj.)*
tiredness	*cansancio (n., m.)*
tiresome	*pesado, -a (adj.)*
tissue	*tejido - skin (n., m.) pañuelo desechable - paper tissue (n., m.)*
to	*a (prep.); para (prep.)*
toasted	*tostado, -a (adj.)*
today	*hoy (adv.)*
together	*junto, -a (adj.)*
tolerate	*aguantar (v.); tolerar (v.)*
tomorrow	*mañana (adv.)*
tongue	*lengua (n., f.)*
too	*también (adv.)*
too much	*demasiado (adv.); demasiado, -a (adj.)*
tooth	*diente (n., m.)*
toothpaste	*pasta dental (n., f.)*
top	*principal (adj.)*
touch	*tocar (v.)*
tough	*duro, -a (adj.)*
toward	*hacia (prep.)*
towel	*toalla (n., f.)*
town	*pueblo (n., m.)*
tract	*conducto (n., m.); tracto (n., m.); vía (n., f.)*
trailer	*casa rodante (n., f.); tráiler (n., m.)*
training	*entrenamiento (n., m.)*
tranquil	*tranquilo, -a (adj.)*
translation	*traducción (n., f.)*
transmission	*transmisión (n., f.)*
transmit	*transmitir (v.); contagiar (v.)*
transmitted	*transmitido, -a (adj.)*
transplant	*transplante (n., m.)*
traumatic	*traumático, -a (adj.)*
travel	*viajar (v.)*
treat	*tratar (v.)*
treatment	*tratamiento (n.)*
tremor	*temblor (n., m.)*
trip	*viaje (n., m.)*
true	*verdadero, -a (adj.)*
trust	*confianza (n.); confiar (v.)*
truth	*verdad (n., f.)*
try	*intentar (v.); tratar (v.)*
tuberculin	*tuberculino, -a (adj.)*
tuberculosis	*tuberculosis (n., f.)*
tug	*tirón (n., m.)*
turn	*turno (n., m.); vuelta (n., f.)*
turn around	*dar vuelta (v.); darse vuelta (v.)*
turnover	*empanada - stuffed pastry (n., f.)*
turn over	*dar vuelta (v.); darse vuelta (v.)*
twenty	*veinte (adj.)*
twin	*gemelo, -a (n.)*
twist	*torcer (v.)*
two	*dos (adj.)*
type	*tipo (n., m.)*
umbilical chord	*cordón umbilical (n., m.)*
uncle	*tío (n., m.)*
uncomfortable	*incómodo, -a (adj.)*
uncovered	*descubierto, -a (adj.)*
understand	*entender (v.); comprender (v.)*
unfamiliar	*desconocido, -a (adj.)*
unfortunately	*desafortunadamente (adv.)*
unhealthy	*insalubre (adj.); enfermizo - sickly (adj.)*
unique	*único, -a (adj.)*
United States	*Estados Unidos (n., m., pl.)*
united	*unido, -a (adj.)*
unknown	*desconocido, -a (adj.)*
unless	*a menos que (conj.); a no ser que (conj.); salvo que (conj.)*
unmarried	*soltero, -a (adj.)*
until	*hasta (prep.)*
up	*arriba (adv.)*
urgent	*urgente (adj.)*
urinary	*urinario, -a (adj.)*
urinary tract	*vía urinaria (n., f.)*
urinate	*orinar (v.)*
urine	*orina (n., f.)*
Uruguayan	*uruguayo, -a (adj., n.)*
use	*usar (v.); uso (n., m.); utilizar (v.)*
useful	*útil (adj.)*
used to	*acostumbrar (v.); soler (v.)*
uterus	*útero (n., m.); matriz (n., f.)*
vacation	*vacaciones (n., f.)*
vaccinate	*vacunar(se) (v.)*
vaccine	*vacuna (n., f.)*
vagina	*vagina (n., f.)*
value	*valor (n., m.); valorar (v.)*
varied	*variado, -a (adj.)*
variety	*variedad (n., f.)*
various	*varios, -as (adj.)*
vary	*variar (v.)*
vegetable	*legumbre (n., f.); vegetal (adj.); vegetal (n., m.)*
vehicle	*vehículo (n., m.)*
Venezuelan	*venezolano, -a (adj., n.)*
ventilate	*ventilar (v.)*
verify	*verificar (v.); comprobar (v.)*
very	*muy (adv.)*
vessel	*vaso (n., m.)*
victim	*víctima (n., f.)*
violate	*violar (v.)*
violence	*violencia (n., f.)*
violent	*violento, -a (adj.)*
virus	*virus (n., m.)*
vision	*visión (n.); vista (n., f.)*
visit	*visita (n., f.); visitar (v.)*
vital	*vital (adj.)*
vital signs	*signos vitales (n., m.)*
vitamin	*vitamina (n., f.)*
vocabulary	*vocabulario (n., m.)*
voice	*voz (n., f.)*
volunteer	*ofrecer(se) (v.); voluntario, -a (n.)*
vomit	*vomitar (v.); vómito (n., m.)*
wait	*esperar (v.); espera (n., f.)*
wake up	*despertar (v.); despertarse (v.)*
walk	*paseo (n., m.); caminar (v.); andar (v.)*
wall	*pared (n., f.)*
wallet	*billetera (n., f.)*
wandering	*deambular (v.)*
want	*querer (v.)*
war	*guerra (n., f.)*
warm	*tibio, -a (adj.)*
warmth	*calor (n., m.)*
warm-up	*calentamiento (n., m.); calentar (v.)*
warn	*advertir (v.); avisar (v.)*
wash	*lavar (v.); lavarse (v.); fregar - scrub (v.)*
watch	*observar (v.); vigilar (v.)*
water	*agua (n., f.)*
way	*camino (n., m.); dirección - direction (n., f.); forma (n., f.); manera (n., f.); modo (n., m.); vía (n., f.)*
we	*nosotros (pron.)*
weak	*débil (adj.); decaído, -a (adj.)*
weaken	*debilitar(se) (v.)*
weapon	*arma (n., f.)*
wear	*llevar (v.); ponerse (v.); vestir (v.)*
wear away	*gastar (v.)*
wear out	*fatigar(se) (v.)*
weariness	*cansancio (n., m.)*
weather	*clima (n., m.); tiempo (n., m.)*
week	*semana (n., f.)*
weekly	*semanalmente (adv.)*
weigh	*pesar (v.)*
weight	*peso (n., m.)*
welcome	*dar la bienvenida (v.)*
well	*bien (adv.)*
well-being	*bienestar (n., m.)*
wet	*mojado, -a (adj.); mojar (v.)*
what	*qué (interr.)*
wheelchair	*silla de ruedas (n., f.)*
when	*cuando (adv.); cuándo (interr.)*
where	*donde (adv.); dónde (interr.)*
which	*cuál (interr.); cual (pron.); que (pron.)*
while	*mientras (adv.); rato (n., m.)*
who	*quién (interr.); quien (pron.)*
whole	*entero, -a (adj.)*
whose	*cuyo, -a (pron.)*
why	*por qué (interr.)*
WIC program	*programa de nutrición WIC para mujeres, infantes y niños (n., m.)*
widow	*viuda (n., f.)*
widower	*viudo (n., m.)*

wife	*esposa (n., m.)*
wild	*alocado, -a - reckless (adj.)*
win	*ganar (v.)*
wind	*viento (n., m.)*
window	*ventana (n., f.)*
winter	*invierno (n., m.)*
wish	*deseo (n., m.); desear (v.)*
with	*con (prep.)*
with me	*conmigo (pron.)*
with regard	*con respecto a (adv.)*
with respect	*con respecto a (adv.)*
without	*sin (prep.); sin que (conj.)*
woman	*mujer (n., f.)*
wood	*madera (n., f.)*
word	*palabra (n., f.)*
work	*trabajar (v.); trabajo (n., m.)*
work excuse	*carta de incapacidad (n., f.)*
worker	*obrero, -a (n.); trabajador, -a (n.)*
world	*mundo (n., m.)*
worried	*preocupado, -a (adj.)*
worry	*preocupar(se) (v.)*
worse	*peor (adj.)*
wound	*herida (n., f.); herir (v.)*
wounded	*herido, -a (adj.)*
wrist	*muñeca (n., f.)*
write	*escribir (v.)*
write down	*anotar (v.); apuntar (v.)*
written	*escrito, -a (adj.)*
wrong	*equivocado, -a (adj.); mal (adv.)*
x-ray	*radiografía (n., f.); placa (n., f.)*
year	*año (n., m.)*
yell	*gritar (v.); grito (n., m.)*
yellow	*amarillo, -a (adj.)*
yes	*sí (adv.)*
yesterday	*ayer (adv.)*
yet	*aún (adv.)*
yogurt	*yogur (n., m.)*
young	*joven (adj.)*
younger	*menor (adj.)*

ANSWER KEY

Unidad 1a

1a-Voc-1

1	acabar	***e***	*to finish*
2	calentar	***g***	*to heat*
3	chocar	***c***	*to crash*
4	congelarse	***f***	*to freeze*
5	cuidar	***b***	*to care for*
6	darse cuenta	***i***	*to notice, realize*
7	golpear	***h***	*to hit*
8	pelear	***d***	*to fight*
9	picar	***a***	*to bite*

1a-Voc-2

1 peligrosa
2 además
3 pobreza
4 obstetra
5 meta
6 darse cuenta
7 casi

1a-Voc-3

"Look, Carmina, this woman lives in a poor and dark apartment with her two children. The children are small, but they don't fight and besides, it seems that they don't notice the poverty. They're happy children. I think that the father doesn't live with them, but the woman is caring for them very well on her own. In any case, she's looking for a new apartment to live in."

1a-Voc-4

Me parece que un amigo de Jaime lo llama y le pide que le dé una medicina para un malestar que tiene. El mismo se ha recetado lo que él piensa que necesita. En los países latinoamericanos la gente puede ir a una farmacia y comprar medicinas sin recetas. Los amigos de Jaime no entienden que en los EE.UU. las cosas son diferentes y que Jaime tiene que obedecer las leyes de este país.

1a-Prin-1

1	¿cuál?	***d***	which one?
2	¿cuándo?	***b***	when?
3	¿dónde?	***c***	where?
4	¿por qué?	***f***	why?
5	¿qué?	***a***	what?
6	¿quién?	***e***	who?

1a-Prin-2

1 ¿Cómo ...?
2 ¿Cómo ...?
3 ¿Dónde ...?
4 ¿Cómo ...?
5 ¿Cuándo ...?
6 ¿A dónde ...?
7 ¿Quién ...?

1a-Prin-3

1 ***c*** ¿Dónde le duele?
2 ***a*** ¿Cómo llegó usted hasta aquí?
3 ***b*** ¿Qué le dijo la enfermera?
4 ***b*** ¿Por qué no vino usted ayer?
5 ***c*** ¿Quién está con este niño?
6 ***c*** ¿Cuándo puedo regresar al trabajo?

1a-Prin-4

1 ¿Cómo se llama usted? OR ¿Cuál es su nombre?
2 ¿Qué le pasó? OR ¿Por qué está aquí?
3 ¿Quién lo va a acompañar a su casa?
4 ¿Usted sabe que necesita regresar en una semana?

1a-Prin-5

1	trabajadores	M/P
2	enfermedad	F/S
3	peligrosas	F/P
4	calentador	M/S
5	oreja	F/S
6	azúcares	M/P
7	temas	M/P
8	golpe	M/S

1a-Prin-6

1 las cortaduras profundas
2 el día largo
3 el problema grave
4 las manos débiles
5 los pacientes estables
6 la decisión difícil
7 las metas posibles
8 las personalidades fuertes

1a-Prin-7

1 *no entendió*; Even though the house where the clinic is housed might be old, putting "*antiguo*" before the noun it modifies means "former" (the clinic is in a building that was once a family home).
2 *entendió*; Used before a noun, "*alto*" means "strong" (the large amount of patients is a strong indication that the clinic was needed).
3 *no entendió*; While Jaime is good-hearted, the sentence means that he is a capable doctor.
4 *entendió*; "*Nuevo*" used after the noun means that it is brand new (and not just new to the patient).
5 *entendió*; Jaime had another job before he was named director.
6 *entendió*; The people who go to the clinic are poor and therefore don't pay very much for the services they receive.
7 *entendió*; "*Raro*" used in front of the noun indicates that this was a sheer coincidence.
8 *no entendió*; The sentence means that unusual diseases are not treated in the clinic but rather in the hospital. It has nothing to do with the age of the patients being treated.

1a-Prin-8

1 media hora
2 una magulladora grande
3 semejante dolor
4 una gran posibilidad
5 la pura verdad
6 un hombre nuevo
7 único problema
8 un nuevo trabajo

1a-Prin-9

1 los
2 el
3 un
4 la
5 el
6 la
7 Las
8 la
9 la
10 el
11 X (no article needed)
12 los
13 Los
14 X (no article needed)
15 al (a + el)
16 unos
17 los

1a-Prin-10

1 The first *"la"* refers to "people" in general. The second one identifies which clinic is being discussed ("the clinic" as opposed to any clinic). **Translation:** People arrive at the clinic every morning.
2 *"El nuevo director"* indicates that he is "the" (not just any) new director. There is no article in front of *"obstetra"* because articles are omitted after the verb *ser* when referring to professions. **Translation:** Jaime Cuenca, the new director, is an obstetrician.
3 *"La prima",* used to describe Laura, indicates that she is "the" cousin (and not just any cousin) in this context. The definite article is used to refer to people by their titles *(la doctora Estrada).* The indefinite article is not used in front of *"trabajo"* because articles are frequently omitted after the verb *tener.* **Translation:** Laura, Dr. Estrada's cousin, does not have a job.
4 The first article, *"el"* is omitted before the day of the week because articles are frequently omitted after the verb *ser.* Definite articles are used, however, to indicate dates. **Translation:** The day after tomorrow is Tuesday, November 11th.

1a-Prin-11

1 esta
2 esta
3 esos
4 aquellos
5 esos

1a-Prin-12 *(Respuesta posible)*

En esta foto vemos que hay tres personas. Esta mujer que se ve en el fondo quiere hablar con esos dos hombres. Aquel cuadro en la pared es muy bonito. Sobre aquel escritorio hay muchos papeles.

1a-Prin-13

1 Nuestros pacientes esperan en la sala.
2 Mi clínica favorita es La Comunidad.
3 Su glucosa está un poco baja.
4 Su amigo está bajo supervisión médica.
5 Nuestra paciente está bajo supervisión médica también.

1a-Prin-14

1 Mi administración es diferente que la tuya.
2 Mi clientela es más grande que la tuya.
3 Mi presupuesto es más pequeño que el tuyo.
4 Mi personal es menos diverso que el tuyo.
5 Mis llamadas telefónicas son menos frecuentes que las tuyas.

1a-Prin-15 *(Respuesta posible)*

No trabajo en una clínica sino en un hospital. El hospital donde trabajo es muy grande y siempre hay diferentes proyectos de construcción. En La Comunidad casi toda la gente habla español: los pacientes y el personal. Donde yo trabajo muchos pacientes hablan español pero casi nadie en el personal lo habla.

1a-Prin-16

1 Emilia y su familia (you could use *"ellos"* here but since this is the first time they are mentioned, it is best to list them out)
2 no pronoun is needed (you could use *"ellos"* but it is not necessary since you are not contrasting them with anyone else and since it is clear you are still talking about them)
3 ella
4 ellos
5 no pronoun is needed
6 the best choice here is *"su familia"* (*"ellos"* is okay but doesn't sound as smooth since it's been so long since the subject for this pronoun was mentioned)
7 ella
8 ella
9 no pronoun is needed since *"estamos"* makes the subject of the verb clear
10 no pronoun is needed; Carmina is speaking with Duna (and probably looking her in the eye) and *"pueden"* makes it clear that the subject of the verb is plural.

1a-Prin-17

1 un veneno peligroso
2 muchas casas norteamericanas
3 pintura vieja
4 niveles muy altos
5 un niño pequeño
6 su boca
7 estas recomendaciones

1a-Prin-18

1 felices
2 en un lugar diferente
3 muy complicada
4 competente
5 el inglés
6 mucho
7 preocupada
8 enamorada
9 ambos jóvenes
10 juntas
11 bonitas
12 buenas amigas
13 la mejor amiga de Ashleigh
14 un hombre simpático
15 listo
16 ciertas preguntas
17 sus amigos

1a-Prin-19

Jaime, me preocupa Emilia Cortés. Ayer vino a verme y tiene todos estos síntomas: sudores nocturnos, tos, pérdida de peso y cansancio. También sufre de fiebres persistentes. Le voy a hacer algunas pruebas para comprobar mis sospechas.

1a-Prin-20 *(Respuesta posible)*

Yo sé que tienes mucho interés en los problemas del medio ambiente. Parece que hay mucha información acerca de este problema que voy a usar para escribir una serie de artículos para *La Voz.* Como sabes, el uso de los pesticidas afecta mucho a la población hispana. Hay un nivel alto de leucemia aquí en el área y muchos creen que tiene que ver con el uso de pesticidas en los campos. Una de las pacientes de mi amigo Jaime está embarazada y está muy ansiosa porque uno de sus hijos mayores padece de leucemia. Es una situación muy triste.

Comprobación

Sección A

1 casados; un
2 muchos; su
3 primas;
4 seria y responsable; rebelede y alegre;
5 buena

Sección B

1 diabética
2 azúcar
3 da cuenta
4 seria
5 Le baja
6 casi

Unidad 1b

1b-Voc-1

1	confiar	***i***	*to trust*
2	diagnosticar	***c***	*to diagnose*
3	enamorarse	***d***	*to fall in love*
4	extrañar	***g***	*to miss*
5	huir	***e***	*to flee*
6	mantenerse	***f***	*to keep oneself*
7	quejarse	***b***	*to complain*
8	retar	***a***	*to challenge*
9	revisar	***j***	*to review*
10	trabajar	***k***	*to work*
11	volver	***h***	*to return*

1b-Voc-2

1	preocuparse	**5**	la guerra
2	mantenerse	**6**	confiar
3	un reto	**7**	enfrentar
4	A veces	**8**	cualquier

1b-Voc-3

"Mis antepasados vinieron a este país para escapar de la pobreza causada por años de guerra. A veces la vida aquí es difícil para nosotros porque tenemos que enfrentarnos a los prejuicios de esa gente a la que no le gustan los inmigrantes, pero tratamos de no quejarnos porque aquí tenemos un futuro. Pero hay veces en las que extrañamos la cultura y costumbres de nuestra patria."

1b-Voc-4 *(Respuestas posibles)*

1 A la gente le sorprende que Duna hable español porque Duna es negra.
2 Su marido le propone que se identifique como negra y no pretenda ser latina.
3 Duna piensa que su marido tiene algunos prejuicios.
4 Duna se siente "entre culturas" pero al final, le gusta.
5 Creo que significa que hay que ayudar a la gente a comprender que se puede ser negra y latina a la vez. Duna acepta su identidad.

1b-Prin-1

1	resulta	**6**	te cuidas
2	sufres	**7**	necesitamos
3	significa	**8**	pienso
4	está	**9**	consumes
5	veo	**10**	te preocupes

1b-Prin-2

1 describe; Ashleigh
2 vigilo; yo
3 produce, se inyecta; páncreas, la señora
4 corres; tú
5 necesito; yo
6 debes; tú
7 afecta; diabetes
8 consumen, reducen; las personas, las personas
9 aumentan; los carbohidratos
10 resultan, tienes; los problemas, tú
11 trabajamos; nosotros

1b-Prin-3 *(Respuestas posibles)*

Carmina

A las 7:30 de la mañana Carmina se levanta. Maneja a la clínica a las 9:00 y ¡llega tarde a su reunión! A las 11:00 de la mañana habla con un grupo de estudiantes.

Jaime (yo) y Ángela

A las 8:30 hablamos sobre el caso de las medicinas que faltan. A las 9:00 asistimos a la reunión con el resto del personal. Y a las 12:30 comemos juntos.

Duna y Ashleigh

A las 9:00 Duna y Ashleigh asisten a una reunión en la clínica.
A las 12:00 comen en un restaurante en la ciudad, y a las 3:30 manejan a la casa de una paciente.

1b-Prin-4 *(Respuestas posibles)*

1 Debe seguir las recomendaciones de su médico.
2 Debe inyectarse en el muslo.
3 La insulina funciona rápidamente.
4 Sí, existen otras formas de insulina pero ésta es la que tiene que tomar.
5 Hay que guardar el frasco en el refrigerador.
6 A veces hay efectos secundarios como el aumento de peso.

1b-Prin-5

1	cuesta	costar; o > -ue
2	merendamos	merendar; e > -ie
3	convierte	convertir; e > -ie
4	duermo	dormir; o > -ue
5	pides	pedir; e > -i
6	almuerzan	almorzar; o > -ue
7	elegimos	elegir; e > -i
8	cuentas	contar; o > -ue
9	pierdo	perder; e > -ie
10	recuerdan	recordar; o > -ue

1b-Prin-6

1	pueden	**9**	pienso
2	podemos	**10**	vuelvo
3	recomienda	**11**	Encuentra
4	quiero	**12**	piensan
5	prefiero	**13**	muestro
6	entendemos	**14**	empiezas
7	vuelven	**15**	sientes
8	puede	**16**	sugiero

1b-Prin-7 *(Respuestas posibles)*

1 Tus recuerdos son muy tristes. ¿Piensas mucho en la guerra? ¿Tienes pesadillas?
2 Te sientes así pero, si te sientes deprimida, debes consultar con un médico. Existen medicinas y otros tratamientos que te pueden ayudar a sentirte mejor.

1b-Prin-8 *(Respuesta posible)*

A veces tengo los mismos sentimientos que Rafa. Es difícil expresarme con precisión en español y aún peor cuando tengo que explicarle algo a un paciente. He descubierto, sin embargo, que los pacientes tienen mucha paciencia y siempre me ayudan.

1b-Prin-9

1 caes—tú; singular; ***you fall***
2 dan—Uds./ellos/ellas; plural; ***you/they give***
3 diagnostica—Ud./él/ella; singular; ***you diagnose*** or ***he/ she diagnoses***

4 eres—tú; singular; ***you are***
5 extraño—yo; singular; ***I miss***
6 hay—indeterminate subject; singular or plural; ***there is/there are***
7 huyes—tú; singular; ***you flee***
8 puede—Ud/él/ella; singular; ***you can*** or ***he/she can***
9 salimos—nosotros/nosotras; plural; ***we go out, leave, exit***
10 se quejan—Uds./ellos/ellas; plural; ***you complain*** or ***they complain***
11 soy—yo; singular; ***I am***
12 tengo—yo; singular; ***I have***
13 terminamos—nosotros/nosotras; plural; ***we finish***
14 va—Ud./él/ella; singular; ***you go*** or ***he/she goes***
15 voy—yo; singular; ***I go***

1b-Prin-10

1	Saben	**7**	mantenemos
2	contribuyen	**8**	es
3	ve	**9**	van
4	tiene	**10**	traigo
5	caben	**11**	doy
6	hay	**12**	pongo

1b-Prin-11 *(Respuesta posible)*
La diabetes afecta casi todos los sistemas del cuerpo humano. Es muy importante cuidarse para evitar problemas. Hay que comer bien, hacer ejercicios regularmente, tomar la medicina que el médico le receta, y revisar el nivel de azúcar en la sangre regularmente. Algunas consecuencias de la diabetes son problemas con los riñones, el corazón, los pies y los ojos. Para evitar problemas como la ceguera y la diálisis hay que seguir las recomendaciones del médico.

1b-Prin-12 *(Respuesta posible)*
Cuando Duna y Ashleigh visitan a la mujer salvadoreña, discuten su dieta para ayudarla a controlar la enfermedad. Ella no comprende todo lo que dice Ashleigh, pero Duna ayuda a aclararlo. Según la mujer, ella no le pone jalea ni mantequilla al pan tostado que come todos los días.

1b-Prin-13
1 ***d*** to express a known fact or truth
2 ***b*** in place of a future tense
3 ***f*** to express the result of a condition
4 ***e*** to express a present event
5 ***c*** to express a habitual action that is still true
6 ***a*** for polite commands

1b-Prin-14 *(Respuestas posibles)*
1 Escribo la respuesta.
2 Me siento en la silla.
3 Todos los días hago los ejercicios que la doctora me recomendó.
4 Tomo la medicina por la mañana.
5 Las pastillas se toman con agua.
6 La diabetes es una enfermedad seria.
7 Si se lava las manos, puede evitar el contagio.
8 Si se toma la insulina, es posible prevenir complicaciones diabéticas.
9 Me dice cuándo es la hora indicada, por favor.
10 Me dices si todavía te sientes mal.
11 Mañana tengo el examen.
12 Lo hacemos a las tres.

1b-Prin-15

1	j	**5**	f	**9**	g
2	b	**6**	h	**10**	k
3	i	**7**	d	**11**	e
4	a	**8**	c		

1b-Prin-16 *(Respuestas posibles)*
Hay = there is, there are. Only use if the English word "there" appears.
Ser = used to express identity, origin, etc. In contrast to *estar*, it is used if the speaker views this as static, without change.
Estar = used to express location, progressive actions, etc. In contrast to *ser*, it is used if the speaker views the action as having changed.

1b-Prin-17
1 está verde
2 rico está
3 Son las tres y media; Es la hora de cenar.
4 está aburrido

1b-Prin-18
1 ***e***; ASHLEIGH: ¿Hay alguien que le pueda ayudar con las inyecciones?
2 ***f***; PACIENTE: Mi esposo está allí para ayudar.
3 ***a, b***; ASHLEIGH: Excelente. Es importante tener apoyo en la casa. ¿Cuántas personas hay en su familia?
4 ***g***; PACIENTE: Hay tres niños y cuatro adultos.
5 ***c***; ASHLEIGH: ¿Cuántos años tienen los niños?
6 ***h***; PACIENTE: Son muy jóvenes.
7 ***d***; ASHLEIGH: Me alegro de saber que está en buenas manos.

1b-Prin-19

1	tiene	**8**	hacen (tienen)	**15**	sabe
2	Tengo	**9**	quieren	**16**	es
3	Son	**10**	comparten	**17**	dice
4	tienen	**11**	se pone	**18**	tiene
5	debe	**12**	doy	**19**	pienso (sé)
6	estoy	**13**	es	**20**	es
7	es	**14**	puedo		

1b-Prin-20 *(Respuesta posible)*
Alex y Laura hacen una pareja inmadura e irresponsable. Los dos son jóvenes. Es la primera vez que Laurita sale de casa y no quiere que nadie la gobierne. Alex es una persona muy insegura y siente celos. Si no aprenden a comprenderse mejor y a tener paciencia van a terminar mal.

Comprobación
Sección A

1	encuentra; es; está	**3**	tiene
2	puede	**4**	es; cuida; va

Sección B

1	recién	**4**	entrar
2	A veces	**5**	enfrentan
3	reto	**6**	cualquier

Unidad 2a

2a-Voc-1

1	d	**3**	a	**5**	c
2	b	**4**	e		

2a-Voc-2

1 ***g*** The bullet probably didn't touch your lung.
2 ***f*** Okay, stay calm; the ambulance is about to arrive.
3 ***e*** Let me make you more comfortable.
4 ***h*** Try not to move, it has penetrated your shoulder blade.
5 ***d*** It seems that the wound is not very serious.
6 ***a*** Do you remember what happened?
7 ***b*** Does it hurt much here?
8 ***c*** I see that you are able to breathe fine.

2a-Voc-3

1 tengo la presión alta
2 hago ejercicios
3 tomo té de yerbabuena para relajarme
4 últimamente tengo más apetito
5 los resultados son buenos
6 hacer otra cita en dos semanas

2a-Voc-4 *(Respuesta posible)*
¿Una noche de salsa?
En vez de una noche de salsa en La Pueblita, tenemos una noche de violencia. Parece que unos pandilleros quieren no sólo bailar y divertirse en el bar, sino también crear problemas para toda la comunidad. Esta noche tranquila hay mucha gente divirtiéndose en La Pueblita cuando se oye unos tiros en el parqueo afuera. Al salir del bar, parece que uno de los pandilleros está herido. Afortunadamente va a estar bien, pero todavía no le quiere decir nada a la policía acerca del suceso. Necesitamos saber lo que pasa en nuestra comunidad para evitar más violencia.

2a-Prin-1

1 últimamente
2 bastante
3 bien
4 muy
5 activo
6 físicamente
7 diariamente
8 anteayer
9 temprano
10 también
11 regularmente

2a-Prin-2

1 fácilmente
2 claramente
3 Probablemente
4 frecuentemente
5 Normalmente
6 adecuadamente
7 cuidadosamente
8 Lentamente

2a-Prin-3

1 anoche
2 a menudo
3 allí
4 Poco
5 Pronto
6 De repente
7 mal
8 Entonces
9 afuera
10 temprano

2a-Prin-4 *(Respuesta posible)*
Tengo un programa de ejercicios que sigo diariamente. Todos los días me levanto temprano y tomo jugo de naranja, cereal y yogurt. Antes de ir al trabajo camino por el parque o ando en bicicleta. Una vez a la semana juego al tenis después del trabajo. El único día que no hago nada físico es el domingo porque siempre estoy muy cansado.

2a-Prin-5

1 ***c*** contribuyendo
2 ***c*** digiriendo
3 ***a*** doliendo
4 ***b*** empezando
5 ***b*** escogiendo
6 ***c*** friendo
7 ***a*** funcionando
8 ***c*** midiendo
9 ***a*** padeciendo
10 ***c*** sucediendo

2a-Prin-6

1 aumentando; *increasing*
2 consumiendo; *consuming*
3 durmiendo; *sleeping*
4 estimulando; *stimulating*
5 leyendo; *reading*
6 previniendo; *preventing*
7 produciendo; *producing*
8 sosteniendo; *sustaining*

2a-Prin-7

1 ***b*** Extraño hablar con mis amigos todos los días.
2 ***b*** A veces paso todo el día durmiendo.
3 ***a*** La gente que dirige los programas tiene mucha experiencia.
4 ***a*** ¿Hacerles daño a tus padres te hace sentir bien?

2a-Prin-8

1 The present participle is used by itself to express the means by which something is done. **Trans**: By working with the youth, we can help the community.
2 The present participle is used in conjunction with verbs as an adverb. **Trans:** Incidents related with violence keep increasing.
3 Present participles in Spanish are not used as verbal nouns. **Trans:** Being part of a gang makes them feel strong.
4 The present participle is used in conjunction with verbs as an adverb. **Trans:** Gang members go on destroying innocent people's property.

2a-Prin-9

1 No. Por lo general, prefiero bailar a mirar la tele.
2 Sí. A menudo hago ejercicio bajando y subiendo las escaleras.
3 No. Dejar de fumar no es fácil para mí.
4 No. Siempre me estiro antes de hacer cualquier ejercicio.
5 No. Una dieta alta en grasas es un factor que contribuye a la enfermedad cardíaca.

2a-Prin-10

1 estoy teniendo
2 están haciendo
3 está esperando
4 estoy analizando
5 está hablando
6 está contando
7 está durmiendo
8 están diciendo

2a-Prin-11 *(Respuesta posible)*
Hoy llega mucha gente a la clínica. Unao de los pacientes de Carmina está entrando en el salón en este momento. Otro paciente está hablando con la recepcionista y ella le está explicando que necesita hacer una cita. Él está tratando de recordar la última vez que habló con la médica.

2a-Prin-12

1 ***d*** compuesto
2 ***f*** decaído
3 ***g*** envuelto
4 ***b*** escrito
5 ***h*** hecho
6 ***a*** padecido
7 ***c*** recetado
8 ***i*** reducido
9 ***e*** retenido
10 ***j*** roto

2a-Prin-13

1 prescrito;	*prescribed*
2 visto;	*seen*
3 tapado;	*stuffed*
4 hinchado;	*swollen*
5 mantenido;	*maintained*
6 sentido;	*felt*
7 muerto;	*dead*
8 vomitado;	*vomited*

2a-Prin-14

1 balanceada
2 adecuada
3 requeridos
4 azucaradas
5 variados

2a-Prin-15

1 ***cantidad***; It's important to receive the recommended quantity of fluoride.
2 ***agua***; You should have the water analyzed to verify its contents.
3 ***gel***; Sometimes fluoride is a gel painted onto the teeth.
4 ***suplemento***; There's also a supplement produced in the form of tablets or drops.
5 ***gérmenes***; Some invisible germs called bacteria convert sugar into acids.
6 ***caries***; For this reason, it is necessary to prevent cavities caused by baby bottles.
7 ***chupete***; It's important not to give the baby a pacifier soaked in honey or sugar.
8 ***dientes***; The teeth remain exposed to sugared liquids.

2a-Prin-16

If you can't go to the store or cook you should contact the programs offered by community groups or organizations dedicated to serving older people. Many times they have a service of food distributed to the home. If you need money, you can buy generic brands sold by the stores. You can also look for canned products because you can keep this type of food for more time. And lastly, my preferred way of saving money is using coupons.

2a-Prin-17 *(Respuestas posibles)*

1 Hay que comer comida saludable y recomendada por un nutricionista.
2 Es importante hacer los ejercicios sugeridos.
3 Es también importante tomar los medicamentos prescritos.
4 Hay muchas enfermedades causadas por dietas malas que usted puede evitar si sigue mis recomendaciones.
5 Al fin y al cabo, no es necesario preocuparse demasiado porque los médicos han descubierto que estas condiciones mejoran con un tratamiento sencillo.

2a-Prin-18

1 No he hecho...
2 Todos hemos llegado.
3 La doctora Estrada ha examinado...
4 Has dicho...
5 Alex ha sufrido.
6 Ustedes han almorzado.
7 Mis colegas han ido.
8 El tratamiento ha sido...

2a-Prin-19

1 ¿Has ido a hablar con la dietista esta semana?
2 Mi hermano ha estado en el hospital tres veces.
3 Mis amigos y yo hemos prometido comer regularmente.
4 El terapista físico ha puesto una barra para que me sirva de apoyo.
5 Los ejercicios han servido para fortalecer los músculos.
6 He terminado la rutina con un período de enfriamiento.
7 Hemos trabajado mucho para adelgazarnos.

2a-Prin-20

1 ¿Cuál es el problema?
2 ¿Hace cuánto ha tenido este problema?
3 ¿Es ésta la primera vez que el niño ha tenido este problema?
4 ¿Otros miembros de la familia han estado enfermos también?

2a-Prin-21 *(Respuestas posibles)*

1 ¿Ha sufrido de molestias en la cabeza?
2 ¿Ha tenido algún problema con la vista?
3 ¿Ha habido días difíciles en el trabajo?
4 ¿Qué ha hecho para controlar el problema?
5 ¿Estas cosas han sido eficaces?
6 ¿Ha traído una muestra del té para mostrarme?

2a-Prin-22 *(Respuesta posible)*

1 ¿Por qué ha venido usted a verme hoy?
2 ¿Ha tenido este tipo de problema antes?
3 ¿Sus padres han padecido de este problema?
4 ¿Qué ha hecho para el dolor?
5 ¿Qué ha comido esta mañana?

2a-Prin-23

1 para	**5** por	**9** por
2 para	**6** por	**10** por
3 para	**7** por	
4 para	**8** para	

2a-Prin-24

1 ***para***; *para* here means "in order to"
2 ***por***; *por* is used to indicate a duration of time
3 ***para***; *para* here indicates a destination (We send the results to the lab.)
4 ***por***; *por* here means "because of"
5 ***para***; *para* means "in order to" in this sentence
6 ***para***; *para* again indicates "in order to"
7 ***por;*** *por* is used for duration of time

2a-Prin-25

1 ***f***; Algunos se hacen miembros *para* recibir protección.
2 ***a***; Lo hacen todo *por* los miembros de la pandilla.
3 ***d***; Los miembros dejan señales de su presencia *por* todas partes de su territorio.
4 ***e***; Muchos jóvenes se hacen parte de una pandilla *por* problemas con la familia, la escuela, o su autoestima.
5 ***c***; A veces terminan en la cárcel *por* su comportamiento violento.
6 ***b***; Uno debe hablarle a su niño al menos *por* media hora todos los días.

2a-Prin-26 *(Respuestas posibles)*

1 Esta receta es para usted.

2 Hoy usted se va para la casa en vez de quedarse más días en el hospital.
3 Para el dolor, si tiene dolor, usted debe tomar Motrin cada seis horas.
4 Debe llamar para decirme si tiene fiebre, hemorragia o dolor abdominal.
5 No puede manejar por dos semanas.
6 Por favor llame mañana para hacer una cita en dos semanas.

2a-Prin-27 *(Respuestas posibles)*
1 El propósito del tratamiento es para calmar a los bebés.
2 La "abuela" no nos dice si es un tratamiento común, pero muchos padres desesperados usan este tipo de remedio para calmar a sus bebés.
3 El tratamiento se administra con el biberón.
4 No estoy de acuerdo con los consejos de la señora. Es muy importante hablar con el médico antes de darle algo a un bebé.

2a-Prin-28
1 present progressive
2 present
3 present
4 present progressive

2a-Prin-29
1 I am feeling; to express a general action that still holds true
2 I have; to express a general action that still holds true
3 I'm doing; to express an ongoing action as it is witnessed
4 I'm going to speak; to express a future event
5 I'm thinking about; to express an ongoing action as it is witnessed
6 I'm thinking about (I'm planning to); to express a future event

2a-Prin-30

PACIENTE:	Recibo inyecciones antibióticas para tratar la infección.
DOCTOR:	¿Ayudan a reducir los síntomas?
PACIENTE:	Sí. También recibo tratamiento de una yerbera. En realidad, la voy a ver después de salir de la clínica.
Doctor:	Veo que las medicinas funcionan y que se está mejorando.

2a-Prin-31 *(Respuesta posible)*
Carmina está atendiendo al herido. Laura también está allí y está preocupada por el hombre. Ashleigh está tratando de ayudar al hombre también, y éste le dice que sólo le duele cuando se ríe. Afortunadamente, Carmina dice que la bala no ha tocado el omoplato y que el herido va a estar bien.

Comprobación
Sección A
1 ocurrido; sido
2 hay; ayudan
3 vienen; sufre
4 visto; peleando

Sección B
1 herido
2 respirar
3 tocado
4 pulmón
5 duele

Unidad 2b

2b-Voc-1

1	arriesgar	f	*to risk*
2	comprobar	j	*to test, make sure*
3	cuidarse	i	*to take care of oneself*
4	dar miedo	a	*to cause fear*
5	dejar de	g	*to stop* (doing something)
6	desayunar	d	*to have breakfast*
7	embaraza	e	*to make pregnant*
8	hacer daño	c	*to harm*
9	ir	b	*to go*
10	sospechar	h	*to suspect*

2b-Voc-2
1 embarazada
2 cuidarse
3 embarazo
4 todavía
5 hacer una cita
6 lo antes posible
7 arriesgar

2b-Voc-3 *(Respuestas posibles)*
1 Ángela, la farmaceútica, sospecha de Alex y por eso ha instalado una cerradura.
2 El hecho de que es un embarazo de riesgo le da mucho miedo a Laura. A veces cree que es demasiado.
3 Laura no se cuida, pero no es por eso que tiene mareos. A lo mejor está embarazada.
4 Carmina le dice a Laura, "¿Cuándo fue tu última regla? ¿No sabes? Por las dudas debes hacerte una prueba de embarazo e ir a ver a Jaime."

2b-Voc-3 *(Respuesta posible)*
Esta vida mía es muy loca. No vas a creer lo que me ha pasado hoy. Descubrí que estoy embarazada. Todavía no le he dicho nada a Alex. No sé cómo vaya a reaccionar. Tengo miedo por lo de la diabetes, pero Carmina me dice que sólo tengo que hablar con Jaime y que él me va a aconsejar. Ojalá que todo salga bien.

2b-Prin-1
1 bebí; I drank
2 comimos; we ate
3 consumieron; they consumed
4 dejó; she left (something behind)
5 nació; he was born
6 permitió; he allowed
7 presionaron; they put pressure (on something)
8 recomendaste; you recommended
9 reconocimos; we recognized
10 respeté; I respected
11 sufrieron; they suffered
12 pensaste; you thought

2b-Prin-2
1 El audiólogo examinó los oídos del bebé.
2 El trabajador social ayudó con los asuntos no médicos.
3 El terapeuta ocupacional trabajó con los problemas de alimentación.
4 El capellán ofreció apoyo religioso.
5 El terapeuta respiratorio revisó las máquinas respiratorias.
6 El neonatólogo administró los primeros cuidados.

2b-Prin-3
1 El esposo se quejó de la condición de la casa.
2 Luego le apretó el brazo y amenazó con darle bofetadas.
3 Salió con otra mujer y al llegar a casa le exigió sexo.
4 Empujó a su esposa por las escaleras y le mostró un arma para controlarla.

2b-Prin-4
1 los niños exhibieron señales de abuso.
2 no identificó el tipo de abuso.
3 alguien golpeó a la niña.
4 no le encontré moretones al niño.
5 demostró un comportamiento nervioso.
6 ellos expresaron sentimientos de temor hacia los padres.
7 el niño respondió con emoción.

2b-Prin-5 *(Respuestas posibles)*
1 ¿Cambió su comportamiento después de visitar a su madre?
2 ¿Habló de un evento traumático?
3 ¿Lastimó alguna parte de su cuerpo?
4 ¿Ocurrió algo específico que le hace pensar que el novio abusó de él?
5 ¿Sucedió algo diferente durante esta visita?

2b-Prin-6
1 mintieron; mentir
2 prefirieron; preferir
3 sirvió; servir
4 consiguieron; conseguir
5 murió; morir

2b-Prin-7

1 dormí	5 sentí
2 sintió	6 pidió
3 Siguió	7 Consiguieron
4 pedí	8 conseguimos

2b-Prin-8

1 *b* contribuyeron	5 *c* pagué
2 *c* busqué	6 *c* se cayó
3 *a* llegaron	7 *c* almorzaste
4 *b* empezamos	8 *c* toqué

2b-Prin-9
1 El bebé llegó temprano.
2 La leche materna contribuyó al buen desarrollo mental del bebé.
3 Comencé a darle la fórmula a los seis meses.
4 Busqué un asiento de bebé seguro para el coche.
5 Distribuyeron cupones en el Departamento de Salud.
6 No castigué físicamente a los niños.

2b-Prin-10
1 Yo busqué un buen médico.
2 Mi esposo colocó la cuna en el cuarto del bebé.
3 Mis padres llegaron de El Salvador para ayudar.
4 Mi madre fregó la casa entera.
5 Mi esposo y yo comenzamos a pensar en nombres.
6 Yo empecé a comer mejor.

2b-Prin-11

1	decir	*d* (-j-)
2	estar	*a* (-uv-)
3	hacer	*c* (-i-)
4	poder	*b* (-u-)
5	poner	*c* (-u-)
6	querer	*c* (-i-)
7	saber	*c* (-u-)
8	tener	*a* (-uv-)
9	traer	*d* (-j-)
10	venir	*c* (-i-)

2b-Prin-12
1 Estuve cansada por nueve meses.
2 Mi esposo fue una gran ayuda durante el embarazo.
3 Él hizo todos los quehaceres por nueve meses.
4 Yo no pude comer ciertos tipos de comida por mucho tiempo.
5 Mis amigos trajeron muchos regalos para el bebé cuando nació.
6 En el octavo mes yo tuve que quedarme en la cama.
7 Mis padres vinieron para celebrar el nacimiento.
8 Mi pobre madre no quiso regresar a casa y se quedó con nosotros.

2b-Prin-13
1 ¿Cuándo supiste del abuso?
2 ¿Les dijo Carlos algo a sus padres?
3 ¿Fuiste a la policía?
4 ¿Qué hicieron?
5 ¿Trajeron alguna prueba del abuso?

2b-Prin-14

1	contribuía	*c* yo
2	daba	*a* la enfermera
3	decían	*c* ustedes
4	contaba	*b* la víctima
5	llegábamos	*a* nosotros
6	mostrabas	*b* tú
7	queríamos	*d* nosotros
8	tenían	*b* las mujeres

2b-Prin-15
1 asistían; ellos, ellas, ustedes
2 caminaba; yo
3 dabas; tú
4 encontraba; él, ella, usted
5 hablábamos; nosotros
6 hacía; yo
7 ponía; él, ella, usted
8 salían; ellos, ellas, ustedes
9 tocaba; él, ella, usted
10 trabajabas; tú
11 veías; tú

2b-Prin-16

1 vivía	4 controlaba	7 metía
2 privaba	5 hacía	8 éramos
3 dejaba	6 íbamos	9 eran

2b-Prin-17
1 Los lunes tomaba sus vitaminas a las 8:00, hacía los ejercicios a las 9:00, almorzaba a mediodía y dormía una siesta a las 2:00.

2 Los martes tomaba sus vitaminas a las 8:00, iba al médico a las 10:00, almorzaba a mediodía y dormía una siesta a las 2:00.
3 Los miércoles tomaba sus vitaminas a las 8:00, hacía los ejercicios a las 9:00, almorzaba a mediodía y dormía una siesta a las 2:00.
4 Los jueves tomaba sus vitaminas a las 8:00, almorazaba a mediodía y dormía una siesta a las 2:00.
5 Los viernes tomaba sus vitaminas a las 8:00, hacía los ejercicios a las 9:00, almorzaba a mediodía y dormía una siesta a las 2:00.
6 Los sábados tomaba sus vitaminas a las 8:00, trabajaba a las 10:00, almorzaba a mediodía y dormía una siesta a las 2:00.
7 Los domingos tomaba sus vitaminas a las 8:00, trabajaba a las 10:00, almorzaba a mediodía y dormía una siesta a las 2:00.

2b-Prin-18 *(Respuestas posibles)*
1 Me levantaba a las siete de la mañana.
2 Le daba de comer a mi hija a las ocho.
3 Atendía pacientes todos los días.
4 Llegaba a casa a las seis.
5 Me acostaba a las 11:00 de la noche.

2b-Prin-19
1 Lleva una hora pujando. Hace una hora que puja.
2 Hace unos días que tengo dolor. Tengo dolor desde hace unos días.
3 Hace años que soy diabético(a). Soy diabético(a) desde hace años.
4 Hace horas que esperamos. Llevamos horas esperando.

2b-Prin-20
1 I've been here since September.
2 I've been sharing a house with strangers for several months.
3 I've been working for this construction company for a few weeks.
4 I've been sending money to my family for a week.

2b-Prin-21
1 b
2 a
3 d
4 e
5 c

2b-Prin-22
1 Carmina parece la mamá de su prima porque se preocupa mucho por ella.
2 A veces Laura se comporta de manera que se causa daño físico.
3 Laura fuma y bebe aunque no debe hacerlo.
4 Carmina espera a Laura mientras ésta tiene la cita con Jaime.
5 Todos los días duerme una siesta tan pronto como llega a casa.
6 Laura siempre se siente mejor después de que habla con Carmina.

2b-Prin-23
1 imperfect
2 preterit
3 imperfect
4 preterit
5 imperfect

2b-Prin-24
Cuando **estaba** embarazada yo **tomaba** ácido fólico todos los días. El médico me **dijo** que **era** necesario cuidarme bien y tomar las vitaminas. Esto es lo que **ayudó** a prevenirle defectos de nacimiento a mi bebé. También **mantuve** una dieta saludable. Por la mañana **bebía** dos vasos de leche porque **necesitaba** calcio para mi bebé. Juan **nació** el 11 de noviembre. Ese día **fue** el mejor de mi vida. Mi esposo y yo **estuvimos** muy orgullos de nuestro primer hijo.

2b-Prin-25
1 ***salimos***—the preterit is used here because the action is completed
2 ***bailaba***—the imperfect is used here because salsa dancing was occurring (presumably for the whole evening) in the bar
3 ***pasamos***—the night is completed according to the speaker so the preterit is used
4 ***conocí***—in the preterit, *conocí* means "I met."
5 ***era***—the imperfect is used to describe where he is from
6 ***se llamaba***—the imperfect is used to tell peoples' names
7 ***invitó***—the invitation was completed so the preterit is used
8 ***conocía***—in the imperfect, *no lo conocía* means "I didn't know him."
9 ***di***—the preterit is used because the action is completed
10 ***fui***—the preterit is used because the action is completed

2b-Prin-26
1 ¿Cómo sabías que algo malo te pasaba?
2 ¿Cuándo empezó?
3 ¿Cuáles eran los síntomas?
4 ¿Recibiste ayuda?
5 ¿Qué hacías antes de que todo empezara?
6 ¿Qué hiciste después de que se detuvo?

2b-Prin-27
Vine a los Estados Unidos porque quería encontrar una vida mejor para mis hijos y para escapar al abuso que sufría. Cuando llegué, no tenía ni dinero ni trabajo y tenía miedo. No sabía lo que iba a hacer. No había nadie que cuidara a mis hijos mientras buscaba empleo. Un día en la iglesia conocí a una mujer que me dijo que había un trabajo en una fábrica. Al día siguiente fui para hablar con el jefe y me lo dieron.

2b-Prin-28 *(Respuesta posible)*
El paciente llegó hace unos minutos. Carmina habló con el por un rato y el señor le hizo una pregunta por lo de la hipertensión. De repente, Ashleigh entró y le dijo a Carmina que Laura estaba ahí. El hombre, que estaba poniéndose la camisa, le dijo que no quería hacerle más preguntas a Carmina. Por eso, ella se fue.

Comprobación
Sección A
1 fue; iba
2 dijo; era; vino
3 Ahora; tuvieron
4 mientras

Sección B

1 sobrino
2 miedo
3 como si
4 creía
5 daño
6 para que

Unidad 3a

3a-Voc-1

1 recién — *b* newly
2 confianza — *b* reliable
3 llegó — *a* arrived
4 pena — *c* sorrow
5 atienden — *c* take care of
6 nivel — *b* level

3a-Voc-2

1 poco
2 servicios
3 sueño
4 da miedo (asusta)
5 pena
6 hace poco (recientemente)

3a-Voc-3

1 Rafa cuenta a los cuatro vientos que los patrones… les proveen viviendas insalubres a los inmigrantes.
2 Carmina sueña con… casarse con un hombre que sepa bailar.
3 Cuando Alex llega a la clínica... va directamente al gabinete que contiene los narcóticos.
4 Ashleigh no tiene mucha confianza… porque no habla bien el español.
5 Laura se asusta porque... le baja el azúcar.
6 Carmina explica que las vacunas… son importantes para los niños.
7 Alex toma muchas pastillas porque… le duelen mucho las rodillas.
8 La diabetes es una enfermedad que… se hereda.

3a-Voc-4 *(Respuesta posible)*

Queridos padres:

Los extraño mucho. Acá todo es diferente. Estamos bien y nos gusta la comunidad aquí, pero es difícil estar tan lejos de ustedes. Pero el bebé está bien y creo que viene muy pronto. Todavía no hemos decidido qué nombre le vamos a poner. Tal vez Lourdes por ti, mami. O Héctor si es varón.

Un millón de besos,
Milagros

3a-Prin-1

1 Sí (Ella la ha tenido.)
2 Sí (La hicieron.)
3 No
4 No
5 No
6 Sí (El niño la toma.)
7 Sí (Las necesitan antes de empezar la escuela.)
8 No

3a-Prin-2

1 Las veo en los dientes.
2 El dentista los llama para hablar del tratamiento.
3 Usted los puede cepillar con un cepillo suave.
4 La uso.
5 Mis hijos los comen en vez de dulces.
6 No lo pongo en su biberón.
7 Mis niños lo miran con temor cuando tienen que ir al dentista.
8 Los niños lo toman.
9 Los selladores dentales las previenen en los dientes permanentes.
10 El uso del hilo dental lo disminuye.

3a-Prin-3

1 Un compañero me trajo.
2 Sí, la recibí en el trabajo.
3 No, no los tengo.
4 No, no las tengo.
5 No, no los tomo.
6 No, no lo tengo.
7 Sí, la he traído.
8 Sí, la necesito.

3a-Prin-4

A mi hijo le encanta jugar al béisbol. Un día lo jugaba cuando de repente recibió un golpe en la boca y se le desprendió un diente. Inmediatamente, lo coloqué en un vaso de leche y llamé a la dentista. La visitamos esa misma tarde. Examinó la herida. La limpió e implantó el diente de nuevo. Después de visitarla, fuimos a comprar un protector bucal. Y desde entonces mi hijo lo usa cuando practica deportes.

3a-Prin-5 *(Respuestas posibles)*

1 ¿El niño demuestra interés en sonidos? No, no lo demuestra.
2 ¿El niño imita palabras simples? Sí, las imita.
3 ¿El niño mira a las personas cuando hablan? No, no las mira.
4 ¿El niño mueve los ojos en la dirección del sonido? No, no los mueve.
5 ¿El niño reconoce los nombres de objetos comunes? Sí, los reconoce.
6 ¿El niño sigue instrucciones? No, no las sigue.

3a-Prin-6

1 No
2 Sí (Me duele el brazo por la inyección.)
3 No
4 Sí (Me molesta el estómago porque comí demasiado.)
5 Sí (Le traje una lista de sus medicinas actuales al médico.)
6 Sí (Le pidieron ayuda al hombre.)
7 No
8 Sí (Quiero examinarle los ojos.)

3a-Prin-7

1 **Le** dan al niño 3 dosis de la vacuna contra el tétanos y la difteria.
2 Con el sarampión **le** salen erupciones a la piel.
3 El médico **nos** dice a nosotros que llamemos si hay cualquier problema.
4 Mis vecinos **me** recomendaron a mí la clínica.
5 Tenemos que ir al doctor si no **le** baja la temperatura al bebé.
6 Debes decir**me** a mí si **te** duele a ti.
7 Algunas vacunas pueden provocar**les** reacciones alérgicas a los niños.

3a-Prin-8 *(Respuestas posibles)*

1 A Rafa le molesta que el señor Anderson les saca un dineral a los inmigrantes.
2 El trabajo de Rafa le da miedo a Ángela porque si el señor Anderson les saca tanto dinero a los inmigrantes por servicios inaceptables, no va a querer que Rafa le diga nada a nadie.

3 El señor Anderson trata mal a los inmigrantes. Les saca mucho dinero por vivir en viviendas horribles.

3a-Prin-9 *(Respuesta posible)*
Elio, hoy me visitaron dos mujeres de la clínica. Ashleigh, la enfermera, me hizo varias preguntas sobre el embarazo. Duna, la trabajadora social, trató de asegurarme que todo estaría bien. Me dijeron también que yo las podía llamar por cualquier razón. ¡Me cayeron bien!

3a-Prin-10

1	a él	***b***	*him*
2	a ella	***a***	*her*
3	a ellos	***e***	*them*
4	a mí	***d***	*me*
5	a nosotros	***f***	us
6	a sí	***c***	*himself*
7	a ti	***i***	*you*, sing., informal
8	a usted	***h***	*you*, sing., formal
9	a ustedes	***g***	*you*, pl.

3a-Prin-11

1 ***a*** a él		**4** ***b*** a ti
2 ***a*** a nosotros		**5** ***a*** a mí
3 ***b*** a ellos		**6** ***b*** a ellas

3a-Prin-12
1 me inyecto; *I inject myself*
2 te cuidas; *you take care of yourself*
3 se sienten; *they feel*
4 nos ponemos; *we put (typically, something on)*
5 se rompe; *she breaks (typically, a body part)*
6 se cae; *he falls down*
7 se van; *you all go (away)*
8 se quejan; *they complain*
9 se divierte; *she enjoys (herself)*
10 se dan cuenta de; *they realize*

3a-Prin-13
1 Normalmente Rafa y Ángela ***se acuestan*** a las 11, pero ayer ***se acostaron*** a las 10.
2 Normalmente Carmina ***se duerme*** rápidamente, pero el otro día no ***se durmió*** tan fácilmente.
3 Normalmente el dolor no ***se extiende*** a la pierna, pero anteayer ***se extendió*** hasta el pie.
4 Normalmente nosotros no ***nos cansamos*** de hacer ejercicio, pero ayer ***nos cansamos*** después de unos minutos.
5 Normalmente yo no ***me enfermo***, pero la semana pasada ***me enfermé***.

3a-Prin-14
1 La madre se preocupaba porque su hijo lloraba todo el tiempo.
2 Todos los años los niños se enferman de gripe.
3 Me apresuraba en llegar a casa para atender a mi hijo enfermo.
4 Por fin, el bebé se calló y se durmió.
5 ¿Se dio cuenta de alguna hinchazón o enrojecimiento?
6 ¿Te acordaste de darle la medicina esta mañana?

3a-Prin-15
1 Se cayó en la obra.
2 No, no se rompió nada.
3 El capataz se asustó.
4 Todos se fueron del hospital porque Federico estaba bien y quería ir a la clínica.

3a-Prin-16 *(Respuestas posibles)*
1 Desde que vino a los Estados Unidos, Laura se ha divertido muchísimo. Demasiado, diría Carmina.
2 La pobre Laura necesita cuidarse un poco más. Ella necesita dejar de beber y fumar.
3 Carmina siempre se ha preocupado por la salud de su prima.
4 Laura se da cuenta de que necesita tomar mejores decisiones.
5 Carmina y Laura se acuerdan de su tío Ramón que murió de diabetes y Laura ha decidido cambiar su vida.

3a-Prin-17 *(Respuestas posibles)*
1 Ahora me acuesto temprano pero antes me acostaba muy tarde.
2 Por eso, ahora me levanto muy temprano; antes me levantaba bastante tarde.
3 Ahora siempre me ducho, antes me bañaba en la tina.
4 Ahora me pongo la ropa antes de desayunar, antes me ponía la ropa después de desayunar.
5 Ahora me cepillo los dientes antes de salir de la casa, antes casi nunca me cepillaba los dientes.

3a-Prin-18

1 recíproco	**3** reflexivo	**5** reflexivo
2 recíproco	**4** recíproco	

3a-Prin-19
1 Carmina y Laura se cuidan entre sí.
2 Rafa y Ángela se quieren mucho.
3 Todos nos conocimos en la clínica.
4 Duna y Ashleigh se respetan.
5 Federico y su familia no se hablan.

3a-Prin-20

1 nada	**3** Nadie	**5** cada uno
2 Todos	**4** Algunas	

3a-Prin-21
Todo el mundo cree que la primera visita al dentista es espantosa, pero con tu ayuda puede ser algo positivo. Se necesita explicarle al niño que alguien le va a examinar y a limpiar sus dientes. Es importante asegurarle que nada malo va a ocurrir.

3a-Prin-22 *(Respuesta posible)*
La mujer quiere preguntarle algo a Carmina. Tiene algunas preguntas específicas. Nadie le había explicado nada sobre las vacunas cuando vino a los Estados Unidos, pero ahora le dicen que es necesario que su hijo reciba algunas vacunas antes de entrar en la escuela. Por eso está algo preocupada, porque no sabe qué hacer. Ella creía que su hijo ya había recibido todas las vacunas.

3a-Prin-23

1 condiciones	**5** clínica
2 aspirina	**6** la que
3 un historial; las vacunas	**7** efectos
4 efectos secundarios	**8** los niños

3a-Prin-24

1 que
2 los que (los cuales)
3 que
4 quienes
5 los que (los cuales)
6 cuyos
7 que

3a-Prin-25

Un bebé cuyo hígado es prematuro puede sufrir de exceso de bilirrubina, lo cual significa que tiene demasiados glóbulos rojos viejos. Esto es algo que causa que la piel se vuelva amarilla y que el bebé esté somnoliento. Sabemos que todos los glóbulos rojos han desaparecido por el cambio del color de su excremento, el cual cambia de verde a amarillo.

3a-Prin-26 *(Respuesta posible)*

Un microbio que vive en la garganta, la boca y la nariz de una persona infectada causa la difteria. Los síntomas que ocurren primero son dolor de garganta, fiebre leve y escalofríos. Por lo general la enfermedad se desarrolla en la garganta. El paciente tiene dificultad para respirar y a veces puede ahogarse. Alguna gente infectada puede contagiar a otros sin mostrar síntomas. Si no se trata la difteria, o si no se la trata lo más pronto posible, puede crear un veneno poderoso. Este veneno, que a veces causa complicaciones serias como infartos o parálisis, puede propagarse por todo el cuerpo. Aproximadamente el 10% de los pacientes infectados de difteria mueren por la enfermedad.

3a-Prin-27

1 diré; *I will tell, say*
2 llorará; *the baby will cry*
3 verás; *you will see*
4 cambiaremos; *we will change*
5 harán; *they will do, make*
6 estarán; *you all will be*
7 dará; *she will give*
8 sabrá; *you will know*

3a-Prin-28

1 daré
2 comerá
3 dormiremos
4 durarán
5 ayudará
6 vendrán
7 estaré

3a-Prin-29 *(Respuestas posibles)*

1 El cordón se caerá durante los primeros días de vida.
2 Usted tendrá dolor por unos días (o semanas si tiene una cesárea).
3 Los senos le dolerán al principio.
4 El niño no sabrá chupar al principio.
5 Los senos se llenarán de leche después de algunos días.

3a-Prin-30 *(Respuestas posibles)*

1 ¿Me moriré?
2 ¿Tendré mucho dolor?
3 ¿Los problemas serán permanentes?
4 ¿Podremos hablar más tarde?
5 ¿Cuáles serán los efectos secundarios?

3a-Prin-31

1 ***c*** probabilidad
2 ***a*** futuro remoto
3 ***b*** predicción
4 ***a*** futuro remoto
5 ***c*** probabilidad

3a-Prin-32 *(Respuestas posibles)*

1 ***Futuro***: Seré enfermera después de graduarme. Predicción: Mis padres creen que trabajaré donde viven ellos. Probabilidad: Viviré en el mismo estado.
2 ***Futuro***: Tendré un trabajo en una clínica rural. Predicción: Creo que el personal y yo tendremos mucho trabajo. Probabilidad: Todos tendrán mucho que hacer.
3 ***Futuro***: Podré trabajar con la población latina. Predicción: Si tengo mucha suerte, podré trabajar con mujeres embarazadas. Probabilidad: ¿Podré trabajar en esta clínica?

3a-Prin-33

1 ***c*** Sí, se las compré.
2 ***a*** Sí, nos la dieron.
3 ***b*** Sí, me lo explicó.
4 ***c*** Sí, se los trajeron.
5 ***b*** Sí, quiero dártelo.
6 ***c*** Sí, estoy buscándotelas.
7 ***c*** Sí, se lo voy a pedir.

3a-Prin-34

1 Sí, se las puse.
2 Sí, me la puso.
3 Sí, se lo dio.
4 No, no me la puse.
5 Sí, te la puedo recetar.

3a-Prin-35 *(Respuesta posible)*

Para protegerse contra las enfermedades contagiosas, todos deben estar vacunados. Es muy importante averiguar con el médico si se han recibido todas las vacunas necesarias. Los niños especialmente necesitan estar vacunados pues no pueden asistir a la escuela sin ser inmunizados. Los servicios ofrecidos por La Comunidad son muy buenos y todo el personal atiende bien a sus pacientes. Los atienden con confianza.

Aunque las vacunas no protegen contra las enfermedades hereditarias, es importante recibir vacunas, especialmente si se sufre de una de estas enfermedades. De esta manera usted puede evitar las enfermedades contagiosas y el riesgo de transmitirlas. ¡Cuídese! Vaya hoy para ser vacunado.

Comprobación

Sección A

1 las
2 quien; que; las
3 encontrará; podrá
4 viven
5 riesgo

Sección B

1 encontrarán
2 positivo
3 por lo
4 urgencia
5 pena
6 Lo peor

Unidad 3b

3b-Voc-1

1 b
2 f
3 d
4 e
5 a
6 c

3b-Voc-2
1 se aprovecha de
2 conseguir
3 ahorrar
4 compartimos
5 la menor idea
6 Además
7 al fin y al cabo
8 culpan
9 arruinamos

3b-Voc-3 *(Respuestas posibles)*
1 Rafa cree que el jefe de una compañía que les provee viviendas a los hispanos, un tal Hugo Anderson, se aprovecha de dichos inmigrantes. Él se dedica a investigar lo que hace este Anderson.
2 Rafa y Ángela acaban de pelear. Los dos creen que tienen la culpa. Ángela le dice a Rafa que estaba equivocada al criticarlo.
3 Eliodoro tiene la idea de que está infectado del SIDA. Para ahorrar dinero, antes de llegar su esposa, compartía una casa con varios hombres.
4 En esta foto, Carmina le dice a Eliodoro que no se puede contagiar del SIDA solamente por compartir una casa. Como Eliodoro no tenía relaciones sexuales con estos hombres ni compartía jeringas con ellos, no hay razón para preocuparse.

3b-Voc-4 *(Respuesta posible)*
Hay que protegerse del SIDA. El VIH, el virus que causa el SIDA, sólo se transmite por vía sanguínea. Por eso es importante nunca compartir jeringas y usar condones cuando se tienen relaciones sexuales. Si usted es portador del VIH, o si cree que lo es, llame a nuestra clínica lo más pronto posible. ¡Podemos ayudarle!

3b-Prin-1
1 elegir; *g → j*
2 comenzar; *z → c*
3 distribuir; *ui → y*
4 llegar; *g → gu*
5 colocar; *c → qu*
6 gozar; *z → c*
7 incluir; *ui → y*
8 alcanzar; *z → c*
9 recoger; *g → j*
10 colgar; *g → gu*

3b-Prin-2
1 no use
2 compren
3 tenga
4 lea
5 no acepte
6 pongan
7 quite
8 guarden
9 sigan
10 no consuman

3b-Prin-3
1 inhale
2 vuelva
3 Recuerde
4 Duerma
5 descanse
6 Haga
7 Coma
8 tome
9 olvide

3b-Prin-4
1 Evite el contacto cercano con miembros de su familia.
2 Duerma en un cuarto separado.
3 Cúbrase la boca con un pañuelo de papel cuando tosa.
4 Ponga el pañuelo de papel en una bolsa y bótelo.
5 Ventile su cuarto y su casa con frecuencia.
6 Tómese toda su medicina.

3b-Prin-5 *(Respuestas posibles)*
1 Entre y siéntese por favor.
2 Dígame, ¿cuál es el problema?
3 Apriete mis dedos.
4 Tome tres cápsulas al día; una cada ocho horas.
5 Llámeme si tiene preguntas.
6 Hable más despacio, por favor.

3b-Prin-6
1 compra
2 usa
3 no compres
4 ten
5 no te pongas
6 No uses
7 Lee
8 sigue
9 No tomes
10 Sé

3b-Prin-7
1 Reconoce los síntomas.
2 Si estás infectada con el VIH, no amamantes al bebé.
3 No dones sangre, plasma, ni órganos.
4 Usa tu propio cepillo de dientes.
5 Deja de fumar y de usar drogas.
6 No compartas jeringas ni agujas.
7 Haz regularmente ejercicios físicos.
8 No te pongas crema con petrolato.
9 Limita el número de parejas sexuales.
10 Ten en cuenta que la píldora anticonceptiva no previene la transmisión del VIH.

3b-Prin-8 *(Respuestas posibles)*
1 Si resulta que estás infectado, ve al médico para recibir consejos.
2 Si quieres un aborto, habla con tu médico.
3 Haz ejercicio todos los días y no comas comida con mucha grasa.
4 Ve al médico y pídele una prueba de tuberculosis.
5 Toma tu medicina a la misma hora cada día.
6 Si ves sangre o pus en la orina, llama al médico.
7 Si se te olvida tomar la medicina, llama al farmaceútico y pregúntale qué debes hacer.
8 Toma jugo de "cranberries" y tómate toda la medicina que el médico te recete.

3b-Prin-9 *(Respuestas posibles)*
1 Limita el número de parejas sexuales.
2 No salgas con gente que no conozcas.
3 Asegúrate de hablar con las mujeres sobre las enfermedades venéreas antes de tener relaciones sexuales con ellas.
4 Siempre usa condones.
5 ¡Cásate con ella y sé fiel! Dile si ya tienes una enfermedad.

3b-Prin-10 *(Respuesta posible)*
1 RAFA: ¡No me digas que no sabes de qué te estoy hablando!
2 ÁNGELA: Sí, sé muy bien de lo que hablas. Pero no me gusta. Deja de escribir artículos contra esta gente.
3 RAFA: Tú no me comprendes. ¡Eres como todas las gringas! Y no me digas que no…
4 ÁNGELA: Pero Rafa, esta gente tiene mucho poder político. Pueden arruinar tu carrera. No hagas nada peligroso.
5 RAFA: Lo peligroso es no hacer nada. Voy a decir la verdad. Vete ahora a la clínica y ¡déjame en paz!

3b-Prin-11
1 exijamos; *let's demand*
2 miremos; *let's watch*
3 no hagamos; *let's not do (make)*
4 disminuyamos; *let's decrease*
5 consultemos; *let's consult*
6 vamos; *let's go*
7 limpiemos; *let's clean*
8 no castiguemos; *let's not punish*

9 midamos; *let's measure*
10 sigamos; *let's continue*

3b-Prin-12
1 Rellenemos estos formularios.
2 Revisemos el presupuesto.
3 Construyamos nuevos edificios.
4 Solicitemos una beca del gobierno.
5 Encontremos maneras para alcanzar a más gente.
6 Contratemos a Federico.

3b-Prin-13
1 Digamos que todo va como esperamos.
2 Hagamos una cita para dentro de un mes.
3 Veamos si hay alguna mejoría antes de cambiar la medicina.
4 Aumentemos la dosis.
5 Recemos por una recuperación rápida.

3b-Prin-14
1 no le digas
2 siéntense
3 dale
4 Ponte
5 no se preocupe
6 Acostémonos
7 Cuídense
8 no te sientas
9 relájate
10 protéjase

3b-Prin-15
1 No me lo muestres.
2 Pónganselo.
3 No lo empecemos.
4 Tráigala.
5 Pídemela.
6 No te lo quites.
7 No nos la diga.
8 No se protejan.
9 Ténselo.
10 Reunámonos.

3b-Prin-16
1 No se lo dé.
2 Háganse una prueba.
3 Sí, vacúnense.
4 Lávenselas.
5 Utilícenlos.

3b-Prin-17 *(Respuestas posibles)*
1 Alex, cálmate.
2 No te enojes tanto con ella. La pobre necesita tu apoyo.
3 Dile que la amas.
4 Explícale que quieres casarte con ella.
5 Vete a su casa y habla con ella inmediatamente.
6 Y finalmente, pídele disculpas.

3b-Prin-18
1 ustedes, ellos, ellas; *you/they would contribute*
2 tú; *you would use*
3 nosotros; *we would give*
4 yo, usted, él, ella; *I/you/he/she would say/tell*
5 nosotros; *we would find*
6 yo, usted, él, ella; *I/you/he/she would speak*
7 tú; *you would pay*
8 ustedes, ellos, ellas; *you/they would support*

3b-Prin-19
1 Emilia, si usted está infectada, tendría que hacerse una radiografía del tórax.
2 La fotografía, o placa, mostraría si las bacterias hubieran causado algún daño a los pulmones.
3 El esputo es un líquido espeso que una persona infectada botaría al toser.
4 Un examen de esputo comprobaría si hubiera bacterias de tuberculosis.

3b-Prin-20 *(Respuestas posibles)*
1 Llamaría la ambulancia.
2 Trataría de quedarme tranquila.
3 Hablaría con la policía.
4 No tocaría al herido, pues no soy médica.
5 Ayudaría a los paramédicos.

3b-Prin-21
1 ***f*** *Would you wait until you were ready to have sexual relations?*
2 ***e*** *Would you be able to take care of a child on your own?*
3 ***c*** *If you kissed each other with your mouths closed you would not get infected.*
4 ***d*** *They probably would not use birth control.*
5 ***b*** *If I were she, I would make an appointment with the doctor.*
6 ***a*** *I would speak with my children if I had time.*

3b-Prin-22
1 *conditional sentence with an "if-clause"; I would consult with a doctor if I noticed any abnormal discharge from my penis (or vagina.)*
2 *refer to the future from the past; According to what the doctor said, without treatment gonorrhea could cause sterility, arthritis, and heart problems.*
3 *probability; I imagine that they would be very happy to know that the results were negative.*
4 *polite request; Please tell me how many partners you've had.*
5 *refer to the future from the past; The nurse told me that there would be a burning sensation when I urinated.*
6 *conditional sentence with an "if-clause"; Irritation, inflammation or sensitivity in the genital area are some of the symptoms that you would experience if you had an STD.*

3b-Prin-23
Un resultado positivo en la prueba de tuberculina señalaría que el paciente ha estado en contacto con la enfermedad y que tiene bacterias inactivas en el sistema. Diríamos que este paciente está infectado aunque no muestre síntomas de la enfermedad y ni siquiera sepa él mismo que está infectado. Si toma las medicinas adecuadas todos los días, mantiene su cuerpo fuerte y es capaz de defenderse de la infección, la tuberculosis no se desarrollará. En un paciente fuerte que está bajo tratamiento, las defensas del cuerpo controlarían las bacterias inactivas, aislándolas del resto del sistema. Las bacterias podrían permanecer vivas, pero inactivas, dentro de un cuerpo por años. Cuando el paciente descubre que está infectado, debe prevenir la enfermedad. Mientras estén inactivas las bacterias que causan la tuberculosis, no podrían hacerle daño al paciente ni contagiar a otros.

3b-Prin-24 *(Respuestas posibles)*

1 Si supiera que mi hijo de 16 años va a ser padre, le diría que estudiara mucho para poder apoyar a su hijo en el futuro... O... le diría que buscara un trabajo para ganar dinero para mantener al bebé.
2 Si mi pareja me dijera que tiene una enfermedad venérea, lo dejaría de inmediato... O... lo llevaría al médico.
3 Si mi mejor amigo me dijera que sufre de HIV, lloraría... O... lo abrazaría y le diría que lo quiero a pesar de su enfermedad.
4 Si el doctor me informara que tengo tuberculosis, le pediría el tratamiento más eficaz...O...iría inmediatamente a la farmacia para comprar la medicina que me recete.

3b-Prin-25

1 *b* usted
2 *a* tú
3 *c* ustedes
4 *a* tú
5 *b* usted
6 *a* tú
7 *b* usted
8 *c* ustedes

3b-Prin-26

1 informal; es Carmina la que habla y son primas
2 formal (usted); es un paciente el que habla
3 informal; Laura habla con Alex, su novio
4 formal (ustedes); no importa que habla con amigos porque en Latinoamérica se usa el formal (ustedes) cuando habla con un grupo de amigos
5 formal (usted); una paciente habla con Jaime, su médico

3b-Prin-27

1 Victor y Manuel, cúbranse la boca antes de toser.
2 Mamá, no me des aquel jarabe con sabor a cereza.
3 Bueno mis queridos angelitos, no se comporten mal.
4 Por favor, doctor, repita las instrucciones.
5 Carmen, tráenos las pastillas de la farmacia.
6 Señor González, póngase de pie.

3b-Prin-28 *(Respuestas posibles)*

1 Señor López, regrese a la clínica en ocho días.
2 Señor y señora Sánchez, vayan a la farmacia a comprar la medicina para William.
3 Cuiden bien a su hijo.
4 William, cálmate. Duérmete.
5 Señor Plata y señorita García, entren. Siéntense.
6 Marta, toma la pastilla una vez al día.
7 Escucha bien lo que te digo y lee este folleto.
8 Señora Perón, coma menos comida azucarada.

3b-Prin-29 *(Respuesta posible)*

Querida familia,
Primero, perdónenme todos por no poder estar allí. Hace tanto tiempo que no los veo que no sé exactamente qué decir. ¡Los extraño mucho! Pienso en todos ustedes todos los días. Vengan a visitarme, por favor. En este momento no les puedo explicar por qué no les he escrito, pero sepan que tengo muchas ganas de verlos. Compren boletos para el viaje con el dinero que les mando. ¡Hasta pronto!

Comprobación
Sección A

1 créame; hágame
2 se preocupe
3 podríamos; culpa
4 cuídela; regrese; sí

Sección B

1 abusa
2 equivocar
3 cabo
4 comparten
5 seria
6 quejas

Unidad 4a

4a-Voc-1

1 *a* agudo
2 *b* tiempo
3 *a* aspirinas
4 *a* daba vergüenza
5 *c* indicaba
6 *b* nada

4a-Voc-2

1 artritis reumatoide
2 renunciar
3 recetó
4 al día
5 nada
6 acompañar

4a-Voc-3 *(Respuestas posibles)*

1 Las contracciones señalan que... pronto viene el bebé.
2 La enfermera le pide disculpas al paciente por... explicarle mal la receta.
3 El paciente grita porque... le duele mucho.
4 La mujer decidió renunciar a su trabajo por... otro que le gusta más.
5 Las medicinas prescritas sólo se obtienen después de... ver al médico.
6 Recibió la dosis equivocada y por eso... sufrió mucho.

4a-Voc-4 *(Respuesta posible)*

Alex acaba de decirle a Laura que a él le gustan las "mujercitas". Laura está gritando porque está muy enojada. Alex realmente quería pedirle disculpas, pero Laura no aceptó sus explicaciones. Después Alex le explica que le duelen mucho las piernas y que ha tomado muchas aspirinas pero que quiere algo más fuerte. Al final Laura lo lleva a la clínica.

4a-Prin-1

1 *c* las limitaciones
2 *d* los planes
3 *c* la tristeza
4 *c* las emociones
5 *c* los desafíos
6 *a* el enojo

4a-Prin-2

1 el dolor es/fue/será controlado
2 las cuentas son/fueron/serán pagadas
3 el trabajo es/fue/será dado
4 un artículo es/fue/será escrito
5 la clínica nueva es/fue/será abierta
6 los archivos son/fueron/serán perdidos
7 la enfermedad es/fue/será prevenida
8 la dosis es/fue/será aumentada

4a-Prin-3

1 es conocida
2 fue examinado
3 fue hecho
4 fue descubierto
5 está caracterizada
6 son causados
7 fueron discutidos
8 serán mostrados

4a-Prin-4

1 Los medicamentos fueron comprados fuera de Estados Unidos.
2 Las instrucciones indicadas en la etiqueta no fueron seguidas por el paciente.
3 El sueño y los dolores de cabeza son causados por las píldoras.
4 Las pastillas para dormir le serán recetadas por el médico.
5 El recipiente con las píldoras es rellenado por el farmacéutico.
6 La medicina equivocada fue tomada por el hombre.
7 La información en español le fue escrita por la enfermera especializada.
8 La venta de algunos narcóticos no es aprobada en Estados Unidos.

4a-Prin-5 *(Respuestas posibles)*

1 Al paciente le fue recetada una medicina por Ashleigh.
2 La receta fue explicada por Ashleigh.
3 La receta fue tomada por Ángela.
4 Ashleigh fue castigada por Ángela.

4a-Prin-6

1 se puede	5 se entrevista
2 se sabe	6 se hace
3 se conocen	7 se ven
4 se puede	8 se debe

4a-Prin-7

1 Se dan sedantes para la ansiedad.
2 No se debe combinar los medicamentos sin consultar al médico.
3 No se crea hábito con el uso de los medicamentos antidepresivos.
4 Se experimentarán boca seca y estreñimiento.
5 Se ofrece la terapia naturista.
6 La depresión no se le quitará rápidamente con terapia.

4a-Prin-8 *(Respuestas posibles)*

1 Se escribe un plan para el futuro.
2 Se analiza la situación completa.
3 Se establecen las prioridades.
4 No se toman decisiones importantes.
5 Se permiten viejas amistades.

4a-Prin-9 *(Respuestas posibles)*

1 Se toman las pastillas todos los días.
2 Se las tragan con un vaso grande de agua.
3 Se toma una pastilla a la vez.
4 Se toman dos pastillas al día.
5 No se come nada una hora antes y dos horas después de tomar la medicina.
6 Se puede llamar a la clínica si hay preguntas.

4a-Prin-10

1 Sí	3 Sí	5 No
2 No	4 No	6 Sí

4a-Prin-11

1 más	4 tanto	7 como
2 que	5 tan	8 tanta
3 de	6 menos	

4a-Prin-12

1 Los músculos de la espalda están tan tensos como los del cuello. / Los músculos de la espalda están menos tensos que los del cuello.
2 Un baño con agua tibia ayuda tanto como uno con agua fría. / Un baño con agua tibia ayuda más que uno con agua fría.
3 Dar un paseo es tan efectivo como hacer ejercicio. / Dar un paseo es menos efectivo que hacer ejercicio.
4 Tengo tantos problemas de dinero como problemas de trabajo. / Tengo más problemas de dinero que problemas de trabajo.
5 Tenemos tantas diversiones como preocupaciones. / Tenemos más diversiones que preocupaciones.

4a-Prin-13 *(Respuestas posibles)*

1 Esta semana Claudia se siente menos apática que antes.
2 Se siente tan desesperada como se sentía antes.
3 Desgraciadamente, se siente tan abandonada como sola esta semana.
4 Se siente más indefensa que apática.
5 Finalmente, Claudia se siente peor esta semana de lo que se sentía antes.

4a-Prin-14 *(Respuestas posibles)*

1 Ashleigh piensa que no es tan profesional como Ángela.
2 Pero Jaime cree que Ashleigh sí es tan profesional como Ángela.
3 Duna cree que el español de Ashleigh es mejor que el de la mayoría de los enfermeros norteamericanos.
4 Ángela cree que sus colegas son mejores que los que tenía antes.
5 Carmina opina que es menos puntual que Jaime.
6 Jaime cree que su vida personal es más complicada que la de Ashleigh.

4a-Prin-15 *(Respuestas posibles)*

1 ¿Cree que sus problemas son más grandes que antes?
2 ¿Tiene tantas responsabilidades como tenía antes?
3 ¿Su esposo le da más o menos apoyo del que le daba antes?
4 ¿Estos sentimientos son peores que los que tenía antes?
5 ¿Sus problemas con insomnio ocurren tan frecuentemente como antes?

4a-Prin-16

1 ***c*** Es el tratamiento más seguro de todos.
2 ***d*** Son los mejores métodos para aliviar el dolor.
3 ***d*** Las medicinas son las menos caras en esta farmacia.
4 ***c*** Mis hijos son las personas más importantes de mi vida.
5 ***b*** Es el peor caso que he visto en La Comunidad.
6 ***d*** Son los síntomas menos severos de todos.

4a-Prin-17

1 la dieta más apropiada
2 los mejores
3 son los menos seguros
4 el tratamiento más efectivo
5 son los medicamentos más útiles

4a-Prin-18 *(Respuestas posibles)*
1 Margarita es la hija mayor y Jorge es el menor.
2 El apartamento es el más grande en el que Gabriela ha vivido.
3 Gabriela escogió el mejor trabajo para ella.
4 Su sueldo no es el mejor de todos, pero es suficiente.
5 Gabriela cree que sus hijos son los más inteligentes y trabajadores de la escuela.

4a-Prin-19
La mejor manera de protegerse es hacer preguntas. Si tiene preguntas o preocupaciones en cuanto a su medicina, lo más importante que puede hacer es consultar a su médico. No se debe ignorar ni la menor duda. Recuerde que se pueden evitar algunas de las situaciones más peligrosas con la información apropiada.

4a-Prin-20 *(Respuestas posibles)*
Rafa
1 Lo más interesante es que tengo la oportunidad de conocer a mucha gente.
2 Lo difícil es que tengo que expresarme muchas veces en inglés.
3 Lo más fácil es escribir los artículos. Me encanta escribir.
Federico
1 Para mí, la cosa más interesante que hago es trabajar con la gente.
2 Diría que lo más difícil es tener que explicarle al jefe que no puedo hacer lo que quiere.
3 Lo más fácil es construir cosas.
Duna
1 Mi trabajo es el más interesante de toda la clínica porque todos los días viajo por la comunidad.
2 Pero la cosa más difícil que tengo que hacer es ayudar en situaciones donde hay violencia doméstica.
3 Lo más fácil es trabajar con Ashleigh porque pone mucho empeño y ganas.
Ángela
1 Me encanta ayudar a la gente y ésta es la parte más interesante de mi trabajo.
2 No me gusta tener que decirle a Jaime que hay un problema con el inventario; ésta es la parte más difícil.
3 Lo más fácil es trabajar con el personal de la clínica; todos son muy simpáticos.

4a-Prin-21

1 ***e*** (sí)	**4** ***f*** (siempre)	**7** ***c*** (ni… ni)
2 ***a*** (nada)	**5** ***d*** (ninguno/a)	**8** ***g*** (sin)
3 ***b*** (nadie)	**6** ***h*** (tampoco)	

4a-Prin-22

1 No	**5** También	**9** no
2 ninguna	**6** alguna	**10** ningún
3 A veces	**7** algunas	**11** tampoco
4 sin	**8** con	

4a-Prin-23
1 Carlos nunca puede concentrarse.
2 Pedro nunca sufre de fatiga.
3 Alguien ha intentado suicidarse.
4 Cristina toma drogas y alcohol.
5 Carmen tampoco sufre de insomnio.
6 Nada le molesta a Carlos.
7 Pedro tiene algunos problemas digestivos.
8 Uno puede mejorar con esperanza.

4a-Prin-24
1 He padecido de algunos problemas del estómago.
2 Él nunca ha sentido ningún dolor en el pecho.
3 Algunas veces ella piensa que está perdiendo la razón.
4 Ni tengo dificultades al respirar ni siento que me ahogo.
5 Ellos también sufren de temblores y escalofríos.
6 Ella siempre se siente aterrorizada sin razón alguna.

4a-Prin-25
1 ¿Ha sufrido depresión de posparto alguna vez?
2 ¿Alguien la ayuda a cuidar a los niños?
3 ¿Siente que tiene algún control sobre su ambiente y su vida?
4 ¿Confía en su familia y en la iglesia?
5 ¿Le hace falta algo en su vida?
6 ¿Podría sobrevivir sin el apoyo de su familia?
7 ¿Tiene el tiempo y el dinero para asistir a clases?
8 ¿Se siente segura en su casa y también en su barrio?

4a-Prin-26 *(Respuesta posible)*
Querido diario:
Soy yo otra vez. No tengo ni la menor idea de cómo ser madre. Sé que puedo contar con el apoyo de Carmina, pero no tengo a nadie en mi vida que realmente me comprenda. Alex es un buen hombre y si decido vivir con él yo sé que me va a ayudar con el cuidado del bebé. Pero no lo conozco muy bien y tengo miedo. ¿Qué voy a hacer?

4a-Prin-27 *(Respuesta posible)*
—Sr. Anderson, usted dice que es responsable de darles viviendas a muchos inmigrantes latinos. ¿De acuerdo?
—Sí, Rafa. No creo que sea mi responsabilidad darles todos de los servicios, pero es importante darles algunos.
—¿Cuáles son algunos de los servicios que su compañía les da?
—Les damos agua, calefacción y electricidad. Nadie puede exigir que les dé aire acondicionado. Algunas de estas viviendas son muy viejas.
—¿No les da este servicio aun si los inmigrantes le dicen que van a pagarlo?
—No. Y nunca lo voy a hacer.

Comprobación
Sección A

1 mucho	**4** gritos
2 asistida	**5** mejor; muy; por; tan
3 no	

Sección B

1 dosis	**4** contracciones
2 corregir	**5** agudo
3 nada	**6** cargo

Unidad 4b

4b-Voc-1

1 d	**3** b	**5** c
2 e	**4** a	

4b-Voc-2

1 tiene	**4** el tratamiento adecuado
2 admitir	**5** se ponga mejor
3 cobran	**6** Prométame

4b-Voc-3 *(Respuestas posibles)*

1 Laura dice que su vida ha sido un infierno. Reconoce que tiene que dejar de fumar. Le agradece mucho a Carmina por su apoyo.
2 La Comunidad va a patrocinar una feria de salud. Jaime va a anunciar que les ha sido otorgado un incremento de recursos.
3 Alex tiene la esperanza de que no le vayan a acusar de nada. Necesita hablar con un abogado para arreglar todo.
4 Rafa dice: "Me complace anunciar que el caso está resuelto." Promete que ya no va a meterse en "estos asuntos insoportables."

4b-Voc-4 *(Respuesta posible)*

Al fin y al cabo, todo le sale bien al personal de la clínica de La Comunidad. Carmina se casa con David y se muda para Gastonia. Laura y Alex se casan y dos meses después nace José Alejandro. Rafa por fin convence a Federico de volver a México. Federico le manda una carta de agradecimiento a Rafael porque está de nuevo con su familia después de tantos años.

4b-Prin-1

1	quite	3	provea	5	corra
2	tenga	4	reclame	6	tome

4b-Prin-2

1 cumpla; *(they doubt that...) I turn (as in so many years old)*
2 establezcas; *(it is important that...) you establish*
3 consuman; *(it is doubtful that...) they consume*
4 preguntemos; *(it is necessary that...) we ask*
5 prepare; *(we hope that...) she prepares*
6 sirva; *(I hope that...) it serves*
7 presionen; *(it is possible that...) they put pressure*
8 recibas; *(we recommend that...) you receive*
9 reconozcamos; *(it is urgent that...) we recognize*
10 necesite; *(he denies that...) I need*
11 provea; *(it is important that...) it provides*
12 pongas; *(she desires that...) you put*

4b-Prin-3

1 Quiero que preparen una lista de nuestras prioridades.
2 Es importante que Rafa escriba un artículo para *La Voz*.
3 Espero que la clínica reciba los fondos necesarios.
4 Pido que compartamos la información con otras organizaciones.
5 Tengo miedo de que nos olvidemos de algo importante.
6 Es posible que la feria no atraiga a toda la comunidad.
7 Es necesario que cubramos todos los asuntos más importantes.
8 Sugiero que distribuyamos información sobre los programas de intervención.

4b-Prin-4 *(Respuestas posibles)*

1 Señor García, temo que usted tenga SIDA.
2 Lo siento que su cáncer sea terminal.
3 Sugiero que ponga usted todos sus asuntos en orden porque le doy unos dos meses.
4 Es muy probable que su esposo fallezca pronto.
5 Temo que sea necesario amputar la pierna.
6 Es posible que su bebé padezca de muchos problemas muy graves porque es prematuro.
7 Es probable que sufras de problemas cardíacos porque estás pasado de peso.
8 Temo que no funcione el tratamiento.
9 Es probable que no valga la pena hacerle la operación.

4b-Prin-5 *(Respuestas posibles)*

1 Lamento que la clínica no esté igual que antes yo irme a México.
2 Ya ven, temo que nada funcione bien en esta casa.
3 Ya tengo bastante con lo que me pasó y por eso sugiero que no vengas a someterme a un interrogatorio.
4 Es una lástima que le caigas mal, pero siempre vienes a hacerme escenas.
5 Pues, a tu edad es probable que cualquiera se preocupe.
6 Dudo que Abe sea "perfecto"; creo que es insoportable...
7 Tal vez sea su actitud, tan machista. Me saca de quicio.
8 Te ruego que no actúes impulsivamente contra gente con poder.
9 ¡Y es dudoso que sean ellos quienes arruinan las viviendas porque son "brutos"!
10 ¡Es terrible que tú seas como todos los americanos!
11 Bueno, mucho gusto, doctor... Verá, es posible que lo que ocurre sea algo... delicado...
12 Abe, siento que Lois Lane ame a Superman y ¡no a Clark Kent!

4b-Prin-6

1 yo—pierda; tú—pierdas; él, ella, usted—pierda; ellos, ellas, ustedes—pierdan
2 yo—me convierta; tú—te conviertas; él, ella, usted—se convierta; ellos, ellas, ustedes—se conviertan
3 yo—comience; tú—comiences; él, ella, usted—comience; ellos, ellas, ustedes—comiencen
4 yo—consienta; tú—consientas; él, ella, usted—consienta; ellos, ellas, ustedes—consientan
5 yo—piense; tú—pienses; él, ella, usted—piense; ellos, ellas, ustedes—piensen
6 yo—entienda; tú—entiendas; él, ella, usted—entienda; ellos, ellas, ustedes—entiendan
7 yo—pida; tú—pidas; él, ella, usted—pida; nosotros—pidamos; ellos, ellas, ustedes—pidan
8 yo—quiera; tú—quieras; él, ella, usted—quiera; ellos, ellas, ustedes—quieran
9 yo—recuerde; tú—recuerdes; él, ella, usted—recuerde; ellos, ellas, ustedes—recuerden
10 yo—me divierta; tú—te diviertas; él, ella, usted—se divierta; nosotros—nos divirtamos; ellos, ellas, ustedes—se diviertan
11 yo—duerma; tú—duermas; él, ella, usted—duerma; nosotros—durmamos; ellos, ellas, ustedes—duerman
12 yo—diga; tú—digas; él, ella, usted—diga; nosotros—digamos; ellos, ellas, ustedes—digan

4b-Prin-7

1	yo, él, ella, usted; morir	7	tú; cerrar
2	tú; acordarse	8	nosotros; medir
3	nosotros; seguir	9	ellos, ellas, ustedes; repetir
4	ellos, ellas, ustedes; servir	10	nosotros; dormir
5	yo, él, ella, usted; probar	11	yo, él, ella, usted; demostrar
6	nosotros; elegir	12	ellos, ellas, ustedes; apretar

4b-Prin-8

1 Le aconsejo que consiga copias de póliza de su seguro de salud o de vida.
2 El departamento de servicios sociales quiere que provea prueba de su estatus migratorio.
3 Ellos requieren que muestre el acta de nacimiento.
4 Es bueno que encuentre documentos de estados financieros.
5 Es importante que lleve copias de todos los talones de su sueldo.
6 Es mejor que pida su tarjeta de seguro social.
7 Pido que escriba una lista de los vehículos que usted posee.
8 Sugiero que tenga prueba de su embarazo.

4b-Prin-9 *(Respuestas posibles)*

1 Laura, sugiero que dejes de tomar alcohol.
2 También es necesario que no fumes más.
3 Recomiendo que le digas a Alex lo más pronto posible que estás embarazada.
4 Es urgente que te cuides mejor.
5 Es importante que tengas una dieta más saludable por lo de la diabetes.
6 Es importante también que empieces a estudiar de nuevo. Necesitas aprender a hablar inglés.

4b-Prin-10 *(Respuesta posible)*

RECEPCIONISTA: Buenas tardes, señor. ¿En qué le puede servir?
SR. GARCÍA: Buenas tardes. Me gustaría saber un poco sobre los servicios aquí en la clínica. Mi esposa está embarazada.
RECEPCIONISTA: Ay, sí, tenemos toda clase de servicios para mujeres embarazadas. ¿Quiere que le dé un folleto?
SR. GARCÍA: Sí, gracias.
RECEPCIONISTA: Si su mujer quiere hacer una cita, recomiendo que ustedes nos llamen lo más pronto posible. Tenemos muchas pacientes.
SR. GARCÍA: ¿Sería posible hacer una cita hoy?
RECEPCIONISTA: Antes de que ella pueda hacer una cita, necesitamos que ella se haga una prueba de embarazo en nuestra oficina. Dígale que venga cuando quiera.
SR. GARCÍA: Gracias. Le voy a decir esta tarde cuando regrese a casa.

4b-Prin-11

1 ruegue; ruegues; ruegue; roguemos; rueguen
2 fuerce; fuerces; fuerce; forcemos; fuercen
3 busque; busques; busque; busquemos; busquen
4 cuelgue; cuelgues; cuelgue; colguemos; cuelguen
5 explique; expliques; explique; expliquemos; expliquen

4b-Prin-12

1 se equivoque	3 te perjudiques	5 goces
2 arriesgues	4 empieces	6 realicemos

4b-Prin-13

1 ¿Es posible que califique para Medicaid?
2 ¿Es necesario que el médico certifique que permanezco en casa?
3 ¿Es necesario que pague el costo íntegro si no recibo aprobación previa?
4 ¿Es importante que busque un plan de salud?
5 ¿Es necesario que un médico de cabecera autorice todos los servicios?
6 ¿Es posible que me nieguen la cobertura?

4b-Prin-14

1 sea	3 den	5 haya
2 sepa	4 vaya	

4b-Prin-15

1 sea	3 estemos	5 estén
2 haya	4 dé	6 sepan

4b-Prin-16

1 No, no hay nadie que me ayude con el cuidado de la niña mientras Eliodoro trabaja.
2 No, no buscamos un apartamento que sea más grande.
3 No, no queremos que la niña vaya a una guardería.
4 Sí, me molesta mucho que mis padres no estén para ver a la niña.

4b-Prin-17 *(Respuestas posibles)*

1 Exijo que mis colegas sean profesionales.
2 Recomiendo que mis pacientes vayan al dentista.
3 Espero que todos mis pacientes sepan que es importante dejar de fumar.
4 Ojalá que todos ellos estén contentos.
5 Dudo que haya mejores colegas y pacientes en el mundo.

4b-Prin-18

1 hayamos vuelto	6 hayas perdido
2 hayan patrocinado	7 haya desarrollado
3 haya sido	8 haya traído
4 haya recibido	9 hayan ayudado
5 haya prevenido	10 hayamos puesto

4b-Prin-19

1 Tal vez sus niños hayan estado en riesgo.
2 Me alegro de que usted haya podido participar en el programa de nutrición WIC para mujeres, infantes y niños.
3 Me gusta que se haya establecido un sistema de prioridades.
4 Espero que hayamos discutido todos los alimentos recomendados.
5 Es bueno que usted haya decidido darle el pecho.
6 No pienso que ellos le hayan mandado el cheque todavía.

4b-Prin-20 *(Respuestas posibles)*

1 Siento que se haya negado a alquilarle el apartamento.
2 Es una lástima que le haya mentido sobre la disponibilidad de la casa.
3 Me molesta que hayan intentado persuadirla para no comprar en cierto vecindario.
4 No me gusta que le haya desalojado de la vivienda.
5 Dudo que hayan querido cobrarle un depósito muy alto.

4b-Prin-21 *(Respuestas posibles)*

SR. ANDERSON: Ojalá que usted haya hecho investigaciones sobre las finanzas de mi compañía. No hay ningún problema.

RAFA: Es posible que usted haya escondido los documentos que necesito.

SR. ANDERSON: No, no he escondido nada. ¡Dudo que mi contador haya tenido tiempo! (Se ríe.)

RAFA: Ojalá que él no haya destruido nada.

SR. ANDERSON: Como le dije antes, no hay nada que destruir. ¡Ojalá que su periódico haya contratado a un buen abogado!

4b-Prin-22

1	fuera;	*(it was a shame that...) I was*
2	llegaras;	*you arrived*
3	murieran;	*they died*
4	trajéramos;	*we brought*
5	llamara;	*she called*
6	comprara;	*he bought*
7	recontaran;	*they recounted*
8	bebieras;	*you drank*
9	cubriéramos;	*we covered*
10	pusiera;	*I put*
11	quisiera;	*she wanted*
12	pudieras;	*you were able to*

4b-Prin-23

1 fuéramos	**5** pudiéramos	**8** tuvieran
2 trajera	**6** ayudara	**9** aceptaran
3 se atrasara	**7** llamara	**10** hubiera
4 pidiéramos		

4b-Prin-24

1. Era posible que una persona viera al médico cuando se sentía enferma.
2. Les importaba que los clientes esperaran privacidad y confidencialidad.
3. No se prohibía que tú cambiaras tu médico de cabecera.
4. Nos dejaron que seleccionáramos un médico de cabecera de una lista de participantes.
5. Estaba bien que un cliente presentara quejas o recomendaciones para cambios.
6. No se permitía que un paciente fuera maltratado.
7. Era posible que los clientes participaran en la toma de decisiones con respecto a su salud.

4b-Prin-25 *(Respuestas posibles)*

1. Pero Laura se comporta como si no fuera diabética ni estuviera embarazada.
2. Pero Alex se comporta como si no sufriera de nada.
3. Pero Carmina sale con Abe como si no soñara con otro.
4. Pero Federico habla como si el personal de La Comunidad fuera su familia.
5. Pero Ashleigh habla como si no supiera bien el español.
6. Pero Ricardito bebe como si fuera un adulto.

4b-Prin-26

1. ***d*** Have him rest a bit.
2. ***b*** Have him loosen his clothing.
3. ***e*** Have him put a wet handkerchief on his forehead.
4. ***c*** Have him sit in the shade.
5. ***a*** Have him drink a glass of water.

4b-Prin-27

1. Que le escriba una carta.
2. Que deje de llamarlo.
3. Que le diga la verdad.
4. Que le presente a otra mujer.
5. Que no acepte sus llamadas.
6. Que le explique que hay otras mujeres para él.

4b-Prin-28

1. Que tu nieto entre en un programa para los que abusan del alcohol y las drogas.
2. Que tu primo/a se mude contigo.
3. Que tus amigos hablen con un trabajador social.
4. Que tu primo/a exija sus derechos.
5. Que tus hijos se conviertan en miembros activos de la comunidad.
6. Que tu tío/a se reúna con un abogado.

4b-Prin-29 *(Respuestas posibles)*

1. Que vaya al médico inmediatamente.
2. Que tome su medicina.
3. Que se quede tranquilo.
4. Que se ponga una inyección.

4b-Prin-30 *(Respuesta posible)*

The indicative mood is used to indicate certainty. It is used to state facts or beliefs or to discuss objective situations. The subjunctive, on the other hand, is used in hypothetical or emotional situations. It is also used to deny the truth of something.

4b-Prin-31

1 Indicativo	**5** Infinitivo	**8** Subjuntivo
2 Subjuntivo	**6** Subjuntivo	**9** Indicativo
3 Subjuntivo	**7** Infinitivo	**10** Subjuntivo
4 Subjuntivo		

4b-Prin-32

1. The subjunctive is used because of the impersonal signal "*es mejor que*" and because "*cuando*" refers to a hypothetical event. **Translation:** It's better that you go to the emergency room only when it's an emergency.
2. The indicative is used because of the certainty implied by "*estaba segura*." "*Eran*" is in the indicative because the information is factual. **Translation:** She was sure that these services did not require the prior approval of a PCP since they were dental services.
3. The infinitive is used because it is the subject of the sentence. **Translation:** It's important to come to preventative care services.
4. The subjunctive is used in the first verb because "*antes de que*" indicates the future (and therefore introduces a hypothetical situation.) The infinitive is used in the second verb because only the infinitive can follow a conjugated verb directly (it is a verb acting like a noun.) **Translation:** Before visiting a specialist, you need to talk with your PCP.
5. "*Escoja*" is in the subjunctive because of "*sugiero que*" which signals an implied command. "*Tiene*" is in the indicative because it follows "*ya que*" and is factual. The idiom "*tener que*" requires the use of the infinitive in the next verb. **Translation:** First, I suggest that you set up your PCP since he has to coordinate your care.

6 After a verb of emotion, the subjunctive must be used. **Translation:** I am sorry we couldn't see her (you) the other day.

4b-Prin-33
Es importante tener un programa de alimentación durante el verano porque los niños no asisten a la escuela durante este tiempo. A través este programa los niños de familias de inmigrantes pobres reciben comida gratis para que las familias puedan ahorrar dinero y comprar otras cosas necesarias para el cuidado de todos los miembros de la familia. Estos niños pueden recibir hasta tres comidas al día y todos los niños de inmigrantes son elegibles a menos que tengan más de 18 años de edad. Como las horas son flexibles, pueden comer cuando quieran. Además, no es necesario que las familias llenen una solicitud.

4b-Prin-34 *(Respuesta posible)*
Señor Ruíz, creo que usted padece de diabetes. Es necesario que busque un trabajo menos difícil. Usted ya sufre de presión alta. Si no deja de trabajar tanto, la presión va a subir aún más. Es urgente también que usted aprenda a revisar el nivel de glucosa en la sangre. Si controla este nivel, no va a tener que tomar medicinas. Coma menos azúcar y menos comida grasosa. Es importante también que haga algunos ejercicios específicos para los pies. El terapeuta físico se los puede enseñar. Por último, vaya al dentista lo más pronto posible si no quiere perder todos sus dientes.

4b-Prin-35 *(Respuestas posibles)*
1 Al principio, es muy importante que decidas a qué gente quieres servir.
2 Después de pensar en esta población, es necesario que invites a las agencias del lugar donde vives.
3 Diles a las agencias que vengan a la feria, a menos que tengan otras citas para ese día.
4 Es sumamente importante que preguntes a los representantes de las agencia qué necesitan: tomas de electricidad, un lugar privado, recipientes de basura, intérpretes, etc.
5 Después de averiguar qué van a requerir, sugiero que te asegures de que el espacio que hayas escogido tenga todas estas cosas.
6 El día de la feria, recomiendo que llegues temprano para que puedas ayudar a todos.

Comprobación
Sección A
1 siga
2 dé; lleve
3 fuera
4 está; es
5 puede
6 resuelva

Sección B
1 admite
2 patrocinan
3 cobrar
4 cepillarse
5 mantener
6 optan

Acknowledgments

The authors would like to thank the following individuals for their contributions:

Leticia I. Romo, PhD, for her excellent proofreading and editorial suggestions
Deborah Bender, PhD, member of the *¡A su salud!* team
Linda Carl, PhD, member of the *¡A su salud!* team
Prem Fort, medical student
Christina Harlan, MA, RN, member of the *¡A su salud!* team
Bob Henshaw, MSIS, member of the *¡A su salud!* team
Carolyn Heuser, pharmacy manager, Carrboro Community Health Center
Anna Kinman, administrative assistant
Claire Lorch, MSW, project director for *¡A su salud!*
Myriam Peereboom, director, Interpreter Services, UNC Hospitals
Elizabeth Shick, DDS
Carl D. Taylor, director of Pharmacy Services, Piedmont Health Services
Amy Trester, MEd, member of the *¡A su salud!* team

The following faculty and staff of the University of North Carolina at Chapel Hill contributed to the development of the multimedia content for the first edition of *¡A su salud!: Spanish for Health Professionals.* A large portion of this content has been incorporated into the text of the *Classroom Edition.*

Julia Cardona Mack
Elizabeth Tolman
Deborah E. Bender
Linda Carl
Christina Harlan
Robert Henshaw
Claire Lorch
Chris McQuiston
Amy Trester

INDEX

Q

R

S

T

V

W